EX LIBRIS

THE ROAD TO VERDUN

ALSO BY IAN OUSBY

The Correspondence of John Ruskin and Charles Eliot Norton (editor)

The Englishman's England: Taste, Travel and the Rise of Tourism

The Cambridge Guide to Literature in English

Occupation: The Ordeal of France, 1940–1944

The Cambridge Guide to Fiction in English

THE ROAD TO
VERDUN

WORLD WAR I'S MOST MOMENTOUS BATTLE AND THE FOLLY OF NATIONALISM

IAN OUSBY

DOUBLEDAY

New York London Toronto Sydney Auckland

PUBLISHED BY DOUBLEDAY
a division of Random House, Inc.
1540 Broadway, New York, New York 10036

DOUBLEDAY and the portrayal of an anchor with a dolphin are
trademarks of Doubleday, a division of Random House, Inc.

The Road to Verdun was originally published in 2002 by Jonathan Cape.
The Doubleday edition is published by arrangement with Jonathan Cape.

Book design by Helene Berinsky

Library of Congress Cataloging-in-Publication Data
Ousby, Ian, 1947–
The road to Verdun: World War I's most momentous battle and
the folly of nationalism/Ian Ousby.
p.   cm.
Includes index.
1. Verdun, Battle of, 1916.   2. World War, 1914–1918—Campaigns—France.
3. Nationalism—Europe—History—
20th century.   I. Title.
D545.V3 O97 2002
940.4'272—dc21   2002019475

ISBN 0-385-50393-8
Copyright © 2002 by The Estate of Ian Ousby

All Rights Reserved

PRINTED IN THE UNITED STATES OF AMERICA

May 2002
First Edition in the United States of America

1   3   5   7   9   10   8   6   4   2

CONTENTS

LIST OF ILLUSTRATIONS

The Voie Sacrée (reproduced by permission of Le Ministère de la Défense/ECPAD).

The Voie Sacrée, drawing by Georges Scott (*Illustrated London News*, 18 March 1916; courtesy of the Illustrated London News Picture Library).

Marshal Joffre at his desk at headquarters (*Illustrated London News*, 3 June 1916; courtesy of the Illustrated London News Picture Library).

Colonel Driant (from Jacques Péricard, *Verdun 1916*, Paris: Nouvelle Librairie de France, 1997).

The civil population of Verdun evacuates the town (*The Sphere*, 18 March 1916; courtesy of the London Illustrated News Picture Library).

The destroyed city center of Verdun at the beginning of the German offensive (photo: AKG London).

The Bois des Caures (from Jacques Péricard, *Verdun 1916*, Paris: Nouvelle Librairie de France, 1997).

Bombardment (from Jacques Péricard, *Verdun 1916*, Paris: Nouvelle Librairie de France, 1997).

French children watch German prisoners captured at Verdun (*The Sphere*, 1 April 1916; courtesy of the London Illustrated News Picture Library).

Fort de Douaumont before the battle (photo: AKG London).

Fort de Douaumont under bombardment (from Jacques Péricard, *Verdun 1916*, Paris: Nouvelle Librairie de France, 1997).

Fort de Douaumont after the bombardment (*Illustrated London News*, 24 June 1916; courtesy of the London Illustrated News Picture Library).

Marianne the revolutionary; detail of "La Marseillaise" by François Rude, Arc de Triomphe, Paris (photo: AKG London/Joseph Martin).

Marianne the republican: "La France belle, forte et fierement sereine," picture postcard, *c*. 1900 (photo: AKG London).

One of the early sketches for *The Raft of the Medusa* by Théodore Géricault (Musée des Beaux-Arts, Rouen; copyright © Photo RMN/P. Bernard).

The eternal quarrel: French or German? Cartoon by Zislin (from Roland Oberle, *L'Alsace au temps du Reichsland, 1871–1914*, Mulhouse, ADM Editeur, 1991).

The Germanization of Alsace; cartoon by Hansi (from Roland Oberle, *L'Alsace au temps du Reichsland, 1871–1914*, Mulhouse, ADM Editeur, 1991).

The landscape of death: corpse in a ravine near the Fort de Vaux (Imperial War Museum Q 23892; reproduced by permission of the Imperial War Museum).

The landscape of death: Le Mort-Homme, April 1916 (from Jacques Péricard, *Verdun 1916*, Paris: Nouvelle Librairie de France, 1997).

The landscape of death: Malancourt (from Jacques Péricard, *Verdun 1916*, Paris: Nouvelle Librairie de France, 1997).

French troops in the Bois de la Caillette (*Illustrated London News*, 27 May 1916; courtesy of the Illustrated London News Picture Library).

French troops at the entrance of Fort de Douaumont, October 1916 (photo: AKG London).

The destroyed village of Ornes (Imperial War Museum, Q 45664; reproduced by permission of the Imperial War Museum).

General Mangin at his headquarters, June 1916 (from Georges Blond, *Verdun*, London: Andre Deutsch, 1965).

Alfred Joubaire (from Alfred Joubaire, *Pour la France: Carnet de route d'un fantassin*, Paris: Perrin et Cie, 1917; British Library 09082.bbb.37; reproduced by permission of the British Library).

"La défense ou l'appelle aux armes" by Auguste Rodin (photo: AKG London).

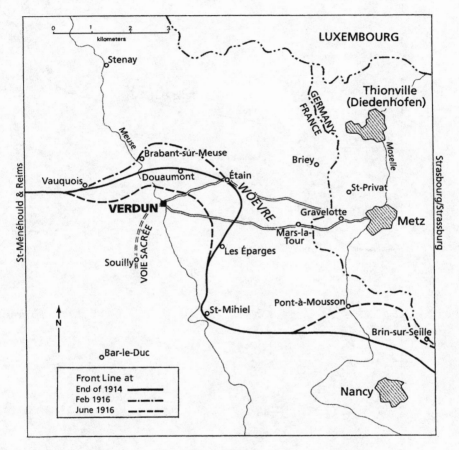

Verdun and Lorraine: The Debatable Lands

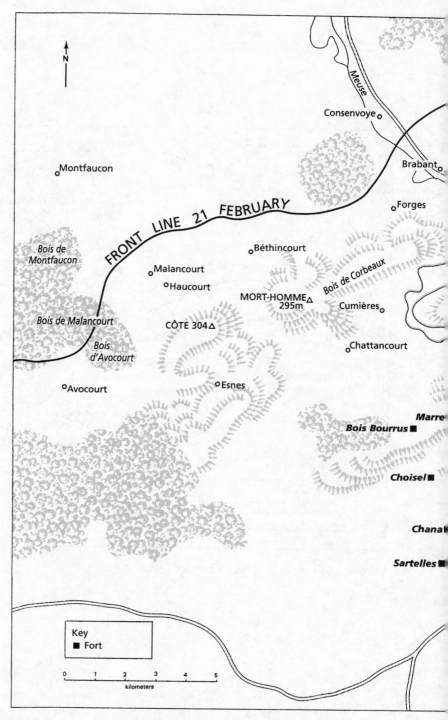

Verdun: The 1916 Battlefield

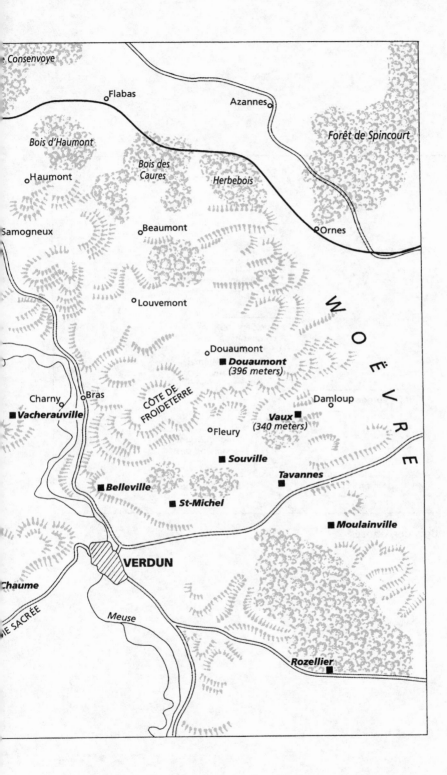

Consenvoye

Flabas

Azannes

Forêt de Spincourt

Bois d'Haumont

Bois des Caures

Herbebois

Haumont

Samogneux

Beaumont

Ornes

Louvemont

W O Ë V R E

Douaumont

Douaumont
(396 meters)

Charny Bras

■ **Vacherauville**

CÔTE DE FROIDETERRE

Damloup

Vaux ■
(340 meters)

Fleury

■ **Souville**

Tavannes

■ **Belleville**

■ **St-Michel**

■ **Moulainville**

Chaume

VERDUN

IE SACRÉE

Meuse

Rozellier

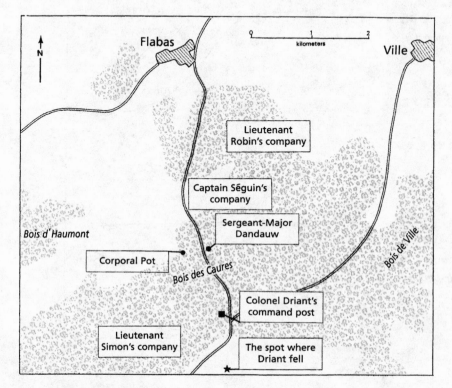

The Bois des Caures

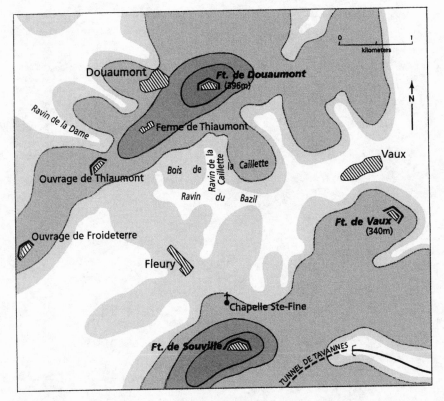

The Central Battlefield around Douaumont, Vaux, and Froideterre

The months are not long nor the days nor the nights.
It's the war that is long.

Guillaume Apollinaire

✛   ✛   ✛

War destroys any conception of goals, including any conception
of the goals of war. It even destroys the idea of putting an end
to the war.

Simone Weil

THE ROAD TO VERDUN

———— ✛ ————

THE ROAD TO VERDUN

Everyone came to Verdun as if to receive some ultimate recognition there; as if all the provinces of the *patrie* had needed to join in one particularly cruel and solemn sacrifice among the sacrifices of the war, exposed to the world's gaze. They seemed to go up the Voie Sacrée like some new form of offertory, to the most formidable altar that mankind had ever raised.

> Paul Valéry, "Réponse au remerciement du Maréchal Pétain à l'Académie française" ("Reply to the Speech of Thanks by Marshal Pétain in the Académie Française"), 1931

✛   ✛   ✛

Across the valley they could make out the ghost of a town in the smoke.

The air trembled.

Blows from a sledgehammer were falling on the town; houses were being scattered as if scraped by hooves, the agony of a cow bigger than the sky that refused to die and that someone kept on trying to club to death. Rubble flew up in the smoke like flocks of pigeons. When it cleared a little, they could see a church of some sort, its legs stiff in the air, its huge stomach bloated, dead.

"Is that Alsace?" said Marroi.

"What is it?" asked Olivier.

"What's that?"

"That town?"

"Verdun," said Doche.

"The slaughterhouse," said Marroi.

> Jean Giono, "Montée à Verdun" ("Going up to Verdun"),
> a discarded chapter from the novel *Le Grand Troupeau*
> (*To the Slaughterhouse*), 1931, published
> in *Refus d'obéissance* (*Insubordination*), 1937

It would almost seem that nature, as well as the destiny of nations, intended Verdun to be a place of battle. There is nothing re-markable about the city itself: like so many of the places where sol-diers have passed the centuries fighting, it holds no special interest, let alone charm. Its terrible prominence has always come from its position by the river Meuse, dominating the only convenient cross-ing for some distance in either direction. This alone has guaranteed that it has stood on the route of invasion. That invasion would be contested here was guaranteed by the hills rising above the right (or east) bank of the river, sometimes called the Hauts de Verdun but more usually the Hauts de Meuse. Even before battle made it deso-late, the countryside—said one historian and soldier who fought here—was already "harsh and melancholy."* Deep and often unex-pected ravines mold the hills into a series of plateaus that seem to invite the wind and the rain during the bitter winters. The hills reach their highest point, a little over 400 meters, where they over-look the dreary plain of the Woëvre.

Beyond, further east, lie the Moselle and another cluster of hills, around Metz; beyond them, Strasbourg and the Rhine. It has always been debatable land. The quarrel reaches back at least to the treaty, bearing Verdun's name, agreed between Charlemagne's grandsons in 843. It divided Charlemagne's Empire into a western

* Notes giving sources of quotations and acknowledging debts to other people's work may be found in the Notes to the Text section near the end of the book; they are not numbered but identified by a name or phrase from the text. Notes at the bottom of the page treat matters more likely to be of immediate interest.

kingdom, corresponding roughly to modern France, and an eastern kingdom, corresponding roughly to modern Germany, but also a short-lived "middle kingdom." This kingdom might soon have vanished from the map but it bequeathed to history more than a name, Lotharingia, which time transmuted into Lorraine (known to the Germans as Lothringen). Lotharingia also left a sinister ghost. Its thin strip of land, running from Belgium, Holland and the North Sea to Provence and the Mediterranean, marked a fault line between the nations of western Europe—a territory of vulnerable small states, unstable boundaries and battlefields, from Agincourt and Blenheim to Waterloo and Sedan.

Nowhere was the land more debatable, the border less stable, than between the Meuse and the Rhine. Germany's annexation of Alsace and part of Lorraine after her victory in the Franco-Prussian War of 1870–71 moved the border from the Rhine to Metz, only 60 kilometers away from Verdun. So the French set about strengthening their natural bulwark with forts on either side of the river but clustered most thickly in the Hauts de Meuse. In the autumn of 1914 Verdun stood at the junction point, or hinge, between the two main arms of the German advance: the attack through Alsace and Lorraine in the south, largely a feint, and the real strike through Belgium and northern France which was brought up short on the Marne at the beginning of September. The German armies had managed to cross the Meuse near the little town of Brabant, only about 15 kilometers north of Verdun, and they dominated the river from Saint-Mihiel, about 35 kilometers south. But Verdun itself held, as it would again resist attacks from the flanks at Vauquois and Les Éparges in 1915.

It had become a salient: a bump in the French lines, or a dent in the German lines, of the Western Front. Any soldier will tell you that a salient is a difficult and dangerous place for both sides. (The other important salient on the Western Front was at Ypres.) For the army on its outer edge—the Germans at Verdun—it poses a continual worry: here the enemy could mass forces and try to break through in any one of several directions. At the same time it offers a continual temptation, for here also the enemy could be attacked from several quarters at once. Even when the salient remains quiet the army inside it usually has logistical problems, since the chances are that the routes available for supplies and communications are limited, at least to one compass point. At worst, and in this regard the French were in the worst of positions at Verdun, all the means of sustenance have to come through a narrow funnel. Once an assault has started, the defenders live with the fear that attack on the wings will leave them encircled, the Stalingrad disaster that had been every army's nightmare since Hannibal's victory over the Romans at Cannae.

The contours of the Verdun salient remained unaltered until February 1916, when the German attack sparked off the largest and longest Franco-German battle of the First World War. Though it haunted the imagination of the French commanders, the nightmare of encirclement was never realized. Yet their problems of communication and supply were immediate, acute and unavoidable. The army in the hills and forts on the east bank of the Meuse did not just fight with the river at its back; it also knew that if push came to shove the river might well prove a greater impediment to safe withdrawal than it would to the onrush of the German advance. The city itself, on the west bank, lay within easy reach of the German guns. And beyond Verdun? In their early stages the road and the railway line running west to the military camps at Sainte-Ménéhould and Suippes, and eventually to Reims, passed perilously close to the German lines. They were among the first targets in the German bombardment that opened the battle. The railway to Bar-le-Duc was a branch line of the sort the French call a *tortillard*, because its course twists and winds; even with urgent refurbishment, it could give only limited help.

All that remained was the road branching from the way to Reims west of Verdun and heading south through villages and rolling downland to Bar-le-Duc, 60 or so kilometers away. Modern maps label it the N35, or Route Nationale 35. Near Verdun it came under threat from the German artillery; even in the safer reaches beyond, it was only a country road, poorly surfaced and at best seven meters wide. For it to serve the defense of Verdun, it needed broadening wherever possible, though many bottlenecks remained when this had been done. Teams of Territorials stood on hand to shovel chippings of the local limestone into the ever-deepening ruts and potholes. Even so, the road was still a sea of mud in the early winter stages of the battle and a haze of white dust in the summer. Its traffic needed continual direction by gendarmes, lest a single breakdown bring the whole flow to a halt.

Against the odds, the traffic did flow. "You'd think you were on the Avenue de l'Opéra," said one lieutenant in the deliberately insouciant tones that soldiers adopt for admiring difficult feats unexpectedly achieved. Before the battle was a month old, vehicles were passing up the road at a rate of one every 14 seconds, day and night. There were staff cars, letter carriers, ambulances and Berliet lorries carrying supplies in cargo compartments that made them look like covered wagons from an earlier time. The drivers, men from the Service Automobile, were judged too old for service at the front yet still worked shifts of 40, 50 and even 75 hours at the wheel in the days immediately after the attack started; even when the battle had settled into its long grinding rhythm they were still doing shifts of anything from 15 to 30 hours.

And, as in any battle at any time in any place, there were always the infantry. In the French army of the First World War the ordinary troops called themselves *poilus*, a word literally meaning the "hairy ones" or "shaggy ones" which expressed the defiant pride they took in the condition to which battle reduced them. Sometimes the *poilus* sat by the side of the road enjoying a rest and a smoke. Sometimes they gathered around a field kitchen. Sometimes they bivouacked for the night in the surrounding fields. Sometimes they rode in the lorries whose flapping tarpaulin covers never quite protected them from the splattering mud in winter and the choking dust in summer. But usually they marched, in two columns: one going up to the battle and one, slower in its pace and thinner in its numbers, coming back.

The Germans launched their attack, on 21 February 1916, with a massive bombardment which gave Verdun, with the Somme, the most dramatic beginning of any battle in the First World War. Yet it had no clear end. The war had deprived battles of the distinct shape, along with the brevity and decisiveness, which the military academies had taught the generals to expect. The Germans had given up any real hope of advancing further by the middle of July, but local attacks dragged on into September. By then the French were welcoming dignitaries from the allied nations to Verdun for victory celebrations, even though they did not recapture the major forts they had lost until late October and early November, or other significant positions until the middle of December. It was autumn 1917 before further fighting brought the French close to the original lines they had occupied. And it was not until 8 November 1918—only three days before the armistice ended the war—that the Germans were pushed from the sector they had first targeted and first captured in February 1916, though the troops who recaptured it were not French but Americans.

So, when historians speak of the battle as ending in November or December 1916, they are drawing an arbitrary line. Nor do the difficulty and imprecision cease when they ask how many of the men who went up the road from Bar-le-Duc between February and December did not return down it. The question was first addressed with scholarly dispassion by Louis Marin and those compiling the official history of the war in the 1920s. Most historians would now accept that the French army suffered somewhere in the region of 378,777 casualties. This term lumps together the wounded, the dead and the missing in the same fashion that commanders in the field do when they calculate how many soldiers remain at their disposal to continue the fight. Of the casualties at Verdun, 216,337 were wounded, 61,289 were killed and 101,151 were missing. Of course, men go missing from battlefields for all sorts of reasons: they get taken prisoner, they get wounded and their arrival at hospital is not properly registered, they fail to come back from leave, they desert, and so forth. But, in postwar retrospect, the term "missing" is a terrible euphemism for the men blown to pieces by shells, those left to rot beyond identification, those who simply vanished into the mud. At Verdun, as in other battles of the First World War, they constituted a disconcertingly large proportion of the casualties.

The number of Frenchmen killed at Verdun, whether officially listed as dead or missing, thus amounts to about 162,440. Responsible German estimates, begun by the work of the Reichsarchiv for its official history, put the number of their dead at about 143,000, out of 330,000 casualties. That German losses should have been so close to the French figures shows just what had happened to the hope of quick victory in the First World War. That the French should have claimed a victory after losses so nearly even shows just what happened to the hope of victory of any sort, indeed to the whole concept of decision by battle. Verdun, then, killed about 305,440 men, out of 708,777 casualties. By any standards, the figures are formidable: almost one death a minute, day and night, for the ten months that the battle lasted. The French dead alone represent almost one-tenth of their one and a half million dead in the whole war. Alistair Horne put the matter usefully in perspective for English-speaking observers when he pointed out that the number of the French and German dead at Verdun did not fall far short of the figure, about 444,000, for all the dead from the British Empire in the Second World War.

Nevertheless, the figures do not in themselves make Verdun the "worst" battle of the war. Statistically, the French losses do not even make it their worst battle in 1916: Frenchmen died at the Somme between July and November at a far more murderous rate. Nor was 1916 their "worst" year in the war. That doubtful honor belonged to 1915, the year of the French attacks in the Champagne and Artois, when about 335,000 men died, as compared with the 218,000 for all of 1916. And the worst period of the war for France (as for all the other combatant nations) was not a full year at all but the four opening months of fighting at the tail end of 1914, when about 307,000 Frenchmen died.

Yet the French regarded Verdun as their worst battle while it was being fought, and they have insisted on seeing it that way ever since. Sometimes they exaggerated the figures, sufficiently chilling in themselves, to match the perception. Verdun left a million casualties, it was said. Verdun, it was even implied, killed a million men. Such claims were common between the wars, even as the bones of the unidentified were being gathered up from the battlefield, and they still sometimes turn up in popular histories and reference books. The sense among the French that Verdun, though a victory, had also been their worst battle did not just come from its sheer length and intensity. It had a statistical basis too, not in the number of those who died but in the number of those who fought. Here Verdun was unique in its scale—or, as the language of the day put it, "supreme." During the ten months between February and December 1916 three-quarters of the entire army that France fielded on the Western Front had marched up the road from Bar-le-Duc.

Indeed, by spring of 1916 most of them were alert to any sign of a new posting or a new deployment, in the expectation that they would be sent to Verdun. The prospect might fill them with dread: "Isn't every unit bound to go marching up that fatal road?" asked the veteran René Naegelen in his novel *Les Suppliciés* (a title best translated, perhaps, as *The Victims*). Yet there were other emotions too. "Our men know where they're going. They've been warned. I don't think they're sorry," noted Major Pierre Louis Bréant, not given to injecting falsely patriotic sentiment into his campaign diary: "Verdun carries such prestige. One will be proud of having been there." Sometimes men spoke of the prospect in exactly the terms that Shakespeare's Henry V sought to inspire in his men before Agincourt. "In our old age we'd be able to say to our families, and to young children being taught the Battle of Verdun, that we were there," mused Marcel Dupont: "And if we've seen such things, and breathed the atmosphere and heard the talk there, people will look at us in amazement."

So by 1918 a majority of the survivors who returned home to post-war life could say *J'y étais* ("I was there") or, in the laconic idiom they often preferred, *J'ai fait Verdun* ("I did Verdun"). Even by itself, this fact suggests why the French have always regarded Verdun not just as another battle or even their biggest battle but as, in some profound way, a national experience. It certainly explains why they should not have remained content to refer to the road from Bar-le-Duc to Verdun by the prosaic label it bears on the maps. Maurice Barrès—novelist, journalist and politician—coined an altogether grander and more resonant name when he visited Verdun in April 1916 and referred to the road by which he reached the battlefield as the Route Sacrée: the Sacred Way.

More closely than anyone else in the public eye, Barrès had been identified with the revival of nationalist sentiment in France marking the years before the war. Indeed, it was he who had first used the word *nationalisme* in what has become one of its most familiar senses: as a key doctrine of the right and extreme right in politics. During the war he found a natural role, through his column in *L'Écho de Paris*, as a propagandist for the cause of France and her ally, Britain. His influence gave wide currency to the label Route Sacrée, which repetition soon altered to the Voie Sacrée. Particularly in this later form, it struck a chord in the public imagination, or at least in the imagination of the civilian public. It helped to build the myth of Verdun by which the home front made sense of the battle—and found supreme significance in it—from the earliest days of the fighting. Presumably, this was not because of its reference to the Via Sacra, the street in ancient Rome on which the chief temples stood, running from the Colosseum to the Capitoline Hill. Rather, the name seemed to evoke the Via Dolorosa, the "Way of Sorrows," and to compare the suffering and sacrifice of the soldiers who fought at Verdun with Christ's journey to Calvary and the Crucifixion.

It was by no means uncommon for soldiers in their diaries and reminiscences to compare their journey up to the front with the Stations of the Cross. For them, the hills of Verdun were a modern Calvary and what they and those around them suffered there was a form of crucifixion. Fifty-odd years of living in a secular republic might have diminished and qualified the modes of thought and feeling that traditional Catholicism had taught, but it certainly had not expunged them. The language of the *poilus* was shot through with religious imagery, just as it also was with superstition, blasphemy, cynicism, despair and a great many other responses for which Barrès found no room in his columns. If troops did not commonly use the name Voie Sacrée, their failure—or refusal—to do so marked their awareness of the gulf between the battle they fought and the battle they read about in the Paris newspapers.

"The general opinion in the trenches was that anything could be true except what the press was allowed to publish," Pierre Chaine testified in his bitterly incisive *Mémoires d'un rat*. The outpourings of the press, and all the other propaganda designed for the home front, had long since been given the contemptuous label of *bourrage de crâne*: literally, "stuffing for the head," or what modern dictionaries now call "brainwashing," though probably the most expressive translation is "eyewash," the slang term used by British troops for nonsense meant to deceive. This did not mean that the troops ignored the newspapers: witnesses agree that they were avid to read anything that came to hand and particularly anything about the war. The *poilu*, said André Bridoux, was trying to discover himself: "He was hungry for some clarification of the confused but powerful sense he had formed of himself in his new destiny; he counted on writers to help him become more precisely aware of what he saw around him and what he felt inside himself." Yet the men were continually angered by what they read, not just in censored news stories about particular engagements but in articles seeking to evoke the life they were leading in their new destiny. They could not recognize themselves or the conditions of battle in what the *bourreurs de crâne* offered the public. Rhetorically, its easy piety and sentimentality were insultingly remote from their harsh plight in the shell-holes of Verdun.

Their reaction to what they read in the newspapers might have made the troops avoid a newspaper-coined term like the Voie Sacrée, but it did not lessen their interest in the road itself. Their diaries and reminiscences dwelt at great length on the approach to Verdun, sometimes giving almost as much space to the business of getting to the battle—let alone the business of getting into position on the battlefield—as they did to the actual fighting. Their experience of the fighting was, after all, every bit as fragmented and disjointed as André Bridoux suggested. Literally, they often did not know where their positions had been, even once they had been relieved, much less know how what had happened to them in their positions might connect with what had happened to other men in other positions, or what it might show about the larger fortunes of the fighting. The road offered them the nearest thing they ever got to a broad view of the battle before it engulfed them.

The sheer volume of traffic around them gave the first real hint of the scale of what lay ahead and often their only glimpse of it, since Verdun was above all a battle of small groups rather than massed battalions. Most soldiers were already used to the distinctive atmosphere of chaos and order, muddle and efficiency that goes with a mass deployment. Yet even veterans of Charleroi and the Battle of the Marne in 1914, or the Artois and Champagne in 1915, had never so powerfully been struck by the sense of being sucked into some vast machine, oblivious and blind to the individual fate and the individual life. The battle—said the priest and theologian Pierre Teilhard de Chardin, who served as a stretcher-bearer—made the soldier into a *monade de guerre*, a "war-monad": "a depersonalized element in a supra-individual activity." The same sense led the Germans, from their side, to speak with weary cynicism of Verdun as "the mill." Above the city of Verdun and beyond the Meuse, the hills were by day covered in a cloud of smoke and dust. By night—and, of course, troops usually made the final approach to their positions by night—flames and flares lit up the sky above the hills. By day and by night, the hills continually gave off the steady rhythmic din of countless batteries discharging their shells, the noise for which the French borrowed the expressive German word *Trommelfeuer*: drumfire.

"As soon as I saw the battlefield," recalled one infantryman who arrived at the beginning of June, "even though I had already spent 14 months at the front, I thought: 'If you haven't seen Verdun, you haven't seen anything of war.' " From their first distant prospect of the battle, men commonly spoke of it as a furnace, or called it a hell, an inferno. Oddly enough, André Pézard, who observed the battle from the Butte de Vauquois overlooking the Reims road, went on to become the finest scholar of Dante his generation produced in France. The poet Laurence Binyon, a Red Cross orderly at Verdun, went on to translate *The Divine Comedy*.* But thoughts of Dante also haunted their less well-read comrades, for whom the journey into battle became a descent into the Inferno as well as a Way of Sorrows recalling Christ's way to the Cross. Above all, borrowing the language of natural disaster, the troops spoke of the battle as a storm, a volcano, and a cataclysm; like the phrases in the Paris press and all the other different sorts of rhetoric prompted by Verdun, their language was quick to develop its own formulae. Hardly original enough to be arresting in the first place yet repeated in diary after diary and reminiscence after reminiscence, the big words soon lose whatever force they once possessed. They convey little more than the difficulty, perhaps the near-impossibility, of conveying what the troops saw and heard on the road to Verdun and what it made them feel.

And that may well be their real point. I have already described the sense of alienation that the *poilus* felt from the press and the readers on the home front who swallowed what the press published. Later I will lay some emphasis on their sense of a gulf separating them from others much closer to hand, whom we might think were part of the battle: the generals directing it, the staff officers disseminating the orders, the gendarmes directing the convoys of traffic,

---

* Binyon wrote "For the Fallen," whose words are familiar from Remembrance Day ceremonies:

> They shall not grow old, as we that are left grow old:
> Age shall not weary them, nor the years condemn.
> At the going down of the sun and in the morning
> We will remember them.

the aviators in the skies above. Nowhere, even in the First World War, did infantrymen feel so helplessly, so infuriatingly remote from the gunners supporting them. Nowhere, perhaps, did infantrymen feel so complete a sense of isolation as they did at Verdun. They felt, quite simply, the solitude of men who occupied positions of acute discomfort and danger, for hour after hour and for day after day, with only (in Maurice Genevoix's phrase) *mort de près*: death close at hand. Death, Genevoix wrote, stopped being a concept and became "a presence as real, for example, as the presence of a wasp which goes buzzing round your head, withdraws a little, comes back, makes your skin crawl with the brush of its wings, and which, at any moment, can sting, is going to sting." The knowledge that others, within arm's reach and scattered in their thousands over the whole of a vast battlefield, had only the same buzzing presence of death close at hand did nothing to diminish the horror of such solitude.

Its only palliative lay in the fierce comradeship that the *poilus* cultivated whenever the slightest relief in their ordeal allowed. Their diaries and reminiscences are often explicitly intended to celebrate this spirit, and to acknowledge the bond they formed with others going through the same ordeal. "I want only to talk about my men, my Zouaves," wrote one officer in a colonial regiment. "In their midst, I felt surrounded by friends. For me, my unit was a family." Such feelings came not just from their common experience but also from their agreement that nobody else could appreciate or conceive what they had been through together. Others, indeed, could never be brought to understand—particularly not after the diet which the newspapers had fed them. "When we get back, it'll be our turn to tell the story of the war, and we'll be in the wrong," prophesied Raymond Jubert in frustration: "More and more, blood ceases to be an argument in favor of those who've shed it." To know what Verdun was really like, you had to have been there, at the sharp end. That was axiomatic, that was part of the claim to authority asserted in the veterans' often repeated *j'y étais*. But if you had been there, so the assertion continued, you knew that Verdun—

and what it had done to you—could not be conveyed by the normal resources of language.

Some hint of this already appeared to the troops on their way up the road to Verdun. They registered awe at the volume of the traffic of which they had become so small a part and at the deafening, smoke-laden battlefield ahead of them. Yet most of all, to judge at least from the written record they left, their interest focused on the columns of survivors returning. Somewhere in the contrast between themselves and those they came to relieve lay the contrast between life before Verdun and life after Verdun. This reflection, indeed, was obvious enough to have struck even the most casual bystander looking at the two columns, one going up and one coming down, and it became familiar in almost all contemporary accounts of Verdun, whatever their source. To put what the combatants themselves recorded in some sort of context, it is worth starting with what could be called the official reading of the contrast, the reading proffered to the same public and in the same spirit as Barrès' articles in *L'Écho de Paris*.

Henry Bordeaux was a friend of Barrès, as well as a member of the literary circles in which Barrès had long been a leading figure. Before the war he had made his reputation with novels set in the countryside of his native Savoie. Serving nominally as a staff officer at Verdun, he in fact became the semiofficial historian of the battle even while it was still being fought. Indeed, he appointed himself the laureate of Verdun, for he intended the three books he published in rapid succession to form an invigorating national epic, a modern *Chanson de Roland*. To him the battle might have been "grim and austere" (on a scale of measurement that managed to discover "all the blitheness of a summer morning" in the Battle of the Somme), yet it still had its beauty. The soldiers were cheerful, going into the attack as if they were holidaymakers setting off on an excursion "from Paris to Saint-Germain or Versailles. Just a walk and a picnic on the grass!" And on their return:

> Are they men or lumps of mud? From their helmets to their boots, they are the same unvarying shade, the brown Verdun clay whose

color and smell are known to every veteran of the battlefield, and which he could never confuse with that of the Artois or the Champagne. It covers their great-coats, their trousers, their leggings, their belts and shoulder-straps, their water-bottles, their haversacks, right up to their rifles and their faces. In these faces—bearded or unshaven, gaunt, lined and sunburned—the eyes shine with pride and hope. Pride in the task they have fulfilled, hope of the rest they have earned.

Few noncombatants who wrote without urgent propagandist intent could satisfy patriotic expectation so conveniently. Louis Hourticq, a lieutenant in the Territorials with plenty of chance to observe the men going into action, found them somber and preoccupied: "their features taut, their eyes fixed; they looked at nothing except a mental image." This was particularly true of the troops who traveled by lorry, he argued, since the passivity of their position gave them a foretaste of the greater helplessness to come:

> The infantryman who marches toward the guns keeps, with his legs, his liberty of movement; he can advance cheerfully and take an interest in the sights he passes; he has less time to ask if he's going to come back. The day has started like any other, so why should it end differently? But men who have been loaded into lorries without warning, to rush them straight toward the furnace, already feel the impotence of infantrymen under shellfire.

"You don't take up your position in a sector at Verdun as you do in other sectors," agreed Marcel Dupont. "Anyone who has to fight in the quarries of Fleury, at the Chapelle Sainte-Fine or the Bois du Chapitre"—these places being among the worst on the battlefield—"feels the hand of destiny weighing on him. You go because you have to go." He added:

> Everybody looks inside himself, listens to internal voices that disturb or console. Some, the weak ones, depress themselves with the thought that death may be only a few hours away; others advance

swearing to sell their skin dearly. Nobody is indifferent, because human nature cannot accept the thought of an infinite amount of suffering without fear or revolt.

One point on which all the troops themselves agreed was that the closer they got to Verdun, the more silent they grew. They might have started out singing: perhaps *Mourir pour la Patrie est le sort le plus beau* ("To die for one's country is the most beautiful of fates") but more likely *Il y a loin à Tipperary* or *Adieu la vie, adieu l'amour* with an extra verse referring to Verdun. But the singing soon died out. The silence that replaced it was prompted as much as anything else by the sight of the columns of survivors returning. Henri Bordeaux's description caught their general appearance faithfully enough—the coating of mud (or, in summer, white dust), the haggard, unshaven faces—but of course the way this external evidence of suffering struck him was very different from the way it could affect men about to undergo the same ordeal. "What disgrace!" exclaimed Marc Boasson, a devout patriot and devout Catholic already beginning to suffer disillusionment. "So this is what men can be made into, machines for suffering. Nothing, nothing so abominable has ever been seen. This is not heroism. It's ignominy."

Such anger was rare. Besides, what most struck the newcomers about the survivors was not the evidence of the physical discomforts they had endured: to see men in such shape was, after all, hardly rare on the Western Front. It was the special look they wore: the look of men who had reached the end of their tether and, perhaps, passed into some territory beyond. Literally, it was a look. Far from being aflame with pride and hope, their eyes were glassy, blank, fixed on the remote distance or on nothing at all, oblivious to the sights around them and even to the surface of the road beneath their feet. The inward gaze of those about to go into battle had retreated further, into unreachable profundity. By the same token, the silence already overcoming the newcomers had in the survivors deepened into complete noncommunication.

Nothing is rarer in the literature of Verdun than the record of words or greetings passing between the two columns of men. Even the exchanges that did take place between those arriving and those departing were terse in the extreme:

"It's a bad one, this spot?"
"Yes, mate, it's a shit."
"Where are the Boches?"
"They're in front of you, mate. Now it's up to you."

In the First World War the troops being relieved and the troops replacing them were usually only too eager to stop and talk. They exchanged news about the progress of the battle or details of a particular position, and they indulged the taste for ironic boasting and jeering, complaint and warning that makes the small talk of soldiers the world over. At Verdun this was not the case. "Sometimes," wrote René Naegelen, "from one of the lorries, a *poilu* stood up, muddy, defeated, terrible, and shouted in a husky voice to the comrades who were heading toward the battle: 'Don't go up there!' " The passage comes from his novel *Les Suppliciés*, so even these few ominous words could be fictional license. On the way into position with his unit of artillery, Lieutenant Pierre de Mazenod met only silence. "Suddenly," he records, "one of the ghosts whom the lorries were bringing back, standing up in his seat, his mouth pursed, his eyes glittering from the depths of their sockets, waved an emaciated arm to take in the horizon. We knew that this mute gesture expressed a horror beyond words."

"The very look of these men," said another officer, "made the questions one wanted to ask die on the lips. They did not seem to belong to the world of the living any longer or had not yet returned to it." Unsure that they were even aware of his presence, he simply let them pass—in the distinctive jerky stride, with its periodic stumbling, that men who fought at Verdun came to recognize. Coming back from the very first days of the fighting, Lieutenant Paul Simon met the troops about to be thrown into battle and was suddenly made aware that he and his men chilled speech in others:

Seeing us, they began to offer the jokes customary when two units
pass each other. Our men, their eyes still full of the hellish sight of
the battle, did not reply. The jokes stopped of their own accord
when the other men realized that the pathetic little company filing
past them was all that remained of a heroic battalion of *chasseurs*.

The First World War was fought in the age of the camera. However blurry the photos and the film footage, and however antiquated
the equipment and uniforms they depict, the very fact that the war
did leave such a record is, for us, a part of its modernity. Even today, it still seems only just out of reach. But then, though cameras
were already sophisticated, they had not yet become an adjunct of
daily life. People still posed for them. This is one reason why they
never quite caught the look on the faces of soldiers coming back
from battlefields such as Verdun that so shocked observers at the
time. Indeed, in the most memorable image I have seen of a soldier
returning from Verdun he wears an expression of relief, tempered
by a blend, familiar from a thousand Victorian portraits, of pride in
being chosen by the camera lens and determination to appear his
best. Some photos of troops after battle in the Second World War,
their faces blank with something more than fatigue, help to bring us
closer to the reality. But, for the rest, we have only the words contemporaries used, and above all their struggle with words.

Today we would say that the soldiers coming back down the
Voie Sacrée were suffering from PTSD, Post-Traumatic Stress Disorder. In the Second World War the British spoke of "battle fatigue" and the Americans of "combat fatigue." In the First World
War the dominant term for the psychic aftereffects of battle was
"neurasthenia" or *neurasthénie*. It did not derive from observation of
soldiers but already occupied an established place in the language of
nineteenth-century science. This, we shall see in the course of this
book, is the case with many of the ways of perceiving the relations
between men and battle in the First World War; indeed, it holds
true of the whole system of thought which helped to guarantee that
men and battle did meet in 1914.

The standard French treatise on *neurasthénie* had been written in 1897 by Gilbert Ballet and Adrien Proust, father of the novelist Marcel. The most common symptoms they identified were weakness, suggestibility, lowered resistance and inability to sustain concentrated, purposeful activity. The cause, they proposed, lay in the strain imposed on the nervous system by *la lutte pour l'existence*—the struggle for existence being, of course, neither their own phrase nor their own concept but part of the common coin of nineteenth-century science. Durkheim advanced a similar view of *neurasthénie* in his essay on suicide when he wrote: "The individual can maintain himself in a society definitely organized only through possessing an equally definite mental and moral constitution. This is what the neurasthenic lacks." According to most authorities *neurasthénie* marked the onset of degeneracy; depending on the ideological bias of the particular authority, the cause was to be sought either in social conditions, the moral state of society as a whole or in genetic legacy.

A predisposition to view life inherently as struggle or battle, whether or not the struggle was conceived in strictly Darwinian terms, a preoccupation with the factors, genetic or cultural, that predispose individuals or whole societies to weakness and eventually collapse: these are not just elements in nineteenth-century scientific thought, but the very hallmarks signifying its whole temper. Later on I will need to evoke this temper in more detail, but it is fitting that we should first meet it in its ready application to the state of the men on the Voie Sacrée—where, of course, it immediately betrays itself as unsympathetic and inadequate. This is not to say, of course, that most people were in practice unsympathetic: their response was usually one of shocked compassion. Yet in formal terms they—and the medical profession, and the military structure that the profession served in wartime—lacked a system of explanation making its focus the horror of the occasion rather than the presumed weakness of the sufferer.

On the whole the troops did not speak of *neurasthénie*; they had nothing to say about degeneracy. When they sought to describe the mental state that battle could induce they had their own, evocative phrases. Louis Madelin (a witness to the battle I shall have further occasion to cite) called it a *crise de tristesse somber*: "a crisis of black melancholy." The universal slang term, however, was *le cafard*. Literally the word meant "cockroach" but in this connection it meant roughly what we would call depression, though perhaps "the blues" better catches its idiomatic force. The trench newspapers wrote of it, without shame or judgment, as a familiar element in the troops' existence, like the mud and the lice and the bad food, and as by no means the worst ordeal they had to face. "*Le cafard* is benign," *L'Écho des marmites* assured its readers in 1917, "except in cases where it is complicated by shell explosions, which can lead to death." It came in varying degrees of intensity, ranging from *la grise* through *le cafard noir* to *le hypercafard* and *le cafard vert*. Everyone knew the symptoms and could describe them (apparently the troops found the causes too obvious to need remarking). It came suddenly and caught you unawares. It made you oblivious of events and sights around you. If you were capable of specific imagining under the weight of *le cafard*, what you saw in your mind's eye was usually a vision of home—your wife and children, your native village—but of home as somewhere remote, unreal, lost rather than somewhere you might return to.

And so when men who knew battle or were about to get to know battle looked at the troops making their way back down the Voie Sacrée they did not call them *neurasthéniques*. They reached back into a richer and more potent language. The survivors—barely more alive than the corpses they had left behind them, unable to communicate even with the replacements who already felt themselves in the shadow of death—were ghosts, phantoms and *revenants*. Georges Gaudy, an NCO who himself saw some of the worst fighting, drew these religious and superstitious hints together into a memorable passage every bit as formalized, even in its detail, as a medieval painting of the Deposition, or Descent from the Cross:

They went past with their heads bowed and their expressions bleak, burdened down by their equipment, carrying their red and muddy rifles on their shoulders. The color of their faces hardly differed from their great-coats. Mud had covered them completely, one layer drying before the next had spattered over them. Their clothing and skin were encrusted with it. Close-packed columns of vehicles roared by, scattering this pitiful flotsam of survivors from the great slaughter. But they said nothing, they were past groaning. They had lost even the energy to complain. When they raised their heads, their faces showed a depth of sorrow one had never seen before. Their dusty features seemed frozen and taut with suffering, as if they screamed out something terrifying: the incredible horror of their martyrdom.

Next to me, some Territorials who had been looking on stayed thoughtful. They had the air of sadness inspired by a passing funeral.

I heard one of them say:

"That's not an army any more! Those are corpses!"

And another, a little old man with a hairy face, murmured:

"One should kneel before them!"

Two of the Territorials were weeping silently, like women.

✛   ✛   ✛

Words today are battles. The right words and battles are won; the wrong words and battles are lost.

General Erich Ludendorff

So there were, in a sense, two roads to Verdun just as there were, in a sense, two Battles of Verdun. Occupying the same ground, they assumed significances that, however much they overlapped, could still be distinguished. The first ground was public. The French did not receive the assault on Verdun as another attack by another army in another war: to them it was a supreme national emergency, making the Voie Sacrée the lifeline of a nation ready to pay a sacrifice so great it was customary to speak of it in the language of religion. The second ground was private. It resided in the experience of soldiers who brought personal hopes and fears to Verdun, including all their personal expectations of what words like "nation," "battle," and "sacrifice" might really mean. They commonly declared what they encountered there inexpressible—to be read, if at all, only in the visual emblems of before the battle and after the battle that the road afforded.

Common to both perspectives is a habit of symbolism; indeed, they share an insistence on symbolism, together with an agreement that religion was a fertile source from which to draw their symbols. When the French speak of Verdun even today, sooner or later they always refer to it as a symbol. They may not always be clear as to what it symbolized, and even when they are specific they often do not agree: Verdun can variously stand for the reserves of strength that France can muster in times of crisis, or the futility of conflict between nations, or much else. But people are still sure it is a symbol. The certainty, it seems, is unavoidable. And it stands in direct descent from perceptions adopted instinctively and immediately in the very first days of the battle.

In none of its various forms has military history ever shown itself comfortable with symbols. It has always had its big words (we hear very little of "honor" and "glory" these days and much more of "tragedy" and "waste") but they have usually sounded peripheral to its real enterprise. They stand at some palpable but unspecified remove from an address to the subject which, in its goal of rendering complex and confused events into the certainties of linear narrative, has always been determinedly literal and scorned language in all but its technical functions. The texts bristle with the jargon of tactics and deployment; they are thick with figures identifying battalions and regiments, locating time and place, tallying the dead. The approach has always had its limitations, whatever marvels of local clarification might result. And these limitations grow all the more apparent as the world wars of the twentieth century recede in time and our standing armies shrink in numbers, leaving fewer veterans or soldiers to write or appreciate such history.

The Battle of Verdun demands a broader approach, if its full significance for the French is to be explored—if, that is to say, it is to be approached not just as a feat of arms but as a complex cultural event. Why should it have happened where it did and when it did? Why should it have taken on the particular character and course it did? And why should the French army, like the German army, have pursued so massive an endeavor with such stubborn determination to the most bitter yet least conclusive of ends? Even the most technical and literal-minded account of the fighting soon frames such questions with particular urgency. The search for answers leads beyond military matters, at least as military historians have commonly understood them, and beyond the immediate confines of the battlefield. The soldiers who came to fight at Verdun brought, along with their weapons, a whole set of cultural assumptions—what the French themselves call a *mentalité*. In its most tangible aspects this *mentalité* had been shaped by the Franco-Prussian War of 1870–71, the first round in the modern Franco-German antagonism. The French themselves had been determined never to forget it or the conditions of peace it had created.

To evoke this context will be the task of the middle chapters in this book. Yet, like any study of Verdun, the book must begin with the feat of arms itself. It must address the facts of the battle. Even here, though, some challenge to the conventions of military history needs to be registered. Battles, so military historians have long agreed, are above all stories; the fact that books about battles have become one of the last refuges of narrative history no doubt explains a good part of their popular appeal. On the battlefield everything is confusion, everything is chaos, and often quite as much so to the general consulting his map at headquarters as to the infantryman crouching in his trench. Military history takes up the challenge of picking its way through this mass of incoherence. It sifts the mistaken reports and the misunderstood orders, the rumors and the scare stories; it compares different and often conflicting interpretations to find out which are reliable and which are not, to establish what really happened. By this process it constructs as best it can an authoritative account, a clear story. Yet in the very clarity of the result lies a profound falsification. The incoherence and the misunderstandings are not simply errors to be explored in scholarly footnotes. They are part of the very fabric of the event, the forces that drive it onwards and give it whatever shape, however disappointingly inartistic, it might come to possess.

Nor are the misperceptions that flourish on the battlefield merely local. Of course, they involve local questions, asked and answered by soldiers in the light of imperfect knowledge: where the enemy is, what his capabilities are, what his intentions might be, and what tactics in general might be expected of such an enemy. But this is far from being the full extent of their life. The questions asked and the answers reached depend on interpretation, equally imperfect, of what has already happened in this battle and this war—and also, of course, on interpretation of what happened in the peace that went before. The French historian Marc Bloch was wise to base his admirably dispassionate inquiry into the rumors, particularly of atrocities, that circulated so freely in the First World War on a simple truth: "a false report is always born out of collective perceptions that exist before its birth." We shall everywhere encounter these collective perceptions, drawn from the experience of the past, as palpable forces on the battlefield.

The conduct of war, then, derives from the conduct of peace. To put the matter another way, the myths of peace feed directly into the experience of battle, thus guaranteeing that battles enact a myth of themselves even as they are being fought. Rather than being distinct from the facts and to be rejected as inferior to them, the myth is at every point bound inextricably to those facts. Indeed, it is a fact, and a determining fact in its own right. So even when seeking to describe the Battle of Verdun, the military event, this book will everywhere be drawn into describing the myth of Verdun, what I earlier called the cultural event. The road from Bar-le-Duc soon ceased to be just a country road, or even a vital supply-line, and became a Sacred Way and a Descent into the Inferno. Verdun, the ground that French and Germans agreed to contest, soon ceased to be just a provincial spot that happened to have found itself a salient—if indeed it had ever been seen in such simple and practical terms alone. The form their contest took depended not just on questions of maneuvers and matériel but on questions of how French and Germans had been in the habit of perceiving themselves and each other. Eventually, it depended on how they perceived war itself.

Verdun was nothing if not a microcosm of the First World War—combatants and witnesses from both sides agreed on this point, at least—and so we should not be surprised that the questions it raises echo the general questions hanging over the whole of the war. Few wars, indeed, have raised so many questions; certainly no war has raised so many questions that resist easy answer. Inquiry into the political causes that lay behind it or the diplomatic circumstances in which it broke out have all too often underlined a sense of bafflement. The more minute the examination, the more likely it is that the First World War will look, paradoxically, like an accident of the most random sort and a collision determined by the most obscure inevitability. Investigations of its course yield little agreement. Blame for the four long years of slaughter can be laid at the door of individuals, usually the intransigent politicians and the blinkered generals. Or it can be placed on the circumstances that combined to give armies the organization and heavy weaponry capable of killing men by the million without achieving the decisive advantage anticipated in 1914.

These matters need to be sifted, in however preliminary a fashion, if what happened at Verdun is to be seen in its context. Wars (to adopt the generalization Clausewitz proposed at the start of his great study) operate on three levels, distinct yet interlocking: the political, the strategic, and the tactical. They are undertaken by political leaders in pursuit of a goal. The goal determines strategy, an overall plan based on the military means available and the means at the disposal of the enemy. The strategy shapes tactics, the orders given and the operations launched where gun confronts gun and soldier confronts soldier. If the First World War has so often seemed mysterious or even senseless, to be ascribed to blind accident or blind fate in its outbreak and its course, it is precisely because of how little resemblance it ever bore to this neat and academic model.

As an instrument of policy, war can serve any number of variously defined goals: protecting endangered territory, acquiring desired territory, reducing the power of a rival or neighbor, and so on. But the point is that the goal had better be defined. Clausewitz's dictum that war is a continuation of politics by other means is sometimes invoked as if it licensed politicians to declare war whenever tempers fray and the normal processes of pressure, negotiation and diplomacy do not answer. In fact, it means quite the opposite. War has to have a goal that war can achieve and only war can achieve; we should hardly need Clausewitz's reminder that it is "always a serious means for a serious object."

No contemporary, let alone historian, of the First World War has argued that the assassination of the Archduke Ferdinand at Sarajevo provided the great powers of Europe with such a goal. It frayed tempers between Austria and Serbia, but the powers who watched their relations unravel in the summer of 1914 had already weathered the Moroccan crisis in 1905 and the Agadir crisis of 1911 in a spirit of political realism sufficient, at least, to preserve their uneasy peace. Sarajevo is commonly just called a "spark." But where, and exactly what, was the powder keg it ignited? France and Britain, nation-states with long histories of ambition and assertiveness, and Germany, a new nation-state with new ambitions and a newly acquired habit of assertiveness, certainly had their jealous interests. When have the nations of Europe not been locked in uneasy rivalry on one score or another? In 1914 their rivalry certainly held a potential for war. Significantly, Europe had spent at least a decade dreaming of the war that might break out, the war that could break out, the war that must sooner or later break out. Yet this is not the same thing as saying that, in practical terms, the necessary conditions had been met. None of the interests to which the powers were committed by policy—whether of economic or colonial expansion—seemed in August 1914 to demand war and war alone.

Nothing betrayed their vagueness about the political reasons for going to war so much as the way that the fighting nations stated their aims, to themselves and each other, once the war had started. War aims spell out the conditions that define victory, or at least the demands to be taken to the negotiating table. The cause of Serbian independence, though obviously a matter to be resolved at Versailles, was in itself not enough to explain what was happening and why. Of all the countries involved in the war Britain should surely have been best able to provide the clearest answers to these questions. Britain, after all, had a record of distaste for continental squabbles and a tradition of "splendid isolation." She had not entered into any formal treaties obliging her to join the fighting. (The Entente Cordiale reached with France in 1904 was just what its label implied—a friendly understanding—and one, moreover, whose original focus had reflected a preoccupation with colonial rather than European affairs.) And in autumn 1914 Britain underwent a palpable moment of hesitation before her army crossed the Channel. So she should have known exactly why she was in the war, if any country did. Yet both her wartime prime ministers, Asquith and Lloyd George, fought shy of formulating precise aims for fear of bringing the differences simmering in their own cabinets out into the open.

The same uncertainty about what was wanted or could reasonably be expected from the war was to be found in France and Germany. Yet nowhere did it make the combatants flexible or keep them silent; on the contrary, it made them all the more intransigent and all the more strident from the start. A good deal of scholarship has been dedicated to reconstructing exactly how the general public in the various nations of Europe greeted the news that war had broken out. In general, its results qualify any simple picture of Europeans engulfed by war hysteria. Yet the public and official utterances of the various countries conspicuously lacked those expressions of regret or reluctance that often accompany the outbreak of war, indicating conditions that the enemy might realistically meet or, more generally, signaling that terms could somehow be agreed. In no previous war did inflammatory propaganda take quite so powerful a role, and in no previous war did it achieve quite such bitter extravagance. Even now that we can compare it with the propaganda of the Second World War—which set out, in this respect as in others, to learn from its predecessor in the worst possible way—its savage extremity can still shock.

So in the First World War rhetoric filled the void left by policy. It is always naïve to set rhetoric aside as "just rhetoric," in the dismissive phrase, though historians make this mistake surprisingly often. It proves fatal to any understanding of a war that offers no political reality in the ordinary sense of the term—no consistently stated agenda of war aims—to use as a yardstick for dismissing its rhetoric. The war was not so much accompanied by rhetoric as driven by rhetoric. Its vague yet potent terms gave people their sense of why they were fighting and what they were fighting for and why they should keep on fighting longer than they had originally anticipated. For their part the politicians, who may privately have regarded rhetoric as a tool to exploit in giving their side of the quarrel the dignity of a cause, looked increasingly like its prisoners. They were not, of course, being taken prisoner by fine phrases and paid hacks but by large cultural forces, in fact by those "collective perceptions" of which Marc Bloch spoke. Wartime propaganda did not need to create a new rhetoric for the occasion, merely to point and burnish a common language with which its audience was already familiar. The contrast with the political level on which the war functioned is striking. The attempt to formulate war aims was fumbling and sometimes divisive, yet propaganda had no hesitation or difficulty in finding just the ideological content it needed.

From whichever side it issued, First World War rhetoric commonly dwelt on two issues: territory and the character of the enemy. These preoccupations resurrected traditional grievances, powerful in their hold over the popular imagination yet largely held in abeyance by the political relations between the European powers during the immediate pre-war years. With little prompting, Germany remembered her discontents with the borders that confined her both in the east and the west. With no more prompting, France spoke of *la plaie béante*, *la plaie saignante* and *la blessure toujours douloureuse*—the gaping wound, the bleeding wound, the wound that always hurts—inflicted by the loss of Alsace and Lorraine after the Franco-Prussian War. As the list of debatable lands grew, so the habit of relying on national stereotypes, on which peacetime Europe had relied too easily and too often, grew into hysterical insistence. To their enemies, the British were obviously suave and unscrupulous in their territorial ambition, the French arrogant and insolent in theirs, the Germans ever-hungry and ever-tyrannical.

Not all the grievances were old. Propaganda was fertile in discovering fresh evidence, further confirmation, new cause for outrage not, significantly, in the events leading immediately to the outbreak of war but in the events of the war itself. The most clamorous instance was Germany's invasion of Belgium, undertaken not because Belgium appeared a desirable goal in itself but simply because it lay on a temptingly convenient route into France. The invasion proved the worst as well as the earliest of Germany's mistakes, and hence the best and most enduring gift to the rhetoric of the Entente Powers in the west. Another patch of ground joined the list of places from which the Germans must be expelled. And it made a particularly poignant patch of ground for it was, in the language of the day, innocent and violated. French and British propaganda, eager to attribute the horrors of war only to the actions of the enemy, dwelt on atrocity stories. Their behavior in Belgium, it seemed, confirmed that Germans were beasts—ready as soon as war stripped the scanty veil from their real nature, to murder civilians, rape women, mutilate children and destroy cultural monuments.

It would be a relief if we could dismiss such propaganda simply as nonsense, unpleasant and embarrassing for Europe to remember even after nearly a century has elapsed, yet incidental to what the war was really about. In fact, it was central, defining what passed for policy and for goals in the absence of anything else. The enemy must be driven from this stretch of ground or that. Yet this alone would not in itself constitute victory, since the root cause of the war lay not in where the enemy was or wanted to be but in what the enemy was. The war had not been started by an action or a program, nor even by a leader or a government, a party or a faction. It had been started by the very character of an entire nation—or, at least, that part of it which French and British propagandists could confidently label, with everything negative it connoted, "Prussian."

Annihilation, *anéantissement*, *Vernichtung*: we readily associate these chilling, absolute words with the Second World War. Yet the rhetoric of extermination is older than that, ready to hand in 1914 and by 1916 or 1917 a familiar staple of wartime literature. "To be or not to be," Clemenceau had warned in 1905, "that's the problem which an implacable desire for supremacy poses for the first time since the Hundred Years War." The implacable desire for supremacy he had in mind was, of course, German; it was already growing axiomatic to speak of her ambitions in these terms. However much they denied or resented the charge, Germans could from their side of the hostile division agree that the tension between Germany and the rest of Europe—not, after all, so grave or urgent in terms of ordinary politics—was still in some sense a matter of life or death for nations, if not their peoples. By 1912 the Kaiser, Wilhelm II, could join Clemenceau in invoking Hamlet's language. The antagonism of other nations toward Germany, he had persuaded himself, was "not a question of high politics, but one of *race* . . . for what is at issue is whether the German race is to be or not to be in Europe."

With the First World War only two months old Winston Churchill was writing that: "This is no ordinary war, but a struggle between nations for life or death. It raises passions between races of the most terrible kind." The young Lieutenant de Gaulle agreed. "What is this war but a war of extermination?" he was asking his mother in a letter written just before Christmas 1914. There was sadness, as well as acceptance, in their tone. But the tone of the propagandist press, in all countries, was enthusiastic. "A Total War: Them or Us": so Léon Daudet entitled an article in *Action Française* arguing that any form of sympathy for Germany or Germans should be considered treasonable. Germans "should be stamped for all time, out of existence," proclaimed Lord Northcliffe's *Weekly Dispatch*. "You cannot naturalize an unnatural abortion, a hellish freak. But you *can* exterminate him," added Horatio Bottomley, most violent of the English *bourreurs de crâne*. The foretaste of the language of the Third Reich in the word "exterminate" was specific, not casual. Bottomley thought that even naturalized British citizens of German origin should be forced to wear a distinctive badge and their children be excluded from school.

By the end of the war the steady diet of propaganda, with its stories of German beastliness and German cruelty and its calls for extermination, had worked its intended effect. It could lead an ordinary civilian like Marjorie Grant, an Englishwoman working at a refuge for the homeless in Paris, to write: "The impression left on one's mind is of despair as to any decent future for the Germans, despair that such an unredeemable race must continue to exist, that it cannot be stamped out like some vile disease." So, even in the casual language of ordinary people—and ordinary soldiers—the enemy was never to be beaten or defeated, much less just outmaneuvered or pushed from his position: he was always to be smashed, to be crushed, to be ground into nothing. Victory would be the end of Germany, the end of France, the end of Britain.

The phrases are vague. Does the end of Germany (for example) mean the end of the German state as presently constituted, the end of Germany as a single and independent nation, or simply the end of all Germans? Vagueness does not make the phrases less powerful in people's minds, and it often makes them more, not less, ominous. The genocidal dream of an end to all Germans is obviously present and, though it grew more intense as the war dragged on, it had been there from the start. The First World War might have begun innocently, in the sense that people believed it would end quickly and decisively, but even at the beginning it was innocent in no other sense. If a certain gravity tempered any impulse to war hysteria in August 1914, it was precisely because few people doubted just how murderous were the hostilities—as well as the power of the weaponry—unleashed.

These points take me ahead of myself in my argument, and into some of its most contentious yet critical reaches. What matters most at the moment is how the failure of policy and the dominance of rhetoric affect the model of war I borrowed from Clausewitz—apart, that is, from making it look increasingly remote from the realities of 1914–18. Plainly, policy did not define and shape strategy. Instead strategy was given the freest of hands by rhetoric. At any time the result would have been dangerous, but it was particularly so when soldiers were singularly barren in their thinking about strategy. Really, the whole conflict saw the enactment of only one big strategic idea, and this had in fact been conceived years before. I mean, of course, the plan which Count Alfred von Schlieffen devised during his tenure as German Chief of Staff, put forward in 1905, and continued to elaborate in retirement; he was still brooding on it on his deathbed in 1912. It formed the basis, at least, for the German advance in August 1914, a great arrow curving west across the map of Europe through Belgium and into France.

Even its shape on the map expresses the love of bold initiative—of *Vabanquespiel*, or playing the game by going for broke—which always came more easily to the German military mind, in the First World War as well as the Second, than to the French or the British. Moreover, it proceeded from an appraisal of Germany's position in the event of war that struck a deep chord with most of the perceptions Germany had been formulating about herself and the outside world since Bismarck had consolidated the state at the end of the Franco-Prussian War. Germany was hemmed in. Talk of *Einkreisung* ("encirclement") and *Deutschland gänzlich einzukreisen* ("Germany entirely surrounded")—even, in the Pan-German slogan, talk of *Feinde ringsum* ("Enemies all around us")—formed the common burden of her worries and discontents. In peacetime she was haunted by what Bismarck himself had called the "nightmare of coalitions," a nightmare that Kaiser Wilhelm II's blundering way with diplomacy seemed expressly designed to make real in the years before the outbreak of war. When war did come, Germany would in all likelihood face the problem of fighting on two fronts: against Russia and France, or, in the charged racial language of the times, the Slavic East and the Latin West.

In this predicament lay the threat of a long and drawn-out war. The danger was most acute in the east. Russia's capacity to absorb and destroy invading armies in its vast hinterland had been notorious since the fate of Gustavus Adolphus and Napoléon. So, in Schlieffen's reasoning, strategy demanded a decisive blow in the west. Yet France was no easy nut to crack. The French themselves remembered the humiliating speed of the defeats they had suffered in August and September 1870. Indeed, they dwelled on it to the point of bitter obsession. For their part the Germans remembered with rancor the long, debilitating endgame to the war. This had resulted from the hasty French *levée en masse*, so it had done nothing to alter their low regard for the French army as normally constituted; contempt for their enemies on this score remained axiomatic in Germany. Yet France's program of fortification in the years since her defeat had made her more than ever, in Schlieffen's eyes, "a great fortress."

France would have been flattered. But her fortresses lay in the Eastern Marches, since 1870 confronting the territories that Germany had annexed, where she most feared further assault and intermittently longed for *revanche*. Schlieffen judged the line from Belfort to Verdun impregnable. So his solution lay in sidestepping the fortresses, just as for Hitler in 1940 it lay in sidestepping the Maginot Line, and going through Belgium. From here the German army would rush across northern France in a great arc, its right flank brushing the English Channel, to capture Paris not by direct assault but by encircling it from the west. Only in this way could Germany achieve a quick victory and a real victory: *Vernichtung* (as Schlieffen inevitably expressed it) in six weeks.

Historians of the First World War used to attribute the failure of the German advance in 1914 to the modifications introduced by the younger Moltke, Schlieffen's successor as Chief of Staff, and the commander of the First Army, General von Kluck.* Their nervous tinkering, it was alleged, robbed the plan of its bold clarity and brought about the check the German armies suffered at the Marne.

---

* General Helmuth von Moltke, German Chief of Staff in 1914, was the nephew of Count Helmuth von Moltke, Prussian Chief of Staff in the Franco-Prussian War.

Yet a good deal of the fault lay in Schlieffen's original idea and its commitment to a route through Belgium—a commitment that Schlieffen himself steadily enlarged in successive revisions from mere infringement of Belgium's southern tip to a broad strike reaching across from the northern Ardennes to the Flanders plain. I have already cited it as a propaganda gift of incalculable value to the Entente Powers. It was also a classic example of what one military historian has called war "shaped solely by the imperatives of military possibilities and free of the overriding controls of political reason."

Moreover, the plan had from the start posed tactical difficulties that Schlieffen himself acknowledged without ever surmounting. A strike on the curve he envisaged, and in the strength and concentration he considered essential, simply crammed too many troops on too few roads, while leaving the French the use of a conveniently disposed railway system in organizing their defense. In their modifications Moltke and Kluck addressed the danger, albeit in a half-hearted fashion. They reduced the number of troops Schlieffen had specified and urged nervous haste on those they did commit. Finally, as the days ticked by and the risk of delay loomed larger, they abandoned the final swing of Schlieffen's arc, meant to encircle Paris from the west. Instead they pulled south short of the capital.

And there, at the Marne, they met the British Expeditionary Force—bedraggled and diminished, rallied for the task only with manifest reluctance by Sir John French—and an altogether more formidable French army. Originally the German deployment had caught Joffre and the rest of the French General Staff unawares, as it was meant to. Their Plan XVII had assumed that the main thrust of the attack would come through Alsace and Lorraine, and had prepared to meet it with a vigorous counterattack. It had thus, in the words of one historian, "fitted into the original Schlieffen Plan like a glove." Overcoming his first reaction of torpid disbelief as the German deployment unfolded, Joffre had readjusted his thinking and was ready to work his miracle. At the Battle of the Marne the Germans were halted and, effectively, strategy died. "I don't know what's to be done. This isn't war," exclaimed Kitchener, Britain's newly appointed Secretary of State for War, when he saw the lines of trenches spreading along the Western Front. Neither the military doctrines in which he had been schooled nor his long years of service suggested any obvious response.

In a fit of youthful bravado Kitchener had actually enlisted in the French army during the Franco-Prussian War. The brief adventure had given him his only taste of warfare in continental Europe, and it made him unique among British commanders.* Veterans of 1870 were naturally to be found in the upper reaches of the French army—starting at the top with Joffre, who had cut his teeth as a second lieutenant in the Engineers. Yet French generals, like their British counterparts, had gained their real experience of command only in colonial wars: relatively small-scale affairs, sometimes no more than skirmishes, usually fought against ill-equipped opponents. All their training and experience made them favor a war of movement. What else indeed was war, or war worthy of the name, if it was not movement? And what else was movement if it was not attack? The British spoke everywhere of "the doctrine of the offensive," to be carried out in a proper "spirit of the offensive," and the French of *attaque à outrance* (attack to the hilt), to be carried out with *élan*.

Of what happened when armies with modern weaponry confronted each other they knew only by report. This is not to claim that, say, the example of the Russo-Japanese War of 1904–05 went completely unheeded; though they despised reading and distrusted learning, the French and British officer corps had at least discovered the idea of military theory and the military academy. Yet knowledge of what the new firepower, with its vastly increased

* "The truth is, that since the Crimean War we have had little or no experience of the kind of effort which will be required of us when next we meet the trained army of a European Power." So Sir John French had written in 1910. He had additional reason to wish the words forgotten in 1914, since they had appeared in an approving preface to the English translation of a book by Count Friedrich von Bernhardi, the German militarist and writer on military affairs. British wartime propaganda liked to denounce Bernhardi as the epitome of everything Prussian, and hence repugnant to civilization.

range, strength and accuracy, could do to the exposed and frail bodies of men did not quench the passion for attack. Attacking had grown more difficult and was bound to be more costly of life, so the response ran, but mind could still triumph over matériel if it were possessed of enough willpower and enough discipline. Indeed, willpower and discipline could triumph over anything that an enemy might pit against them. In speculating why so shaky a premise should have been so eagerly accepted, and so grimly adhered to, more than one historian has suggested that the emphasis on *élan* was in fact a "rationalization of weakness." It held reassurance for a country such as Britain, lacking any tradition of conscription and conscious of how small her professional army was. France did have a tradition of conscription and hence the capacity to mobilize a mass army, but France had also spent the decades since the Franco-Prussian War brooding on the alarming rate at which both German industry and the German population were expanding by comparison to her own.

In France the doctrine of *élan* became central to military thinking. It was promulgated by the École de Guerre founded in 1878 (whose most perfect product, among the generals of the First World War, was Foch) and by the influential Colonel de Grandmaison, Chief of the General Staff's Troisième Bureau:

It is always necessary in battle to do something which would be *impossible* for men in cold blood. For example: march under fire. Such things only become possible for men in a high pitch of excitement against men in low morale. The experience of every age shows that in the offensive, safety is gained first by creating this depression in the enemy that renders him incapable of action. There exists no other means but attack, immediate and total. . . . Our conclusion will be that we must prepare ourselves and others by encouraging with enthusiasm, with exaggeration and in all the infinite details of training everything that bears—however little— the mark of the offensive spirit. Let us go as far as excess and this will perhaps not be far enough.

So military training consisted less in advocating strategy or tactics than in inculcating and celebrating a warrior code. Commanders must be inspiring in their leadership, capable both of inculcating ideals and of rousing the beast within the men they ordered to attack. For their part, the troops must be taught how to believe, how to obey, how to kill with passion and how to look calmly, even proudly, on the prospect of their own death.

Just how thoroughly these injunctions had permeated the army by the eve of the war can be judged from a speech made to incoming conscripts in 1913. By then the offensive spirit had become identified above all with the savage romanticism of the bayonet charge and by then, too, it could be openly taken for granted that the enemy on the receiving end of the bayonets would be the Germans. The speaker was Charles de Gaulle, fresh from his officer training at Saint-Cyr and still highly orthodox:

> Everywhere, always, one should have a single idea: to advance. As soon as the fighting begins everybody in the French army, the general in command, the officers and the troops have only one thing in their heads—advancing, advancing to the attack, reaching the Germans, and running them through or making them run away.

It was single-mindedness of this sort that generals and officers of the First World War usually had in mind when they judged their troops' morale.

From such doctrine stemmed the belief that the war was going to be short, if costly of human life. So it left the victors at a loss after the Marne, when the Germans dug themselves in to defend the line where they had been stopped. French and British troops had little option but to follow suit, and thus the Western Front was established. Its trenches announced a stalemate; its trenches signaled that the war of movement was over and the war of position had begun. In a very real sense the military history of the next four years was the history of the generals' frustration with the war of position and of the price that their frustration could force their armies to pay. Officially, the name for the response they adopted was "attrition." (The French *usure* and the German *Ermattungsstrategie* carry the same meaning.) If the enemy could not after all be crushed at a blow, it seemed, he could at least be worn down to nothing. Slowly, his positions could be weakened and eroded, his troops could be killed in such numbers that the flow of replacements ran dry, and eventually his economy could be brought to ruin by the whole effort of sustaining the war.

This is how the case for attrition was promoted. Yet attrition never really achieved the status of strategy, let alone of successful strategy, and always looked more like a fig leaf worn to conceal an absence of strategy. In the mouths of those who first used it, it signified little more than "It's not going to be a short war, after all." Sometimes it meant no more than "Wait and see." That is what it seems to have meant to Kitchener, who (to give him his due) had been almost alone in Britain—alone, certainly, among her cabinet—in prophesying a long war from the start. The uncharacteristic prescience made him gloomy but prepared for the task of raising a mass volunteer army from a nation that had always preferred to leave the job of warfare to a small professional force. French commanders still had strong doubts whether reservists and hastily trained civilians could muster the same spirit as professional soldiers. Privately the spirit they most inclined to admire was still *élan*. Publicly they grew more likely to enjoin *patience*, *détermination* and *fortitude* on their troops. Journalists and propagandists recommending the doctrine of attrition to the home front—which had, after all, given its support to the war in the belief it would see a quick victory—set about promoting the moral qualities demanded by what the historian Ernest Lavisse called *l'épreuve de la durée*: the long haul.

Not victory today, after all, nor even victory tomorrow, but victory if we can hang on longer than the enemy. The shift is not so much conceptual as rhetorical, designed to promote a new morale rather than to present a new idea. Lavisse spoke of *l'épreuve de la durée* in a volume of essays bringing together the most distinguished

French intellectuals mobilized in the propaganda effort. It appeared in the spring of 1916. With the war 16 months old and Verdun underway, the need to address morale had grown more pressing. Joffre had addressed it, and rather effectively, when he spoke of his strategy as *gringotage*: nibbling away at the Germans. Soldiers always love to speak of their trade in metaphors of eating—they bite, they swallow or they gulp their enemies—and *gringotage* certainly sounded more invigorating than the glum *usure*. Yet Joffre used the word to characterize his strategy throughout 1915, and nothing could be more misleading than its suggestion of patient, small-scale activity. 1915 had been a year of big attacks and no useful result. It had killed even more French soldiers than 1916, the year of Verdun and the Somme.

The big French attacks of 1915—like the Somme and all the big French and British attacks of the war—were really failed attempts at breakthrough. Pulverize the enemy with an artillery bombardment, take his positions with an infantry assault, roll up the trenches on either side and drive your army through the gap: in one massive hammer-blow the frustrating war of position would be transformed into the exhilarating war of movement. If it did not work this time, then surely it must work the next time, in another sector or a wider front, with more resources, a more carefully prepared bombardment, troops filled with more zeal, an advance carried out with more *élan*. The hope continued to animate commanders in whose mouths attrition was usually just a convenient word to disguise their repeated failure to break through.

What made the breakthrough, if not impossible, at least infinitely more difficult and less likely than commanders thought was the simple fact that modern weaponry had shifted the odds quite decisively in favor of defense rather than attack. No amount of willpower and discipline in the attackers, no warrior code carried to whatever extreme of zeal, could level the odds against defenders now equipped with (among other advantages) concrete, long-range rifles and machine guns. Lengthening the artillery bombardment that preceded the perilous moment when the infantry advanced, making it yet more massive, increasing its accuracy as much as the primitive state of battlefield communications allowed: all these expedients the generals tried. But the more carefully prepared the bombardment, the more forewarning the defenders had of the time when the opposing infantry would come out of their trenches. And, horrifying though the bombardment might be for the enemy in their trenches, it still did not destroy enough of the defenders' heavy equipment to change the odds in favor of attack.

Such factors, of course, did not just baffle the attempt at breakthrough. They vitiated the argument for attrition, making nonsense of it even as a fallback justification after the attempt at breakthrough had failed. For attrition to work as a battlefield doctrine, it was not enough for the attackers to kill a lot of the defenders: they had to kill more defenders than they themselves lost in the process. In his draft plan for the Somme offensive Sir Henry Rawlinson defined his purpose: "to kill as many Germans as possible with the least loss to ourselves." Even the unreliable statistics of battle issued while the war continued showed that this was not happening. The sums could be done. We will see in a later chapter how André Maginot could add the figures up quite easily by the summer of 1916 and use them to devastating effect against the claims being made for progress in the war against Germany.

To revert once again to that remote and ideal model of war I borrowed from Clausewitz, an absence of political goals passed the burden for conducting the war down to the level of strategy, and an absence of strategy passed the burden down yet further to the level of tactics—and of worn-out tactics blindly repeated, at that. In the process political leaders showed a sinister reliance on their military commanders. We expect politicians to fancy themselves soldiers in wartime; the delusion is usually one of war's sorriest and most disastrous spectacles. Yet one striking feature of the First World War was that it showed men as different as Poincaré, Clemenceau, Lloyd George, and the Kaiser willing, not just to suspend their judgment or stifle their doubts when their chiefs of staff spoke, but almost to be held in thrall by the mystique that attached to them. Events nevertheless ensured that the mystique was usually short-lived. The French Miracle of the Marne finished the younger Moltke, who had launched the German strike at France, and Verdun finished Joffre, his reputation already shrunken since the Marne, as well as Moltke's successor in Germany, Falkenhayn. Of the supreme commanders only Haig, whatever other qualifications he might have lacked, showed real tenacity in clinging to office.

Before their departure, these chiefs of staff usually excused their failure to deliver the military possibilities they had successfully urged on their masters by blaming their war ministries for not having equipped them properly or the generals under them for not having carried out their orders properly. After misreading the Schlieffen Plan as it had unfolded before his gaze, Joffre took advantage of the months following his victory at the Marne for witch-hunting among his subordinates. Of the 48 commanders of infantry divisions before the war, only seven were still in place by January 1915: one had been killed and one seriously wounded, several had been advanced to command corps, and the rest had been demoted. (Their fate originated the verb *limoger*, for they were sent to Limoges to report for rear duty.) And before their departure these subordinates had charges of their own to level. Regimental colonels and junior officers, they pointed out, were sometimes men promoted beyond the rank their age or training would normally have justified; the men in the ranks, hastily drawn from the undisciplined and suspect masses whom democracy had bred, could make poor soldiers.

And the regimental colonels, the junior officers and the troops? By and large they were stuck with the job of holding positions, if necessary to the last man, and attacking positions, if necessary to the last man. Even when they are not worn out and blindly repeated, tactics are almost always about positions. Most commanders in or near the field—a general of a division briefing his staff, a colonel addressing the officers in his regiment, a junior officer deploying his battalion or company or unit—are thoughtful enough to know that what they do is meant to play its part in some larger design. It usually helps if they are aware of this dimension; it also helps if they see the design as serving a cause to which they are wedded. But they know that these issues do not belong essentially to the language of command. They don't tell the troops to go and engage the enemy so that his attention is distracted from another sector, and they don't tell them to go and defend liberty. It might be reassuring to remind them that there is a larger design, and it is often appropriate to make encouraging reference to the cause they all serve. But the core of what they do is to draw a line and say, "Don't let them take this position," or to indicate toward a distant spot and say, "Take that position." Tactics are about holding ground and capturing ground.

So the reliance on tactics, in its preoccupation with ground, produced a result agreeing with the rhetoric which, for want of a clearer goal, concentrated on territory. They reinforced each other. Don't let the barbarians get an inch further, said the rhetoric to anyone who would listen: push them from what they have already taken, push them from Belgium, push them from the annexed provinces. Don't let them push you out of your trench, said tactics to the men at the front: push them out of their trench. Whatever its particular vantage point, serious treatment of the First World War or any of its major battles must surely begin and will probably need to end with somber, bemused reflection on how much suffering was expended and how many lives were lost over strips of ground so small, so insignificant.

✛ ✛ ✛

A battle? . . . But Verdun is a complete war in itself, inserted in the Great War, rather than a battle in the ordinary sense of the word.

> Paul Valéry, "Réponse au remerciement
> du Maréchal Pétain à l'Académie française"
> ("Reply to the Speech of Thanks
> by Marshal Pétain in the Académie Française"), 1931

In one way and another, most of what I have to say about Verdun in this book will affirm the truth of Valéry's description—though not always in quite the spirit that led him to offer it when welcoming one of Verdun's heroes into the ranks of the 40 *Immortels* who make up the Académie Française. The generalizations I have just been making about the war as a whole, often admittedly in large and perfunctory terms, hold true in the detail of their local application to the battle. It too began in hopes of a quick victory, hopes that lingered disastrously in the minds of commanders even as it turned into a long haul mimicking the course of the larger war. Fought in a political and strategic vacuum, it was thus conducted in the language of tactics and rhetoric—above all in its preoccupation with the significance of ground.

It will already be obvious, I hope, that tactics are shaped by considerations far from being as strictly practical as the generals and military theorists would sometimes have us believe. Certainly it is difficult to identify any great practical value in the ground of Verdun in 1916. Neither side seriously claimed it held such value. Neither the Germans in their wildest hopes nor the French in their wildest fears really believed that Verdun was the key that could unlock the way to Paris. Indeed, each side was given to mocking the other as irrational in attaching significance to Verdun as a military position. Yet the Germans attacked it and kept on attacking it while the French defended it and kept on defending it, even as the months dragged by and the cost mounted to figures chilling even by the standards of a wasteful war. The French determination to defend the east bank of the Meuse, with its hills and fortresses, can seem particularly curious in the light of what I said at the start of this chapter about the practical difficulties and dangers faced by an army inside a salient. Even without a German attack, the French could profitably have withdrawn across the Meuse; the maneuver would have shortened, simplified and secured their front line. Yet even at their most acute moment of danger this was the very maneuver they set their faces against.

Plainly, ground has an emotional content in tactics as well as rhetoric. In principle it is usually considered more valuable and in practice it is often easier to hold or to capture if it is "home." Failing that, it helps if it can be claimed as ground once belonging to the homeland. This is a simple matter of morale. One reason why the French fought so stubbornly at the Marne was because they were Frenchmen with their backs to Paris. And one reason why the British Expeditionary Force, at least in the person of its commander Sir John French, fought with comparative reluctance was because of a residual distaste for getting embroiled on the soil of continental Europe. In their hearts, the British felt that the last battle, the one that counted for everything, would be the one that took place across the Channel.

The emotional significance invested in a particular spot of ground by an army's knowledge that it is home or was once part of the homeland can be intensified by its larger historic associations. By far the most potent of them are the previous battles that have taken place there. Their memory is often already familiar, from the military academy if not the schoolroom, and it can easily be pressed into service. Since politicians and commanders readily acknowledge the force of such association, they can even use a little sleight of hand with the evidence. The victory scored by the German Eighth Army, under Hindenburg and Ludendorff, over the Russians in East Prussia toward the end of August 1914 was a spectacular achievement in itself. It came, moreover, as a particular relief to Germany after the opening stage of her campaign on the Eastern Front had threatened to bear out all her deep-seated fears of war with Russia. But the Germans did not choose to celebrate their victory as the Battle of Frögenau, though that was where their field headquarters lay. They turned instead to a tiny village several miles away and called their victory the Battle of Tannenberg. Apart from chiming harmoniously with Hindenburg—their first and always their most lustrous war hero—the name of Tannenberg recalled the battle some centuries earlier (in 1410) in which the Poles and Lithuanians had defeated the Teutonic Knights. Modern Germany, it appeared, did not just revive the old Teutonic spirit: it avenged history.

Few corners of the globe have a map more thickly clustered with the crossed swords that mark historic battlefields than western Europe. And in western Europe the crossed swords cluster at their thickest in the broad vertical swathe of land where the modern France and the modern Germany face each other, the territory where Lotharingia, the Middle Kingdom, had once lain and the Western Front now lay. These past associations did not always help the Entente Powers, and particularly not in their relations with each other. At the very start of its campaign the British Expeditionary Force disembarked at Boulogne within sight of a statue of Napoléon, marking the point from which the Emperor had planned his invasion of England.* When the troops arrived at Rouen they struck the French president Raymond Poincaré—and he surely cannot have found himself alone in the thought—as coming to "perform a rite of expiation in honour of Jeanne d'Arc." With memories of traditional Anglo-French enmity written into the very landscape around them, it was hardly to be wondered that relations between these inexperienced and unlikely allies should have been so fraught with discord in the early months of the war.

Joffre, however, could exploit history to his advantage as cannily as the Germans did in the naming of Tannenberg. Watching the German advance in autumn 1914 and calculating where he could best rally the French army to confront it, he brought all his massive calm to bear on his staff, his soldiers and the public. He predicted that the battle would probably take place on 2 September and that its scene could well be the little town of Brienne-le-Château, near the river Aube, in the open country of Champagne. In fact, he was wrong about the date as well as the place, though not too far out, and he went on to work his miracle at the Marne on 6 September. But his oddly and unnecessarily specific prophecies had made their point. No Frenchman or woman needed reminding that

* To commemorate the arrival of the BEF a statue of Britannia was erected at the entrance to Boulogne harbor in 1938. In his speech at the unveiling ceremony, Pétain described Boulogne as "a point of contact for the French and British peoples" and chose to remember its associations with Dickens, Blériot and cross-Channel swimmers, rather than Napoléon. The German occupiers destroyed the statue in July 1940.

2 September was the anniversary of the day in 1870 when Napoléon III had ridden out from Sedan to surrender himself and his army to the Prussians. The date itself warned of the national emergency. And Brienne was the site of one of Napoléon's battles, against the Prussian Blücher. Even more significant, it was where France's greatest soldier in modern times had first attended military academy.

And Verdun? Obviously it was "home" for the French and, moreover, a part of the homeland in the vulnerable and battle-torn Eastern Marches. Past conflicts lent its name resonance. Yet these factors still fall short of explaining the determination to defend it at such cost in 1916—one should say, the French obsession with defending it at any cost. A good part of "home" was already in German hands by then: "Messieurs les Allemands sont toujours à Noyon" ("The Germans are still at Noyon"), Clemenceau never ceased reminding the readers of his paper. As for the historic associations, they cannot be ignored but by themselves they had not already made Verdun a compelling symbol to the French. It was not Orléans, where Jeanne d'Arc had raised the English siege; it was not Rouen, the coronation place of kings, where the English had burned her at the stake. It was not Sedan.* Yet Verdun was potentially a symbol. It offered enough associations to be exploited by a wartime rhetoric expert in playing on such things. Exactly how the rhetoric and the friction of the battle itself worked together to make Verdun a name as resonant and compelling as any of the names I have just mentioned, later chapters will need to show.

In fact, the French in 1916 preferred to dismiss the suggestion that they were influenced by Verdun's history of battles. Their denial was understandable, since recent centuries offered a record only of French defeat. During the Revolutionary Wars of the 1790s the citizens of Verdun had insisted on surrendering to the Prussians despite the vow that the commander of its garrison had made not

---

* Ironically, Sedan had already been taken in the German advance in the autumn of 1914. Its symbolic life was not finished, though, since in planning his *Sichelschnitt* operation against France in 1940 Hitler was at one early stage captivated by the idea of making Sedan a major target for Rundstedt's army group.

to yield. And it had surrendered again during the Franco-Prussian War, in the aftermath of the decisive German victories at Gravelotte, Saint-Privat-la-Montagne and Mars-la-Tour which had left General Bazaine bottled up in Metz with a good part of the French army. The latter occasion was a particularly impolitic memory to evoke (though, of course, few memories of 1870 were comforting to the French) since Verdun's lack of preparedness could prompt questions which, as we shall see, were uncomfortably to the point again in 1916. Such events, the propagandists liked to claim, held no weight with the French. It was the Germans who had been influenced by them. The Germans, it seems, could not forget the past— a morbid preoccupation in contrast to French reasonableness—and, in particular, could not forget the glorious occasion in 1792 when their national poet Goethe had accompanied the Duke of Saxe-Weimar's army to the gates of Verdun.

Maurice Barrès, who did so much to determine the line that French propaganda followed during the First World War, pioneered this argument when the battle was only five days old:

> Verdun exercises a sort of fascination over the minds of our enemies. . . . The simultaneous fall of Toul and Belfort, we gather, would be nothing to the capture of the old town with which Goethe has made every schoolboy familiar by the account he left of his time there in his *Campaign in France*.* Memories of 1792 are still lively. . . . The Argonne and Verdun still seem the Thermopylae of France.

Where Barrès led, others were quick to follow. They quoted his words or simply borrowed his references to Goethe and Thermopylae, the Greek pass that had seen several battles, most famously when Xerxes and his Persian army met Leonidas and his Spartan defenders in 480 B.C. The German obsession with Verdun

---

* Though Goethe called his book *Campagne in Frankreich*, Barrès insisted in the original French of this passage on referring to it as *Kampagne de France*—the letter K being, in French eyes, an epitome of German barbarity.

was treated virtually as dogma in the histories of the battle rushed into print even while the battle was still being fought.

It remained a staple of the French military histories and memoirs that fell abundantly from the press in the years immediately after the war. But then the memoirs of Erich von Falkenhayn, the Chief of Staff responsible for the attack, permanently modified accounts of German intentions at Verdun. Generals' memoirs are notoriously unreliable documents, and none more so than those by First World War generals. Commonly they are rambling and self-justifying, eager to place whatever blame needs to be dispensed on the shoulders of politicians, colleagues and subordinates; by comparison, the enemy is usually treated rather mildly. For all the disappointments of his wartime career, and those of 1916 in particular, Falkenhayn did not give way to these temptations. His memoirs aspired to impersonal objectivity right from their title, *General Headquarters 1914–16 and Its Critical Decisions*. The claim extends even to his habit of referring to himself in the third rather than the first person. Naturally, the result is no more trustworthy than any other account a First World War general offered after the event, but its unreliability lies always in its acute reticence. Falkenhayn drew a veil over the circumstances in which he became Chief of Staff—he had previously been the Kaiser's Minister of War—after the younger Moltke had led the German army to its check at the Marne. A yet thicker veil covered his loss of the job at the end of August 1916, amid the failures at Verdun. Of the growing doubts about the wisdom of the offensive, let alone the real scale of German losses in proportion to French losses, he was careful to mention nothing pertinent.

Yet on the original decision to attack Verdun Falkenhayn offered something much more to the point: a draft of the memo he had written arguing the case for the Kaiser's benefit sometime in December 1915. As suave and apparently dispassionate as anything else in his book, it was a model position paper from a man whose previous career had shown him to be a politician in uniform rather than a working soldier. It certainly betrayed no trace of the obsession with Verdun that the French were so eager to attribute to the Germans. Nor did it have any truck with symbolism or the emotional resonance of ground, except insofar as they might affect the French response. It was fundamental to his plan that the place chosen for attack should be, for whatever reason, an objective "for the retention of which the French General Staff would be compelled to throw in every man they have."

Indeed, Falkenhayn's main argument was not that Verdun must be attacked but that something must be attacked. The way he broached and developed his theme shows how differently the whole question of attack was debated among the Kaiser's entourage than it was among those directing the military effort in France and Britain. When I spoke earlier of the inflexible attachment to the doctrine of the offensive that characterized the First World War, the burden of my aspersion fell on France and Britain. German military thinking was more flexible. In describing the German army as a vast machine, soulless yet aggressive, boneheaded at the top and devoid of initiative below, in attributing to it all the characteristics that went to make up the current definition of Prussian, the French and the British were in fact describing themselves more precisely. Germany had indulged her love of *Vabanquespiel* in August 1914 in carrying out the attack that her military planners had been refining on paper for more than a decade. After the Marne she changed her tune.

It was the Germans who first started digging trenches. It was the Germans who first worked out the need for reserve trench lines and other refinements of their hastily adopted posture of defense. It was the Germans who, after the Somme, resolved to yield their forward positions and withdraw to the prepared fortifications of their Hindenburg Line. Even the official British history of the war conceded that they had done a better job of adjusting to the realities of "siege warfare in the field" than the Entente Powers. Indeed, it went further in its tribute:

> With their usual thoroughness, having decided to stand upon the defensive, they gradually evolved a system which amounted to something more even than defensive strategy and tactics, and may be described as a philosophy of the defensive.

The proof lay in the simple fact that, while the British and the French vainly expended themselves again and again in the hope of breakthrough, the Germans launched no large-scale attack between August 1914 and Ludendorff's spring offensive in 1918.

Except at Verdun in 1916. Verdun originated in the problems left unsolved by the German philosophy of the defensive. It might have avoided the appalling level of waste incurred by the French and British habit of attack, but it had also left the stalemate of autumn 1914 unchallenged and unbroken. This the Germans regarded with growing dread, the dread they had always felt of a long war. German thinking had begun with the premise that war in the east could easily be long, yet it had never lost sight of the fear that war in the west might be long as well, and that this would prove equally a disaster. In proposing his plan Schlieffen had everywhere implicitly reckoned from German weakness; he had stressed that the best, if not the only, chance lay in forcing the issue to a quick result. By 1914, when Germany's sense of weakness had if anything deepened since Schlieffen's day, Moltke and Kluck's enactment of his plan had betrayed anxiety, not confidence. By Christmas 1915, with the chance Schlieffen had put in her hands long since dead, Germany was very far from being about to crumble, as the propaganda of the Entente Powers liked to portray her. Yet her underlying fear had been confirmed and her anxiety given time to grow.

Falkenhayn's memo did not dwell on these factors in any detail. It did not need to, for his audience was already familiar with them. Nor did it argue at length his belief that decisive action should be taken in the west rather than the east. Germany—like Britain—had its Westerners and Easterners in debate about strategy, and Falkenhayn had already made his position known, just as Hindenburg and Ludendorff, his rivals and soon to be the beneficiaries of his failure at Verdun, had established themselves as advocates of action on the Eastern Front. Falkenhayn merely urged, as a fundamental premise, that Britain was the main enemy and that Britain was still strong. Russia might be shattered and Serbia all but destroyed, Italy might be prone to second thoughts and France weakened by fruitless offensives, yet Britain was undiminished. She remained powerful in her grip on her allies and powerful in herself. Indeed conscription would soon swell the ranks of her army. Falkenhayn did not feel the need to remind his audience of the likelihood of renewed French and British offensives. (He did not know it but virtually as he wrote, on 6 December, Joffre was sitting down with the British at his headquarters in Chantilly to secure their commitment to the Somme offensive.) Even without special intelligence or special gift of prophecy, Falkenhayn could still warn tellingly of approaching crisis, the moment "when the balance of numbers will deprive Germany of all remaining hope."

Britain, then, was the enemy who must be assailed as soon as possible. Yet she was difficult to assail and impossible to assail directly. Land invasion could be ruled out now more than ever. Even the British sectors of the Western Front should be avoided, either because of a lack of German divisions in the right places or because of the muddiness of the terrain until mid-spring. By spelling out these difficulties, Falkenhayn proceeded with rigorous logic to two proposals. The first, for unrestricted submarine warfare against Britain, took some time to gain acceptance. When it was adopted, it gave the Entente Powers their best fodder for propaganda—particularly propaganda directed at the USA—since the subjugation of Belgium.

Falkenhayn's second proposal did gain immediate acceptance. It was to attack Britain by attacking France, in the southern sector of the Western Front, and so knocking Britain's "best sword out of her hand." Two possible targets proposed themselves: Belfort and Verdun. In his dispassionate way, Falkenhayn said nothing of their history for French and Germans. He made no mention of the Prussian victories at Verdun in 1792 and 1870. He made no mention of Belfort's successful resistance in the Franco-Prussian War, nor even of the fact that Bismarck had originally demanded Belfort in the brisk negotiations about the extent of the territory he would annex. Either place would do, Falkenhayn thought, though he inclined to judge Verdun better because it lay closer to railway lines under

German control. Both answered his criterion in being "objectives for the retention of which the French General Staff would be compelled to throw in every man they have." And if they did so:

> the forces of France will bleed to death—as there can be no question of a voluntary withdrawal—whether we reach our goal or not. If they do not do so, and we reach our objectives, the effect on French morale will be enormous.

Bleeding the forces of France to death: the image leaps from its dry surroundings in Falkenhayn's prose. It compelled the attention of the first historians of Verdun who encountered it, and it still compels attention. Many recent histories take it for granted that, even in its conception, Verdun was something appalling, something unprecedented: a battle simply undertaken to slaughter the enemy in the largest numbers possible. Taking Falkenhayn's phrase so completely at face value might suit our ready inclination to believe the battles of the First World War senseless, and hence fitting preludes to a century of senseless warfare, but it nonetheless misses the point. Appalling Verdun certainly was, and was always bound to have been from the moment Falkenhayn laid out the idea in his memo. Yet it was not unprecedented in its conception. Far from being novel and chilling in its clarity, Falkenhayn's thinking followed the familiar pattern of its time—and not least in being, at the core, vague. That was what made it so dangerous.

Exactly what sort of battle was Falkenhayn proposing, in its purpose and likely form? Obviously he did not have in mind a battle aiming to capture a specified position because of its local, tactical significance. Nor did he promise his master an open road to Paris. Indeed, he went out of his way in the memo to cast a very skeptical eye on any such scheme:

> Attempts at a mass breakthrough, even with an extreme accumulation of men and material, cannot be regarded as holding out prospects of success against a well-armed enemy, whose morale is sound and who is not seriously inferior in numbers.

This was sensible, given the French and British failures to break through and the readiness among the German leadership to take note of their failures. It was also typical of Falkenhayn's prudence: he was not a man to promise, even for temporary advantage, a success that he did not believe he could deliver.

Yet what he suggested instead was, after all, not so remote from the thinking of the French and British. Indeed, it was essentially the same as what Sir Henry Rawlinson would shortly be proposing at the Somme: to kill as many of the enemy as possible with the least loss to his own side. Bleeding the French army to death was really *Ermattungsstrategie*—attrition—in its battlefield application, albeit described in unusually blunt and pointed language. Yet I have already stressed that, however it was expressed, attrition was always at best a flawed concept. Often it was deliberately muddled, the muddle providing convenient room for excuse after failure. Falkenhayn, always the politician, was plainly aware of this advantage; much less the soldier, he glossed over all the dangers. As a result he promised himself and the Kaiser the luxury of a win-win situation at Verdun. He promised a battle that would be massively involving and murderous for the French yet not for the Germans. He promised a battle that would at once be decisive and yet low in risk. He promised a battle that would succeed whether it was short or long. And he promised a battle that would be a victory whether Verdun fell or not.

Such easy reassurances served their turn in promoting the idea in general terms and they evidently helped Falkenhayn to win the Kaiser's approval, granted at an audience in Potsdam shortly before Christmas 1915. Then they were embodied in the impressively melodramatic codename chosen for the operation: *Gericht*. Alistair Horne, the most distinguished of recent historians who have assumed that Falkenhayn's stated purpose of bleeding the French army to death explains more than it actually does, would have us translate *Gericht* as "execution ground." But this is among the rarer and more specialized meanings of a word that usually means "judgment." Verdun, then, was to be in some large but unspecific sense a judgment for the French army and for France: the moment of truth, the big crunch.

The difficulties began when it came to hammering out the specifics of a battle plan in the weeks after the meeting at Potsdam. The task of carrying out Operation Gericht was assigned to the Kaiser's son, Crown Prince Friedrich Wilhelm, and his Fifth Army. On the face of it, they were the logical choice: they had battered against General Sarrail's French Third Army at Verdun in 1914, though without effect, and they had remained in the sector facing the salient ever since. Indeed the choice was so logical that one cannot help finding a courtier's compliment to the imperial family in Falkenhayn's final decision to make Verdun rather than Belfort his target. Yet it was also questionable, since the Crown Prince himself commanded so little respect. Far more than his failure to take Verdun in 1914 stood against him, though it made an additionally depressing augury. The French naturally exploited it in this light once the battle had started. But by then the point was often lost in comprehensive derision hinging on an English pun on his name, so obvious as to be irresistible: the Clown Prince.

Friedrich Wilhelm certainly appeared the very model of the playboy soldier. His youth (he was 34 at the time of Verdun) put it beyond doubt that he owed his rank to his position in the imperial family and to his father's insistence that he play a leading role in an army where lesser German royals (like Crown Prince Rupprecht of Bavaria) were winning respect. His habit of conducting indiscreet affairs with French women from German-occupied regions several times threatened embarrassment. Even in uniform his bearing let him down. His awkwardness on horseback earned him the contempt of his father, let alone of brother officers schooled to attach particular importance to parade-ground display. His lean, gangling body and wizened schoolboy face at once contrived to suggest the stereotype of the Prussian aristocrat while falling a long way short of the handsome elegance that was supposed to go with it. Physically, the Crown Prince was a gift to hostile cartoonists.

In the circumstances there was little reassurance to be taken from the common report that he was allowed to do nothing without the express agreement of General Schmidt von Knobelsdorf, the chief of staff his father insisted on assigning to him. All the blame for the failures of the Verdun assault seemed to beg to be laid at his door. More detached historians have still sometimes accused him of misunderstanding or going rashly beyond the brief that Falkenhayn had placed in his hands. Yet in fact the problems lay in the brief and, while exposing them, the Crown Prince's consultation with Falkenhayn did nothing to answer or remedy them. A man whose real gift always lay in quick instincts and the inclination to trust them, the Prince had a bad feeling about Verdun from the start.

He certainly appreciated that what Falkenhayn envisaged was a limited offensive, not an attempt at breakthrough. The Prince knew that what he and his army were being asked to conduct was what soldiers call a "bite and hold" operation: attacking a piece of the enemy's ground and making him waste his resources in defense, holding it and making him waste his resources in counterattack. At Verdun the obvious way to carry this out would have been by en-circlement, the fate that salients always invite, the fate that the de-fenders of Verdun were in fact to spend months dreading. The more patient the process, the more damaging it would have been to an enemy given time to pour men and matériel into a closing trap. Yet Falkenhayn at first denied the Prince the resources to attempt encirclement, and only later and halfheartedly granted the Prince permission to spread the offensive to both banks of the Meuse. Al-ternately bold and cautious in proposing the assault, Falkenhayn would quickly show himself indecisive in overseeing its progress.

Falkenhayn's reasons for denying the resources in the weeks be-fore the battle are revealing of the confusion he generated. He needed divisions in reserve, he said, to meet the counteroffensives that would surely be launched elsewhere on the Western Front in response to the Verdun assault. The argument did not convince Crown Prince Rupprecht of Bavaria, commanding the Sixth Army facing the British in Flanders, or his chief of staff General von Kuhl. Their own, far more realistic view was that the British would not have rebuilt their army sufficiently by spring to undertake any such action. Indeed, the more he listened to Falkenhayn, the more Rupprecht—a far more substantial and respected royal commander than the imperial Crown Prince—grew uneasy. Verdun, he gathered, would start a process decisive in restoring the war of movement, but his diary recorded the impression that Falkenhayn

> was not clear what he really wanted, and . . . was waiting for a stroke of good fortune which would bring about a favorable solution. He wanted a decision in the spring, while declaring a breakthrough impossible, but how else should the change from the war of position to the war of movement be enforced?

Forced to concentrate his opening move on the east bank alone, Crown Prince Friedrich Wilhelm had little option but a fast and furious assault in one sector. It would presumably have to be as fast and furious as possible. If the attackers were not simply to linger in a dangerous salient they had carved for themselves inside the original salient, they would need all the force they could muster to push ahead to the goal they had defined. The Prince later claimed to have realized and complained virtually at the start of battle that Falkenhayn was denying him resources adequate to this operation as well. The criticism was certainly justified, even if the emphasis the Prince later attached to it might well be the memoirist's habit of self-justification. The temptation was particularly acute for a man who in later life came to believe that, though it might have been the war that robbed him of his crown, it had been Verdun that robbed him of his reputation as a man of honor.

Hindsight certainly showed up, and tempted aggrieved participants to dwell on, the inadequacies lurking in preparations that at the time struck all those involved simply as massive. Verdun was to be the biggest thing the Germans had conceived, let alone attempted, since the opening moves of the war. Yet no consideration of the scale proposed for the assault—whether it emphasized the grandeur of its first thoughts or the niggardliness of its second thoughts—could disguise the uncertainty about what exactly it was supposed to achieve. Falkenhayn had not properly defined his goal in terms of ground, the only terms that would really matter once this battle, like any battle, had started.

His memo had contrived to suggest it was optional whether the city of Verdun itself should fall. All that was needed was for the French to be drawn into battle among the hills and fortresses of the east bank by the threat of the city falling. If Verdun were taken, well and good; if it were not, still well and good. The Prince did not suffer from such unsoldierly vagueness. He was soldier enough to grasp the practical point I have already spelled out: that the language of command must speak about ground and speak precisely. It can talk of bleeding the enemy to death if it wants, but not as the core of the orders it gives. There, it is not even enough to tell troops to push ahead as far as they can. If the troops were to be invigorated and sustained for a battle of this magnitude, they must be shown a prize. And at Verdun the prize could only be the city that bore the name.

So, in the orders coming from the Prince and his staff as the battle started, the assault was about taking Verdun and taking it quickly. Regiments were encouraged to bring their flags forward in the expectation they would soon be parading them in the city. Such hope soon backfired on German morale, but this is not to say the Prince's orders misinterpreted or distorted or exceeded Falkenhayn's original plan. They simply translated his equivocation into the only form that might make sense on the battlefield. In fact, it hardly mattered what the orders said on this point. As soon as battle was joined, whether Verdun fell was bound to become the only criterion for victory or defeat—in the eyes of the soldiers who fought and suffered on either side, in the eyes of the public which watched from the home front, in the eyes of the rest of a world which found in Verdun a critical test of strength. Each day the French held out would look, or could be made to look, like another day's success. Each day the Germans stood short of Verdun would look like another day's failure.

"Everything is very simple in war, but the simplest thing is very difficult," said Clausewitz, admitting the limits to the clear-cut theoretical framework which his meditation on war had begun by proposing. Few organized human activities are more intricate than a battle, more at the mercy of accident and the unforeseen, and in consequence few show the gap between intention and execution more glaringly. Launched with a muddled intention, the Battle of Verdun was bound to reveal this gap at its widest. Attack met with defense, disorganized but determined, so immediate as to be virtually without thought. Both attack and defense grew quickly into desperate habit, and then into sullen habit. Habit was what kept the battle going, rather than any definable purpose beyond the local exigencies of the moment, and it took many months and many deaths before it gave way to exhaustion. It was, by definition, a tragedy that needed time to unfold. Yet the seeds of the tragedy had been sown even in the opening days.

PART ONE

FRICTION AT VERDUN, FEBRUARY 1916

The whole conduct of war is like the action of a complicated machine, with an immense amount of friction; so that combinations which are easily made on paper can only be carried into execution by very great exertion.

Carl von Clausewitz, "Summary of the Instruction
Given by the Author to His Royal Highness
the Crown Prince [of Prussia]
in the Years 1810, 1811, and 1812,"
printed as an appendix to *Vom Kriege* (*On War*), 1832

1

—✛—

THE BOIS DES CAURES

To foresee "the war of tomorrow" was not difficult: it was bound
to come. To predict this attack on Verdun . . . was more daring.
We're about to have it.

Lieutenant Colonel Émile Driant, letter to a friend,
20 February 1916

Surprise and speed, assets that military commanders have always been schooled to prize above virtually all others, were
rarely at their disposal in the First World War. The Germans still
hoped to enjoy them at Verdun, but first they had to put their faith
in the lessons of mass warfare as they had learned them since 1914.
Elaborate preparation, it seemed, was the key to victory. Falkenhayn might have hesitated to provide resources on a scale that met
the large promises of his memo to the Kaiser or the specific needs
that the Crown Prince discerned, yet what he authorized in the
compromises hammered out immediately after Christmas 1915 was
still a massive concentration of force. Indeed, it was the most massive yet gathered in a war that had already proved a deadlock of concentrated force.

The salient where this force gathered in the New Year described
a 60-kilometer curve around Verdun. Prominent hills marked the
tips of either wing: Cote 304, in French hands, and the Butte de
Montfaucon, in German hands, on the left bank of the river, and

Les Éparges, which the Germans had vainly tried to take early in 1915, on the right bank. Louis Madelin—a native of Lorraine and scholar of Napoleonic history as well as one of several staff officers who set out to chronicle Verdun—compared the landscape to an intermittently rocky coastline facing the sea. This, indeed, is exactly what it had been at some remote point in geological history. The effect is most clearly marked in the eastern and southern sectors, from the village of Ornes down to Les Éparges, where the Hauts de Meuse overlook the Woëvre. Here the French and Germans confronted each other on the plain, but the bulk of the French defense lay in the commanding hills behind them. For their part, the German positions still enjoyed the advantages for which the attackers of a salient naturally look. All were well served by supply-lines for bringing in extra troops and equipment, and many lay in deep forest offering cover to new deployments.

"Build no more fortresses, build railways": the elder Moltke's dictum had been a guiding principle of the German army since the days of the Franco-Prussian War. That war had given the Germans control of the long-distance lines leading to Metz, a major railway center, and their advances in 1914 had given them command of those serving Charleville-Mézières, Longwy and Briey. All came within 100 kilometers of Verdun. In the New Year of 1916 the Germans set about extending them down to the towns, villages and woodland fringing the salient. Here they added a further network of narrow-gauge tracks penetrating the forests; at some points these came within half a kilometer of the front lines. With the belief in railways went a belief in artillery, particularly the heavy artillery unmuzzled in the advance through Belgium which had begun the war. The most notorious of the German siege weapons was the Krupp 420mm howitzer, the *Dicke Berta* (or Big Bertha) that had flattened the forts of Liège.* Over seven meters long, it was transported to

---

* Nonmilitary readers may appreciate being reminded that artillery weapons are formally designated by the caliber of the shells they fire: thus the Big Bertha fired a shell with a diameter of 420mm, or about 16½ inches, and a 77 fired a shell with a diameter of 77mm, or about 3 inches.

the battlefield in sections and took almost a day to assemble for firing; its shells were nearly as tall as a man and many times as heavy. Almost as powerful were the Krupp 380mm naval gun—the Germans, like their enemies, were turning their naval weaponry for use on land as the war at sea proved less important than expected—and the Austrian-made Skoda 305mm howitzer, or *Schlanke Emma* (Slim Emma).

They positioned this heavy weaponry well to the north of the battlefield, behind the crests of hills offering both concealment and points of observation. Its job was to pound the forts and city of Verdun from long range. Closer to the front line were 210s and 150s, whose shells the French called *marmites*, or stewpots, and flat-trajectory 130s and 77s, whose shells the British called whizzbangs and the French *miaulants* or *miaules*, from the noise they made in flight. They were supported by a whole range of field and trench mortars—*Minenwerfer* to the Germans, *crapouillots* to the French—which could fire gas and incendiary shells as well as explosives. Their job was to tackle the French field artillery, strip cover from the forests, knock out local strongholds of resistance, flatten trenches, kill infantrymen, mangle them, choke them, demoralize them and stun them into submission.

In all, the Germans moved about 1,200 artillery pieces up to Verdun, over half of them heavy caliber, and equipped them with two and a half million shells, enough for six days of bombardment in a battle they still hoped would quickly prove decisive. Men were deployed on the grand scale as well. By the early weeks of February, the Crown Prince had at his disposal a total of some 17 divisions, or perhaps 300,000 men. They included elite units such as General von Lochow's 3rd Corps, which had forced the British back from Mons and was in 1916 fresh from success against the Serbs. Rather than digging the jumping-off trenches which so easily betrayed the imminence of an attack to the enemy, these and the other infantry units destined for the front line were concealed in *Stollen*, underground barracks specially dug deep in the woods. The largest could hold more than 1,000 men, and some lay less than a kilometer away from the French front they would soon be attacking.

Formidable though it was, this array of firepower and fighting men did not leave the Crown Prince and his staff a free hand in fixing their plan of battle. Falkenhayn had insisted on keeping divisions in reserve for imagined counterattacks from the British sector of the Western Front. In doing so he had deprived his army at Verdun of the weight needed to launch, on so wide a front, the battle of the wings that would have been required by military wisdom about how to attack salients. While opening his artillery bombardment on all the sectors between Montfaucon and Les Éparges, the Crown Prince needed still to focus the real thrust of his assault on one part of the French line. Inevitably he chose the northern tip of the salient, a 12-kilometer sector stretching from the right bank of the river almost to the village of Ornes. Here he concentrated the bulk of his artillery and the strongest of his front-line forces: about 850 guns and well over 100,000 men. It was here, after all, that a puncture in the French lines promised the speediest way to the forts in the hills and to the city of Verdun itself. And it was here, in the Bois de Consenvoye and the Forêt de Spincourt, rather than in the more open country of the Woëvre, that the dense trees and the winter mists clinging about them gave the best chance of concealment and surprise.

It was also here that the French were at their most vulnerable. In fact, they were more vulnerable than the Crown Prince had any means of realizing and, moreover, weak throughout the entire salient. Perhaps the most curious feature of the buildup to the battle was the poor intelligence that the enemies possessed of each other's capabilities and intentions. The Germans, as the scale of their preparation testified, simply took it for granted that Verdun was strongly defended. The French, who had spent several decades pointing with pride to Verdun as a showcase of defensive fortification, became aware only at the last minute of the peril to which its present state now exposed it. Yet how on earth could Verdun have been allowed to grow weak? The reasons lay in policy rather than simple accident, and they cast a good deal of light on both the theory of warfare as it had come to be understood and the politics of warfare as it had come to be practiced by 1916.

The strategic importance of its position had made Verdun a fortress and garrison for many centuries, but the decision to fortify the surrounding hills was of much more recent date. It arose from the disasters of the Franco-Prussian War, which had brought the German border closer to Paris and left Metz, traditionally France's main bulwark on her Eastern Marches, in the hands of her newly powerful rival. In the early 1870s General Séré de Rivières proposed that the new line of defense should run from Verdun to Toul, Épinal and eventually Belfort. Ironically, the forts were built by Italian laborers who came, as *frontaliers*, across the new border from the provinces to the east. Across that border, military activities seemed to justify the need to fortify Verdun in particular. Elsewhere less interested in forts than railways, the Germans chose to complete the system round Metz already begun by the French shortly before 1870, naming each of its new bulwarks after victorious commanders in the war.* Following decades saw the Verdun forts periodically elaborated in obedience to crises in Franco-German relations and to advances in technology. As Minister of War in the 1880s and 1890s, the former engineer Charles de Freycinet took a particular interest in bringing Verdun up to date with the changes that had produced artillery shells better capable of shattering stone and reinforced concrete better capable of withstanding them. Thus did France turn *la plaie béante*, the gaping wound of her eastern frontier, into the "great fortress" that so impressed Schlieffen.

By the time war came some 19 forts and as many more *ouvrages*, or smaller fortified positions, protected Verdun. Clustered most thickly on the right bank, they were disposed in concentric rings marking successive lines of a defense whose center, or last ditch, lay in the city itself. Here the Citadelle originally designed by the Marquis de Vauban in the seventeenth century had been made into an

---

* Subsequently, in 1893–1913, the Germans fortified Thionville (which they called Diedenhofen), another city on the western edge of their newly acquired territory. Their arrangements thus mirrored French provisions at Verdun and Toul, guarding the Moselle and its gorges, and behind it the Rhine, against approach across the lowlands of the Moselle.

underground labyrinth, set beneath several meters of stone, where 2,000 men could be garrisoned. Of the forts the most formidable were Douaumont, and its slightly smaller twin, Vaux. Set on a plateau where the Hauts de Meuse rise to their highest point at almost 400 meters, Douaumont dominated the terrain of the future battlefield—as, indeed, it dominated the military architecture of its day.

The aerial reconnaissance photographs that would make its image familiar to most of the world in 1916 emphasized the sullen, determined simplicity of a design which had served fortification since the days of Louis XIV's military architect, the Marquis de Vauban. The view from above revealed an outline in the shape of a polygon, or star, with its apex pointing north and its entrance in the center of the inwardly recessed southern wall. Zones of barbed wire, a line of metal spikes and a dry moat that could be covered by enfilading fire from the corners of the polygon defended the approaches. The flat surface of the roof, made of reinforced concrete below a heavy layer of soil, was broken by revolving turrets housing machine-gun posts, a big 155mm gun and several 75mm guns, two of them sharing a so-called Casemate de Bourges. They could all be retracted under the protection of huge metal domes, leaving little or nothing to be seen from the air of the fort's real strength. This lay belowground, where the gloomy, echoing maze of galleries and rooms, still lit only by kerosene lamps in 1916, could house a working garrison of about 1,000 soldiers.

S'ensevelir sous les ruines du fort plutôt que de le rendre, proclaimed the motto inscribed in the underground corridors of Douaumont and the other Verdun forts: "Rather be buried beneath the ruins of the fort than surrender." After mobilization in 1914 there were in fact about 500 men in Douaumont to contemplate the prospect of sacrificing themselves in this fashion. Yet the French high command soon judged that the opening stages of the war had made their position irrelevant and outmoded. The ease with which the Germans had taken the Belgian forts of Liège and Namur and the French fort of Manonviller had seemed to demonstrate the ineffectiveness of any fort against the new generation of artillery, so the men and weaponry lodged in Douaumont would be more safely and usefully deployed in the field.

This lesson overlooked the fact that the business of subduing Liège had at the time seemed to the Germans an agonizing hitch in their advance, as well as the fact that the Verdun forts had withstood the assault of autumn 1914 without suffering serious damage. Yet Joffre and his staff soon converted it into dogma because it suited their assumptions, and Joffre, in particular, was never a man to question his assumptions. The whole bias of his thinking, like that of virtually all his contemporaries, inclined to offensive and not defensive strategy. "Whatever the circumstance," said the first sentence of Plan XVII, Joffre's counterpart to the Schlieffen Plan, "it is the Commander-in-Chief's intention to advance with all forces united to attack the German armies." So little time did he have for the very concept of defense, indeed, that he insisted on describing his last-ditch defense at the Marne as an attack. This curious blurring of distinctions, moreover, answered not just to the temper of military thinking but to the whole temper of the nation.

To retreat for safety behind concrete walls, even to bury oneself in the bowels of the earth, was a natural enough reaction when the wounds of the Franco-Prussian War were fresh. France would do so again, with the Maginot Line, when she emerged victorious yet even more deeply wounded from the First World War. But these nervous precautions were always less than reassuring. Even in its tactical detail Séré de Rivière's line was pessimistically drawn, since it left the city of Nancy exposed as a sacrificial pawn to attack from the east. Its reliance on siege warfare also carried disturbing reminders of 1870, when the French armies had allowed themselves to be bottled up in Metz and Sedan, which the elder Moltke had with relish called a "mousetrap." General Ducrot, caught inside the mousetrap at Sedan, had his own vivid image for the prospects of the French: *Nous sommes dans un pot de chambre, et nous y serons emmerdés* ("We're in a chamber pot and we're going to get covered in shit").

Even in the immediate aftermath of 1870, so memorable a warning made it hard to trust entirely in fortification or to contemplate siege warfare with confidence. In the longer term a purely defensive stance did little to assuage national pride. Accepting the truncated eastern border was painful enough in itself; marking it with such massive permanence made people yet more uneasy. What the wounds of 1870 really cried out for was *revanche*. Aggressive war with Germany might not be politic and any sort of war with Germany might not be welcome. But if it did come, it should at least be a war of attack to wipe away the humiliations of the past. The French might not have been as interested in building railways as the Germans, but in their hearts they took little consolation from building fortresses. What they wanted was a war of movement that would carry the fight into the provinces they had lost: much better than hiding soldiers underground was to take their graduates from cavalry school up to the blue line of the Vosges so that they could view the slopes down which they would one day charge in triumph.

Later chapters will need to dwell further on these attitudes, and the ambiguities with which they clouded the very concepts of attack and defense, for they emerged from deep within the French experience of history and they affected even the day-to-day course of battle at Verdun. What matters here is that, after the opening stage of the war, they licensed the systematic downgrading of fortresses originally built with such effort and pride. By the autumn of 1915 Joffre had further, and more precise, reason for ignoring Verdun in his growing preoccupation with the Somme offensive. He proposed it to British commanders at much the same time that Falkenhayn was commending the attack on Verdun to the Kaiser. The Somme, Joffre remained sure, was where the effort of war should be made; the Somme was where French resources would most be needed. Just as he had stuck serenely to Plan XVII as the Schlieffen Plan unfolded in Belgium and northern France in 1914, so again he showed himself reluctant to let events or the enemies' intentions disturb his vision. By the New Year of 1916 the Verdun fortresses had been deprived of their autonomous status as Places Fortifiées and subsumed into a larger Région Fortifiée, and the new region had been put under the general command of the Groupe d'Armées du Centre. These bureaucratic maneuvers made it easier to strip the heavy artillery—even the guns in their ingenious retractable turrets—in readiness for use on the Somme.

So a policy of benign neglect gave Verdun the reputation of being a quiet part of the front, a sector where units—sometimes makeshift and understrength—could be left to rot in their positions. When new troops did arrive, they were told it was a good posting for the father of a family. It was "a very tranquil and peaceful place," a sergeant reported in June 1915:

> From their trenches, some two hundred meters apart, French and Germans exchange occasional rifle fire to keep themselves occupied. The artillery exchanges shells which swish high above us. The village is in ruins, but a charming stream runs through it and, miraculously, its church tower is standing. Our normal schedule here is four days in the trenches and four days rest, the one amounting to about the same thing as the other.

Another soldier added to this picture: "We have almost nothing to worry about, we often play cards and sometimes we have to drop them and jump for our rifles. Bang, bang. False alarm. And back we go to our seats and our cards, our minds completely on the game again."

Such an atmosphere encouraged "live and let live" arrangements, allowing both sides to go about their daily tasks with the minimum of trouble and risk. At least one commander found it necessary to censure these "communications" with the Germans, as he discreetly called them in an order of the day issued during September. Such contact, he reminded his men, was necessary only when receiving deserters; in all other circumstances it merely served the enemy's designs. He ended with a ringing declaration meant to restore a high sense of purpose and a proper spirit of antagonism:

> To understand how obnoxious they [the Germans] are, infantrymen have only to remember the shootings of innocent people, the

massacres of wounded men, the rapes and the burnings, in short the atrocities perpetrated in France by the Germans when, believing victory certain, they thought that they could commit their crimes with impunity.

So not everybody at Verdun was complacent. Lieutenant-Colonel Émile Driant, who issued this order of the day, would later achieve a semi-legendary reputation for the prescient unease he had felt in the months before the battle began. Yet, to a degree, his concern was shared by most of the commanders in the field. They could hardly have been expected to watch calmly as the defenses for which they held responsibility were progressively weakened. General Herr, appointed Governor of the newly defined Région Fortifiée in August 1915, repeatedly urged the need for more artillery, only to have more artillery taken away. On assuming command of 30th Corps, General Chrétien judged Verdun a place ready for catastrophe. Yet there was a strict limit to the protest such men could make against the decisions of their commander-in-chief. General Herr was driven, in muted desperation, to concentrating his meager resources in organizing the defense of the left bank—thus nominating himself as a convenient scapegoat once the attack on the vulnerable right bank had begun.

Colonel Driant was not so restrained in his protests. He was every inch the professional soldier; the photographs show a neat and self-possessed figure, the tributes of junior officers portray a firm yet compassionate leader. Yet he had pursued a checkered career and come to make a habit of outspoken prediction. As a young lieutenant in the 1880s he had served as aide to General Boulanger, the Minister of War whose brief hour of popularity had made him imagine himself a Napoleonic alternative to the messy democracy of the Third Republic. Driant had left the General's staff to serve with a Zouave regiment in Tunis by the time the political crisis broke and Boulanger's star plummeted. But he appears to have stayed in touch with right-wing groups that flew the Boulangist flag, such as Paul Déroulède's Ligue des Patriotes, and anyway the original connection with Boulanger was kept alive in people's minds by his marriage to the General's daughter.

His career showed no sign of flourishing in an army increasingly forced, as its misconduct in the Dreyfus Affair came to light, to purge itself of dissident elements and conform to Republican values. In 1905, finding himself still a mere major at the age of 50, Driant left the army for politics and literature, combining the two vocations in much the same spirit as his friend Maurice Barrès. As deputy for Nancy, a city that Barrès himself had previously represented before he transferred his seat to Paris, Driant built his political career on France's need to defend her Eastern Marches. As writer, he turned to fiction. He took his inspiration, he said, from *Salammbô*, though the novels he wrote under the pen name of "Capitaine Danrit" bore little obvious resemblance to Flaubert's tale of Carthage after the first Punic war. Driant's métier lay in producing bulky fantasies of future warfare.

The popularity such fantasies enjoyed in the prewar years, when writers from all the nations that would later meet in battle were busy turning them out, stands in striking rebuke to any attempt to portray the public mood as complacent. The fantasies themselves supplied an index to public apprehension. Their point of origin had been the Franco-Prussian War: the pioneer work, Sir George Tomkyns Chesney's *The Battle of Dorking*, had sounded the note of warning by transferring the scene of Prussia's victory to the southern counties of England. Chesney's imitators followed him in alarmed reflection on what the war had shown about the strength of the German army and the power of the new weaponry. In speculating about modern warfare, they sometimes proved themselves rather more prescient than the generals and military planners— partly because soldiers and ex-soldiers like Driant often used them to voice concerns that had gone unheeded in the upper reaches of their own profession and to explore military scenarios that might, in more thoughtful armies, have formed the basis for memoranda or position papers.

In proposing political scenarios that led to war, the novelists

played freely on old national fears in the light of current international tensions. British writers, predictably, were preoccupied by
the threat of invasion and the lack of an army of reservists to meet
it; to these themes they would later add the fear of infiltration by
Continental (usually German) spies in the guise of barbers and
waiters. For their part, French writers made favorite themes of the
need for *revanche* in regaining the eastern provinces France had already lost to the Germans and of France's continued vulnerability
in the neighboring provinces—including, of course, Driant's own
seat at Nancy. So when the adolescent de Gaulle tried his hand at
the genre in 1905, it required no great originality on his part to
imagine a German army crossing the Vosges. (The distinctively
personal touch lay in casting himself as the general commanding a
French army which saved Nancy, besieged Metz and marched on
Strasbourg.) Driant's novels, which de Gaulle had evidently read,
offered a more sober and adult version of this fantasy. *La Guerre en
forteresse*, particularly successful in its time and given special interest by later events, was a novel of siege warfare plainly conceived
with the Verdun defenses in mind.

The larger theme of Driant's utterances, common to his work as
novelist and politician, was the need for France to recover her military strength, her preeminence in European politics and, above all,
her sense of national pride. Together these would free her of the obligation to placate her new enemy, Germany. Nor would she need
to cultivate the protective friendship of Britain: so far was Driant
from forgetting the old *ennemi héréditaire* that his fertile scenarios
for future wars included, in *La Guerre fatale*, a Franco-British one.
At the heart of this book, as of all his novels, lies what one critic has
tellingly described as a vision "of a noble people, united in true
brotherhood, engaged in the great task of winning for the nation its
rightful place in the world."

Driant found this vision unrealized by the nation that the Third
Republic was building, and he found it nowhere more glaringly absent than from the army of the Third Republic. Unconventional
though some of his prophecies about future war may have been, he

nevertheless agreed with other military writers from Britain and Germany as well as France in attaching critical importance to the "moral qualities" demanded of soldiers. Yet, depending as they did on a traditional sense of hierarchy, these qualities were inimical to the democratic ethos fostered by the Third Republic. "In an inconceivable aberration," he wrote contemptuously of the new social values, "it is these very qualities that are under attack, setting private soldier against officer, destroying trust, sapping discipline, wiping out the whole ideal of the profession of arms."

It does not seem that Driant's experience of the First World War caused him to change this gloomy diagnosis. By autumn 1915 he had managed to escape from the staff job in the Verdun garrison originally judged appropriate to his age (he was then coming up to 61) and returned to his natural milieu as a regimental officer in the field. The units he commanded were two battalions of *chasseurs à pied* (or light infantry) stationed to defend the Bois des Caures— the very center of the northern tip of the Verdun salient which would soon take the brunt of the Crown Prince's assault. What he found there plainly horrified Driant. His men were for the most part experienced troops, but uneventful months in disregarded corners of the front had taken their toll on what he thought of as their moral qualities. Hence the need to condemn and forbid "communications" with the enemy. The physical state of the defenses which Driant found gave him even greater cause for concern. Here, as elsewhere in the salient, the downgrading of the forts and the removal of their guns had not been accompanied by any sustained effort to make alternative provision. In many places the front-line trenches were makeshift affairs unsupported by a second line, if only because the Territorials who should have dug them had been pressed into service swelling the thin ranks of the front line.

Driant set about making his own arrangements in the Bois des Caures. Instead of continuous trenching, he organized three lines of defense artfully scattered about the shady recesses of the forest. The front consisted of Grandes Gardes, concrete redoubts capable of holding a platoon (about 60 men), sporadically linked by short stretches of trench. Behind it lay a line of support, also broken up into carefully sited stretches, and behind that lay a final line of resistance whose redoubts included Driant's own command post. Events would show his system to be as effective as anything in the Verdun region, and indeed far more effective than most sectors could boast, yet it left Driant far from satisfied. The poverty of the resources at his disposal, combined with the vulnerability of his position in the north of the salient, still troubled a man who had spent so many of the prewar years envisaging scenarios of future battles.

Toward the end of August he wrote to his friend and colleague Paul Deschanel, president of the Chamber of Deputies. His letter predicted that, now that their successes against Russia had freed their hand in the west, the Germans would make a hammer-blow attack somewhere along the line between Nancy and Verdun. He underlined the terrible effect that the loss of either or both of these cities would have on the morale of the French. Near the close he descended from grand warning to specific complaint, dwelling on the many inadequacies he could observe throughout the salient: "Should our front line be overrun in a massive attack, our second line is inadequate and we're not managing to build it up: *not enough men to do the job*, and I add: *not enough barbed wire.*"

In obedience to Driant's request Deschanel passed a summary of his points to General Galliéni, the Minister of War, and in December Galliéni wrote to Joffre expressing concern at reports he had received of "defects" at various points along the French front, Verdun among them. Specifically, Galliéni asked for confirmation that French defenses everywhere included a second trench line. More generally, he advanced a carefully worded warning: "Breakthrough by the enemy would be a matter not of your responsibility alone but of that of the entire government as well." Joffre's reply scorned discussion of military detail but contented itself with the large assurance that French defenses were stronger and better organized than those of their enemy. Much more forcibly and at much greater length, Joffre dwelt on his annoyance at being thus challenged by the Minister. He demanded to know exactly what Galliéni's sources had alleged and exactly who they were:

I cannot permit soldiers under my command to make their complaint or discontent about my orders known to the government through channels other than those which the military hierarchy has established. . . . The very fact that the government welcomes communications of this sort coming, directly or indirectly, from officers serving at the front or from politicians in uniform, is likely to do serious damage to the spirit of military discipline.

Exactly how much of this lofty and stinging rebuke reached Driant's ears we do not know. During the winter he certainly admitted to one of his lieutenants in the Bois des Caures how deeply disheartened he felt by the struggle against staff officers and career officers who resented his status as a politician. He was even thinking of resigning his command and returning full-time to the Chamber. Yet his protest, and the milder voices of other commanders at Verdun, had not been entirely without effect. By 1916 Joffre was still to the general public the man who had saved France at the Battle of the Marne; his grandfatherly calm still inspired trust, even awe. But the disappointments of 1915 had already begun to erode the olympian freedom from accountability to government and elected politicians he had once enjoyed. In Galliéni he already had a determined and powerful enemy, and among the deputies in the Chamber the number of his critics was steadily growing. So the unease about Verdun he had sought to dismiss out of hand refused to go away.

Near the end of January General de Castelnau, Joffre's brisk and cheerful chief of staff, was despatched to Verdun to examine and report on the state of its defenses. What he found led him to share the concern felt by local commanders and to establish a reputation, valuable in the coming weeks, for a sympathy with their plight that others high up in the chain of command had so signally failed to show. Certain matters, at least, could be taken in hand. Extra divisions could be posted to Verdun, or at least moved closer to the salient in readiness. Work strengthening the first line of defense and constructing the second line could be pushed ahead, particularly on the right bank which General Herr's husbandry of his resources had forced him to neglect. Luminaries like President Poincaré and even Joffre himself could briefly show their encouraging faces to assure the defenders that they had not, after all, been forgotten.

Of course, it was all too little and too late, as the critics would afterward point out. Numerically the advantage still lay over-whelmingly with the Germans. The Crown Prince had about 300,000 men and over 1,000 artillery pieces at his disposal. For all the last-minute maneuvers and reinforcements, General Herr had perhaps 180,000 men and 270 artillery pieces. In the crucial north-ern sector of the right bank the Crown Prince had concentrated about 830 guns and 150,000 men. Here General Herr had only Chrétien's 30th Corps of some 35,000 men. And at the very tip of the sharp end, where the Germans confronted the French in the Bois des Caures, 10,000 men from the 21st Division of General von Schenck's 18th Corps stood ready to attack Colonel Driant, who had 1,200 men in his two battalions of *chasseurs* and about 100 extra men from the 165th Infantry Regiment under his command.

Nor was the disparity just a matter of numbers. Of the French heavy artillery, the Banges were old and the Rimailhos short-range; most of the French guns, anyway, were light compared to the ar-mory now assembled against them. The 75mm field piece was not just a staple of the artillery in the way that the Lebel rifle was a sta-ple of the infantry at Verdun. The Soixante-Quinze had virtually become an article of faith in military circles. "You talk to us about heavy artillery," a representative of the General Staff had told the budget commission of the Chamber of Deputies in 1909: "Thank God, we don't have any. It's the lightness of its guns that makes the French army what it is." Nothing heavier than the 75 was appro-priate to an army with *élan*. Two years later, the generals had blocked the Minister of War's attempt to replace it with the 105. At first their faith had appeared justified. Easily transportable and quick-firing (it could manage an amazing rate of 30 rounds a minute, at least for short bursts), the 75 had done sterling service at the Battle of the Marne while the Germans were having trouble bringing their heavier pieces into position. Subsequent battles betrayed the disadvantages of its flat trajectory, unsuitable against deeply set fortifications and in hilly country, like the Hauts de Meuse. So even had the 75s been better deployed at Verdun—and in greater numbers, and with greater reserves of shells—their familiar sound would no longer have brought the reassurance it had once given the infantry.

Now it signified a lack of preparation and lack of foresight which was all too apparent, even in the composition of the infantry. Where the Crown Prince's troops were well prepared and well chosen, the defenders were ill prepared, haphazardly assembled and sometimes organized into makeshift units. Far from being a crack unit, Chrétien's 30th Corps was—in the contemptuous words of one officer—*bric à brac*. Colonel Driant had the previous autumn seen the danger in padding the ranks of the front line with Territorials who should have been digging trenches for the reserve lines of defense. Now the result of such weakness was growing apparent to ordinary soldiers without his tactical experience, and it was taking its toll on morale. Men were losing trust in their generals as the rumors of impending attack grew.

However dismaying, the rumors at least showed that the Germans had lost the advantage of surprise. It had always been naïvely optimistic to hope that an army of the size they had assembled could creep undetected into position. To begin with, they had been helped by the weather. The short days and the poor light, the frequent flurries of snow and the mists that hung over the woods, had kept their troops and guns concealed from observation planes—of which the French anyway had pathetically few. But to launch his attack the Crown Prince himself needed clear weather and good light for observation, particularly by the *Drachen*, or balloons, that would help to guide artillery fire to its target.* The date he had originally fixed, 12 February, arrived without the skies of Verdun obliging and the days continued to pass in snow and mist. Each evening he issued the order to attack, only to countermand it the next dawn. In their

---

* The French called the balloons *saucisses* (sausages) or *biroutes* (a northern slang word for penis).

Stollen the infantry grew cold and bored; the artillery began to betray its presence by longer and longer bursts of ranging fire. French observers remarked the destruction behind the German lines of landmarks such as church bell towers which could be useful to French artillery. The growing trickle of German deserters reported that the hospitals at Metz had been cleared in readiness for an influx of casualties.

On the French side of the lines, the new troops arriving and the old ones returning to their posts noted the air of nervous expectancy. Paul Voivenel, an army doctor taking up his post near Chattancourt on the left bank, watched people fleeing from the nearby villages with their valuables. What instinct was it, he wondered, that prompted them to wear their Sunday-best clothes? Once the battle had started, the few thousand civilians who had remained in Verdun itself would swell the columns making their way against the tide of troops and vehicles headed for the battlefield. Coming up the road from Bar-le-Duc—not yet labeled the Voie Sacrée—Henry Bordeaux would meet:

> women carrying babies or dragging along little children whose legs were giving way, wagons piled with mattresses and furniture. People had taken what they could, at random. Two old folk, husband and wife, side by side, were panting horribly and in the cold air their breath hung round them like a halo in the cold. Dogs followed the procession, tails down.

The suburbs of the city were soon empty, save for the occasional looter at work: "In the streets you see the houses locked up, with their windows broken. Everything is silent; suddenly, you hear a racket from inside, like furniture falling; a face appears at the window and disappears when it catches sight of you."* Troops march-

---

* Rumors of the looting obviously reached Paris, where they angered Maurice Barrès, like any suggestion that the behavior of France and her army was less than immaculate. Reporting his visit in April, he took special care to mention that he had been asked by an eight-year-old girl who had fled the city to retrieve her dolls. (She was in fact his niece Anne Boidot.) He found them where she had left them, undamaged and untouched.

ing through Verdun at night on the way to the battlefield found it an eerie ghost town.

Marc Stéphane, a corporal with Driant's *chasseurs* returning from sick leave on 18 February, noted with approval new 120mm guns in position as well as newly dug and newly strengthened trenches on the right bank—*réseaux Castelnau* (Castelnau networks), the men were calling them in tribute to the General's last-minute intervention. Up in the Bois des Caures he was met with grim jokes ("Any news? They say there's going to be a war") and panic stories picked up from the German deserters making their way through the lines. Waiting for an attack to start can play havoc with the nerves of even well-prepared units, and those at Verdun knew they were still badly prepared. The rumors flying around were getting more and more ominous. Some of the men were saying that the bombardment which nobody now doubted was about to start would last for 100 hours.

In fact, the bombardment on the afternoon of 20 February was bad enough. Even for André Pézard, the Dante scholar perched on the Butte de Vauquois just beyond the western tip of the salient, it made "a terrible day." In the course of a few hours his position had been ravaged, he lamented in his diary: "My poor 11th Company falls from the stalk, it falls from the stalk! Eleven more wounded, three of them already dying. . . . My most experienced gunners, the good comrades who survived last winter, the best Boche-killers, are getting wiped out along with the rookies." For "rookies" Pézard used the expressive slang word *bleusailles*: troops so fresh that their uniforms kept their pristine blue and had not faded into a dusty gray.

Up in the Bois des Caures some of the *bleusailles* cheered when silence fell at the end of the afternoon and no attack materialized. Experienced men who, in the troops' idiom, "knew the music" felt anything but reassured. Stéphane, a 46-year-old reservist whom the younger men called *grand-père*, could recognize the sound of enemy artillery making its final preparations, and he could distinguish the note of 210s as well as 130s and 150s in the din. He knew what these signs warned about the weight of the blow that was about to fall. The Crown Prince—his army starting to lose its edge and his enemy alerted to its peril—had seized at the promise of clear weather. He was determined to attack the next morning.

✢ ✢ ✢

One holds one's ground and dies at one's post.

> Colonel Driant, letter to General Bapst,
> commander of the 72nd Division,
> 18 February 1916

As dawn approached on 21 February the overnight snow had given way to a clear frost. The German bombardment opened up, apparently at 7:00 in some sectors and at 7:15 in others; this, at any rate, is the obvious way to explain the discrepancies in what witnesses recorded.* But there was no disagreement about the shocking intensity of the effect. In distant sectors of the French front troops listened in awe; up in the Vosges, 150 kilometers away, General Passaga felt a steady rumble in the earthen floor of his shelter, punctuated by a heavy pounding. Closer to hand, André Pézard could only be sure of the general direction from which the racket came. At first he was uncertain whether the French or the Germans were firing, but decided cynically that if it were the French much more reliable rumors would have been in circulation about when it was going to start. Was the target Saint-Mihiel, he wondered, or Verdun or, nearer still, the woods of Malancourt below his own position? He looked at his men, pledged to defend mangled trenches and shelters choked like rat-traps at whatever cost, and wondered what would become of them if the storm moved their way.

In fact most of the salient was under fire, from the Reims road in the west to the forts on the hills in the east. In the city of Verdun a shell from one of the Krupp naval guns crashed into the courtyard

---

* I use French time in my account of the battle; the German army, of course, observed German time, an hour later.

of the Bishop's Palace and damaged a corner of the cathedral—the very first shell of the barrage, or so a slightly whiskery tradition maintains, and yet more evidence for French propaganda to cite as proof that the Germans loved vandalizing cultural monuments. In fact it had been aimed at the nearby bridge. Before they were chased from the skies, the handful of French planes sent up to pinpoint the location of the German guns reported simply that the woods beyond the French lines had erupted in an almost continuous line of smoke and flame. Defenders could only watch as the landscape around them was struck by a convulsion. The sheer number of the shells and the systematic rhythm in which they fell—saturating one stretch of ground before moving on to the next—made it look, some said, as if the forests were being doused by a hosepipe that destroyed everything it touched. Frozen snow cascaded from the branches. Whole trees were uprooted and blown into the air, or snapped in two, leaving only their mutilated stumps standing. Men already began to grope for metaphors to describe the devastated landscape. One compared it to a vast asparagus bed; most said it looked like the surface of the moon.

Nowhere was the bombardment more intense than in the Bois des Caures and its neighboring forests, the immediate target of the planned attack. Here the men of General von Schenck's 18th Corps, flanked by Zwehl's 7th Reserve Corps and Lochow's 3rd Corps, stood poised to advance on General Chrétien's 30th Corps. More certain than ever of the prediction he had first made the previous autumn, Colonel Driant had risen early at the house he was renting by the river in Samogneux. He took care to leave behind his wedding ring and a letter to his wife when he rode over to his headquarters at Mormont. From there he went on to R2, the concrete bunker on his line of resistance which he had selected in advance as his command post in the field. He arrived just in time to see the defenses he had so carefully devised collapse into chaos, and most of the surrounding forest with them.

Within minutes smoke, churned-up earth, snow and the débris of splintered trees had thickened the air into an impenetrable curtain of white, brown and gray. The ground shook so violently that it seemed to pitch and toss. The noise was soon so deafening that men had to shout to make themselves heard by someone standing only a couple of paces away. The field telephone wires were cut in the first hour of the barrage, so the only chance that units had of keeping in touch with each other was by runner. For most of the day it would be impossible for them to cover even the shortest distance. When Corporal Stéphane, with Lieutenant Robin's 9th Company at the northwestern corner of the wood, tried to run the ten paces or so separating two shelters he was half-choked and half-stunned by clods of soil from the *marmites* landing all round him. The whole atmosphere enveloped him, and soon his clothes and body too, stank of chemicals. Worse than that, he decided: they stank of death.

"If I listened only to my instinct," Jacques Péricard wrote of his own experience under fire a few days later, "I would throw myself flat on the ground at the bottom of my shelter and cover my ears and wait until it was over." Most men did just that, or the closest thing to it they could manage. Commonly, they crouched in a fetal position, with their back bent over and their heads tucked between their knees or their haversacks clutched over their heads. Sometimes they prayed or talked mechanically to themselves: "Ah! Mon Dieu! . . . Ah! Mon Dieu!" or "That one's coming straight at me." Even if they covered their ears, they could not block out the noise all round them. It still came at them like a physical assault, kneading the body, dissolving the will. In *In Stahlgewittern (Storm of Steel)*, the most famous German memoir of the war, Ernst Jünger likened the sensation to being tied to a post that was struck repeatedly with a sledgehammer. Corporal Stéphane struggled with italics and capitals to convey what he went through even after he had made it to his shelter:

> Imagine, if you can, a storm, a tempest, growing steadily worse, *in which the rain consists entirely of cobblestones, in which the hail is made up entirely of masonry blocks*. Remember that a mere 120, at the point of impact, has gathered the same energy and releases, just as

instantaneously, the same destructive force as an express train hitting the buffers at 90 kilometers an hour. . . . And we're underneath it, you follow? UNDERNEATH IT, as quiet as Baptists, smoking our pipes, waiting from *moment to moment* for the inevitable, fatal moment when our wretched carcasses are going to be squashed, flattened, ground instantly into dust.

For most of the troops who fought at Verdun prolonged bombardment constituted the very heart of their ordeal. It brought not just death close at hand, in Genevoix's phrase, but obliteration. Men found themselves looking on sights that could turn the most hardened stomach, that could appall even a doctor like Paul Voivenel, used to the casualty wards. He and his comrades went in search of a friend and found that he had been blown to pieces by a 305: "In the clear air I could make out a trouser leg on the highest branches of a tree. . . . About 20 meters beyond, a shredded greatcoat . . . a few unrecognizable fragments of the man who had been our friend were vanishing beneath the snow." Captain Charles Delvert came upon the aftermath of a similar catastrophe:

> A long pool of blood, purple and sticky, has congealed near the trunk of a tree. Helmets full of blood, disembowelled haversacks, spades, rifles splashed with blood. A white shirt, spotted with red, stands out from a heap of indistinguishable débris. Near the tree a head that nobody has had the time to collect up. Doubtless that of poor little D—, reported missing.

When a group of soldiers near Raymond Jubert took a direct hit, the result was surreal in its horror: "A great pile of earth, round, shaped like a pyramid, with a hole gouged out all round. Sticking out of it, symmetrically, to a distance of about 40 centimeters, were legs, arms, hands, and heads like the bloody cogs of some monstrous capstan."

Paul Dubrulle, who followed Stéphane into battle only a few days later, described the cycle of terror and relief that those who survived were forced to endure:

When a shell bursts a few meters away, there's a terrible jolt and then an indescribable chaos of smoke, of earth, of stones, of branches, and—too often, alas!—of limbs, flesh, a rain of blood. Immediately a frightful concert breaks out, the wounded screaming as if their souls were spilling out of them. For a few seconds you are overwhelmed by extreme terror and then, very soon afterward, blessed relief. The crisis has passed; you can breathe again for a few moments; you come back to life.

And then, almost immediately, fear returned—fear of the next shell and the death it might bring, the prospect not just of dying, but of "being torn apart, quartered, squashed to pulp," suddenly reduced to "nothing."

When people had imagined war during the years of peace before 1914—and they had certainly spent a great deal of time imagining war—they had often found the prospect seductive, even exhilarating. This was not because they had supposed it would be clean sporting fun; despite what many of the history books would have us believe, the prewar years were not an innocent age. Rather, people had imagined war as an intense, savage process that cleansed, reinvigorated, enlarged the scope of life's possibilities. Peace was passive; it brought mean constraints. War was active; it brought supreme freedom. As well as liberating the nation in political terms, it liberated the individual in spiritual terms. Easy though it was to indulge this simple dream in time of peace, it had already been given the lie by the new technology of warfare—and not even by the technology that looked new in 1914 but by the technology available to the combatants in the Franco-Prussian War. "This war is particularly brutal, without soul, without discernment, without heart," George Sand had written in September 1870, as a mere civilian observer of a conflict that had yet to reach its most sinister intensity: "It's an exchange of projectiles in greater or lesser numbers, having greater or lesser range, which paralyzes individual worth, nullifies the soldier's awareness and will. No heroes any more, just bullets."

There was, then, a terrible irony for the soldiers of 1914–18 in the discovery that battle was above all an experience of supreme

helplessness. At Verdun men sat, or crouched, or lay, and waited for
the shell that would pound them into nothing. They could hardly
speak, they could hardly hear, they could hardly move, and soon
they could hardly think. Bombardment battered their minds and
senses into numbness. In this state, some began to hope that the
next shell would finish them. Some grew so indifferent to danger
that they stopped trying to protect themselves from it: they would
crouch for hours, refusing to move, beside piles of live shells.
"Bah!" exclaimed Pierre de Mazenod, "this death or another! . . .
It's no time for coquetry. I'll stay where I am." Others grew openly
mad and simply wandered off. In the coming months soldiers taking up position would often meet these pathetic vagrants, desperately asking where their wife and children were, screeching like
circus clowns, or mechanically going through their rifle drill with a
branch torn from a tree. Yet the most common reaction was also the
most natural: men simply withdrew into profound sleep.

In one fashion or another, the troops under bombardment began
to sink into the strange world of shadows, itself a sort of death,
which still marked them off from the living as they made their way
back down the Voie Sacrée. Stéphane and his comrades were entering this state by one o'clock, when the German artillery had been
firing for six hours and still showed no sign of stopping:

> Barely able to hear, our eyes bulging, we hang tightly on to things,
> we bump into each other, we stagger about; around us everything
> is shaking, everything is breaking apart, everything is about to
> capsize, and it's as if we are in a ship scraping its bottom on a reef
> in a sea of mud. And, right down into the depths of our bowels, we
> are choked by the stench of the charnel house.

At least one other veteran of Verdun would compare this condition to the effects of chloroform: "it puts you partly to sleep while
leaving your brain full of torments and dreams."* But several would

* The same comparison occurred to an English soldier, Private T. Jacobs, after the German
offensive in spring 1918: "Nobody would stand more than three hours of sustained shelling
before they started feeling sleepy and numb. You're hammered after three hours and you're
there for the picking when he [the enemy] comes over. It's a bit like being under an anaes-
thetic; you can't put a lot of resistance up."

be struck by the same metaphor that occurred to Stéphane when he spoke of being on board ship. If, in the minds of those who endured them, the artillery bombardments made Verdun a storm, it was above all a storm at sea. It gave men "the sensation of being in a cabin on a liner and hearing huge waves beating against the hull." Paul Dubrulle put the matter even more dramatically:

> Perhaps the best comparison would be with seasickness, but an "aggressive" seasickness, caused by the unceasing attack of breakers sweeping over shipwrecked men on their raft. It's then that one gives up, that one can't even summon up the energy to put one's haversack over one's head for protection from explosions, that one can hardly manage to commend oneself to God.

Colonel Driant commended himself to God when he received final absolution from the unit's chaplain, Père de Martimprey, around midday. Many of his men were already beyond such aid. The trenches and the temporary shelters for machine-gun units offered defenders virtually no protection, and even the concrete bunkers were proving little safer. Those guarding the southwestern corner of the woods, manned by Lieutenant Simon's 8th Company, suffered in particular: their bunker at R3, and the 90mm gun and ammunition store nearby had been hit in the opening rounds of the shelling. In the course of the afternoon Driant's command post at R2, crowded with refugees from the destruction elsewhere, had one of its concrete corners almost flattened. The colonel himself escaped injury, but at least nine men were seriously hurt and Lieutenant Petitcullot died from his wounds soon afterward. The losses that Corporal Brassard estimated were probably typical of what was happening throughout the woods: "of five *poilus*, two are buried alive under their shelter, two are wounded in one way or another, and the fifth is still at his post." Driant had begun the day with 1,300 men under his command. By the time the bombardment lifted his "effectives"—to use the dreadful military term—numbered perhaps 300 or 400.

The lull came at about four o'clock, when the German guns lengthened their range and the shells fell on the French positions behind the Bois des Caures. Snow had started to fall again and dusk was fast approaching. Survivors stretched frozen limbs, unplugged the dirt from clogged rifle barrels, and waited for normal hearing to return and the ground to feel stable again under their feet. Some began to emerge cautiously from their shelters and take stock of the wreckage around them: mangled bodies, useless equipment, and a landscape rendered unfamiliar, almost unrecognizable, where trees had disappeared and craters left by shells had taken their place. Some remained deeply asleep, or numb with shock, and would be found in this state by the Germans who took them prisoner. At least outwardly as calm as ever, Driant left R2 to survey the scene and, in the few cases where it was possible, to bring up his meager stock of reinforcements. "We're here," he told his men: "It's our position, and we're not moving from it." Nobody needed to be reminded what would happen next. Artillery prepares the ground by destroying the enemy's positions, and then the infantry captures it. Defenders in First World War battles were all too familiar with the unnerving rhythm of attack: first the shelling, then a pause, and then the first sight of foot soldiers advancing toward them.

The German assault followed this pattern, but the attacking troops did not come in the huge waves or the long skirmishing lines that the British used at the Somme. This uninventive style of deployment reflected the commanders' distrust of their troops' training and discipline, for infantrymen who know their job prefer to advance by crouching, zigzagging and pausing in order to avoid the defenders' fire. At Verdun the Germans had chosen their front-line units with care, and thought carefully about the best way to deploy them. They came forward in small groups, probing weakened points in the French defenses, ready to push at points where they still might meet resistance.

The first units consisted of infantrymen with grenades and pioneers with flamethrowers. The grenade, not the bayonet, was always the favored weapon in hand-to-hand fighting—the French call it *corps à corps*, body to body—in which, of course, the aim was to get no closer to your opponent than you had to. Propagandists on both sides liked to describe any advance by the infantry as a bayonet charge, but as Jean Norton Cru—veteran of Verdun and a relentless debunker of battlefield myths—testified:

> I never saw the bayonet being used, never saw the bayonet stained with blood or stuck in a corpse. It was the custom to fix bayonets at the start of an attack; but that was not a reason for calling it a bayonet charge, any more than a charge in puttees.

Unlike grenades, flamethrowers were an unfamiliar and terrifying weapon: one of the first French soldiers to get hit was blinded on the spot and died several days later in captivity. Yet, as the French soon realized, the petrol cans strapped to the operators' backs made easy targets. The operators themselves often ended up being burned to death, spraying the comrades around them with flame in their agony.

In the northwestern corner of the woods, where French and German lines lay closest to each other, Lieutenant Robin, Corporal Stéphane and the men of 9th Company were caught by surprise and forced out of the bunker where they had sheltered from the barrage. In the fighting at least one of them died and several more were seriously wounded—a jaw smashed by a bullet, a face disfigured by the blast of a grenade, a stomach ripped open—though Robin himself escaped with only a wound in the foot. He and his men had been cut off since the start of the bombardment, unable to plead for reinforcement or artillery support, even to report their plight or find out what was happening elsewhere. The runners he had dispatched—15 of them, says one account—had died almost as soon as they set out.

Under cover of darkness Stéphane succeeded in making the journey down to R2: a man in his mid-forties, suffering from bronchitis, crawling most of the way across almost a kilometer of frozen ground. Driant, who had spent much of the day cursing the silence of French artillery and the absence of French planes from the sky, had no solace to offer: "To tell you the truth, corporal, old fellow, I don't think there's anyone we can count on anymore except ourselves." By then Robin had managed to recover some of the positions he had lost. In the darkness both French and Germans were now blundering around like men blindfolded, equally capable of surprising each other's positions or simply stumbling on each other by chance. Robin's nerves were obviously fraying. Near midnight, when Driant managed to visit him on one of the patrols he made throughout the night, the lieutenant asked: "What on earth can I do here, with my 80 men?" The colonel struck his characteristic note of gruff and kindly pessimism: "My poor Robin, your orders are to stay here."

Privately Driant's judgment was as dark as it could be: "Everything's smashed, there's no way we'll be able to hold on." The Germans who had taken Robin by surprise had come not from the north but from the sides. Driant's main worry had always been that his positions might be outflanked in the Bois d'Haumont to his west or the Bois de Ville and Herbebois to his east. Both sides had been as badly battered by the German artillery as the Bois des Caures. Sent out to survey the damage in the Bois de Ville, the young and recently promoted Lieutenant Étienne Gilson and his sergeant-major were visiting a dugout when it was hit by a shell that killed everyone but themselves: "The two of us returned to the captain, each carrying a machine-gun. He asked us what was going on. We are, we said, bringing back to you all that is left of the company." In the Bois d'Haumont several companies had been reduced to two or three men each, and Colonel Bonviolle's 165th Infantry Regiment was being forced out of the woods. Its attempts at counterattack were quickly extinguished, and the next day the village of Haumont itself fell to the Germans. By then Bonviolle, who had started the battle with almost 2,000 men under his command, had scarcely more than 60 left.

These developments posed immediate danger, not just to Robin's 9th Company but to Captain Séguin's 7th Company and

Lieutenant Simon's 8th Company on the western flank of the Bois des Caures. Even Driant's command post at R2, not far behind them, stood in peril. Just as light was on the point of failing altogether on the first afternoon of the fighting, Lieutenant Simon saw German infantrymen emerging from the Bois d'Haumont. There were over 100 of them to start with, quickly joined by more, all heading unopposed toward the French lines. Their sudden appearance took him so much by surprise that he had no time to take any action before they stood in the same line of fire as Captain Séguin's men. Also taken by surprise, Corporal Pot and the crew of machine-gunners guarding the exposed tip of Séguin's company fell hurriedly back on the position held by Sergeant-Major Dandauw and his unit. Dandauw panicked and fled with his men down communication trenches until he reached R2. There an exasperated Driant firmly told him to rest his men and then return to his position in the morning.

This, at any rate, is the clearest version of the incident that can be pieced together from the evidence of various eyewitnesses, starting with Lieutenant Simon. Contemporary reports did not mention it; postwar histories touched on it as lightly as they dared, without identifying Dandauw by name. Georges Becker, a staff officer with the 30th Corps, maintained in the history of the battle he published some 16 years afterward that the Germans who prompted Dandauw's flight had been disguised as French soldiers. So the discrepancies between accounts, which started with the trivial matter of whether the German artillery had opened fire at 7:00 or 7:15, soon extended to much deeper questions—questions about the conduct to be expected of Germans and the conduct to be expected of Frenchmen. The Germans played dirty tricks but all the French, or at least all the French fighting in the Bois des Caures, were heroes. The very idea made Marc Stéphane, who relished playing the role of cynical old sweat, explode with angry laughter:

> Heroes, us? You must be joking! Well, to get the real measure of our heroism, the heroism of us trench-fighters *who were fed up with it all*, all you had to do in the first days of February 1916 was to let

us choose where we wanted to serve. How quickly we would have swapped a ticklish spot like Verdun for the Bordeaux sector, for instance, or the Place Pigalle!

Certainly Colonel Driant, with his calm reaction to Dandauw's flight and his bleak prognosis, had few illusions, though none of Stéphane's earthy cynicism: only a settled determination to do his duty and get others to do theirs. The next day brought no relief to his fears but also apparently no weakening in the example his conduct offered his men. This time the bombardment was briefer, ending at midday, but it seemed to achieve a new intensity. The infantry followed even more closely on its heels—so closely that the Germans were sometimes shelling their own men—and in much greater numbers. Rather than relying on the small patrols of the previous day, General von Schenck was now committing the entire 21st Division directly to the task of securing the Bois des Caures. Increasingly these men were joined by troops infiltrating from the west and the north.

Lieutenant Robin's fragile hold on his corner of the woods crumbled when he and the men with him at Grande Garde 2 were captured. Again, there is a discrepancy between official and unofficial accounts of his fate. The versions offered to the public have him being taken by the enemy *fusil à la main*: with his rifle in his hand. The phrase is a purely formulaic one, denoting heroic resistance until the very last moment; it appears in innumerable accounts of innumerable incidents at Verdun and other battles, sometimes accompanied by the additionally reassuring phrase *et baïonnette au canon* (and with bayonet fixed). Its function was to remove any taint of shame that might otherwise attach to a soldier who had not actually died at his post, any faint suggestion that he might have allowed himself to be taken prisoner or actually chosen to surrender.

The French did not do such things. On this point a good number of the soldiers in the front line, as well as the armchair warriors of the home front, were firm—just as they were firm that surrendering was the German thing to do. Cowardice in defeat was the reverse of the brutality that the Germans could display in victory.

"Dreadful, dreadful race; the more one sees them close up, the more one detests them," wrote Captain Augustin Cochin, not otherwise a strikingly prejudiced witness to the battle. "The groups of prisoners are ignoble to see, debased, eager to ingratiate themselves, delighted to be captured." In affirmation of this view French troop slang disowned the very act of surrender by calling it *faire Kamerad*: throwing one's hands in the air and calling out *Kamerad!* in the German way.

Étienne Gilson, forced to surrender in the Bois de Ville the next day, knew just how humiliating it could be. The feeling had nothing to do with the way his captors treated him, for they reassured him on the spot that "wir sind keine Barbaren" ("we're not barbarians"). Such civility was far from uncommon. When his turn came, Stéphane was told that it was his lucky day, since he'd be out of the war for good; another *chasseur* who had fought at Driant's side was offered liquor and cigarettes and congratulated, in French, on having proved himself "unkillable." Looking back from old age on the way he had been treated, Gilson wondered if the Germans were under special orders meant to deprive the Paris papers of fodder for stories of their brutality; at any rate he thought them typically German in not being barbarians and in being eager to make the fact clear to him. Though it might well have softened his view of the Germans, the passage of time had done nothing to soften his memory in other respects. He still vividly recalled the ordeal of being led under guard through the enemy lines as a "way of the Cross"; its worst moment came when a Frenchwoman from one of the villages jeered at him for having allowed himself to be taken.

Such attitudes help explain why it was important for the public record that Lieutenant Robin should last have been seen confronting the enemy *fusil à la main*. Corporal Stéphane did not actually see Robin captured; when confusion descended on Grande Garde 2 he quickly found himself surrounded by his captors. But Stéphane had been with Robin almost continually from the start of the bombardment, and he left a highly circumstantial description of the last moments of their freedom together. Robin was a young career officer, heavily dependent on his fellow officers and, in their absence during the previous 24 hours, "like a soul in pain." When the Germans appeared only a few meters from their bunker, he ordered his men to open fire. Several demurred. Robin grew hesitant, wept tears of rage and asked, "What should we do, then?" The question, Stéphane felt, was directed at himself, presumably in his capacity as an older man and an NCO. It betrayed Robin's inability to face up to a decision: "he didn't have the guts . . . to take responsibility for the outcome of a situation so desperate that it could issue only in senseless death or humiliating surrender."

By the middle of the afternoon Colonel Driant held a conference of his officers in R2 to address the same dilemma. The Germans were close at hand on three sides and would soon be all around them. "In a few moments we're going to have to die or be taken prisoner," Driant said, "unless we try to save some of these brave men." Captain Hamel agreed: "That would mean more survived to fight again tomorrow." Captain Vincent was heard to say that he preferred to die fighting. Major Renouard took little part in the debate, except to confirm that he had destroyed any papers which might be of use to the enemy. (A former pupil of Driant's at Saint-Cyr, he was a staff officer temporarily seconded to service in the field; Stéphane had described him the previous day as looking "whiter than candlewax, with a panic-stricken expression.") Eventually the group adopted Driant's proposal that each of them lead a column of the survivors out of the woods.

Lieutenant Simon had reached the same decision and led the remnants of his company down to the village of Beaumont. The officer in charge of the command post there told him: "You're all cowards, you're clearing out. Give me the order and I'd retake the Bois des Caures tonight with my battalion." In his memoirs Simon claimed that he managed to reply: "I just hope that tomorrow you'll hold your positions in Beaumont as we held ours in the Bois des Caures." Even if he did not achieve such dignified articulacy on the spot, one cannot doubt that he already felt a sense of isolation—it was to be characteristic of the battle—depending on much finer distinctions than the gulf between *l'avant* and *l'arrière*, the front and the rear, soldiers and civilians. Really, the *poilus* used to say, there were at least four distinct categories: *l'arrière de l'arrière*, *l'avant de l'arrière*, *l'arrière de l'avant*, and *l'avant*. Only those at *l'avant* knew the true meaning of war. Even those immediately behind them, who had heard, seen and suffered the artillery bombardment, and would be the next to confront the attacking infantry, did not yet understand it.

Captain Hamel and his men joined Simon, and together they moved further south to Louvemont, where they gathered other survivors from the Bois des Caures around them. Simon was already starting to realize that he and the rest had a look that stopped others asking them questions. It struck Louis Madelin when he saw them, as it would strike so many other witnesses who saw the columns of survivors in the months to come:

> They fixed their gaze straight ahead, indifferent, expressionless and, apparently, dead, and I was reminded of the *grognard* who, after Russia, said in a faint voice; "Now, I won't die any more!"

The parallel was ominous, for the *grognards*—or grumblers—had been the rankers in Napoléon's Grande Armée. Was Verdun going to be as disastrous as the retreat from Moscow?

It might well have seemed so to Lieutenant Simon and Captain Hamel when they took stock of their losses. Out of the original 1,200 *chasseurs* in the Bois des Caures only 118 were left. The officers included Captain Vincent, who had said he would prefer to die at his post, but not Renouard or Driant. A question mark hung over their fate for several weeks, while Maurice Barrès' column in *L'Écho de Paris* began the job of making Driant a national hero. Then statements from eyewitnesses, some by then prisoners of the Germans, confirmed that both men were dead. Only a few hundred yards away from his command post, Driant had paused in the tricky business of picking his way from one shell-hole to the next in order to put a dressing on a wounded comrade. A machine-gun bullet had struck him square in the forehead. Murmuring "Oh! là, mon Dieu!" (at least in one report), he had died on the spot. Soon after these facts became available the Germans conveyed assurances to Madame Driant by neutral diplomatic channels that his body had been given a decent burial nearby.

2

✛

THE FALL OF DOUAUMONT

Douaumont! Douaumont! No longer the name of a village, it is
the cry of distress from the depth of sorrow.

Charles Laquièze

It did not need Maurice Barrès to make a national hero of Driant,
though his endorsement certainly helped. The French seized on
the example of Driant's death because they desperately needed
something to give them pride and consolation during the first days
of the battle. Their admiration had nothing to do with the awkward
integrity of Driant's protest at the inadequacy of Verdun's defenses
the previous autumn. This embarrassing episode remained private,
to be raised only months later by those determined to force Joffre
from his position as Commander-in-Chief, or at least to shear away
some of the power he had assumed. Nor did the public's admiration
of Driant necessarily imply agreement with the political views he
had aired before the war, scornful as they had so often been of the
whole temper of republican France.

Yet the admiration was something more than tribute to gallantry
pure and simple. It was tribute to a gallantry that the French liked
to believe was peculiarly French, gallantry of a sort that fitted the
nation's image of itself. The Germans, everyone knew, were strong,
efficient and soulless. They organized and deployed their forces
with massive care but no spark of inspiration. The French, on the
other hand, had grace and verve. They might be inefficient, and

sometimes badly organized, but they were expert at *le système D*: the art of inspired makeshift. Driant's practice of *le système D* in the Bois des Caures, backed up by the patriotic guts that made the Germans pay in blood for each further step forward they took on the soil of France, had not won a victory. Yet it had given the Germans a nasty surprise, and it had bought time for the rest of the French army.

Whatever one may think of these assumptions about national character, and whatever one may surmise of the real feelings behind the desperate note of national self-praise, the conclusion cannot be entirely dismissed. Even at the start, the battle was not going exactly as the Germans had planned. Success, the Crown Prince had concluded, depended on surprise and speed. First the weather had robbed him of surprise (and even after the clear spell on the morning of 21 February it was still not smiling on his endeavors). Then Driant's *chasseurs* had robbed him of speed. It might have been supposed that they would be swept aside as soon as the infantry advanced; German officers had certainly encouraged the men in the front ranks with just this prospect. Yet in the event the whole of Schenck's 18th Corps had taken the better part of two days to get through the Bois des Caures—just a couple of kilometers of ground.

Part of the failure, perhaps, had come from the caution with which the infantry had moved forward as dusk began to gather on 21 February. Most of it, though, had come from a snag that all the mass assaults of the First World War met. However murderous the attackers might make their opening artillery bombardment, it never proved quite murderous enough. The technology that had given the artillery its new weight and range was still far in advance of the technology for assuring that shells found the right target at the right time. Observation was still a primitive science, fallible in better conditions than the Verdun winter offered. Without the advantage of field radio, communication was always a problem and the lack of coordination between artillery and infantry could slow down an assault, or worse. The French might have been cursing their inability to summon artillery support, but German infantrymen were getting hit by shells from their own side as they surged forward in frustrated haste on 22 February.

Defenders could suffer terrible losses, but some of them always survived. After a particularly heavy barrage from the German artillery in April, Major Bréant took stock of the losses to his battalion: five lieutenants wounded and a captain dead, 150 of the men in the ranks wounded and another 80 dead or missing, 16 machinegunners wounded and 17 of them dead. The list was appalling but "given the bombardment that took place it's more astonishing that anyone was left alive." Others would feel the same surprise, and be surprised too at how efficient a defense a handful of survivors could muster. By the late afternoon of 21 February the German artillery had killed or seriously wounded perhaps three-quarters of Driant's men; some of the rest had lost their weapons, while others were stunned or demoralized. Yet the armed and able-bodied men still in position had shown just how much trouble they could give the enemy.

The process of technological advance that had given the attacking artillery a massive yet blundering power had left defenders— even small groups of unsupported infantrymen defending isolated positions—better equipped as well. They had machine-guns, reinforced concrete and barbed wire, even if not in the quantities that a commander like Driant desired. Their rifles fired more rapidly, more accurately and over a longer range than those of a generation before. In battle the advantage had always tended to lie with defense rather than attack; now the new technology had increased it. The implications of this truth, challenging the doctrines and frustrating the plans of the commanders, hovered over all the battles of the First World War.

It was, indeed, to answer the resulting problems for attackers that Heinz Guderian would advocate the use of tanks which the German army adopted in the Second World War. Panzer divisions supplied the need for accurate, mobile and responsive artillery so efficiently as to make the heavy guns of the First World War look like dinosaurs. In February 1916 Guderian was a young intelligence officer serving with the Crown Prince's staff. Like everyone else at Verdun, he was impressed by the sheer scale of the damage the artillery inflicted: it "converted the beautiful countryside into a moonscape." But he also grew disappointed by its inability "to break down enemy defenses quickly and thoroughly enough to secure more than a simple incision." Just when his doubts crystallized his biographers do not record, though it seems unlikely to have occurred in the very first days of the assault. Then he probably shared the slightly qualified optimism still reigning in the German command.

From the French point of view, the consolation available was more apparent to those who listened to the desperate optimism of the *bourreurs de crâne*—the propagandists in the press—than to those who surveyed the disarray of the battlefield itself. Pierre-Alexis Muenier, the son of a portrait painter who himself went on to become a literary critic, was then an ambulance driver. He spent the days in the immediate aftermath of the attack ferrying the wounded to safety. Or rather he tried to, since the roads were clogged with fleeing soldiers, dying horses, broken-down vehicles and a litter of shelled and abandoned equipment. Sometimes they had turned into a sea of frozen mud, and sometimes they had disappeared beneath the lunar pattern of shell craters that was fast becoming the characteristic landscape of the battlefield. Muenier was lucky if he could manage a couple of kilometers an hour, just to reach a handful of wounded men, already half frozen by the cold, and start the journey back to a hospital where they would still be in danger from German shells and would still not receive the treatment they so desperately needed.

Muenier's diary is, implicitly, a testimony to his own bravery. The men he was trying to help seem to have lapsed into a numbed patience, beyond bravery or cowardice, hope or despair. Other reports from the first-aid stations and hospitals confirm the impression. They tell of one man shot in the knee but still walking, another with hands crossed over his stomach to hold in his guts but still somehow managing to stay on his feet, and another hit by a bullet that had entered behind his right ear and exited through his left eye, still talking and behaving as if he were not badly hurt. Arriving at one of the hospitals on 27 February, Georges Duhamel found wounded men who had been left lying on the floor for up to four days with nobody even to change their field dressings. When he began to operate, he discovered that the bandages and even sometimes the wounds themselves were crawling with lice. "The unfortunate men apologized," he noted, "as if they were to blame for the infestation."

Yet what Muenier's account most conveys is the hopelessness gripping the entire army in the field. Troops from the front lines described how they had been pinned down by the shelling, hour after hour, without even glimpsing their enemy. Those who had encountered the enemy directly had felt scarcely less impotent. "There were so few of us left. . . . We didn't have any orders," one lamented: "We didn't dare to keep on firing, for fear of getting ourselves killed. And suddenly the Boches were legion. Behind us as well as in front of us they were swarming in the darkness without *any hurry*." In the coming months such stories would grow familiar, but in February they carried a special note of panic. Most of the time the Germans were invisible. When they did appear, they came not just in force but, like insects, in swarms: numbers too great to be calculated, much less resisted. "Nothing can stand up against this," a fellow ambulance driver told Muenier on 23 February. "It wouldn't take anything," warned another colleague the next day, "just a slightly harder blow, for everything to collapse."

French commanders shared the fear and had little enough at their disposal with which to avert catastrophe. They had lost more than the Bois des Caures and its neighboring woods in the opening two days of battle. Eager to make up for the time they had lost at the start, the Germans were busy exploiting the breach they forced in the center of the French lines. By midday on 23 February they had taken Brabant, on the bank of the Meuse, and by the early hours of the next morning they had moved further south to occupy Samogneux, thanks partly to the misguided French artillery fire which fell on the last French defenders. Beaumont, where the battalion commander had been eager to retake the Bois des Caures, fell

later on 24 February. Further east, the French had been pushed
back to Bezonvaux. The line they now sought to defend ran across
the Côte de Talou and the Côte du Poivre via the village of Louvemont, still stubbornly managing to hold out. It was perilously close
to the forts at Douaumont and Vaux, and, by comparison to the line
only a few days before, uncomfortably close to Verdun itself.

Moreover, on 24 February it looked like crumbling at any moment. The destruction of Driant's *chasseurs* in the Bois des Caures
had begun the destruction of the larger unit to which it belonged,
General Bapst's 72nd Division, and the loss of the neighboring
Herbebois had marked the beginning of the same fate for its sister
division, the 51st. General Chrétien's 30th Corps was dying. When
they were not wasted in vain attempts at counterattack, its remaining units were being brushed aside, virtually disappearing in the
face of the German advance. Toward the end of the afternoon two
brigades of General Balfourier's 20th Corps arrived, bringing with
them a famous reputation, for the corps had previously been commanded by Foch and was nicknamed the Iron Corps. But on
24 February they had marched about 50 kilometers in 36 hours,
making much of their journey on icy roads and some of it without
proper food. All Chrétien could do was to remind their commanders what tired and hungry troops had been required to do—and
had succeeded in doing—at the Battle of the Marne, and then throw
them into the gaping holes in his line as quickly as possible.

On their way into position these men passed soldiers fleeing the
battle, bareheaded, sometimes without their weapons, looking nervously behind them for signs of pursuit, crying out that the Germans had broken through, that the Germans were impossible to
stop, that "*They* have got it into their heads that they want Verdun
and *they* are going to have it." Ammunition carts thundered past;
the guns had been abandoned but, as one driver pointed out in cynical desperation, the Germans would no doubt find a use for them.
Mingled with these fugitives were the last country people abandoning their homes in the hills, with as many of their goods as possible
piled on to carts, and sometimes their most precious farm animals

hitched to the tailboard. The villages they left behind bore lingering traces of their previously quiet existence among all the signs of
the recent attack. At Douaumont the fountain still played and the
church clock kept time. At Fleury, where holes gaped in the walls of
houses, meals were still laid out on the tables. Livestock and pets
still wandered about its long main street; from the barns came the
noise of cows complaining of full udders. A few days later an old
lady insisted on coming back to fetch her laundry, or so a story
among the troops claimed.

Of the troops they were supposed to relieve and the positions
they were supposed to occupy, the reinforcements often found
no trace beyond shattered and abandoned equipment, corpses,
and wounded men calling out piteously for water from the craters
left by shells. So, at the end of their long journey they had to set to
work setting up shelters for their machine guns and, often with
bayonets rather than proper trenching tools, digging shallow holes
or grooves in the soil in lieu of proper trenches. Jacques Péricard,
later a historian of the battle but on 24 February a lieutenant taking
up a position on Cote 347 outside Douaumont village, insisted that
the need for these desperate expedients had, paradoxically, an invigorating effect on men who had only just before been tired and
dispirited. The very absence of established defenses seemed to
bring a promise of fighting out in the open, where soldiers were
supposed to fight, rather than being stuck in a battle of fixed position where men died in holes. "And about time too," one commented at the prospect. Others were transformed from "tired
cattle" into "raging lions." "O mystery of the French heart!" Péricard exclaimed later: "O miracle of the race!"

As we shall have reason to remember later in this chapter, Péricard is something of a special witness among the combatants. Even
Ceux de Verdun, the account of the opening days of battle he published during the war—let alone the history he compiled from veterans' accounts during the interwar years—stands as a striking (and
discomfiting) reminder that the attitudes and even the very language of the *bourreurs de crâne* did not always belong just to the

Paris press at the rear of the rear. Indeed, by February 1916 Péricard was already a minor celebrity linked with Maurice Barrès'
name by the incident which had become known as *Debout les Morts!*
While serving in the Bois Brûlé sector, south of Saint-Mihiel, in
April 1915 Péricard had found himself facing apparently overwhelming attack. He had restored his courage by addressing the
dead men in the trench around him: their souls, he felt, joined and
strengthened his own. He did not claim to have uttered the words
Debout les morts! ("Rise up ye dead!")—let alone that the dead came
to his aid in any literal fashion—but he did not disown them or the
increasingly fanciful embellishments of the story that gained currency. In *L'Écho de Paris* Barrès made large claims for the incident,
promoting it to the same status enjoyed by the British myth of the
angel or angels (or, in some versions, archers from the field of Agincourt) who had come to the aid of the troops at Mons.* In a lecture delivered in July 1916 he proffered it for consideration by the
British Academy: "The soil of the trenches is holy; it is impregnated
with blood, it is impregnated with spirituality."

   There was, then, enough of the mystical nationalist about Péricard—and enough of the self-publicist, as even Henry Bordeaux
suspected—to mean that his testimony needs to be treated cautiously. Yet the reaction he attributed to his men on Cote 347,
which he stressed took him by surprise, is by no means implausible.
The inadequacy of the defenses ensured that Verdun was never going to fit into the conventional mold of trench warfare; the chaotic
flux of its early days could be taken as a signal, by French as well as
German soldiers, that a battle of movement had at last broken out
in a war of stagnation. And even Péricard conceded that the rein-
vigoration of his men was grounded in a particular sort of despair:

---

* This myth originated in "The Bowmen," a short story by Arthur Machen first published in
September 1914, and he had been prompted by reading newspaper accounts of the retreat
from Mons. His first idea bore a strong resemblance to the holocaustal imagery which I go
on to discuss: "I seemed to see a furnace of torment and death and agony seven times heated,
and in the midst of the burning was the British Army. In the midst of the flame, consumed
by it and yet aureoled by it, scattered like ashes and yet triumphant, martyred and forever
glorious. So I saw our men with a shining about them . . ."

"We had the clear impression of being alone, abandoned by the rest of the army, sacrifices chosen for the salvation of Verdun," he wrote in *Ceux de Verdun*.

"Sacrifice" is a word that war memorials and tributes to the war dead have rendered pale and dignified. But for "sacrifices" in this sentence Péricard wrote *holocaustes*, a word that in English we associate only with Nazi atrocities against the Jews in the Second World War. In French it is used of people as well as events, and it means "burnt offerings." In contemporary writing about the First World War, and nowhere more than in writing about Verdun, it took on particular force in conveying just how unspeakably savage a ritual could be the sacrifice demanded of the troops fighting for their country. "We are lost!" exclaimed Paul Dubrulle. "We have been thrown into the furnace, without food, almost without ammunition. We were the last resort. We are lost! We have fought bravely, but our struggle will be in vain."

It was Dubrulle who elsewhere compared the sensations of troops under bombardment to those of shipwrecked mariners on a raft. Virtually the same metaphor for the plight of the troops was forming in the mind of Pierre Drieu La Rochelle, infantry sergeant and future novelist of the First World War. It emerged to remarkable effect as he was on his way to take up a position north of Douaumont village on 26 February, close to where Péricard and his men were still fighting on Cote 347. "We marched for six hours without a break, gnawed by the cold, worn down by solitude. There were thousands of us marching along and each one of us felt as lonely as a little child, in the middle of this landscape of frozen meadows, passing through villages abandoned a thousand years ago." On the way Drieu saw the last pitiful remnants of the 51st Division, tossed about by the battle since its first day:

> These men were no longer men, and to recognize men in us kindled a flickering light in their eyes, ready to die out again. They were more desperate than men shipwrecked at sea or lost in the desert, than men buried alive in a mine or a submarine, because

they knew that we were not saving them and that they would return, after we had fallen, to this vast burial amid the iron rain. I remember one man above all, a great big fellow, thin and bent over.
With his goatskin coat, his eight-day beard, his gray hands, his
eyes as vacant as a prisoner's, he made me think of Robinson Cru-
soe. Yes, we were Robinson Crusoes, poor people engulfed in the
chaos that we ourselves had unleashed.

If Verdun was a storm at sea, the French troops were not just
shipwrecked mariners on their raft but something more pitiable:
Robinson Crusoes in their ragged and unkempt appearance, and
also in the terrible fact of their abandonment. Sensible officers
commanding men in the field or preparing them to take up their
positions made no bones about the extremity of their plight. Had
not Driant told Stéphane they had nobody to count on except
themselves? Some days later General Deville spelled out the message in detail when he briefed officers of the 42nd Division in the
town hall at Verdun before they led their men into position:

> I'm not going to hide the truth from you, we've been taken by sur-
> prise. . . . I'm not going to hide the mistakes from you, it's up to
> us to put them right. . . . The situation is desperate; it's not yet
> been stabilized. . . . The sector we're going to? Chaos. . . . The
> life that awaits us there? Battle. . . . The trenches? They don't
> exist. . . . Don't ask me for equipment; I don't have any. . . . Or
> reinforcements: I don't have any.

Not the least significant part of this speech is its mention of mistakes. Suffering under long-range bombardment and encountering
the enemy so rarely in person, it was easy for the French to see the
battle in elemental terms, as a force of nature. Yet when they looked
at the poverty of their resources and the weakness of their positions,
they were reminded that it was man-made and made by the mistakes of man. Obviously the generals at the top had let them down.
All that they could offer was high-flown rhetoric in their orders of

the day: the *style Joffrette*, as Paul Voivenel contemptuously called it. Obviously heads were going to have to roll: rumors that General Herr had been sacked anticipated the event by several days. "It breaks one's heart thinking of the responsibility borne by those who deceived us," wrote one lieutenant: "So it's easy to understand the anger rising in the hearts of those unfortunates . . . who know very well that they're going to pay with their lives for the lies and the culpable negligence."

From such perceptions came the mood of the battle or, rather, the succession of moods that the different stages of the battle called forth. Anger among the French, anger against themselves and each other, played a role as well as anger against the enemy. It marked the vast distance separating Verdun from those ideal battles envisaged by military theories of prewar days, fought by charismatic leaders and admiring troops. It went far beyond the usual grumbling and cynicism which, sensible commanders have always known, can be a sign of health in an army. From the start it contained the seeds of bitter doubt and disillusionment. Yet these seeds did not necessarily germinate amid the overwhelming emergency of the opening days. Then, the troops' anger could easily crystallize into a stubborn pride in relying only on themselves and a stubborn determination to pull a few chestnuts out of the fire into which others had so carelessly thrown them. That in effect was the example Driant and his men had set in the Bois des Caures. Doing their best despite the generals, doing their best in contempt of the generals, doing their best almost against the generals is not, after all, something that comes unnaturally to men stuck at the sharp end.

Yet on 24 February the best the *poilus* could do still looked pathetically little; even the most determined of them had every reason to fear it was scarcely more than a matter of allowing themselves to be sacrificed. At the same time that reinforcements were being thrown hastily into battle, and the formalities of transferring responsibility for the critical sectors from Chrétien's 30th Corps to Balfourier's 20th Corps were being put in hand, the Germans had achieved a position of decisive advantage. That day they had advanced further than in the previous three days put together, and the prospect of more gains lay just ahead. Only the most scanty and disorganized opposition barred their route toward the main forts and even beyond to the Fort de Souville, perilously close to the suburbs of Verdun itself.

They failed to seize the moment. Postwar French historians, who saw all too clearly how the outcome of the battle had hung in the balance on 24 February, liked to claim their cause had been saved by the Germans' lack of audacity, their failure of nerve. For his part the Crown Prince, whose brooding on Verdun had served to confirm just how weak the French defenses had been at this juncture, pointed bitterly to Falkenhayn's niggardliness in granting him the men he had needed. His army might still have been superior in numbers and organization but four days of fighting—a good deal of it unexpectedly bitter and intense for the front-line troops—had left it by no means fresh and unscarred. Another all-out push forward would simply have been too great a strain. Yet no explanation of the Germans' reluctance to capitalize on their advantage is complete unless it remembers the uncertainties they had betrayed from the start. They had planned an attack that was to be big and bold yet perhaps not so big and bold after all, and they had made their advance through the Bois des Caures alternately by putting out cautious feelers and throwing in every man they could muster.

So they began 25 February in a spirit of caution, and it was only luck that made it end with their most significant gain in the battle so far. General von Lochow's elite 3rd Corps, which had fought its way south through Herbebois to the Bois la Vauche, was charged with the task of advancing to the Bois Hassoule. In effect, it was to engage the French on the line of defense they had marked out in front of their main forts—a line consisting more of hopes on paper than of men in the field. Yet by the end of the afternoon the German flag was flying from the sullen outline marked in the earth by the roof of the Fort de Douaumont. The Germans had not just exceeded their modest goal: they had captured what had once been the pride and guarantee of the whole system of defense the French had spent several decades throwing around Verdun.

Nothing could disguise the significance of Douaumont's fall, but the legends and propagandist claims rising immediately up from both camps did an effective job of smothering the details of how it had actually fallen. Reconstructing them took many years and the work of several historians. Douaumont had in fact withstood the German bombardment remarkably well, as—in defiance of prevailing wisdom—it would continue to withstand bombardment throughout the battle. The previous year a German shell had shattered its main entrance, reducing the name incised over the arch to the letters MONT. The rest of what stood aboveground was beginning to look like a ruin, almost a battered outcrop of rock, less and less distinguishable from the ravaged countryside around. Yet this was only superficial damage. Belowground, where the shelling echoed through the corridors like giant hammer-blows, it remained intact.

Yet on 25 February these corridors were virtually empty. The fort which could house 1,000 men, and had in fact held 500 at the outbreak of war, was now manned only by the elderly Sergeant-Major Chenot and about 50 Territorials. They did not even constitute a garrison in the proper sense of the word: most of them were merely using Douaumont as a convenient barracks. Even worse, full knowledge of the fort's weakness and responsibility for doing something about it had slipped down the cracks in the handover of command from 30th Corps to 20th Corps. The oversight came naturally to generals still used to regarding the Verdun forts as autonomous, but it invited disaster. The men inside Douaumont, designed as the linchpin of just such a battle as now raged around them, were left without reinforcement, without information and without orders.

Chenot later claimed that on the afternoon of 25 February he was in the turret from which the big 155mm gun was operated. He might have been telling the truth, but most of his men seem to have been sheltering as deep as they could in the bowels of the earth. The near-silence of the fort's guns, and the lack of direction to the

The Voie Sacrée.

(*Above*) The Voie Sacrée, *drawing by Georges Scott.*

Marshal Joffre at his desk at headquarters.   *Colonel Driant.*

(*Above*) *The civilian population of Verdun evacuates the town.*

(*Below*) *The destroyed city center of Verdun at the beginning
of the German offensive.*

(Left) The Bois de Caures.

(Below) Bombardment.

(Right) French
children watch
German prisoners
captured at Verdun.

(Above) Fort de Douaumont before the German offensive.

(Below left) Under bombardment. (Below right) After the bombardment.

(*Above left*) *Pétain at the time of the battle.* (*Above right*) *The hero of Verdun.*

(*Below*) *Pétain at the parade celebrating the French repossession of Metz, 19 November 1918.*

(Above) Equestrian statue of Kaiser Wilhelm I on the Esplanade at Metz.

(Below) The statue torn down from its plinth, the day before the French celebrations.

(*Above*) *Busts of Pétain, as leader of the Vichy government, on the production line at the ateliers of the Musées Nationaux in 1943.*

(*Left*) *Charles de Gaulle during the First World War.*

fire that did issue from them, struck Jacques Péricard and his company, less than a kilometer away on Cote 347. The failure puzzled them, but their own beleaguered position left them with too much else to think about and they were, besides, already resigned to failures of coordination that left them unsupported. It also caught the attention of several companies from the 24th Brandenburg Regiment which had penetrated the French lines far more easily than expected and were now ahead of their planned advance, still not meeting serious opposition. Reckless curiosity rather than any precise intention, much less direct orders, drew them right up to the outer defenses of the fort.

The first to arrive were Sergeant Kunze and a company of pioneers, whose job was to clear barbed wire and other obstacles from the path of the infantry. Once the unit had cut its way through the barbed wire guarding the northern perimeter, Kunze and just two of his pioneers discovered, to the amazement of their less hardy companions, that they could climb down into the dry moat without being greeted by fire from defenders. They entered by a window and were exploring the galleries inside, surprising and being surprised by the scattered handfuls of French inside, when they were followed first by Lieutenant Radtke and his men, then by Captain Haupt and his men, and finally by Lieutenant von Brandis and his men. The Germans inside Douaumont—by now about 90 at most—made contact with each other and finished the job of rounding up the French. The prisoners were scarcely more incredulous at what had happened than their captors. They would not have surrendered had they known how few Germans were involved in the assault, complained one of the Territorials. "Too late" came the reply. And so the battle for Douaumont ended, not with a bang but a whimper.

The fort had fallen by sheer inadvertence on the part of both French and Germans. Arguably this shabby reality was dwarfed by the significance of the result, in terms of both tactics and morale. The Germans had taken a great prize. They now controlled a landmark dominating the battlefield that they sought to conquer: a position for their artillery, a garrison for their troops, a hospital for their wounded, a depot for their supplies and, perhaps above all, an observation post unmatched in the landscape around. After the loss of Douaumont, the French would feel that they could not take up a position or dig a trench or move their field artillery without being under German eyes.

Such a gain tempted the Germans out of the guarded note they had deliberately struck since the beginning of the battle for fear of raising public—and particularly international—expectations too high. The official communiqué announcing Douaumont's fall identified the fort as "the north-east pillar of the permanent fortifications of the Verdun fort system," which was accurate and dull enough in its phrasing to satisfy the most technically minded reader. But it went on to remind readers that the battlefield lay "to the south of the *route nationale* from Metz to Paris," as if the way to the capital might just be opening at last, after all the months of frustration since the beginning of the war. At home bells rang out from church steeples and a national holiday was declared. The Kaiser paid a visit to the troops. Regiments brought their flags forward in anticipation of a victory parade outside the cathedral in Verdun.

Such celebration demanded a tale of a heroic victory that the exploits of Kunze and the rest did not satisfy. The tale found its willing and eager focus in Captain von Brandis, leader of the last group to reach Douaumont, though also the man entrusted with the job of conveying the news of its fall to battalion headquarters. He shared with Captain Haupt the honor of being awarded Germany's most coveted medal, the *Pour le Mérite*.* The two senior officers present at Douaumont were acknowledged over a lieutenant and a mere sergeant. Photographs revealed Haupt as middle-aged, bald and meekly clerical in appearance, while Brandis was young and dashing; the artist's idealizing pen could easily emphasize the combination of dreamy poetic gaze and firm soldierly jaw. He was photographed with the Crown Prince and had a village named after

* Created by Frederick the Great of Prussia, and hence named in the language he favored over his native German.

him. In 1917 he published *Die Stürmer von Douaumont* (*The Men Who Stormed Douaumont*), a memoir of his company's adventures from the start of the war to the Somme. Its account of the fall of Douaumont is necessarily brief—after all, nobody could claim that a great deal had happened on the afternoon of 25 February—but appropriately self-glorifying. It managed to mislead even conscientious historians, French as well as German, almost until the Second World War.

For their part, the French took some time to absorb even the fact of their loss, much less its significance. At staff headquarters the next day there was still hope that the Germans would quickly be dislodged. It informed the official communiqué and gave it much-needed aid in playing down what had happened. Douaumont was identified merely as "an advance element in the organization of the former Verdun fort system," in murky reference to the bureaucratic changes made to the status of the forts in the previous autumn. Douaumont had fallen, it seemed, only after several fruitless assaults that had cost the Germans heavy losses. And, by the time the communiqué was issued, French troops whom the Germans had been unable to repel had succeeded in reaching the fort and moving beyond it. *Atteindre* and *dépasser*, the French verbs chosen for this curious phrasing, were obviously meant to give casual readers the impression that Douaumont had actually been recaptured.

Not all the difficulty that the French experienced in reacting to their loss stemmed from the chaos of the battlefield, which made it hard to get precise intelligence of what was happening even in so crucial a sector, or the need to cobble together reassuring phrases to counter German propaganda. It stemmed from the ambivalence that they had come to feel toward forts—which was, of course, a part of the larger ambivalence they had come to feel toward defense as opposed to attack. The fort, after all, could be an essential bulwark of the nation's borders, a static refuge incompatible with the military *élan* that expressed itself in movement and attack, or just an outmoded encumbrance in the new age of artillery. To the French it had certainly seemed all these things before the loss of

Douaumont. And yet, once news of the loss had sunk in, it was bound to give Douaumont a simple and central significance it had not possessed before.

In French hands, the fort might have been so much concrete and metal, a mere object to be assessed in terms of its practical value. In Germans hands, it became a living being, a captive to be freed—as in the title of the third book in Bordeaux's trilogy about Verdun, *Les Captifs délivrés*—and, increasingly, a beautiful woman calling for rescue from those who violated her. The language was profoundly suggestive. Whatever the French most valued about their nation, they had long been in the habit of personifying, and personifying as a woman. It was thus they had spoken about Liberty since the Revolution. And it was thus they had spoken of the annexed provinces since the Franco-Prussian War. Douaumont the fair, Douaumont the ravished: the soubriquets identified the fort with the nation's most precious values and its loss with the nation's most painful memories of catastrophe. The symbolism lay close to the heart of the symbolism with which the whole battle was rapidly being endowed. "O Verdun!" exclaimed Paul Voivenel, a few days after the fort had been captured:

> Your heart quivers. Be as proud as a beautiful woman! Rather die than let yourself be lost! For nine days the men of France have been defending you with a love that the whole world admires. Your children from the provinces of France have come to defend you, O queen! The barbarians shall not defile you.

Such resonance intensified the need for legend and propaganda more effective than the communiqué of 26 February to assuage the sense of catastrophe and, particularly, to still the uneasy suspicion that it had been brought on by mistakes the French themselves had made. Lieutenant von Brandis' eager self-aggrandizement was inadvertently of some help, since it did at least convey the impression that there had been a battle worth the name over Douaumont, but it never came close to answering the French need at all adequately.

One legend determinedly proffered at the time came from Jacques Péricard. He was an obvious—indeed, an ideal—source, since his position on Cote 347 made him virtually a witness to Douaumont's fall and his role in the *Debout les Morts!* episode had already shown him, if not willing to launch legends, at least content for his name to be attached to them.

Ceux de Verdun, the account of his experiences in the early days of Verdun that Péricard published in 1917, had a curious story to tell. At about four o'clock in the afternoon of 25 February, when the various units of Germans were entering Douaumont, flares fired from the northern side of the fort caught the attention of Péricard and the men in nearby positions. Then they saw not German troops but Zouaves, or French colonial troops, making their way on to the glacis. They were about 200 meters away and, to start with, numbered about 100. Their sudden appearance and their behavior were inexplicable, since they had appeared from the direction of the German lines—where no Zouaves should have been—and marched confidently ahead despite the risk of fire from both sides. In fact, the guns of Douaumont remained silent and, more suspiciously, the German guns grew silent as well.

Péricard and his sergeant-major, Durassié, waved at the Zouaves to warn them of their danger but received only friendly waves in return. With no sign of hurry or concern, the men continued their advance. Smelling a German trick, Captain Delarue ordered his machine-gun unit to open fire. For the next few minutes Péricard alternated between watching the Zouaves through his binoculars to determine if they were genuine and making frantic pleas to Delarue and Colonel de Belenet to stop the shooting. Eventually they agreed to do so for long enough to allow Durassié to approach the Zouaves. Their hostile reaction and the obviously German accent in which one of them pronounced the command "Pose fusil" ("Drop your rifle") as "Posse fusil" immediately betrayed their true identity. Durassié signaled for the French to resume fire, threw himself to the ground and was himself miraculously spared in the slaughter that ensued.

Even the most hard-fought and bitter battle does not obliterate the notion that battles are governed by a code. It may differ from culture to culture and from period to period, it may even be differently defined by the enemies confronting each other, but in some fashion the code is always there. It was present on the battlefield long before the late-nineteenth- and twentieth-century conventions that sought to render it international law, and it survived even the worst atrocities of the Second World War. It is, of course, in the name of the code that warring parties are able to accuse each other of dirty tricks. The allegation that the enemy has disguised himself in false uniform has a particularly long and stubborn history. In August 1792 (to look no further back in history) French Revolutionary soldiers had excused their massacre at the Tuileries palace by claiming that aristocrats returned from exile had donned the uniforms of the Swiss Guards, responsible for protecting the King's person. At the start of the Crimean War, in 1854, it had been suggested that Russian warships achieved their victory over the Turkish fleet at Sinope by flying the flag of Britain, Turkey's ally.

It was inevitable that the First World War, rooted in hostile stereotypes of the enemy and systematically fueled by propaganda to a virtually unprecedented degree, should have vastly extended the list of examples. Even the first day of Verdun had already produced, however fleetingly, the suggestion that the Germans who routed Sergeant-Major Dandauw had come like wolves in sheep's clothing. Bordeaux's history and other contemporary accounts charge them with the same trick on several later occasions in the battle, as well as masquerading as stretcher-bearers (complete with machine-guns concealed beneath the blankets of their stretchers) and faking surrender in order to take the French by surprise. The accusations are usually made in passing, with little or no serious attempt to substantiate them. Péricard's story of the false Zouaves is plainly of a different order, in its length, its circumstantial detail and the sheer passion of its telling.

None of these features makes it any more plausible. It makes no allowance for the fact that there were stray Zouaves on the battlefield; a whole regiment thrown into action had virtually disappeared beneath the German advance on the previous day. It brushes aside the difficulty in being certain of any identification amid the chaos, the gathering dusk and the falling snow. It ignores how often the French troops at Verdun were struck by the strange ways in which their comrades from different regions spoke. Nor does it help to suggest, as Alistair Horne has done, that what Péricard saw were German soldiers with the spikes removed from their helmets to help them make their way through tangled undergrowth. Even without their spikes German helmets do not look much like the distinctive Zouave *chéchias*, or fezzes, and Péricard repeatedly insists that what he saw were *chéchias*.

In the course of his story Péricard portrayed Captain Delarue as ruthless in acting on the mere suspicion of a German trick and Colonel de Belenet as brusquely reminding him that people get killed in war. Yet even battle-hardened troops find the suggestion that they have fired on their own side profoundly disquieting; they will go to considerable lengths to avoid facing it, or to exonerate themselves. And the particular length to which Péricard went already had a long history, not just in the claims and counterclaims of the First World War but in French perceptions of their national enemies. During the quiet days in the Bois des Caures the previous autumn, Colonel Driant knew that he was pushing a familiar button in reminding his men that atrocities in Belgium and northern France had confirmed the Germans as unprincipled brutes. Claiming that Germans disguised themselves in French uniforms had already offered a convenient way of excusing Dandauw's flight from his post in the first day of fighting in the woods. Convincing himself that the Zouaves who died under French fire had really been Germans assuaged whatever personal guilt Péricard might have felt and also denied the Germans a moral victory in taking Douaumont. They had managed it by a dirty trick.

The charge also distracted attention from French mistakes, and this would no doubt have seemed a crucial task to an officer as concerned with morale as Péricard. What success the story enjoyed as it circulated round the battlefield in the aftermath of 25 February we have no means of knowing. Indeed, we have few reliable means of knowing how the troops at the front viewed their enemy. As alien degenerates capable of any atrocity? This is certainly what the *bourreurs de crâne* wanted them to believe, but *poilus* were commonly reluctant to swallow what the *bourreurs de crâne* wanted them to believe. As fellow orphans of the storm? This is what some veterans claimed, though usually some years after the event, when wartime hysteria had given way to a mood tinged with pacifist internationalism.

All we do know for certain in this particular case is that Péricard felt confident in setting his story out in his 1917 book, aimed presumably at an audience of soldiers and veterans of Verdun as well as civilians, but discreetly omitted it from the monumental history of the battle he published during the interwar years. Durassié did not let the matter die so easily. He had privately written his own account of the incident while it was still fresh in his memory, slightly different from Péricard's in points of detail yet still squarely attributing the fall of Douaumont to German trickery. It turned up in General Rouquerol's book about Douaumont's role in the battle, also published in the 1930s, and Durassié himself was still sticking vehemently to it when Alistair Horne arranged a meeting between him and former Lieutenant Radtke in 1963. But Rouquerol, without dismissing the story of the false Zouaves or even treating it with any marked skepticism, did not regard it as explaining the disaster. In his account, as in Péricard's second version and in virtually all French accounts that appeared once the dust had begun to settle, the real explanation lay in French negligence.

Even at the time people's thoughts were running along those lines, though they could not be explored in print. The elegant pens of Maurice Barrès and the *bourreurs de crâne* sought to put a better gloss on the matter. This they did by invoking the suspicion of fortresses and siege warfare which dated back to the *souricière* of Sedan in the Franco-Prussian War and had been revived in the decision to downgrade the Verdun forts. The Germans who now held

Douaumont were not just in a precarious situation, since the fort would be retaken any day; they were also, it seemed, redundant. In fact, they were not holding Douaumont at all but being held there, virtually as prisoners. The really important thing to remember, Barrès added, was that the French lines were holding: they remained firm. Other *bourreurs* were more ready to concede what could hardly be denied, that the French had moved, but they insisted that the loss of ground had simply been a strategic withdrawal: reserve positions were often much better than the front lines fixed by the mere accidents of battle. In *L'Oeuvre* Jean Brunhes invoked the encouraging views of General Verraux: "The position to which we have withdrawn seems to me as good as our original position which, dominated by a ring of heights and its field of fire restricted by woods, was bad."

If General Verraux's opinion held any precise meaning at all, it could only be that the Verdun forts had been built in the wrong place. One should not look for intellectual honesty or rigorous logic in wartime propaganda, particularly the propaganda that seeks to gloss over a setback like the Germans' capture of Douaumont. Its muddle and inconsistency are all too obvious. Douaumont, to judge from the Paris press during the battle of Verdun, mattered and did not matter; it was an asset and a liability. Its loss was no defeat to speak of, yet its recapture would be a great victory. If it were recaptured tomorrow the French would have cause for national celebration, yet if it remained in German hands they need not worry.

Somewhere in this mishmash, one central point was entirely clear. The loss of Douaumont had changed the temper of the entire battle, had cemented a determination that was no longer just a local but now a national commitment. Verdun must be held. On this point there was unanimity, at precisely the moment when realization was dawning that it might not prove a short battle, any more than the war was turning out to be a short war. Just as the propagandists of 1915 had settled into the business of reconciling the public to *l'épreuve de la durée*, so Barrès was already by the beginning of March warning his readers that Verdun would itself be a long haul. The watchword was *tenir*: specifically, hold Verdun, but also more generally, hang on.

On the battlefield it had been the watchword from the start. "Tenacity, yet more tenacity," General Bazelaire had urged the troops on the left bank on 24 February, in the order of the day that made Voivenel smile and speak contemptuously of the *style Joffrette* favored by generals. Even then it had been no mere rhetorical flourish. It had been all that officers in the field could tell their men to do in the chaos of the moment. "My poor Robin, your orders are to stay here": in one form or another, Driant's words were being echoed all over the battlefield. Every order that Jacques Péricard received routinely ended *il faut tenir*. Every time his commanding officer spoke to him he added: "Even if I am killed, even if things look desperate to you, *il faut tenir*." The phrase was not just a preoccupation, Péricard thought: it was growing into an obsession. Now, after Douaumont, it had become a national obsession as well.

✛ ✛ ✛

Because of the considerable forces hurled by the Germans at the 72nd and 51st Infantry Divisions, 30th Corps has been in reality reduced to playing a covering role in the defense. Through the sacrifice of all its units, 30th Corps has gained time for sizable reinforcements to rush to the battlefield.

Remembering its glorious traditions, the infantry did not submit passively to the enemy assault; it responded energetically with counterattacks. Despite its losses, and by deployment of its reserves, it was able to contest the ground inch by inch up to the last moment.

The artillery also conducted itself heroically.

The infantrymen and artillerymen of 30th Corps have earned the admiration of France.

Faced with heavy losses, the commander takes solace from the knowledge that every soldier has carried out his duty to the *patrie*.

General Chrétien, commander of 30th Corps,
reporting on the events of 21–25 February

Yet what, really, did *tenir* mean? In the German decision to attack Verdun lurked confusion and uncertainty which the battle had already begun to expose, even before Douaumont fell. The French determination to hold Verdun concealed equivalent confusion and uncertainty, and they too were already being exposed. Neither side would ever resolve them in the months that followed. Instead they remained at the very heart of the battle, as part of the friction shaping the course of the fighting and dictating, too, how little its course conformed to military theory and military planning.

The first commander to fall victim to the friction was Colonel Driant's divisional commander, General Bapst of the 72nd Division. Faced with the overwhelming threat to Brabant which had developed by the end of 22 February he asked for permission to withdraw his men to Samogneux, where their added presence could help make the French line of defense tenable. What he proposed was no more than what Driant, at his lower level of command, had proposed that afternoon at the desperate council he convened in the Bois des Caures: to save the lives of men who had fought bravely in a desperate position so that they could fight in better positions on another day. Yet the request appears to have thrown General Chrétien into a paroxysm of indecision. After some delay, he allowed Bapst a free hand; then, once the French had withdrawn from Brabant, he changed his mind and ordered Bapst to retake it. His second thoughts came far too late, for Brabant was already secure in German hands. Indeed Samogneux, which Bapst had hoped to save, was under such immediate threat that he believed it had already fallen; he summoned artillery fire which, for once delivered and for once accurate, fell on its last few defenders. All that Bapst had achieved by withdrawing from Brabant was to make himself a scapegoat in the hunt for men to blame for the deficiencies at Verdun. He was relieved of his command the next day, before even General Herr, the other commander whose neck lay temptingly on the chopping block. There was talk of court-martialing him, but in the event he simply became the first of the *limogés* of Verdun.

Given the scale of the disasters already unraveling and about to unravel, the fates of Bapst and even Brabant looked insignificant enough. Yet they highlighted unresolved questions beneath the mantra of *tenir*. Did holding Verdun mean holding the entire region, the right bank as well as the left, or just the main ring of forts, or just the left bank? And did holding any of these different stretches of ground mean simply trying to keep the line intact at whatever cost? Should new men be thrown into action to stand in the shoes of the dead, and should they always be ordered to retake any lost ground as soon as possible? Or did holding Verdun mean husbanding resources, accepting inessential losses of ground in order to preserve what was essential, waiting for the advantage that the morrow might bring? The ruthless logic of battle urged these questions without leaving time to debate the answers. It urged them, moreover, on an army whose commitment to the offensive left it as unversed in the mentality of defense as it was unprepared in its practical dispositions.

By the end of 24 February, the black day when French fortunes were sinking to their lowest point, the questions had spread to the largest issues and the highest level of command. General Herr faced that he could no longer hope to hang on to his positions in the low-lying Woëvre and his request to withdraw from them was transmitted to Joffre via General Langle de Cary, commander of the Groupe d'Armées du Centre. The order to withdraw was confirmed by midnight. Yet the fate of even so large a stretch of ground, no mere village like Brabant, was already lost in the larger question of whether the entire right bank should be held. Could it, indeed, be held? Many of the French, and not just the demoralized remnants of units pushed back from the front lines, thought their army was about to withdraw across the river *en masse*. Ominously, the guns of the Fort de Vaux had already been spiked during the afternoon. Though it could merely have been precautionary, Herr's order to pull back as much heavy equipment as possible to the left bank intensified the gloomy conjecture. Among staff officers there was panicky talk at headquarters of the Meuse bridges being blown.

It has never been clear exactly what positions the various commanders adopted in their attempt to fix on a tactic. The paper trail of written orders leaves little clue of what was really said in hasty counsel and, above all, it leaves Joffre's role obscure. Was he originally inclined to leave the decision to Herr? Did he briefly give permission for Herr to withdraw to the left bank before countermanding his instruction? Did the decision not to withdraw come from him or his chief of staff de Castelnau? By the summer his enemies in the press and the Chamber of Deputies would be making all these accusations to damaging effect. The suspicion that Joffre had not been alert to the gravity of the situation, or had hesitated in resolving to defend Verdun to the hilt, was enough to mark another stage in his fall from grace. Yet none of the accusations ever stuck decisively. Joffre had always owed his longevity in command to his silent imperturbability, his sleepy and noncommittal manner and his habit of cloudy utterance.

In the event, the uncertainties about how Verdun should be defended and what, indeed, should be defended were ended by de Castelnau rushing a second time to the front, whether on Joffre's orders or at his own insistence. After inspecting the battlefield and conferring with the generals on the spot, he announced, even as Douaumont fell: "The defense of the Meuse must be made on the right bank; there can be no question of anything except stopping the enemy on the right bank at any price." There is more that is revealing in this sentence than just the phrase "there can be no question," which of course concedes just how much questioning there had been and how firmly de Castelnau intended to put a stop to it. He did not do so by reasoned argument. It was not the moment for reasoned argument and, anyway, chiefs of staff do not make flying visits to engage in dialectic. They go to give orders.

Yet de Castelnau's order did not affirm what he thought best: it affirmed what he thought inevitable. It made no appeal to tactics, which speak of feasibility, but referred the issue beyond tactics to the realm of moral obligation. Honor, pride and morale—and implicitly the power of the nation's opinion over those whom it entrusted with its honor, pride and morale—left the French no choice but to stand where they now stood. So at Verdun *tenir* was to mean literally what it said, and to mean that for the highest-ranking general and the lowest-ranking *poilu*. It was simply to be the doctrine of the offensive, inverted to the unwelcome circumstance of defense but essentially intact. Attack to the hilt because the code demands it; defend to the hilt because the code demands it. Hold the most desperate position, at any price, without thought of withdrawal.

This, at any rate, was always to be the official theory of Verdun, always to be the official order at Verdun. Yet armies know that in the pressure of battle they do not operate exactly according to the letter of their orders; they operate according to whatever approximation of them the circumstances allow. Negotiating the gap between the two is what makes up the real business of battle. At Verdun it would always be the trickiest of tasks, for the gap opened between particularly inflexible orders and particularly unpromising circumstances. So how was it to be negotiated? Where did acceptable conduct, a realistic way of fighting, for general or *poilu* actually lie? Driant had got himself not just killed but canonized while trying to lead his men out of the Bois des Caures. Lieutenant Simon had managed to lead his men out of the woods and had been called a coward by the first officer he met. General Bapst had proposed a small strategic withdrawal and been consigned to outer darkness. So the question of what could be demanded of an army, what an army could demand of its men, would hang over the battle from the start. It would be manifest not just in the large rhetoric of "sacrifice" that attaches to any battle and attached with particular force to the battles of the First World War. It would be manifest as a daily uncertainty in expectation and accountability.

The inflexible resolve that de Castelnau spelled out on behalf of Joffre and the French high command, signaling that the vacillation of previous days was over, clearly demanded the appointment of a new general to lead the effort. Herr was already marked to follow Bapst into disgrace. Yet the choice of Philippe Pétain was, on the face of it, surprising.* Unlike (say) Foch, he was no rising star; his

---

* Unusually for a Frenchman, Henri Philippe Benoni Omer Pétain commonly used his second name, a habit that confused French journalists in the early days of Verdun and would confuse some foreign ones to the end of his life.

name brought no immediate assurance to the troops embroiled in the battle and no particular luster to the national effort that had been declared. A man without reputation outside military circles, and few prestigious contacts in the higher reaches of the army, he had in 1914 been a regimental colonel only a few years away from retirement. The mass sackings with which Joffre celebrated his victory at the Marne had brought him the command of a brigade and his performance in the course of 1915 had earned him respect. Yet he was still largely unknown to the wider public and remained sufficiently so even after several weeks at Verdun that the press, eager to promote his reputation, had difficulty in finding engraved portraits of him to publish.

Pétain apparently had not rushed to assist, his caustic contempt for journalists and politicians being a point of compatibility with Joffre. His background and the personality that went with it marked further affinities. Pétain came from a village near Béthune in the Pas de Calais—his family were long-established farmers, secure and even modestly prosperous but without substantial fortune to help his progress in the army—and, long after he had left home for Saint-Cyr and beyond, he had kept many of the traits associated with the northern French peasant. Indeed, with the passage of the years, he may deliberately have cultivated them. Often taciturn, he was always brief and sometimes sharp-tongued in his speech: a straightforward and businesslike officer who demanded the same behavior from his subordinates and expected it from his superiors. A love of good food with the occasional good cigar and a bachelor career of womanizing aside, he was modest in his habits. He reserved his weaknesses for the relative privacy of the officers' mess. To the men he commanded he made a point of displaying the spartan side of his nature, arriving at Verdun in homespun woolen stockings as protection against the cold. In following years, a promotion and honors accumulated in the form of a marshal's baton, seven stars on his sleeve and a *képi* with oak-leaf braid, he still by preference wore the simple *horizon bleu*. In this uniform he rode his white horse beneath the Arc de Triomphe at the Victory Parade in 1919; in this uniform he appeared in 1945 before the court that judged his role as leader of the Vichy régime treasonable.

By 1945 Pétain had become a figure not so much controversial as baffling to the French people. In 1916 he still bore all the identifying traits of a good Republican general. In its brief history the Republic had already suffered a good deal of trouble from soldiers of zealous Catholicism or (the characteristics were often found together) aristocratic lineage, right-wing views and Napoleonic ambition. The discredit which the army had brought on itself by the Dreyfus Affair had prompted a purge, controversial but effective, of officers whose sabers, in Clemenceau's contemptuous phrase, were sprinkled with incense. The noble and devout de Castelnau—he kept a private chaplain and was nicknamed "the booted Capuchin"— survived in striking exception. Most of the generals whose careers flourished, however briefly, in the First World War were like Joffre himself: men with views acceptable to the new order and often with personalities that enabled the press, when occasion demanded, to present them to the public as true sons of the people.

Yet it seems unlikely that such factors carried special weight in the late-night deliberations between Joffre and de Castelnau at Chantilly on 24 February. Good peasant Pétain may have been, as well as acceptably lax in his Catholicism and, for all his dislike of politicians, discreet in his political views; even during the Dreyfus Affair he had voiced no emphatic loyalties. But in all likelihood his vital qualification was simply that he was available. He and the Second Army he commanded had already been withdrawn from the front in preparation for the Somme offensive; in February they were in a training camp at Noailles, near Beauvais, uncommitted and ready to hand. So, even when it came to finding a suitable commander, Verdun was from Joffre's point of view a distraction—unwelcome and, he earnestly trusted, short-lived—from his pet project.

Hastily made, the choice of Pétain would prove at once apt and ironic. His undistinguished record before the war did not betoken mediocrity but a habit of independent and unfashionable thought in military matters, as well as an occasional bluntness in making his opinions known. Against the grain of current theory, he had con-

centrated on developing a strategic philosophy that was in effect a
philosophy of the defensive. Where others celebrated attack and the
willpower that could subdue all obstacles in its way—dramatic
means aiming at quick results—Pétain instead stressed an elementary dictum: *le feu tue*. Firepower kills. You cannot expect men to
withstand matériel and you cannot throw men against matériel. Defense therefore should not be a matter of do-or-die heroics in crumbling trenches, much less of desperate counterattack to retake
ground as soon as it was lost. It should rather depend on marshal-
ing and deploying artillery, letting it wear down the enemy until
limited counterattacks with precise goals could finish the process of
destruction step by careful step.

Such views made the man and the occasion seem ideally suited
for each other, which is considerably more than one can say of any
other commander and any other battle in the First World War. It
was almost as if Pétain had been waiting for Verdun, or it for him,
during the long and unrewarding years of garrison life when he had
attracted only a small circle of admirers and protégés. Even though
his winter journey from Paris via Joffre's headquarters at Chantilly
on 25 February gave him a cold that soon turned to pneumonia, he
brought with him from the moment of his arrival an air of compe-
tent authority. Louis Madelin described the meeting he convened
with staff and field commanders the next day:

> He walked into the meeting room, shook a few hands, and went
> straight to the big map on the board, picked up a stick of charcoal
> and began tracing out the different sectors with as much serenity
> as if he was sketching a landscape on a peaceful morning. After the
> first fighting everything on the battlefield had ended up in confu-
> sion; now, above all, order had to be reestablished with a firm de-
> lineation of responsibilities, starting with the sectors at the front:
> "Bazelaire here. Guillaumat here. Balfourier here. Duchêne here."

Obviously Pétain's businesslike way of getting down to work
carried conviction. In fact, this first meeting did little more than
confirm the disposition of the troops in the lines and reaffirm the

spirit of de Castelnau's order. Yet, despite the illness that forced him to his bed, Pétain soon applied himself more closely. His immediate worry was for the left bank and it would never completely leave him: it was here, if Verdun was to follow the classic form of a battle of the wings, that an attack should already have developed and could still develop at any time. (The Crown Prince was in perfect agreement.) Worry, indeed, was central to Pétain's method and what he brought to Verdun. Even the most hero-worshiping descriptions of his almost statuesque calm—and they were legion—remembered to note the nervous tic in his eyelid, furiously active when he was tired. It was the betraying mannerism of a commander whose approach depended on relentless, unceasing attention to detail. It was in the detail that the devil lay, and nowhere more than in the detail of amassing and organizing artillery, munitions and supplies. Hence the vital need for the Voie Sacrée, a country road made to serve as a major artery down which they could flow.

And with them the troops. Pétain's philosophy set him apart from contemporaries in his attitude to the ordinary troops as much as in his attitude to the new firepower. By rejecting the conventional belief in what willpower alone could achieve, he was partly escaping the narrow definition of morale that other generals too often adopted. Of course, he was no less a disciplinarian than they (subordinates had long ago nicknamed him *Précis-le-sec*), no less willing to lament the lack of soldierly virtues in the newly trained conscripts increasingly swelling the regiments at his disposal. Yet to Pétain the troops were, at least, a resource to be husbanded as carefully as possible, and a tool whose strength and breaking point needed to be estimated as carefully as that of any of the other tools on the battlefield.

This is just what he had been doing even before he was posted to Verdun. Preparing the units under his command for the Somme after the grueling attacks of 1915 had demanded more than building up their numbers and resources; it meant gauging their morale and, since Pétain did not like what he found, repairing it. The mood of the men, he had concluded in November, was "volatile": "under the least influence it is susceptible to deep depression or rapid improvement." This state he joined other thoughtful contemporaries in labeling "resignation." In spelling out what had bred it, one of them made clear how much it consisted of exhaustion rather than determination:

> The soldier of 1916 is not fighting for Alsace, or to destroy, or for his country. He fights out of honesty, habit and necessity. He fights because he has no choice. He keeps on fighting because, after the initial enthusiasm, after the discouragement of the first winter, has come, with the second winter, resignation. What we hoped would only be a temporary state . . . has become, even in its instability, stable.

Pétain's distinctive style toward the men at Verdun was announced in the very decision to make his headquarters at Souilly. It lay closer to the battle than many generals of his day would have thought necessary, or comfortable, and it lay directly on the Voie Sacrée. By standing on the steps of the *mairie*, which he made it his custom to do whenever his work permitted, he could see and be seen by the men who marched into battle and the men who straggled back. In the same spirit, he made a point of visiting the hospitals from which fellow commanders, such as Joffre and Haig, recoiled in dismay. His contact with the troops was largely ceremonial—a salute here, a medal pinned on a wounded man there—and his dignified bearing on these occasions carried little hint of earthy rapport. Pétain was never one to chat or joke or swear with men from the ranks, as other generals much less mindful of their welfare and their lives sometimes were. Yet he conveyed a paternal concern, left behind the suggestion that here was a general who, while every inch the *chef*, really cared.

His most important step was in introducing the system that came to be known as the *noria* or, more often, the *tourniquet*. A *noria* (the word is the same in English) is an endless chain of buckets on a wheel or loop, while a *tourniquet* is a turnstile. The troops were to be relieved as quickly as possible. Ideally they would spend only eight days in the front line. In practice, of course, they were often stranded in position much longer, for lack of fresh troops to replace them, or sent back for a second tour of duty after only a few days of rest and recuperation. But in general they were relieved more quickly than troops on other battlefields and more quickly than the Germans. By the beginning of May, 37 French divisions had served at Verdun (eight of them for two tours of duty) as compared to 26 German divisions. By the middle of July the disparity stood at 64 French divisions (11 of them serving twice and three of them serving three times) to 46 German divisions. By the end of December, 125 French divisions had served, though some had become virtually a permanency (like the luckless 37th, 38th and 128th Divisions, which had each done five tours of duty). About three-quarters of the French army on the Western Front had fought during the long course of the battle—and, as I have already suggested, this fact alone explains why Verdun permeated the national consciousness and the national memory to an unprecedented degree.

Even apart from the strain it placed on French manpower elsewhere, and the check it offered to Joffre's plans for the Somme, the *tourniquet* had serious disadvantages. Troops are at greater risk when they are being moved around a battlefield than when they are in position. Of this truth, the fate of just one company in the 119th Infantry Regiment is sufficient reminder: it numbered 150 when it left the Bézaux barracks on 1 June, but only 30 of them lived to reach the front line, without yet having seen their enemy. And, naturally, troops perform more effectively when they know their position thoroughly and are in properly established contact with neighboring units. Some of the blunders at Verdun, and the appalling casualty rate that always went with them, happened when troops had no time to make the most elementary reconnaissance of the terrain or had no idea where, or who, neighboring units were. Pétain was doubtless aware of these drawbacks to his *tourniquet* but thought them less important than the benefit to morale. Armies are most likely to reach their breaking point when the troops feel trapped in battle, when they come to see death as their only way out. So at Verdun they were offered the promise that, if they survived their allotted time in hell, they would be taken out of hell for good.

The *tourniquet* also signaled that Verdun was going to be a long battle. All the other measures that Pétain took, even in the first days of his command, carried the same message. And the likely length of the battle was literally the message in the words ending his order of the day on 10 April: *Courage, on les aura!* ("Take heart, we'll get them!"). They were meant to stick in the memory and they did, as a catchphrase to be repeated with grim relish by *poilus* and *bourreurs de crâne* alike. Here was the *style Joffrette* but with a difference: an echo of Jeanne d'Arc's encouragement to the French during the siege of Orléans combined with an informal use of *on* rather than *nous*.* Yet the content of the message was unlikely to appeal to Joffre, for beneath the heroic phrase was all too plainly a counsel of caution and patience, a warning to the French that they should settle down to play a waiting game.

And here lay the critical point of disagreement between Pétain and more or less everyone else he had to deal with, both his superior officers and his subordinates in charge of divisions, brigades and regiments. The differences between his approach and theirs had, of course, been wide and fundamental from the beginning. The philosophy of defense he had spent his career evolving had little in common with the doctrine of *defense à outrance* they had hastily converted from *attaque à outrance*. Pétain's philosophy allowed for strategic withdrawal and, left to himself, he would have chosen to abandon the right bank and husband his energies on the left. This heretical possibility had been forever ruled out by the very terms of his command. Pétain's philosophy viewed with skepticism

---

* Colloquialism did not come naturally to Pétain, whose contributions to the Académie Française in later years identified him as a purist in matters of usage, and he was persuaded by his staff to use *on* only after objecting, "That isn't French." Jeanne d'Arc's words at Orléans were: "Nos ennemis, fussent-ils pendus aux nuages, nous les aurons! Et nous les bouterons hors de France!" ("Our enemies, even if they hung from the clouds, we shall get them! And we'll drive them out of France!")

the immediate and ill-prepared counterattacks that others were only too eager to launch. Here at least he could compromise, discouraging them on the right bank but licensing them on the left, where his worries left him ready to show the Germans that every inch of ground they attacked would be as hotly contested as possible. But on the question of how long the battle might last—and what reserves of energy, men and matériel it might use up—there could be no question of disguising the difference of opinion.

But surely the rest of the French were already reconciled to the prospect of a long battle? It all depended on what you meant by long. Maurice Barrès, among the first and most influential voices speaking of the need for *tenacité* and seeking to prepare the public for the long haul, was still thinking in terms of weeks rather than months. Many, if not most, commanders were reluctant or unable to shed the thinking of a lifetime: the itch for bold gesture and surprise maneuver could not be quelled, the belief that somehow victory might be obtained tomorrow could not be banished. In foreseeing a battle that might last out the year, in betraying no sign of impatience even as it eventually moved into its laborious endgame, Pétain was probably alone among contemporaries whose opinion mattered. And he was certainly unpopular in upholding what could so easily appear a timid, negative and gloomy view. Joffre, absorbed in his plans for the Somme, certainly arrived at this exasperated opinion as Pétain's requests for more men and more guns continued to flow in while the promise of results, and when they could be delivered, remained as cautious as ever.

So Verdun was never really to be Pétain's battle after all, however ideally the man and the occasion might have seemed matched for each other. He could never fight it entirely on his own terms and in May, when he had been at Verdun only for ten weeks, Joffre seized the chance to remove him from effective command. Pétain did not hesitate to use the word *limogé* of his fate but, of course, there was never any question of his following Bapst and Herr into disgrace. During his brief tenure he had won too much respect, and simply become too well known, to make open reproof or demotion politic. So he was kicked upstairs to General Langle de Cary's job commanding the Groupe d'Armées du Centre, which left him still nominally in charge of the battle but put effective day-to-day control in the hands of General Nivelle, a man altogether more attuned to the current temper of military thinking. Yet Pétain—disregarded for most of his career, still an obscure colonel as he approached 60—had always looked like the tortoise who would eventually outrun the hare. When Nivelle's reputation came crashing down with the failure of his Chemin des Dames offensive in 1917, Pétain again returned to favor as a *chef* whose combination of sternness and kindliness might heal the wounds of an army now demoralized to the point of open mutiny.

In establishing himself as the doctor of the army he retrospectively confirmed his reputation as the victor of Verdun. By the end of the war his name had become indissolubly wedded to that of Verdun: he personified the occasion when France had faced her worst hour in battle, had made her greatest sacrifice and had achieved her greatest glory. So Verdun, as national symbol, was fed into the processes of history that would make Pétain return to power in 1940, apparently as national savior, to lead the Vichy government during the German occupation. This is how national symbols function, not as safe and static entities whose role, like that of flags or statues, is purely ceremonial. They have an unpredictable life, and above all an unpredictable political life of their own. They do not embody the safe truisms on which the nation can agree; rather, they mark the chosen grounds of contention where the nation can conduct its deepest quarrels, even its most bitter strife, with itself. And what, for a national symbol in this sense, could be more appropriate than a battle?

Pétain's role at Verdun, and its long-term consequences, were the most striking evidence of how central and how complex a status the battle, both as event and symbol, occupied in the life of France. Yet they were far from being the only evidence, since it was a focal point in the troubled history of the Third Republic, past and future. Reminders of what had troubled the Republic in its prewar phase were brought to the battlefield in the person of Colonel Driant, author of future-war fantasies and former associate of General Boulanger. The most troubling name of all from that era was represented by Pierre Dreyfus, son of Alfred, who fought near Douaumont for 21 days without relief during the opening phase of the battle. (Captain Dreyfus himself, by then a major and reservist, was denied the active posting he sought for fears his presence in the field would reopen memories of the Affair.)

Driant's role as protector of the Eastern Marches would be taken up in June 1916 by another politician-soldier, André Maginot, who had in fact been badly wounded in the leg while serving at Verdun in November 1914. He wore the disability with pride—"I am like my leg, it won't bend, and neither will I"—and made it the mark of his authority as scourge of the military establishment for its lack of preparedness in February 1916. After the war he became a veterans' leader and finally the Minister of War who gave his name to the defense system modeled on the Verdun forts. All these associations and their place on the field of Verdun were acknowledged in 1935, with the unveiling of a monument to Maginot a few kilometers south of where Driant had fallen and just beyond the furthest point the German advance had achieved. By the Second World War other veterans of Verdun were playing, with Pétain, roles in public life—never amounting to consensus, a single lesson drawn from the Verdun experience, but rather the range of contention the battlefield had encompassed. Such figures included: Édouard Daladier, the Prime Minister who joined Chamberlain in reaching the Munich pact with Hitler in 1938; Jacques Duclos, wartime secretary of the Communist Party; and, most tellingly of all, de Gaulle.

Ironically, it had been his youthful admiration for Pétain that led de Gaulle, on graduating from Saint-Cyr, to request a posting to the 33rd Infantry Regiment, which the future Victor of Verdun then commanded. On 1 March 1916 he was with the 33rd, commanding its 10th Company in the sector round Douaumont village where Jacques Péricard and Drieu La Rochelle had been fighting shortly before. During three days of fighting the regiment lost more than half its men, and first reports put de Gaulle among the dead. Recommending him for the Légion d'Honneur—posthumously, as he believed—de Gaulle's colonel described him as having died leading his beleaguered company forward in a last desperate charge against the Germans. Replete with all the heroic imagery of a nineteenth-century canvas, the account spoke of shattered rifles and exhausted ammunition, of hand-to-hand struggle with the closely packed ranks of the enemy, and of 10th Company "selling its life dearly and falling gloriously." Endorsing the recommendation, Pétain wrought its language to an even higher pitch and mourned him as "an incomparable officer in all respects" who had embraced "the only solution he thought compatible with military honor."

In fact, de Gaulle had been seriously wounded—for the third time since 1914—and captured. Even by the time he was released in 1918 he was ruefully aware of "contradictory pieces of information" circulating about exactly what had happened, some glamorizing and some apparently disparaging his conduct. He himself never set down anything like a full account for public consumption; Verdun, as well as being a place of national commemoration to which he returned each year during his presidency in the 1950s and 1960s, was also an intense experience in the life of a man who guarded his privacy with massive silence. So the legends proliferated. By the end of the Second World War they included a claim from a German veteran of the battle that de Gaulle and his men had surrendered under a white flag improvised from a shirt on the end of a rifle. Another version had de Gaulle treating his captors arrogantly, as if it were he who still gave the orders. Yet another account had him engaging in prophetic dialogue with the soldier who took him prisoner. The man was supposed to have remarked that de Gaulle's name had once been the name of France and been told, "It's still the name of France."

To judge from what he privately told his colonel in 1918 and his son Philippe in later life, de Gaulle had been in no state for arrogance or badinage, much less for flags of surrender. But he had not been leading the remnants of his company in a last charge against the enemy in the approved manner either. Instead, and much more sensibly, he had been trying to get his men out of danger and into contact with neighboring French units. Coming unawares on several Germans sheltering in a trench or shell-hole, he was wounded in the thigh and either lost consciousness on the spot or was concussed a few seconds afterward by the blast of a grenade. The grenade was probably one he had just been in the act of throwing.

De Gaulle spent the rest of the war as a prisoner, "buried alive," as he gloomily put it after one of his five attempts to escape had failed. He whiled away his time by giving a series of lectures on the war to his fellow prisoners. It offered a blunt indictment connecting the French mutinies of 1917 with the mistakes he had witnessed in the *usure* of 1915:

> The subsequent breakdown of certain units which you have all heard about had, in my humble opinion, no other cause than the demoralization resulting from these lamentable experiences, in which I know for sure that the infantry reached the depths of despair. It was caught every time between the certainty of a futile death within ten meters of the jumping-off trench and the accusation of cowardice from commanders too nervous and in any case without illusions themselves . . .

In such remarks lie the germ of his postwar writings, and particularly his advocacy of the use of tanks—a conclusion in which de Gaulle joined his fellow veteran of Verdun, Guderian.

De Gaulle's views on tactics betrayed few, if any, points of agreement with Pétain, the commander who had been his first hero. There was little in his temperament to make him warm to the idea of cautious defensive strategy; his approach was always Napoleonic in its determination to take the fight into the enemy's camp without delay. Yet his stance was every bit as independent-minded as Pétain's theories had been in the previous generation, and it proved just as unhelpful to his chances of promotion. Much as Pétain's thinking in the years before the First World War had prepared him for the role he had played at Verdun, so de Gaulle's prepared him for the role he played after the fall of France in 1940. Then, of course, de Gaulle and Pétain were antagonistic voices, clashing in their rival claim to speak for France, yet oddly linked by their shared experience and the personalities this experience had molded.

It would be only too easy to extend the list of famous veterans of Verdun; many of their names will crop up, in one context or another, in the pages that follow. Yet it would be misleading, fatally so, to imply that such a list accounts for the national significance of the battle or even begins to describe the real network of connections that bound the battle to the nation's history. Verdun never belonged to politicians and generals, any more than it could ever have belonged to a single general like Pétain, however closely his name and reputation might have been wedded to it. It belonged to the *poilus*, as the politicians and generals themselves—Pétain among the more generously eloquent of them—were always constrained to testify. It was the *poilus* who took the first shock of the attack, in the absence of adequate preparations and properly maintained defenses. It was they who took the burden of continued attack in the months that followed. Their haggard, dirty, unshaven faces and their figures, in tattered clothing that bore less and less resemblance to soldiers' uniforms, spoke more eloquently of the battle than the portraits of their commanders in the public prints.

Their chests were the true fortresses of Verdun, said the *bourreurs de crâne*, putting the best gloss they could on the matter. Yet glorifying the *poilus* required an adjustment of rhetoric in writers who were always most comfortable when they could sanitize the fighting with the imagery of nineteenth-century heroic paintings or endow it with the glamour of knightly combat. It was no accident that Henry Bordeaux should have taken exception to the word *poilu* itself. He claimed that the men joined him in disliking an epithet that referred so insultingly to their unkempt and unshaven state:

> It is a nation of respectable people fighting for its hearths, for its
> endangered soil, for its rights and its liberty, for all the past which

it has inherited, for all the future which it holds in trust, and not a herd of half-savage gypsies, outside the law, without house or home.

His reasoning was far removed from the milieu in which the ordinary soldiers fought and died. The poor bloody infantry have always taken relish in adopting derisory terms for themselves, like *grognards* (the "grumblers" of Napoléon's army) or "Old Contemptibles" (the men of the British Expeditionary Force in 1914) or indeed, "poor bloody infantry." Sometimes they even adopt names that suggest they are, or have been made into, animals: German soldiers in the First World War called themselves *Frontschweine*, literally "front-pigs" and presumably an ironic distortion of *Frontsoldaten*, while a later generation of American GIs would call themselves "grunts." The hearer is left, deliberately, to decide whether the men who answer to such names are animals by nature or just being treated like animals by uncaring superiors.

So despite what Bordeaux would have had people believe, the *poilus* never disavowed the term, though they had other words for themselves as well: *bonhommes*, *biffins* and its slang diminutive *biffs*. Even *biffin* means, literally, "rag-picker." And even a writer like Marc Stéphane, who avoided *poilu* and preferred in the subtitle of his memoir to identify himself as a *tranchérien* (roughly, "trench-man"), took pleasure in using the savage phrase, *les cons qui se font tuer*: "the assholes who get killed." Nor, despite Bordeaux's claim, did the *poilus* entirely resent their appearance. Indeed, they made a cult of beards and, particularly, of luxuriant, unbarbered mustaches, redolent with associations of virility, ferocity and brigandage. Some may deliberately have been invoking memories of the early Revolutionaries, with their curving mustaches and clay pipes; many may have been taking comfort in their resemblance to conventional depictions of Gallic warriors.

"The social being of former times was no longer recognizable in the modern fighter," Paul Voivenel and Louis Huot wrote in *La Psychologie du soldat*, "long-haired, bearded, covered with mud and dirt, chewed by lice, wearing sheepskin pelts and shod in trench boots." The sheepskin was greatly prized during the Verdun winter, and those who could not lay their hands on one made do by wrapping themselves in old quilts or blankets. Most wore a huge dirty scarf wrapped round the face to conceal everything except the eyes. Strapped across the back in the infantryman's traditional *barda* (harness), or a makeshift bundle, were spare equipment and possessions: blankets, a canvas for sleeping on, a spade for digging trenches, perhaps a pair of shears for cutting barbed wire, a couple of hundred rounds of ammunition, a handful of hand grenades, a billycan and a small stewpot, emergency rations for three or four days, some wine, perhaps some coffee grounds and, often most prized of all, pipe tobacco (cheaper and easier to get than cigarettes) and letters from home.

Fewer and fewer items survived from regulation equipment to identify them as soldiers who had once passed muster on parade. Gas masks, when the army got round to issuing them, were often treated carelessly; there are accounts of men under gas attack desperately fumbling for the nearest mask they could find on a corpse, French or German. The steel "Adrian" helmet which had replaced the *képi* for troops in combat the previous autumn had seemed an oddity at first: "You would think we were firemen" was one comment.* But its benefit was quickly appreciated and it became as essential to the infantryman as his Lebel rifle—though, with a cork from a wine bottle plugged in the muzzle and a handkerchief or an old rag wrapped round the trigger guard to protect it from mud and dust, the rifle was far from being the shining ornament of the parade ground.

In their whole appearance the *poilus* asserted a return to the savage, almost a reversion to the animal. When Raymond Jubert seized the chance of a brief, unexpected leave to eat at a smart restaurant

---

* The helmet had been introduced thanks in part to a press campaign conducted by Maurice Barrès. While Verdun was being fought he was further urging the introduction of shoulder armor and shields—as if to complete the resemblance he liked to detect between the modern soldier and the medieval knight.

in Bar-le-Duc he suddenly became aware of the contrast he and his companions presented to the civilians and staff officers around them: "we were Red Indians." At first he felt acutely embarrassed but then he noticed the looks of admiration, almost of envy, that the other diners were stealing at his party. Tired and unshaven faces, ragged and dirty clothes, were at once marks of degradation and badges of pride. The *poilus* might look like outcasts and, if they were not sacrificed like beasts, they were bound to be ignored or misrepresented afterward. (Admire the *poilus* as "immortal heroes," Barrès was already telling his readers at the beginning of March, but don't listen to what they say about the battle.) Yet they were needed far more than Barrès and the other *bourreurs de crâne*, or the politicians, or staff officers, or the generals. They were all that these luminaries—and the rest of France—had to save them.

So the crisis in the terrible days of 24 and 25 February was only superficially a disagreement about tactics, an uncertainty in command, and a shuffle in leadership. Really, it was a crisis somewhere in the complex spirit of a mass army, realizing that it now represented—and, in however distorted a fashion, was acknowledged by others as representing—whatever real reserves the nation possessed. This, at any rate, was how the matter seemed to Pierre-Alexis Muenier, vivid eyewitness to the chaos and desperation on the battlefield. What he saw prompted the darkest fears and imaginings, not just for the immediate fate of the soldiers around him but for the fate of France. But for him the turning point came when he witnessed the first elements of 20th Corps trooping into their temporary barracks at the Caserne Marceau, near Verdun.

On the face of it, the sight of them offered little encouragement. Any reinforcements were welcome but Balfourier's men had arrived in small numbers, tired and hungry. Now, before being thrown into battle, they were seizing the chance to rest for a few hours on planks or concrete floors in a temperature of eight degrees below zero. Yet, to Muenier's amazement and relief, they looked calm and strong. Above all, he noted, their manner was not that of dumb beasts or fearful serfs, but of thinking men who knew perfectly well what lay in store and agreed, however grimly and reluctantly, to their fate. It seemed a microcosm of what the Republic was about, or supposed to be about: a voluntary, intelligent association capable of holding together, and perhaps at its strongest in the worst hours and the worst circumstances.

To Muenier the character of 20th Corps was also a microcosm of the Republic, for it was heterogeneously made up of men from the Aube, Lorraine and Paris. Most contemporary observers of France, and particularly of its army at war, were intrigued by regional differences. They noted the local accents and patois, varying from the northerners' habit of pronouncing *ce-toi-moi* as *chtimi* to the Languedocien habit of saying *ta miliou* for *tant mieux*, and from these details they liked to construct theories of regional temperament and character. It was customary to end such surveys by insisting and marveling that all these different sorts of people were still French, identifiably of one nation.

For Muenier contemplating the troops in the Caserne Marceau this well-worn train of thought now took on special urgency and brought special reassurance: "20th Corps wouldn't be what it is without the Parisians, just as the Parisians might not give their all without the men from Lorraine. The warrior calm of the one group and the generosity of the other are brought together, mixed and enhanced in their common life." This surely was what the Republic, what France was all about: not just a voluntary association but a unity, a common life, that derived its strength from the differences of its component parts. It was what made France able to weather crises, able to survive the threat of her destruction. It had been tested and it had been proved before.

PART TWO

THE ENDLESS CRISIS, 1870–1914

The passions which break forth in war must already have a latent existence in the peoples.

Carl von Clausewitz, *Vom Kriege* (*On War*), 1832

✝ ✝ ✝

It would seem that nations still obey their immediate passions far more readily than their interests. Their interests serve them, at most, as rationalizations for their passions; they parade their interests as their justification for satisfying their passions. Actually why the national units should disdain, detest, abhor one another, and that even when they are at peace, is indeed a mystery . . .

Sigmund Freud, "Zeitgemässes über Krieg und Tod" ("Thoughts for the Times on War and Death"), 1915

3

✛

The Raft of the Medusa

An immense disaster, a peace of despair, griefs that nothing could console, the state without foundations, no army save the soldiers returning from enemy prison-camps, two provinces snatched away, an indemnity of billions to pay, the victor occupying a quarter of the territory, the capital running with the blood of a civil war, Europe cold or disdainful: such were the conditions in which a defeated France resumed her march toward her destiny.

> Charles de Gaulle
> describing France at the end of the Franco-Prussian War,
> *La France et son armée*, 1938

✛ ✛ ✛

Oh! what heart we had in those days. . . . Lord, how cold we are these days! You would think an Ice Age had begun. Who would show such fresh feelings now? Alas, France, what has become of you?

> Jules Michelet
> comparing France in the 1870s with France
> under the Revolutionary Directory in the 1790s,
> *L'Histoire du XIXᵉ siècle*
> (*History of the Nineteenth Century*), 1872–75

By 1870 Parisians had almost a century of coups and revolutions behind them, as well as a tradition of carrying them out in the rain. Sunday 4 September might have been the balmiest of early autumn days, but it was nevertheless time for the Empress Eugénie to flee her palace at the Tuileries and seek safety in exile. The fate of its previous occupants already hung over the building. When a mob of revolutionary soldiers had attacked it in 1792, overcoming the Swiss Guards sworn to protect the King, Louis XVI had fallen permanently into the hands of his enemies. When Napoléon I returned from Elba in 1815, Louis XVIII had fled the Tuileries for England; Louis-Philippe had followed the same humiliating path during the Revolution of 1848. Now, in the opening days of September 1870, the Second Empire was all too plainly in ruins, its collapse brought about by the failure of its armies in the Franco-Prussian War.

Eugénie's husband Louis-Napoléon had founded the Empire by a *coup d'état* in the aftermath of the 1848 Revolution. The taint of charlatanry and adventurism always lingered about his reputation but, as Napoléon III, he had seemed to restore a measure of greatness to France in the middle of a century of misfortune which had begun with the rise and fall of his uncle, the first Napoléon.* At home, the wide boulevards that Baron Haussmann had blazed across the map of Paris seemed to epitomize his achievement. Abroad, Napoléon III had allied successfully with the old enemy, Britain, in the Crimean War and profited from intervention in Italy to acquire Nice and the Savoie. Yet in 1870 he had allowed himself to be provoked into war by a passing disagreement with Prussia known to historians under the richly absurd label of the Hohenzollern Candidature. It concerned the choice of a constitutional monarch for Spain. Neither the Emperor nor Prussia's chief minister Bismarck took a critical interest in the question but each seemed

---

* Though formally remembered by Bonapartists as Napoléon II, Napoléon I's son the Duc de Reichstadt had never ruled. He had died in his early twenties in 1832.

bent on using it as the occasion to snub the other; the style of their quarrel soon overshadowed its substance.

Napoléon III led his armies off to battle at the end of July. Their enemy, of course, was not just Prussia, even though the French were in the habit of talking as if the Prussians were the real and only enemy. Ranged against them were the Protestant states of the Norddeutscher Bund (or North German Federation) which Prussia had forged in 1867 and several states from southern Germany, of which Bavaria was the most powerful. Brought together under King Wilhelm of Prussia, Bismarck and their military commander-in-chief, the elder Moltke (uncle of the First World War general), this coalition proved considerably more effective than anything the French could muster in the field. "Three absurd weeks" in August exposed their weakness. Mobilization, transport and supply of the troops were all chaotic; the Emperor showed himself the least Napoleonic of commanders. By the beginning of September Marshal Bazaine's army was bottled up in Metz after its failure to break out along the road to Verdun; it would remain there, humiliatingly inactive, until its capitulation at the end of October. Napoléon's indecisive blundering had led him and Marshal MacMahon's army into the mousetrap of Sedan. On 2 September he surrendered—not, as he had hoped, personally to Wilhelm but to Bismarck—and was taken into captivity.

"One should not, in general, rely on gratitude," Bismarck told his defeated enemies at Sedan, "and especially not on that of a people." He was rejecting pleas that France be treated leniently. Parisians saw little reason to be grateful to Napoléon III and were not inclined to be lenient. After greeting the outbreak of war with confidence, they had been depressed by conflicting rumors and unconfirmed reports of military disaster. When the news of the Emperor's surrender reached the capital, their mood hardened decisively. Less than 24 hours later, on 4 September, a group of politicians led by Jules Favre and Léon Gambetta left the Palais Bourbon, where their assembly held its meetings, and made their way to the Hôtel de Ville to proclaim a republic. It was the same spot where revolutionary governments had been proclaimed in 1789 and again in 1848, and the same spot where de Gaulle would declare the republic restored after Paris had been liberated in 1944.

By the afternoon crowds were gathering outside the Tuileries palace to chant *Déchéance*: "Abdicate!" As an ardent Catholic, the Empress was associated with those policies of the Second Empire least acceptable to republican sentiment. As a foreigner, known to the French as *L'Espagnole*, she risked becoming the target of the same anger that revolutionary mobs had directed at Marie Antoinette, the "Austrian whore." Though nervously mindful of her danger, the Empress was still reluctant to leave. With the front gate blocked by the crowd, she finally slipped out by a side gate, took refuge with her American dentist and made her way across the Channel. The details of her flight are unimportant except in one particular. The side gate from the Tuileries led to the Louvre, already the nation's art gallery but then almost bare, since its treasures had been sent to the naval arsenal at Brest for safekeeping at the beginning of the war. Of the few works still in their places, too large or too heavy to be moved, the most imposing was the canvas by Géricault known as *Le Naufrage de la "Méduse"* or *Le Radeau de la "Méduse"*: *The Shipwreck of the "Medusa"* or *The Raft of the "Medusa."* Despite the urgency of her flight, Eugénie paused and stood in front of it for several minutes, as if thunderstruck.

Well she might have done. Even before Géricault took it as the subject of his most ambitious work the fate of the *Medusa* had bitten people's imaginations. When the frigate was wrecked off the coast of Senegal in 1816, about 150 of her crew and passengers had scrambled onto a makeshift raft and drifted at sea, without food or water, until they were picked up 13 days later. By then only a tenth of their number were still alive. Heat, thirst and hunger had taken their toll, together with a terrible struggle for survival: the strong had thrown the weak and the wounded into the sea, and even (it was hinted) eaten the flesh of the dead. Géricault chose a monumental scale—the picture measures about five meters by seven—and a heroic composition after the manner of his master David to depict the shipwrecked men adrift on the raft at the extremity of their suffering. A macabre light plays over a pyramid of contorted, intertwined figures; from its apex supplicant arms and hands point in desperation at the sail of a ship passing across the horizon, oblivious of their fate.

Eugénie did not forget the painting during her long years of exile, first at Chislehurst in Kent and then at Farnborough in Hampshire. "Here we are on the raft of the *Medusa*," she confided in a letter. "There are moments when we feel like eating each other." It was not just in the minds of squabbling exiles that the image lingered. From the time it had first been exhibited at the Paris Salon in 1819, Géricault's painting had always been received as allegorical. History as allegory, and in particular as political allegory, was a familiar genre in nineteenth-century art of the grander kind. And the French naturally found in shipwreck and what ensued after shipwreck an image for their own recurrent condition since the Revolution, struck by external disaster and torn apart by dissension among themselves. The image still came readily to de Gaulle's pen in describing the double tragedy that France suffered in 1940: defeat by the Germans followed by the ascendancy of Pétain and his Vichy régime. "Old age is a shipwreck," he wrote in his war memoirs. "That we might be spared nothing, the old age of Marshal Pétain was to identify itself with the shipwreck of France." And before that, in 1916, the troops whom Pétain commanded at Verdun had imagined themselves sailors tossed helplessly about in a storm, shipwrecked men as remote from hope of rescue as Géricault's figures pointing toward the distant, indifferent sail.

To the *débâcle* of 1870 the French already brought an experience of shipwreck; from it they would take a memory lasting through two world wars. Yet the *débâcle* itself came as a shock. When Napoléon III had declared war, the general expectation, abroad as well as at home, was of a French victory. Even his critics shared the belief, opposing the conflict not because they foresaw disaster but because they did not want to see him consolidate his reputation. Among his supporters the mood looked very like thoughtless arrogance. "The army is ready to the last buttons on its gaiters," boasted Marshal Leboeuf. "We are declaring war with a light heart," announced Émile Ollivier, first minister in Napoléon's newly appointed cabinet. The words would soon guarantee his permanent disappearance from the political scene.

Such incautious utterances could be disowned, along with the emperor whose incautious policy had brought about the war. Yet the war itself could not be disowned. Napoléon's downfall was personal: he surrendered on behalf of himself and his army at Sedan, not on behalf of France. What remained to be fought was between nations. Prussia and the states allied with Prussia had perceived the war in this light since it began. Behind the present Napoléon stood the first Napoléon and behind him Louis XIV in a long French tradition of making war against their neighbors across the Rhine. The memory of French victories, and the need to guard themselves against their repetition, gave the German states their impetus to federate with each other; nationalism and the memory of Napoléon I's defeat of the Prussians at Jena in 1806 always went hand in hand. Bismarck, who knew this well, had already brought the dream of nationhood several steps toward reality before 1870. Napoléon III's declaration of war and his rapid humiliation had brought it yet closer. By completing the victory Germany would at last realize herself.

War has always been the cradle of nations, and potentially their grave as well. The politicians who stood on the steps of the Hôtel de Ville on 4 September 1870 understood both halves of this truth. The knowledge was already part of the republican tradition that they sought to revive. They had no option but to continue the princely folly they had inherited, but they would continue it as nation against nation, French against German, in a different temper and a different language. "We will not yield one inch of our territory, nor one stone of our fortresses," announced Jules Favre, Foreign Minister in the provisional Government of National Defense. Posters on the walls of Paris repeated the slogan as the German armies began their encirclement of the capital. Léon Gambetta, the Minister of the Interior, made a dramatic escape by balloon in the first week of October to call for a *levée en masse*. Literally, this meant a mass mobilization of all available reserves; in a wider sense it summoned the whole nation to arms. It invoked the days of the Revolutionary Assembly in the 1790s not just in its letter but in its spirit. The nation always resides in the people, and so in time of crisis the nation's strength and its hope of survival lies in the people, not their leaders.

Disillusionment with their leaders had been widespread among the troops even before Sedan. "We didn't deserve this," they grumbled as the early days of the war revealed the muddle of French preparations. "We've been betrayed": the refrain that would accompany the fall of France in 1940 was already the refrain of 1870. Virtually from the start, the Franco-Prussian War was for the French a war without heroes. Or rather, it was a war in which the heroes were to be found among the rank and file of the army or among ordinary civilians. Alphonse de Neuville's paintings *Les Dernières cartouches* and *Le Cimetière de Saint-Privat*, hugely admired in the years after the war, celebrated desperate last-ditch defenses carried out by men let down by their commanders. A thousand eulogies paid tribute to the inhabitants of Metz, whose gallantry under siege stood in stark contrast to the criminal inactivity of its military commander Marshal Bazaine.

And so the spirit of 1870 laid the groundwork for the spirit of 1916: a national crisis met by the nation in spite of, almost in defiance of, its official leadership. The ragged and unshaven *poilus* offering their flesh to defend Verdun could feel, and were certainly encouraged to feel, a kinship with the *francs-tireurs* whom Gambetta had summoned to France's aid. They were linked in a distinctively republican tradition of militancy depending on the citizen as patriot and soldier. Yet, for all the stubborn pride attaching to the tradition, the precedent of 1870 offered little comfort. Gambetta's *levée en masse* did not succeed and never looked like succeeding, even in its immediate goal of relieving the siege of Paris. Its do-or-die rhetoric was every bit as remote from the military realities of the battle as the mantra of *tenir* seemed in the first days at Verdun.

In the Franco-Prussian War those military realities had already
been settled by the German victories in the autumn of 1870. Besieged and with no help at hand, Paris managed to hold out until
the New Year. An armistice was agreed in February, leaving the new
French government—once elections had made its status official—
with the task of ratifying peace on terms that amounted to humiliating surrender. The attempt at continued resistance had merely
added a long and bitter endgame to the fighting. The war which
had begun in a spirit still recalling the cabinet wars of an earlier era
reached its conclusion in a spirit anticipating the total wars of the
twentieth century. In total war the issue, as the opposing parties express it to themselves and each other, is not victory or defeat with
political consequences to be interpreted at the conference table. It
is destruction or survival.

It was, Karl Marx observed from across the Channel, "a truly
Hohenzollern idea that a people commits a crime in continuing to
defend itself once its regular army has disappeared." King Wilhelm,
Chancellor Bismarck and the propagandists who echoed their
words might have declared from the start that they held "France in
its entirety" rather than Napoléon III responsible for the war, but
by this formula they usually meant that their enemy was not just
a particular régime but a historic entity: the France of the first
Napoléon and Louis XIV and the record of arrogant aggression
that had left the German states and principalities a weakened patchwork still struggling to achieve nationhood. So they were, in a
sense, surprised to find themselves taken at their word and to meet
opposition from "France in its entirety" after the collapse of the
Second Empire and the formally constituted armies it had so in-
eptly fielded.

In France in 1870–71, as again in Belgium in 1914, the Germans
reacted to continued resistance, and particularly to makeshift civilian resistance, as a form of cheating designed to rob them of the
clear-cut victory to which they were entitled. It was as if the outcome of wars was meant to be settled only by men in uniforms—
and that, of course, is a view to which history, even the history of

cabinet wars, gives little support. Moltke and his fellow generals looked with intense frustration on the prospect of a drawn-out campaign, of unspecified length and cost, following on the heels of engagements that had appeared so decisive. From such reactions atrocities are born. So too is the readiness on the part of those who fear they will become victims to accept the most exaggerated atrocity stories. In believing them, they are not just succumbing to temporary hysteria, but settling into assumptions about the norms of their enemy's conduct, even about the real and permanent character of their enemy. A vital part of those "collective perceptions" which Marc Bloch found ready and waiting in his countrymen at the start of the First World War went back to the character assumed by the Franco-Prussian War after the fall of Sedan.

At the end of December the German guns encircling Paris shifted their aim from the forts on its perimeter to the monuments that were the capital's pride. Civilian resistance elsewhere was already labeled *Kriegsverrat* ("war treason") and being met with increasing savagery. "The very severest treatment of the guilty as regards life and property can alone be recommended to your Excellency," Moltke instructed his commander in Burgundy, "whole parishes being held responsible for the deeds of their individual members when these cannot be discovered." A poster in Saint-Quentin spelled out the message to the French: "The German authorities give notice that, if a single shot is fired at a German soldier, six local people will be shot." By November one German officer, stationed on the Loire, was reporting in dismay: "The war is gradually acquiring a hideous character. Murder and burning is now the order of the day on both sides, and one cannot sufficiently beg Almighty God finally to make an end to it." Yet increasingly rhetoric could conceive the end of the war only in the most apocalyptic terms. "It will come to this, that we will shoot down every male inhabitant," exclaimed Bismarck. His wife went further, suggesting that all the French should be "shot and stabbed to death, down to the little babies."

Later the nationalist Paul Déroulède would suggest that her

words should be inscribed on the walls of every school in France. In fact no such reminder was needed, and certainly not while the war still raged. "You want to destroy France!" Jules Favre exclaimed on his first, futile meeting with Bismarck in September 1870. It had quickly become axiomatic to the French, as to the Germans, that the war was not a dispute between leaders or governments but a life-or-death struggle between nations. The enemy sought the end of France, and the threat could be met only in the same terms. By the New Year Gambetta was writing to Favre:

> The whole country understands and wants a war to the end, without mercy, even after the fall of Paris, if that horrible misfortune must befall us. The simplest clearly understand that since the war has become a war of extermination covertly prepared by Prussia for 30 years past, we must, for the honour of France and for our security in the future, finish for good with this odious power. . . . We shall prolong the struggle to extermination.

And so in the spring, when Paris had fallen and no alternative remained but to admit defeat and sue for an armistice, it could seem as if the end of France had indeed come. "Tout est fini," cried Victor Laprade: "Everything is finished." "It was the end of everything," Zola wrote in echo at the end of his novel *La Débâcle*, "fate pursuing its relentless course in a series of disasters greater than any nation had ever undergone."

This, one might say, was just the rhetorical extravagance of the moment. Such despair was inviting but, even at the time, few adopted it as more than a brief, passionate outburst. Otherwise no peace, however harsh its terms, could have been brokered or accepted. Indeed, the newly elected National Assembly which ratified the Treaty of Frankfurt as its first public task, greeted the prospect of peace with relief as well as depression. The effort and suffering of the war had been too great to sustain. Yet the rhetorical extravagance of the moment also leaves a permanent mark, and the fears that 1870–71 had so acutely aroused would remain. Nations, or so the nineteenth century had believed since Hegel delivered his lectures on the philosophy of history, have a life-cycle like that of the individual: they are born, they grow and they die, by disease or violence. So France could end, and there was special reason to fear that she might be near her end, whether through her own weakness or the malice of others. In the new German state forged by the victory she certainly had an enemy which sought the end of France not so much for reasons of policy as out of natural instinct—the same instinct, the French said after the bombardment of Paris, that made the barbarians want to destroy Rome.

Reflections of this sort, muted as memory of the war faded but never abandoned, would play their part in the life of France for the next half century and beyond. They were not less powerful for being only a loose set of assumptions, often vague as to why it should be the natural impulse of one nation to seek another's death, almost always unspecific about exactly what did constitute the death of a nation. Though undefined, the ominous word *anéantissement*—like its German equivalent *Vernichtung*—had stubbornly attached itself to perception of what struggle between nations involved. Nor were such reflections less powerful for being partly subterranean, in the sense that they found only intermittent expression in political debate which, inevitably, focused on immediate circumstances and practical measures. They helped to mark the broad direction of the road to Verdun—a road always signposted less by policy, or even the mistakes of politicians, than by the latent beliefs and fears that war could mobilize.

The Franco-Prussian War might not have destroyed France but the prospect confronting her was still, in sober reality, bleak. In international terms she was *la grande blessée*: the wounded giant. In 1814–15 it had taken a coalition of virtually the rest of Europe to defeat her; now she had been beaten by just one neighbor. Defeat, moreover, had exposed the isolation to which the policies of Napoléon III had reduced her. In her suffering she had found not a single ally: not Britain nor Italy nor Austria. At home, thanks to the conditions exacted by the Germans in the Treaty of Frankfurt, she faced a massive war indemnity, the stages of its payment linked to a phased withdrawal of German troops from French soil. Most permanently galling of all, she had to suffer helplessly the annexation of Alsace and the northern part of Lorraine.

All these misfortunes were the consequences of war but, as if in fulfillment of a natural rhythm, the shipwreck at sea had been followed by the struggle on the raft. The men who brought together the Government of National Defense and founded its formal successor, the Third Republic, had been careful to limit leadership to politicians already holding elected office under the Empire's tentative concessions to representative government. Yet the street protests prompted by the fall of Napoléon III were not so easily stilled, for they marked the reemergence of hopes left quiescent since the days of 1848. The hardships of the siege lent them added bitterness. By the summer of 1871 they flared up in the July Commune, the bloodiest uprising France had seen since her first Revolution in the previous century. The Commune was suppressed, though at the cost of yet more blood and, incidentally, more damage to the city's monuments than the German bombardment had caused (the Tuileries palace was among the landmarks destroyed). France, said the historian and philologist Ernest Renan, discovered "a wound beneath the wound, an abyss below the abyss." And she received a warning too obvious to ignore: humiliation in a foreign war had not stilled but, if anything, reawakened her tendency to tear herself apart from inside. It would be hard to think of a government that endured a more agonizing birth or inhabited a more uncomfortable cradle than the Third Republic.

✛ ✛ ✛

The essence of France's political sensibility is . . . a revolutionary instinct. No party has this instinct to a greater extent than any other: they all have it. They are all revolutionary because they all want not to improve, modify or perfect, but to destroy everything and sweep the floor clean. Some say that they want to do this in order to put the clock back 5, 25 or 100 years; others say they want to create a completely new society. Whatever the motive or pretext, the instinct is always the same: total destruction.

Comte Arthur de Gobineau,
L'Instinct révolutionnaire en France
(*The Revolutionary Instinct in France*),
written in 1877

In fact it would be hard to think of any government in recent history which had started promisingly or lasted long. The nation was locked, said Renan, in a "fatal circle of revolutions." Since guillotining its king, Louis XVI, in 1793 it had seen at least ten different coups and been ruled by two emperors (the Napoléons, uncle and nephew), three monarchs of differing constitutional bias (Louis XVIII, Charles X and Louis-Philippe) and various forms of provisional, revolutionary and republican government. Even by 1848 a political cartoon could show a civil servant hastily consigning an official bust of Louis-Philippe, the latest leader to be deposed, to a shelf already crammed with the busts of his recent predecessors. Soon afterward the republic which the 1848 Revolution had ushered in would be swept aside by the *coup d'état* establishing the Second Empire. Now the Second Empire had gone and the new republic had already been faced with the threat of the Commune.

What (Renan had asked in despair, even before the Franco-Prussian War and the Commune) could one say of a nation which, after climbing out of the abyss, plunged back in again twice, even three times? Somewhere in this unstable career lay the development of a republican idea, but France's experiments with republicanism, at least under that name, had always been particularly short-lived. The French, the socialist Louis Blanc remarked, were in the habit of strangling their republics in the cradle. It would have been more accurate to say that the Bonapartes were in the habit of strangling republics in the cradle, for it had been Napoléon I who rose to power over the corpse of constitutional experiment in the 1790s, just as Napoléon III rose to power over the corpse of 1848.

If the third attempt at a republic looked bound to suffer a similar fate, it was not just because of the desperate mood in France in the aftermath of the war. Léon Gambetta and Jules Favre had strongly republican credentials, but other early servants and even makers of the Republic manifestly lacked conviction. An ominous precedent had been set even before it had come formally into being, in finding a leader for the provisional government declared at the Hôtel de Ville in September 1870. The obvious candidate was General Trochu, the Imperial Governor of Paris known for his antagonism to Napoléon III. Yet Favre persuaded him to accept the post only with difficulty, and during his brief tenure Trochu never concealed his lack of enthusiasm. Even Adolphe Thiers, though he shared with Favre the burden of negotiating with Bismarck and went on to become the first president of the Republic, declined to hold formal office in the provisional government. And Marshal MacMahon, Thiers' successor as president of the Republic for most of the 1870s, was himself no friend of republicanism. Like a large number of the politicians elected to the National Assembly in the early years, he saw the Republic merely as a makeshift arrangement, to be replaced by a more stable system as soon as the time was ripe.

A good part of the problem lay in the history of aborted republican experiments. If the Republic was not a distant ideal, to be realized only at some future point, then it was an interim, a way that France marked time before a new convulsion and a new constitution. The thought did not just give heart to its enemies. It dimmed the enthusiasm of those whose enthusiasm the Republic seemed most urgently to need: those liberals and radicals sympathetic to parliamentary democracy and the whole republican experiment, old enough to remember not just the failings of the Second Empire but all the hopes that the Revolution of 1848 had briefly inspired. The novelist Flaubert voiced a common feeling among them when he looked up from his writing desk for long enough to consider what, politically, the events of 1870–71 had created: "I defend the poor Republic," he said, "but I don't believe in it."

With its friends in the middle ground of political opinion often lukewarm in their support, the Republic had no lack of enemies. On the right, looking to the monarchist past or the constitutional example of Britain, they yearned for a traditional form of government; on the left, lamenting the defeat of the Commune, they yearned for a republic that would truly embody the ideals and legacy of the Revolution. Many, complex and volatile in their groupings, these enemies were led by the representatives of all the other constitutional arrangements proposed or attempted in the last century. As exiles, they watched jealously from abroad for the next coup, the next turn in France's shifting fortunes. There were the surviving Communards in Geneva and London, where they came increasingly under the influence of, respectively, anarchism and Marxism. There was the Comte de Chambord, descendant of the Bourbon kings and *légitimiste* pretender to the throne, keeping pious and gloomy court in Austria. There was the Comte de Paris, grandson of the constitutional monarch Louis-Philippe and *Orléaniste* pretender to the throne, at his house in Richmond. And there was Napoléon III, released from German captivity into exile at Chislehurst with the Empress and their quarreling entourage, adrift together on their own particular raft of the *Medusa*.

Napoléon III did not long survive his fall from power. He died in 1873 after an operation on the gallstones which had already been plaguing him during the campaigns of the Franco-Prussian War, forcing him to conceal the pallor of his complexion from the troops by rouging his cheeks.* During his brief years in exile he was never high on the list of threats that the Third Republic needed to worry about but, like any exiled prince, he could still dream of a return to power. Even his dreams, though, were troubled by thoughts of the pain his gallstones gave him when he sat astride a horse. The con-

---

* The Bonapartist claim passed to his 17-year-old son, the Prince Impérial whom he had proudly led off to war in 1870. Louis joined the British Army and died fighting the Zulus in 1879. On his death Prince Victor, son of Napoléon III's cousin Jérôme, inherited the claim but the Bonapartist cause, always a matter more of clannish interest than coherent ideology, had effectively disintegrated.

sideration spoiled any prospect of reentering Paris in triumph. "I cannot walk on foot at the head of the troops," he told Eugénie. "It would have a still worse effect to enter Paris in a carriage. It is necessary that I ride."

Of course he would have needed to ride. Just as France had experimented with different constitutions over the years, so her leaders had experimented with different personal styles. Louis-Philippe had even affected an umbrella in proof of his bourgeois credentials. But, at some level of the popular imagination, the leader of France was still supposed to be a man on horseback. The first Napoléon had made sure of that. When he embarked on his Austrian campaign in 1800, he had crossed the Saint-Bernard Pass in the customary and sensible manner, on a mule. The mule did not feature in the picture of the episode by his court painter David, for Napoléon appreciated how important was the visual drama of leadership, the sheer spectacle of power in action. (Indeed, he grasped the importance of these things more thoroughly than any other modern European leader except Hitler.) He wanted an image expressing the conception of himself that had inspired him to overthrow the Revolutionary Directory and rule as First Consul, then as Emperor: no "mere general" but "a man called upon to influence the destiny of the people." So in David's painting, *Le Premier Consul franchissant le mont Saint-Bernard*, Napoléon sits astride a rearing white charger with flowing mane and tail.

It took a long time for France to rid itself of the image and all the romantic promise it seemed to hold. In the aftermath of 1870–71 it could still attract a nation nervously aware of its history of political instability and actively smarting with the humiliation of defeat. To both problems the strong, charismatic leader could seem a more effective answer than career politicians in suits. And so a succession of candidates offered themselves in the next few decades, embodying the threat from an anti-Republican right that found its natural base in the army and the Church. Initially its sympathies were monarchist, though as time passed its monarchism was muted in a populist appeal to the economic discontents of the urban working class. In the 1870s the candidate was Marshal MacMahon, the president who sought to convert the Republic into a "Republic of Dukes" and so pave the way for the *légitimiste* pretender, the Comte de Chambord. Though modestly conceiving himself as General Monk rather than Cromwell, he made such use of his own appearance on horseback that a contemporary newspaper published a cartoon of him with the caption: "The horse looks intelligent." In the 1880s the candidate was General Boulanger, or perhaps one should say the candidates were Boulanger and his charger Tunis, for except in its company the General had no obvious qualifications for the role he sought.

MacMahon was forced out of office in 1879. Boulanger botched his planned coup in 1889, fleeing the country for Brussels, where he soon afterward committed suicide over his mistress's grave. When Marx said that history happens twice, the first time as tragedy and the second time as farce, it was French history he had in mind: he was referring to the coups launched by the two Napoléons. He might have added that, with further repetition, history sinks further into farce. It had certainly done so by 1899, when President Félix Faure died at a particularly tense moment in the Dreyfus Affair. Paul Déroulède, former Boulangist and founder of the right-wing Ligue des Patriotes, chose the state funeral as the occasion to stage a *coup d'état*. He and his supporters—Maurice Barrès among them—waited in the Place de la Nation for the guard of honor to pass on its way back from the graveside, hoping to persuade their commander to march on the Élysée palace. In the event General Roget merely brushed Déroulède aside with his sword and afterward had him arrested for disturbing the peace.

By then the quasi-military posturing of men like Déroulède looked less of a threat than the bomb outrages—plaguing Paris like other European capitals—from anarchists on the far left. Somehow the Republic had grown a little stronger against attack and conspiracy from the right. Monarchism was on its way to looking marginal. By the turn of the century both the Church and army, those bastions of right-wing sentiment, would emerge bruised and chastened from their role in the Dreyfus Affair; the eventual triumph of the *Dreyfusards* would give added heart to the republican project of curbing their influence. Yet the Affair, a rhetorical civil war seeming at times to threaten actual civil war, also demonstrated the continuing tensions of French society. It left its own legacy of bitterness to add to the accumulations of the past.

Nor did the political processes at the heart of the Republic ever look substantial, much less impressive in their operation. The political parties claiming the loyalties of deputies in the Assembly proliferated in mazelike intricacy, restlessly shifting in their coalitions and disagreements. So did a succession of governments. Between 1871 and the First World War, the Third Republic saw 50 different ministries come and go, an average of more than one a year. (In Britain, which the French sometimes cited for comparison in the workings of democracy, the average life of a ministry was just over three years.) One cause, though not by any means the only one, for their frequent rise and fall was the prevalence of scandal and corruption.

To believers in democracy and skeptics alike the Third Republic had given little reassurance. Its operations looked unstable, its practitioners weak or tainted. Where it was not actively hated, it was frequently despised: the right-wing nickname of *la gueuse*—the whore—gained currency outside right-wing circles. Nor was there much about the Republic's continued life in the twentieth century, between the two world wars, to change such impressions. The rise and fall of ministries accelerated in its pace; the Panama Scandal gave way to the Stavisky Affair. The men on horseback had not ceased to threaten, and with the street politics of interwar fascism as their guiding example, their threat no longer seemed risible. The riots of 6 February 1934, led by Colonel Roque and his supporters in the Croix du Feu, represented the most serious outbreak of civil disorder since the days of the Commune; they succeeded in frightening an elected government out of office.

It was an ominous sign of the way Europe, and France with it, was tending in the 1930s. And in 1940, in the immediate aftermath of France's defeat, the Third Republic itself was frightened out of existence. Appropriately enough, it chose as the setting for its voluntary suicide the Grand Casino at Vichy, where it voted by an overwhelming majority to suspend its machinery and its constitution. And Pétain, the man to whom it handed over power, was the last but by far the most effective of the men on horseback who had dogged its career. To the public he was a man on horseback in a very real sense. He had earned many laudatory titles over the years, and with them several heroic epithets—among them, of course, the Victor of Verdun for his achievement in 1916. Yet the image of Pétain that most people carried in their minds, the reassuring picture that made them trust him in the hour of their need, was of his appearance at the ceremonies marking the end of the First World War. At Metz in November 1918, when he was made a Marshal of France, and again at the Victory Parade in Paris in July 1919 he had worn a simple *horizon bleu* uniform, matching the color of his eyes, and ridden a white charger.

Like almost everything else about Pétain, the image and the appeal it exerted were highly complex. In turning to him in 1940, were the French turning to what had always stood in opposition to the Republic or what, however little, could then be rescued from the Republic? In 1916 he had been regarded as a good Republican general, or at least a good enough Republican general. Though it might not have earned him his command at Verdun, the reputation had certainly helped to make him available as a candidate for command. In carrying out his command he had shown a concern for the lives and welfare of his troops which, though justified by military appreciation of the need for thrift and efficiency, had seemed very like the spirit of republicanism in action: here at last was a general who treated his troops with a democratic compassion, a democratic respect. This appeal was still relevant in 1940, when he offered himself to the nation on the grounds of his proven ability to husband its diminished and beleaguered resources, to share its suffering.

And yet at the same Pétain offered strong leadership of precisely the sort that critics charged the Third Republic with failing to deliver. He promised to end the shabby failure that had betrayed

France into her present crisis. It was all too familiar a promise. Indeed, as Pétain made it in 1940, it sounded positively old-fashioned, redolent of opposition to the Republic in its early rather than its later career. Pétain's Vichy régime had about it little trace of the raucous street demagoguery of 1930s fascism. Far from celebrating the end of republicanism and what would succeed it, far from embracing the modern in all its violent beauty, it harked deliberately back to a world older than the Republic, older even than the Revolution: safe, hierarchical and pious. Having passed for much of his career as the good Republican general, Pétain proceeded after 1940 to surround himself and the régime of which he was leader with all the paraphernalia of Catholicism and monarchism. Not for him the floodlit public rallies of Berlin and Rome. He preferred to be photographed examining the Christmas cards sent by the schoolchildren of a grateful nation, or making his way to Mass on Sunday; he even proposed to make the festival of Saint Philippe a public holiday. The stance he strove to adopt toward the French was that of an ideal king toward his subjects: kindly yet occasionally stern, the good father feeling for his children even when he found it necessary to rebuke or punish them. The novelist Céline dubbed him *Philippe le dernier*. It was as if the Republic, the turbulent events which had brought it to life and the whole complex milieu in which it had survived, had never happened.

✛ ✛ ✛

That an emblem may be a useful rallying point, for any sort of group, is unnecessary to point out. It makes everybody aware of social unity by expressing it in a material form and, for this reason in itself, the use of emblematic symbols must quickly have gained currency once the idea had been conceived. Yet this idea should spring spontaneously from the conditions of common life; for the emblem is not only a convenient device for clarifying what a society feels about itself; it serves to create the feeling; it is itself a constituent element. . . .

So, in all its aspects and at every moment in its history, social
life is possible only thanks to a vast symbolism.

Émile Durkheim, *Les Formes élémentaires de la vie
religieuse: Le système totémique en Australie*
(*The Elementary Forms of Religious Life:
The Totemic System in Australia*), 1912

It is not hard to write off the Third Republic in the harshest terms.
The span of its existence determined by the two great national ship-
wrecks of 1870–71 and 1940, it was just another raft of the *Medusa*:
fragile from the start, kept continually unstable by the tensions of
French political life, always an arena for conflict rather than cooperation. Even while the Republic survived, it rarely commanded
respect; once it had gone, it was so unlamented as to be expunged
from memory. There are many objections to be lodged against so
dismissive a summary, but the most important is also the simplest.
The Third Republic lasted nearly 70 years. Despite France's previous record of short-lived constitutions, and despite the prophecies
of its own early death, the Republic survived longer than any system of government France had adopted since the Revolution. The
achievement left a permanent mark. Its memory was far from being
expunged, for (thank God) the political life of France did not end
with Pétain and Vichy, however loudly they might have announced
an end to modern experiment. All France's postwar constitutions
have been the Third Republic's offspring and heirs.

In fact the Republic had always been a good deal stronger than
it looked, though its strengths, like its virtues, were largely negative.
They were those of a compromise: inhabiting the middle ground,
doomed to look timid, incapable of attracting passionate loyalty, always susceptible to attack, and yet, when it came to the crunch,
preferable to the alternatives on offer. In the sheer number of those
alternatives lay its safety; the Republic, one might say, was fortunate
in having so many enemies. In practice the threat did not come
from the legacy of the Bonapartism, monarchism and the Commune, for these were abstract entities. It came from Bonapartists,

monarchists and Communards, and these were faction-ridden clans, given to quarreling with themselves and each other, sometimes managing to form conspiratorial alliances and on occasion seeking rapprochement with elements in republicanism. Even before fate had cast him on the raft of the *Medusa* Napoléon III had reviewed the various tendencies of his family and their immediate supporters with some bewilderment: "The Empress is *légitimiste*, my cousin is republican, Morny is *Orléaniste*, I am a socialist; the only Bonapartist is Persigny and he is mad."

Parliamentary parties behaved in the same fashion, of course, but their apparent chaos signified deep-seated instability only if one assumed that it was the destiny of all parliamentary democracies to develop a party system on the British model. In their gloomy contempt for the maneuverings of politicians, the French sometimes fell into exactly this mistake. But they did not mistake the frequent changes of government for violent changes of direction. Governments might rise and fall but their personnel remained all too familiar; the name of the game they played was not revolution but musical chairs. The record holder for sheer durability among the servants of the Republic was Aristide Briand who, between 1906 and 1932, held office in 25 different cabinets; in the process he served 11 times as Prime Minister and 17 times as Foreign Secretary, on several occasions occupying both posts at the same time. Of the 561 men who served as ministers during the lifetime of the Republic, 103 did so twice, 71 three times, 48 four times and 122 more than four times. It was no wonder that Clemenceau, taxed with making a career of bringing down governments, should have replied: "I have overthrown only one. They are all the same." And it was no wonder that the French, who called the Republic *la gueuse* in moments of anger, should more commonly have known it as the *République des camarades*: the Republic of Cronies.

Politics and politicians, the Third Republic helped to teach the French, were to be suffered. Meanwhile people got on with their lives. The years after the Franco-Prussian War soon brought signs that the French were getting on with their lives again, and to good effect. Even those who had feared or prophesied the end of France in 1870–71 admitted that she had again shown her ability to pull herself out of the abyss. The most tangible sign of recovery was economic, enabling her to pay the massive war indemnity imposed by the Treaty of Frankfurt far sooner than anybody had foreseen, the Germans included. For this achievement the Republic, its leaders and its politicians received little or no thanks. The credit, of course, belonged to "the people." It was in the people that the strength of France lay. I have already quoted the lurid end of *La Débâcle* in which Zola, looking back on 1871 from the vantage point of 1892, saw "the end of everything." In fact what he saw, though undoubtedly disaster, was not quite the end of everything. He also saw his hero Jean, bowed but not broken by the German victory, uncorrupted by the frivolity of the Second Empire or the savagery of the Commune: "the very backbone of the nation, the sensible peasant, wanting peace so as to return to work, earn some money and get strength back again."

France, then, was not its government nor its leaders nor its politicians but its people. "They" are ineffective or contemptible; "we" embody profound resources, the real resources of the nation. Gambetta had invoked this belief, loosely declined from the values of the Revolution, in his call to arms after the fall of Napoléon III. It continued to dictate the mood of the peace that followed the Franco-Prussian War as well, and so paved the way for how the *poilus* reacted at Verdun. They have failed and left the job to us: this signaled a crisis, beyond doubt, yet it was after all a familiar sort of crisis, a half-expected sort of crisis, a French sort of crisis. If the Third Republic had done nothing to change the perception in the years between 1871 and 1916, and if anything had confirmed it, this was not just because of its limitations and obvious failings, as a weak government of cronies inhabiting difficult times. It was also the result of policy; it was even, in a sense, the major and enduring achievement of the Republic.

Suspicion of government and leaders was certainly a safeguard against the caesarism of the men on horseback. In this respect a decisive moment came with the threat posed by MacMahon, not just the first but, because of his respectability, the most formidable.

MacMahon exploited the status given to the President in the Republic's original constitution: directly elected by the voters, he was able to appeal to "the people" over the heads of fellow politicians, in true caesarist fashion. In one of remarkably few constitutional amendments, and undoubtedly the most significant, the National Assembly responded by reserving to itself the power of appointing presidents. The president thus became a figurehead or, as de Gaulle put it, "a Head of State who is not a Head and does not have a State." Clemenceau, too active a politician to seek an office which would have made him "a useless organ, like the prostate," liked to say that when there was a choice of candidates he always voted for the most stupid. The results only just fell short of bearing out his claim. Who today in France (much less anywhere else) remembers Émile Loubet, Armand Fallières or Paul Doumer? In 1940 politicians paid so little heed to Albert Lebrun that they forgot to tell him that the Republic of which he was President had just ended.

In the same period when it made this amendment to its constitution the Republic also passed another piece of legislation, apparently quite trivial, prohibiting public statues of living people.* MacMahon, of course, had erected a statue of himself; the ban was in rebuke to his example and to the whole cult of personality. Arguably it was quite as important as the diminution of the presidency. Statues mattered. The emblems or symbols by which a régime presented itself to the nation and encouraged the nation to define itself mattered. Napoléon I had made the lesson unforgettable. Indeed nothing better expressed the instability of the recent past, and the continuing tensions they had left, than the discordant litter of national emblems and symbols France had acquired by the 1870s. Was she the *tricolore*, the white flag of the Bourbons (or even conceivably the black flag of anarchy)? Was she the Gallic cock, the fleur-de-lys or the imperial eagle?

* Exceptions could be made, as in the case of the composer Saint-Saëns, whose statue was erected in his birthplace, Dieppe. At the unveiling he remarked: "Since one only puts up statues to the dead, it follows that I am now counted among their number. You will excuse me therefore from making a speech."

Establishing a set of national emblems, then, was no hollow formality but a process fraught with ideology in every detail. That the Republic should have embarked on it as firmly and thoroughly as it did in the period following the fall of MacMahon says a great deal about its commitment to a cultural project more fundamental than its immediate political concerns. The project, of course, was to shape and remold the identity of the nation into a secure and coherent form, and to wed the idea of the Republic—no longer an experiment or a régime but an institution—indissolubly to the idea of the nation. Its choice of emblems and symbols favored abstract values rather than individual leaders; in particular it concentrated on values harking back to the Revolution.

Part of the legacy of the Revolution was inescapable, already central in those traditions to which the Republic owed its being. The *tricolore*, with its three abstract bands of color, echoing the tripartite slogan of *Liberté, Egalité, Fraternité*, perfectly expressed the rejection of a monarchist past when flags had carried religious symbols or the heraldic devices of noble families. The vibrant militancy of *La Marseillaise* had always made it, in the first Napoléon's phrase, republicanism's greatest general—perhaps, indeed, France's greatest general. The Republic officially adopted it as the national anthem in 1879 but long before then it had spontaneously assumed this status. Inevitably Napoléon III had tried to stamp it out, substituting instead a pious little piece of medievalism about a knight setting out on the Crusades, supposedly written by his mother Hortense. The feeble strains of *Partant pour la Syrie*, as it was called, had quickly been drowned out by *La Marseillaise* even at the very start of the Franco-Prussian War, when the Empire still ruled and victory was expected.*

Other choices proved more complex and more revealing, none more so than the adoption of Marianne as the official personification of the Republic. She too had her roots in the Revolution, for Marianne had been the nickname of the first Republic in 1792; it

---

* *Partant pour la Syrie* vanished so completely that at the Empress Eugénie's funeral in 1920 the band did not know the tune. It played *La Marseillaise* instead.

had quickly become synonymous with Liberty. Yet, like Liberty, Marianne could take different forms. In one tradition, the earliest, she is portrayed as the very image of revolutionary zeal: young, marching, with her mouth open, her hair floating freely and her breasts bare. Sometimes she wore a Phrygian cap, the headgear of free Roman slaves; sometimes she brandished the cap at the end of a pole or a pike. In this guise she had been invoked by Delacroix in his painting *La Liberté guidant le peuple* (*Liberty Leading the People*) and by François Rude in the bas-relief head, popularly known as "La Marseillaise," on the Arc de Triomphe.

It was in this guise, too, that Marianne was most hated by the conservative right as *la gueuse* herself. "Let her be hanged," wrote Verlaine in his religious and counterrevolutionary phase: "Horizontal in life and vertical in death!" Yet her street-fighting militancy could be equally unsettling for politicians who wished to present Liberty, and the Republic, no longer as a cause to be fought for at the barricades but as an achievement already secure. The presence of the Phrygian cap on the statue of the Republic unveiled in the Place de la République in 1883 was judged controversial, and President Grévy did not attend the ceremony. By then a muted portrayal of Marianne was preferred; it could be seen, for example, in the busts displayed in town halls throughout France. In them she was more likely to be matronly than young; her hair was neat rather than disordered; her mouth was closed and her expression calm. She had become a figure of serene and classical dignity.

In one of the most savage pamphlets prompted by the Franco-Prussian War the German historian Heinrich von Treitschke compared his own country's sense of history—long and continuous, reaching back to ancient times—with the brevity of the French perspective. "It is here," he concluded,

> that the essential and fundamental feature of modern French political sentiment, and the ultimate source of the disease pervading the French State, is to be sought. The nation has broken with its history; it accounts what lies behind the Revolution as dead and done. . . . All that happened before the sacred date of '89 belongs

to archaeological research, and no bridge remains to connect to-day with yesterday.

On the face of it, this was an odd charge to level, for France's post-revolutionary historians—Michelet is the obvious example—had never ceased to take pride in the sheer length of the national record, the 20 centuries of civilization in France. Yet Treitschke also had a point, and a damaging one.

Each of the different régimes under which France had lived since the Revolution had announced a discontinuity that went far deeper than just the surface of political life. Each had in some way sought to expunge a portion of the past, if only the past as repre-sented by the immediately preceding régime. And each attempt had in some measure recalled the original Revolutionary effort of the 1790s to break with history and start again from the year nought. Custom, habit and popular memory—all the various channels through which a sense of the past, however hazy, persists despite ideological command—had made the endeavor futile. They were forces too stubborn to be denied by a republic that sought to ex-press a settled order, to wed itself to the ways in which the nation already thought of itself. And yet how could a republic reach safely back for symbols into a pre-Revolutionary past that was, in this re-spect, the territory of kings and saints?

The question, inevitably, focused on the figure of Jeanne d'Arc. She had never been forgotten, and her claims were growing stronger and stronger as she became the object of fascinated admiration to intellectuals from Michelet to Péguy. To the Republic she repre-sented a focus of sentiment too potent to be allowed to flourish be-yond the official boundaries, a cultural resource too precious to be ignored. It finally acknowledged Jeanne in making her feast day a day of national homage in 1920. But the proposal had taken a good 30 years to gain acceptance and its slow progress had moved virtu-ally in tandem with the procedure that led, in the same year, to her canonization by the Catholic Church. If there were two different versions of Marianne, there were radically different Jeannes as well. Even more plainly, her case emphasizes how national symbols are often built not on sites of easy and universal agreement but on sites of contest.

The Jeanne d'Arc originally proposed for canonization in 1869 was a figure venerated by the disaffected Catholic right. Her cult had strong parallels with the cults of the Sacré-Coeur and Sainte Bernadette of Lourdes, both of which flourished in the aftermath of the Franco-Prussian War.* National, as well as personal, healing was to be sought by pilgrimage to the grotto at Lourdes; devotees of the Sacré-Coeur called for penitence and expiation by a nation that had abandoned true piety and been punished for its sins. The Jeanne d'Arc whom cultists venerated was an abiding example of traditional virtues in her fidelity to God's call and her fidelity to her sovereign. Yet plainly this was not the only heroine whom the story contained. There was another Jeanne in the simple peasant who led an army, the lonely patriot who suffered desertion by her king and the stubborn heretic who defied the power of the Church in holding to her conscience.

Expressed thus starkly, there was not just difference but opposition between the Catholic heroine and the radical, or republican, heroine. Jeanne, it would seem, did not unite the French but divide them. Yet that, surely, is to misread the significance of Jeanne—and of communal symbols—just as it would misread the issue to say that the Church canonized one Jeanne and the Republic acknowledged the other. At a certain point the two Jeannes overlapped and agreed, and their point of meeting was, of course, France. In both readings she was above all a national heroine who had emerged, as if in embodiment of the residual strength of France, in time of crisis. She had fought to repel the foreign invader and—the coincidence was too strong to be ignored after the Franco-Prussian War—she had

* The adolescent Bernadette Soubirous experienced her visions of the Virgin Mary in 1858. She was canonized in 1933 but her cult had attracted a following before the Franco-Prussian War. The cult of the Sacred Heart stemmed from the visions of Sainte Marguerite-Marie Alacoque at Paray-le-Monial in the seventeenth century but did not become widely popular before the 1870s. Then its celebration made the Burgundian town scene of what one historian has described as "an enormous festival of the political right" and disfigured the Paris skyline with the basilica of Sacré-Coeur in Montmartre.

fought under the banner of the cross of Lorraine, the emblem of her native province, now partly annexed by the Germans.

It was no accident, then, that the Franco-Prussian War should have served to reinvigorate and the First World War to test the cult of Jeanne in both its strictly religious and its strictly republican aspects. "What troubled the minds of the Kaiser and his General von Kluck?" asked a field chaplain after the German army had been stopped at the Battle of the Marne. He proceeded to speculate about the miraculous powers of intercession in the most devout terms:

> Was it gentle Geneviève who stopped this new Attila? Was it Jeanne d'Arc, angry at seeing him violate Compiègne and Reims? Was it Our Lady who wanted to expel him from the land where her sanctuaries flourish? . . . I await strategic explanations of the victory; but I certainly have the right to see our heavenly allies hovering over the battlefield of the Marne.

At the same time the philosopher Henri Bergson could agree that "Jeanne d'Arc won the Battle of the Marne," finding in her name and memory the embodiment of a national will. It was in the same spirit presumably that Pétain invoked her words at the siege of Orléans to encourage the troops at Verdun ("Our enemies, even if they hung from the clouds, we shall get them! And we'll drive them out of France!"). And it was in the same spirit that the troops themselves came to view her (in the words of one observer) as "their older sister, their own particular little saint, involved by her generous patriotism in their sufferings."

To involve the object of a religious cult so loosely and emotively in the language of patriotism might have been intellectually imprecise, yet it proved sufficient for all but the most doctrinaire Catholics and doctrinaire republicans. Most people were neither, but lived somewhere in that middle ground where the Republic sought to root itself. It had already strengthened its appeal in adopting *La Marseillaise*, the *tricolore* and the figure of Marianne as its own; *Partant pour la Syrie*, the imperial eagle, the Bourbon flag, even the previous ways of portraying Marianne faded into the past as redundant attempts at national self-definition. From the start there was a claim to permanence in the achievement, and indeed the Republic did succeed in giving France the constellation of national symbols by which she still knows herself and is known by the world today. In adopting Jeanne, the Republic achieved something further. Without ceasing to be republican, it gained a stake in history that was, literally, pre-republican; it declared its affinity, its continuity, with the nation's larger past. And at the same time it gained another sort of territory as well. It partly appropriated to its own use a figure who had previously appeared to belong to religious cultism. It took Jeanne from the candlelit world of the Mass into the world of civic festival and ceremony. Under the Republic, the language and sentiment attached to religion were increasingly being claimed for the nation.

4

---··---

A Certain Idea of France

All my life I have held a certain idea of France. Sentiment inspires me to it as well as reason. My emotional side naturally imagines France, like the princess in the stories or the Madonna in the frescoes, as dedicated to an outstanding and exceptional destiny. Instinctively, I have the feeling that Providence made her for complete successes or exemplary misfortunes. If, however, mediocrity marks her acts and deeds, this strikes me as an absurd anomaly, for which the French can be blamed, not the genius of the country. But, at the same time, the positive side of my mind convinces me that France is not really herself except in the first rank; that only great enterprises can compensate for the disruptive ferment her people carry in themselves; that our country, being what she is, among the others, being what they are, should aim high and hold firm, even at risk of mortal danger. In short, as I see it, France cannot be France without greatness.

In France today there are still people who know these words virtually by heart and cannot recite them without emotion; the idea of France they evoke strikes the deepest of chords. If I could begin to unpack all their inflections, all the resonance that the name of France holds for the writer, a good part of my work in this chapter, and indeed this whole book, would have been done. The writer, of course, is de Gaulle and the passage opens his memoirs of the Second World War, in elegant, lofty explanation of his refusal to accept

France's defeat in 1940 in the spirit of "realism" (or defeatism) that led Pétain and his Vichy government down the path of compromise to humiliation and self-betrayal.

Recurrent among the many difficulties de Gaulle had to contend with as leader of the exiled Free French was the fear that he was yet another of the men on horseback who had threatened the Third Republic while it survived. (Nor did the difficulty vanish in 1944, for the fear lingered throughout his postwar career in politics.) Churchill was frequently exasperated by de Gaulle's imperious and autocratic conception of himself, while the Americans were ready to dismiss him as a political general from a country which had already produced too many political generals and suffered too much at their hands. Their doubts soured his relations with the Allies and permanently reduced his standing. Among his countrymen, left-wing *résistants* like Jean Moulin frequently suspected him of being a "fascist"; by no means all proved as willing as Moulin to abandon the suspicion. Despite being Pétain's antagonist, de Gaulle could look disconcertingly like his twin—not least in his identification of France with himself and his belief that her destiny lay in his hands. And yet, nowhere more strikingly than in his words at the start of his war memoirs, de Gaulle's idea of France showed him to be a true child of the Republic.

Born in 1890, de Gaulle was certainly a typical child of the Republic. His father Henri had served in the Franco-Prussian War and seen action in an unsuccessful attempt to break out from the siege of Paris. He used to take his young son to the war memorial near the spot where he had been wounded. It depicted a broken sword with the inscription: "The sword of France, broken while in their valiant hands, shall be forged anew by their descendants." Such sentiment formed a common strand in public rhetoric of the years following 1870–71; war memorials and the ceremonies attaching to them provided the ideal place and opportunity for its expression. It exercised a profound influence on de Gaulle's generation, growing up in the shadow of a defeat it had not directly experienced, imagining another war that would expunge the shame. It helped to breed a new militancy that found a natural vehicle in an army being remodeled, in the wake of the Dreyfus Affair, along republican lines. De Gaulle's choice of soldiering was made at an early age: by the time he was 15, he was already dreaming on paper of leading France to victory in the Eastern Marches. The acceptance of the Republic that went with his chosen career was, said his monarchist mother, the only serious disappointment he ever gave her.

In 1914 de Gaulle was a recent graduate of the military college at Saint-Cyr. With many of his peers he found in the First World War a necessary test—not quite the same thing as a welcome test—of the strength of the sword that the Republic had forged and that they now wielded. This time the sword did not break. France held at the Marne, and above all France held at Verdun in her longest hour of crisis. The achievement validated republican values and the larger view of France and her history which went with them. Writing in the 1930s de Gaulle could remember those who had prophesied the "end of France" in 1870–71 with an indulgent smile, for they had reckoned without "that hidden force which, always, pulls us out of the abyss." France was not helplessly adrift on the raft of the *Medusa*, however much she might have seemed so in the previous century. She did not simply racket from disaster to disaster, as her enemies and critics might have claimed. Rather, she had a destiny that scorned the safe and mediocre course; it demanded high ambition and it courted great risk. The elements went together, in a virtually inevitable rhythm: greatness and shipwreck, disaster and recovery.

There was consolation to be taken from this view of France in 1940. In its power, a good deal of the consolation came from the language in which the view was now clothed, the ground on which it staked its claim. It might have been rooted in the events of 1870–71 and 1914–18, and in the way those events were read from the vantage point of a Republic avowedly secular, yet it was no longer a lesson in history—if indeed it had ever been anything so dry. Evoking it at the beginning of his war memoirs, de Gaulle appealed not to reason but to sentiment and spoke of France as a princess or a Madonna. In this rhetorical mode France is always female and always belongs to the world of fable and religion. There was, it seemed, a masculine France to be grasped in terms of fact and argument and abstract concept. Yet there was also a more essential France, a female goddess or saint, to be loved sensuously and worshiped with all the force of religious belief.

In 1940 the same sort of faith, though professed in rhetoric of a lower key and a rather different temper, could sustain other children of the Republic, nurtured in the same ethos as de Gaulle. Perhaps the most remarkable case was Marc Bloch, among the most respected historians of his time. His book *L'Étrange Défaite* (*Strange Defeat*) was not so much a history of the fall of France at the hands of the Third Reich as a testament—he called it a *procès-verbale*—written virtually while events unfolded before his eyes. All his science and his professional skill, he stressed, did not permit him to see the future and, anyway, as an "old historian" he might not live to witness the outcome of what had been set in motion by France's defeat. (In fact he did not, though it was not old age that killed him: his body, identified by the false papers he carried, was found with the bodies of 27 other *résistants* from the Lyon area in 1944.) Much of the chaos in the spring and summer of 1940 which Bloch recorded, in a fashion at once vivid and reflective, was already familiar from the first days of Verdun, from the opening month of the First World War itself, from the absurd weeks of August 1870: a lack of preparation, a failure of organization, a collapse of leadership leaving the ordinary people to muddle through as best they could. He remained sure, though, that even in that muddle lay "deep resources"—like the "hidden force" of which de Gaulle had written—"intact and ready to revive."

So for Bloch, as for de Gaulle, the disasters of France belonged to a cycle that also promised her recovery. Yet Bloch was acutely aware that the rhythms of the cycle could be expressed in different terms, already habitual and now heard more loudly than ever: not simply as disaster and recovery but as punishment and reform. Observing the penitential mood of 1940 Bloch was reminded, with a historian's gift for salient detail, of a brief passage in the memoirs of

President Poincaré referring to the end of August 1914, just before Jeanne d'Arc had won the Battle of the Marne, when his postbag had been full of letters calling for France to dedicate herself to the cult of the Sacré-Coeur. Many of them the President had found touching, but "others seemed unhappily inspired by political passion rather than religious sentiment. In them our defeats are depicted as rightful punishment, inflicted by God on the Republic."

I have already mentioned the popularity that this cult enjoyed in the 1870s. Then, of course, the punishment had been defeat in the Franco-Prussian War; the sin that prompted it was the Second Empire. To the Catholic right Napoléon III's régime had never been Catholic enough, despite the example of devotion set by the Empress Eugénie. Abroad, it had betrayed the Papacy in its policy toward Italy; at home, it had fostered a mood of shallow materialism. Indeed, the Empire was everybody's favorite scapegoat in the 1870s, whatever their perspective. To some it had not been Catholic enough; to others it had been too Catholic. To some it was objectionable because it had been anti-republican (had it not come into existence by murdering an infant republic in its cradle?); to others the objection lay in its belated and timid concession to democracy. Beneath their partisan differences the common theme of these indictments was that the Empire had been frivolous and degenerate. Under its sway France had become "a fire without flame or light; a heart without warmth; a people without prophets able to say what it felt; a dead planet, following its orbit with a mechanical movement."

These words were written by Ernest Renan and they come from an essay, "La Réforme intellectuelle et morale de la France" ("The Intellectual and Moral Reform of France"), which gave the title to a volume of essays he published in 1871. It set a precedent for Bloch's L'Étrange Défaite in expressing the reaction of a scholar and historian to present disaster, though the comparison underlines Renan's readiness to indulge the habit of national self-chastisement of which Bloch was skeptical. A good deal of Renan's savagery in framing his indictment comes from the unmediated shock of events, yet by no means all. In 1869 he had already written in gloomy presentiment, not specifically of war, much less of defeat, but of some inevitable and necessary rebuke that history had in store:

> France can do anything, except be mediocre. What she suffers, all in all, she suffers for having too boldly challenged the gods. Whatever misfortunes the future may hold, and should the fate of the French, like that of the Greeks, the Jews, the Italians, one day excite the pity of the world and almost its amusement, the world will not forget that if France has fallen into the abyss of misery it is through having made bold experiments from which everybody benefits, through having loved justice to the point of madness, through having embraced with generous imprudence the possibility of an ideal that the miseries of humanity do not admit.

If at first reading the passage sounds very like the opening of de Gaulle's war memoirs, the similarity is more superficial than real. Renan and de Gaulle might both have seen the extremes of greatness and misery in the destiny of a country that could never simply be mediocre, but they agreed on little else. Where de Gaulle could meet the nation's dark night of the soul with a ringing profession of faith, Renan had only the hollowest consolation to offer. In his grudging account France's greatness fell a long way short of the "complete successes" to which de Gaulle alluded. Bold experiments, a love of justice pursued to the point of madness, the embrace of ideals that could never work: French history, at least since the Revolution, was a record of dangerous folly rather than achievement. To de Gaulle France's misfortunes were "exemplary": the French have always been in the habit of regarding their nation, in her greatness or her misery, as a pattern for other nations, and it was not just at Verdun that a consciousness of being under the gaze of the world could make an additional burden. To Renan in 1869 the prospect already added a final touch to anticipated discomfort: France would be chastised, deservedly chastised, and in the most humiliatingly public fashion.

Such gloom could not fail to deepen after 1870–71. The project of national self-indictment could not fail to broaden, even amid the signs of France's economic recovery and the tributes it brought to the underlying resilience of her people. Strictly speaking, of course, nations do not indict themselves. The description implies a communal agreement and a willingness to shoulder individual responsibility that defeat and disaster do not encourage. The activity is always partisan, always divisive. People go looking for scapegoats: first individuals, usually generals or political leaders, and then groups. One reason why Marc Bloch remained wary of the whole ethos of "punishment" and "reform" in 1940 was the ease with which he could foresee Vichy's whole program of witch-hunting Jews, Communists and Freemasons. After 1870–71 the luckless, and stubbornly unrepentant, Marshal Bazaine would be put on trial; the Second Empire would be condemned. Yet as Renan had already shown, there were far larger axes to grind. France had not been punished because of a general or even an episode in her history. Perhaps she had been punished because of her history—even, in a sense, punished by history?

No work shows more massively how this indictment could be framed than Hippolyte Taine's *Les Origines de la France contemporaine*. An ambitious multivolume history dealing with the period from the *ancien régime* onward, it occupied its author from 1875 until his death in 1893 and confirmed his position among the most respected historians of his time. He undertook it as an act of diagnosis, starting from a simple proposition: "Our faults caused our reverses." Chief among the faults, embracing all the others, was that the French were impractical. In itself, the point was hardly surprising, for even in moments of self-congratulation the French have never been given to listing practicality among the virtues on which they pride themselves: imaginativeness, inventiveness and energy certainly, and also a stubborn resourcefulness in adversity, but not practicality. But the charge of impracticality had never been made so urgently and so relentlessly as it was by Taine. In his account, most vividly of the Revolution, the French are absolutist in their love of ideas, besotted by theory: they pursue wild, fantastic, anarchic dreams to the bitter end.

"It was the scientific spirit that defeated us," wrote Zola in 1879, while Taine's history was still running its lengthy course. He had in mind far more than the modern efficiency that Moltke's army had shown on the battlefield, of course, and more than the reputation for science that the German universities had established. To him, as to many contemporaries, it was not so much Germany which had threatened the ruin of France as something in France herself. For Zola, like Taine, the "something" was a sort of impracticality: a scornful neglect of the procedures of science and of the laws that science discovered. The French had never lacked the capacity to produce new ideas or good ideas (Zola on this point being some-what more charitable than Taine), but they lacked the capacity to develop them systematically or effectively. "This is why we, who ought to be at the summit after the seeds of truth we have ceaselessly thrown into the wind, are now weakened, crushed by duller and more methodical races." The lesson to be drawn from this fate, as Zola spelled it out, was obvious: "All we have to do is to school our-selves in science. No more lyricism, no more big empty words, but facts, documents. Ascendancy in the world will belong to the nation with the most precise observation and the most powerful analysis."

Zola made this call in an essay cast specifically as a "Lettre à la jeunesse"—a letter to the young—and he plainly intended his mes-sage to be stern but optimistic. Taine wrote his history in precisely the scientific spirit that Zola advocated, opposing hard fact to the idle theories of the Enlightenment and Romanticism, insisting that history itself proceeds by laws that science can trace, laws that have nothing to do with the idealistic hopes of those who had sought to shape the recent course of France. There was little, if any, trace of optimism in the result. I said just now that Taine's intent was diag-nostic; in fact, his work often reads more like a *post mortem*. The ac-count it gives is of a nation apparently dying, if not already dead, pursuing an inevitable trajectory of decline, a victim of its weakened and unstable temperament.

Even those among the young who did not reject Taine's anti-republican bias could find his defeatism unpalatable. Defeatism, indeed, could seem all that the established generation of thinkers and intellectuals offered by way of teaching in the 1870s and beyond. Too often their view of France's disasters as deserved punishment or inevitable rebuke could lead to a view of France as helpless in the face of history, helpless in the face of what she had become. Renan, claimed Maurice Barrès in disgust, had remarked to the would-be conspirator Paul Déroulède: "Young man, young man, France is dying; don't disturb her in her agony." So from the 1890s onward the familiar cry of "We have been betrayed" would take on a new dimension. Leading thinkers and academics who occupied the chairs in the great universities would often be joined to the list of leaders remote from the real spirit of their country and incapable of upholding it.

"We have been continually betrayed by our teachers and our leaders," wrote Charles Péguy. "We will not at any price allow our children to be betrayed in their turn, and by the same teachers and the same leaders." The betrayal had made his generation, already grown to maturity before the First World War, a *génération sacrifiée*. He did not mean, of course, a generation sacrificed to the horrors of war, though it would shortly become just that, and Péguy himself would be one of the earliest victims. He meant a generation sacrificed to the horrors of peace, or at least to a passivity and readiness to capitulate that had brought the advantages neither of war nor of peace. His complex, republican militancy made Péguy an intellectual hero to his juniors and perhaps to none of them more than to the young de Gaulle. Yet how exactly was the idea of France that animated de Gaulle achieved? How could the impulse to see France as fatally weakened by her mistakes and faults be turned into a vision of France, held with the clarity of faith, as capable still of strength and greatness? In the 1870s the task could seem all but impossible. It would always remain daunting yet essential, a matter of political survival for the Republic and, in the wider sense, a matter of cultural survival for the French.

✛ ✛ ✛

German historians had, for fifty years, united and toughened
Germany; French historians, partisan in their work, had divided
our hearts. . . . On the one side, discipline, order, the courage of
the group; on the other, individual courage, distrust, indiscipline,
division.

> Numa-Denis Fustel de Coulanges,
> "De la manière d'écrire l'histoire en France et en
> Allemagne depuis cinquante ans"
> ("How History Has Been Written in France
> and Germany for the Last Fifty Years"),
> published in *Revue des deux mondes*, 1 September 1872

The French did not just have a history of behaving divisively: they
had a history of writing history divisively. Instability and national
weakness were thus confirmed and perpetuated; they had become a
tradition and now seemed almost a destiny. Germans, by contrast,
had found in their historians willing servants of the drive toward
unification. Their service might have given the lie to any claim to
scientific objectivity, betraying the standards of a discipline which
should ideally remain serene and impartial, but perhaps it could
teach French historians a lesson. "In an epoch of war . . . it is surely
time for France at last to think of parrying the blows." In making
the suggestion in 1872 Fustel de Coulanges (himself a distinguished
historian, recently exiled from the University of Strasbourg) judged
the French habit of indulging in divisive historiography to be some
50 years old. So the axe-grinding of Renan, reacting to contemporary events, and of Taine, speaking the contemporary language of
science, was no innovation after all. In fact, the habit was more than
50 years old. Though strengthened by the Revolution, it went back
beyond 1789, the date which the French usually liked to identify as
the beginning of all their bad habits. Indeed, it was almost ancient.
Certainly, it concerned itself not just with the modern clash be-

tween monarchist and revolutionary or republican principles but with ancient history and the very origins of France.

All groups, communities and nations develop a narrative of their ancestry, and usually they do so very early in their life, if not actually at the moment of coming to regard themselves as a group. It answers an elementary need; it constitutes an act of self-definition. So when academic historians direct their gaze back beyond the modern history of their nation, they are walking in the footprints already left by myth and fable, poetry and chronicle. And what they say has a significance beyond the academic, a potency as great as that of earlier narratives. In France, as in all nations, traditional accounts had begun by addressing an obvious fact: that the territory of what at some later point became the nation had earlier been inhabited by different groups of people, whether as first settlers or as arrivals in successive waves of migration and invasion. Three groups were taken to be the most important: the Gauls, or Celts, conceived as aboriginal; the Romans, whom Caesar's conquest of Gaul made dominant in their turn; and, with the collapse of the Roman Empire, the Germanic tribes from across the Rhine, chief among them the Franks who (sometimes to the later embarrassment or irritation of the French) had given France her name. Together the Gauls, the Romans and the Franks in some way constituted the ancestors of the French.

The problem was to determine in what way. It remained as great a problem for academic historiography as it had been for the earlier narratives which academic historiography replaced. Indeed, for all the refinements of scholarship they introduced, historians often worked inside the same framework of assumptions that had generated previous accounts. It remained their habit, for example, to regard the three groups as utterly cohesive and distinct from each other: each one a tribal unit, closely linked by blood, language, custom and character, and so unmistakably different from other tribal units. The Gauls, Romans and Franks were not just "groups" or "peoples" but "races," to use the slippery and contentious word I have so far deliberately been avoiding. The historians I am referring to did not avoid it. Sometimes they applied the label so casually that it is impossible to say what particular meaning, if any, they attached to it; increasingly they devoted a central part of their labor to defining and refining it, always on the assumption that in "race," as applied to the early life of the nation, was a palpable historical fact requiring exhaustive definition and refinement.

Hand in hand with assumptions about race went assumptions about the primitive. The Gauls, the Romans and the Franks might each have built civilizations, to be praised as great, noble and refined, yet they were also in some sense "primitive." This did not necessarily mean that they were inferior and it could mean that they were superior: broadly speaking, the question hinged on whether historians viewed the trajectory of history in terms of progress or decline. Yet the term "primitive" did carry reasonably constant meanings as applied to behavior. To be primitive was, above all, to be violent. Primitive violence could issue in simple unruliness. The Romans might be exempt from this failing and also the Franks, to a lesser extent to be measured by the individual historian, but the Gauls were in most accounts downright fractious. Yet however unruly the group might be, it always possessed a terrible solidarity in its battles with other groups. Fighting other groups, apparently, was what primitive violence was all about; fighting other groups was what primitive life was all about. So ingrained was this assumption in historians that they were always prone to label new arrivals on any particular patch of soil invaders rather than migrants. The primitive peoples they studied might have been farmers, fishermen, hunters, builders or artists, but they were of consuming interest in their capacity as warriors.

Assumptions about the nature of the past were further complicated by assumptions about the nature of the present. Tracing a connection between the ancient and the modern was always a part of the historian's purpose, implicit even in the driest and most recondite inquiry. When the inquiry was not dry and recondite, and the purpose avowed, the precise nature of the interchange taking place between past and present could still be difficult to grasp. Take, for instance, this summary of the Gallic character in a popular history of France from her beginnings to the present:

> The Gauls were lively, quick-tempered, bold, always ready for a fight, above all in the presence of their wives, who willingly joined in their quarrels and did not shrink from combat any more than their husbands. They prided themselves on frankness and generosity, and punished lying and deception. They had a great appetite for news, and used to wait in the town squares and on the highways to question travellers. Excessive curiosity made them credulous.

The Gauls do not sound a very attractive crowd but, then, the writer does not sound a very good historian either. This much is obvious. It is less obvious just what impels the happy speculation that in his case substitutes for scholarly knowledge. Is he simply imposing on the Gauls unexamined notions about how primitive people behaved? Or is he imposing on them his observation of violence and turmoil in his own time? He was, after all, writing in 1803, only a decade after the execution of Louis XVI and a few years after the first Napoléon had seized power.

In fact, this particular writer did not lay special emphasis on the Gauls as ancestors of the modern French. By no means all historians did. The tripartite origins of France lent themselves to manifold, as well as fanciful, interpretation from which no settled agreement emerged—except perhaps in the decision to regard the French language as a Roman legacy and to praise its Latin purity. Yet the opposition between the original Gauls and the Franks, conquerors of their Romanized descendants, remained too fundamental to be ignored. Did it not suggest an ancient basis for the social divisions of pre-Revolutionary France? Perhaps over the centuries tribal difference, and antagonism, had been transmuted into class difference, and antagonism, between a Gallic peasantry and a Frankish aristocracy. This view had already grown current before the *ancien régime* ended, giving the longest of perspectives to contemporary debate. When Montesquieu praised the Franks for their role in establishing the law and the constitution, Voltaire responded by dismissing them as "ferocious beasts in search of pasture."*

So the Revolution could portray itself as an act of justice righting the largest and oldest of wrongs, the wrong done to the Gauls by the Franks. Writing in 1789, the Abbé Sieyès put up only a brief show of reluctance to get involved in questions of history and race before urging the Third Estate, made up of the People, that it had nothing to fear from reviving them:

> It will go back to the year before the conquest, and since it is to-
> day strong enough not to let itself be conquered, its resistance will
> no doubt be more efficacious. Why should it not drive back into
> Franconia all those families who maintain the absurd pretension of
> being issued from the race of the conquerors, and of having suc-
> ceeded to their rights? The Nation, thus purified, will not regret
> being reduced to believing itself composed exclusively of descen-
> dants of Gauls and Romans.

Race war reenacting itself as class war a thousand years later: the vision would permeate the work of later historians, regardless of their political perspective. In 1820 Augustin Thierry did not claim any originality for himself in discovering the

> sombre and terrible truth, that there are two enemy camps on the
> soil of France. It has to be stated since history is its witness: what-
> ever physical mingling of the two primitive races might have oc-
> curred, the constant opposition between their spirit has survived
> to this day in the two distinct parts of the population . . .

Nor did François Guizot, professor of history at the Sorbonne as well as Louis-Philippe's most influential minister, hesitate in agreeing:

---

* French commentators (Augustin Thierry above all) were naturally aware that British history and society lent itself to a similar interpretation, in which the defeated Saxons were ancestors of the working class and the conquering Normans ancestors of the ruling class.

The struggle continued in every age, under every form, with every army, and when, in 1789, the deputies from the whole of France were reunited in a single assembly, the two peoples were quick to take up their ancient quarrel. The day of victory had at last arrived. . . . The people defeated in ancient times became the conquering people.

It was no wonder, then, that Fustel de Coulanges should have charged historians with dividing the hearts of the French while German historians had been uniting the hearts of the Germans. Inevitably, he went on to supply the need for patriotic history as he conceived it in the work he contributed in the 1870s. And yet his call had already been answered, and on an epic scale, in the work of a historian significantly different in temper from those I have so far described. Jules Michelet belonged to the same generation as Victor Hugo: born amid the Revolution and inheriting its central ideals, living through their revival and disappointment in the Revolution of 1848. For him the Second Empire marked a period virtually of internal exile, just as it drove Hugo literally into exile. If Michelet did not receive the vast popular acclaim that greeted Hugo on his return after the fall of Napoléon III, nor live to see the fledgling Republic far beyond its difficult birth (he died in 1874), he exerted a critical influence on what the Republic attempted. His vision of French history was not merely congenial to the Republic's aims; implicitly, it shaped the act of national self-definition that the Republic undertook in its public symbols and, above all, in the campaign of school education that lay at the center of its project. To be a child of the Republic was to be a pupil of Michelet.

The great history of France that occupied the bulk, though not the whole, of his formidable energy from the 1830s until the 1860s began conventionally enough. It continued in this spirit until about halfway through the first volume, where Michelet summed up her origins: "Such was the accumulation of races in our Gaul. Races on races, peoples on peoples: Gauls, Cimbri, Belgae; on the one side

Iberians, on the other Greeks and Romans; the Germanic tribes are the last to arrive." At such a moment, the historian could proceed to argue his particular case for the civil war generated by these discordant elements, or to trace the different strands of French life descended from these various groups, or to claim one particular group as the true ancestors of the modern French. Michelet did none of these things. Instead he posed a challenging question and developed a challenging answer:

> That said, has one described France? Almost everything remains to be described. France is made of elements that could have resulted in a completely different mixture. Oil and sugar are made up of the same chemical principles. The principles given, all is not given; there remains the mystery of the particular and special existence. How much more should one take this into account when considering a living and active mixture such as a nation; a mixture likely to work on itself, to modify itself. This work, these successive modifications, by which our country kept on transforming itself, are what the history of France is about.

He again glanced back at ancient history but briefly, to dismiss it without nostalgia:

> So we should exaggerate neither the primitive element of Celtic genius nor the additions from abroad. Doubtless the Celts had an impact, also Rome and Greece, the Germanic tribes as well. But who united these elements, dissolved them and changed their nature? Who transmuted and transformed them, made them into a single body? Who drew our France from them? France herself, by that internal labour and mysterious childbirth, mingling necessity and liberty, which history must take into account.

I have quoted this passage at some length because it marks a central moment, not just in Michelet or in French historiography but in how it became possible for the French to see France and themselves in the nineteenth century. Where others had so often insisted, and would later continue to insist, on finding divisiveness, Michelet discovered a principle of fusion at work. Turbulence and failure were not the consequence of some ineradicable weakness or some inescapable cycle of conflict but of creative ferment. The key to this essentially optimistic view lay, perhaps, in the reference to "necessity and liberty." It identifies Michelet as the heir at once to the ideals of the Enlightenment and the fervor of Romanticism, the two traditions combining in his thought as they had in the impulse of the Revolution. Origin and ancient legacy are not determinants. They are rather the givens, or *fatalités*, which a nation transforms and transcends in the very act of becoming a nation. The process is an act of liberation, both philosophically and politically: made possible by free will, guided by love of freedom and taking full achievement of liberty as its eventual goal.

This is to spell out by abstractions what Michelet preferred to grasp by metaphor. To him France was always a person, a living being with a head and a heart, a temperament and a character. As such it could be at odds with itself without ceasing to be one. Its organic unity was always implicit in its diversity, revealed as much through geography as history. Reluctant to attach too great an importance to difference as it had first manifested itself between her ancient peoples, Michelet was always willing to concede it as it survived in the provincial types he detected among the modern French. Indeed, a good deal of his writing is devoted to rapt celebration of the patchwork of local variety that the nation had come to embrace. It was at its most emphatically marked on her territorial borders, in "the ingenious races of the Midi, the Roman or Iberian blood of Provence and Languedoc which links France to Italy and Spain," "the victorious and quarrelsome Normans, the most heroic people in heroic times, the most industrious in the industrial era," and in Alsatians whose "blue eyes and blond hair" made him look hopefully on "French Germany, thrown like a bridge between two civilizations and two races."

The evidence of such links, with other nations as much as with the past, were to be admired precisely because they had been modified and united through the operation of France's center, the Île de France and the capital:

> Here can be found the proof and guarantee of the living organism, the power to assimilate in its highest form: French France has been able to attract, absorb and make its own the surrounding Frances which were English, German, Spanish. French France neutralized them one by one, converting them all into her own substance. She subdued Brittany through Normandy, Franche-Comté through Burgundy, Guyenne and Gascony through Languedoc, Provence through Dauphiné. She made Northern France southern and northernized Southern France; to the Midi she brought the chivalric spirit of Normandy and Lorraine, to the North she brought the Roman character of the city of Toulouse, the Greek industrialism of Marseille.

Paris itself, of course, was the supreme achievement of the fusion through which the identity and personality of the nation expressed itself. Parisians' very neutrality—their lack of indigenous character or marked traits of ancestry, even of distinctive physique or features, going with their ready aptitude and universal capacities—made them "the head and the thought of France."

In strictly political terms these views endorse the centralizing tendency, expressed in the dominance of Paris over the provinces, that marked a continuity between the pre- and post-Revolutionary phases of French history. Yet Michelet preferred to celebrate it as the result of a cultural impulse to federation, even simply as the expression of a natural sociability. And to him the Revolution itself was the supreme expression of the same drive. His achievement was to read the Revolution simply as one event, the moment when the French came together as one in shared ideals of liberty and fraternity. Local consciousness merged and expanded into national consciousness, its growth being signaled by a widening spirit of festivity, culminating in the great national *fête* held in Paris at the Champ de Mars on 14 July 1790:

On that day everything was possible. All division had ended; there was neither nobility nor bourgeoisie nor people. The future was present . . . that is to say, time was no more. . . . A lightning bolt and eternity.

Nothing, it seemed, could stop the social and religious age of the Revolution, which still recedes before us, from being made real.

If the heroic goodness of this moment could have been sustained, the human race would have gained a century or more. It would, with one leap, have freed itself from a world of sorrows.

Here, more openly even than in anything that de Gaulle had to say of France, is patriotic belief raised to the pitch of a religious faith designed to meet and survive the world of sorrows in which France, like other nations, is still destined to live. To affirm such faith was always the purpose of Michelet's work, and we have already seen how it could nourish the children of the Third Republic when the sorrows of the world were at their most intense. "Give us festivals!" Marc Bloch could still exclaim in 1940. For him as for Michelet, the real and abiding spirit of the nation lay in the "beautiful surges of collective enthusiasm" that brought the French together, whether to crown their kings at Reims or to celebrate Liberty at the Champ de Mars. To Pierre-Alexis Muenier, the ambulance driver crouched in his freezing barracks at Verdun in February 1916, the arrival of 20th Corps gave heart in bringing not just reinforcements to the battlefield but a reminder of what France was really about. Its mixture of men from the Aube, Lorraine and Paris, brought together in willed and voluntary unity, presented in microcosm the same spectacle that Michelet had so lovingly evoked in his sweeping panoramas of the nation.

✦ ✦ ✦

It is not a matter of a temporary crisis, but of a completely new situation in the world. Another race of men has appeared on the stage.

Edgar Quinet, letter of 9 September 1866

Yet it is, after all, in de Gaulle's voice at the beginning of his war memoirs that we hear the echo of Michelet most clearly. "France certainly undertakes so ambitious a flight, is carried so high, that a fall is inevitable": this could be de Gaulle writing about the fall of France in 1940, but in fact it is Michelet writing about the *débâcle* of 1870–71, still preferring France's twin destiny of greatness and misery, her "precocious and sublime impulses," to the "uniform mediocrity, often flat, often in thrall to the follies of the past" achieved by duller nations. And in no respect were Michelet and de Gaulle closer than in speaking, at root, of France rather than the French.

In their mouths, the two were far from being identical. De Gaulle draws the distinction with particular clarity, reserving his praise for "the genius of the country," France in the abstract, made alive in his imagination since childhood by its association with the princess in the stories and the Madonna in the frescoes. She is beyond censure. The French themselves, on the other hand, are open to blame, for they embody the spirit of France at best in a partial and imperfect form: they let it down by their failings and, above all, by the "disruptive ferment" that they—not the princess or Madonna—carry within themselves. "De Gaulle loves France," Georges Bidault would remark, while serving as his foreign minister after the war, "even if he doesn't like Frenchmen."

The same charge could not be leveled at Michelet, whose praise of the French always carries a sensuous relish, an earthy warmth, that makes de Gaulle's temperament seem remote and chilly by comparison. Yet it was never in the French that he placed his ultimate faith, rather in something called France which lay above and beyond them. France was never simply the sum total of the French at any given moment in their history, nor even the sum total of the French at all the moments in their history. She might by glimpsed, however fitfully, in the French and their acts—gathering, for example, at the Champ de Mars in 1790—but she belonged neither to people nor to history. She was an ideal, aspired to though never achieved and perhaps, like the revelation briefly granted on the Champ de Mars, never capable of permanent achievement.

By the same token, she was an ideal which had preceded the attempt to embody her, preceded even the French. The French did not make themselves out of the Gauls and Romans and Franks whom Michelet waved aside in the first volume of his great history, however much their voluntary and enthusiastic participation in their making might make Michelet love them. France herself made the French, France as both idea and destiny. As such she was, if not imperishable, vital to the life of the world:

> Doubtless all great nations represent an idea important to the whole human race. But, good God, how much more true is this of France! Imagine for a moment that she were eclipsed or had ended; the sympathetic tie holding the world together would be weakened, dissolved and probably destroyed. Love, which is the life of the world, would have been attacked in the very place where she had been most alive.

At such moments the very grandeur of Michelet's conception of France also signaled its limitation—or at least the limited power it could command after the Franco-Prussian War. Its consolatory force in moments of crisis might have been undeniable, yet its relevance to *l'épreuve de la durée*, the long haul out of disaster that France confronted, was far more questionable. It was more than just its rhetorical mode that could sound out of key, though Zola had certainly struck a contemporary nerve in his weary distrust of lyricism and big empty words. France as a beacon of civilization, France as a pioneer in the discovery of values from which everyone benefited: those proud boasts had been easier to make amid the philosophical enthusiasm of the Enlightenment or the untested zeal of the Revolution. The nations of Europe as a family linked by sympathetic ties: such internationalism had always seemed more than a little remote from the rivalries dictating *realpolitik*. Michelet himself had always let his fair share of resentments and prejudices against France's neighbors show through; suppressing them grew impossible in the few years of life left to him.

Amid the particulars of the present in 1871, even the attempt looked antiquated. France had always had jealous rivals and enemies; now she had a new and powerful one. Victory had not just strengthened the enemy but in a very real sense summoned the enemy into being. Nobody in France could overlook the obvious fact that German victory and German unification had occurred simultaneously, that they had in fact been one event. The Germans had driven it home by an act of political theater. They formally declared the new Reich, forged from the alliance that Prussia had led into battle, on 18 January 1871, between the fall of Paris and the negotiations bringing an end to the war. So the new Germany made imposing its terms of peace its first major official act, just as France's new government made swallowing them its first major official act. The place chosen for declaring the new Reich was every bit as resonant as its timing. King Wilhelm of Prussia was formally exalted to Kaiser Wilhelm I in the Galerie des Glaces at Versailles—Louis XIV's great stateroom in Louis XIV's great palace. Revenge for the past was also warning for the future.

It was as if France had acquired a new *ennemi héréditaire* overnight. Previously the label had always been applied to Britain (though she was always called England), opponent on so many battlefields, rival over so many centuries for the privilege of being the dominant nation-state in Europe, and hence something more. In a striking phrase Michelet had called England *l'anti-France*. He was not, he rushed to make it clear, talking about "national hatred" or "blind malice" but rather an opposition of temperaments, values and cultures: "two conflicting magnets, pulling in opposite directions . . . two electrical forces, positive and negative." Like so many French writers he had been in the habit of enforcing his characterization of the French—light, witty, imaginative, energetic, erratic—by pointing out the contrast with the English, solidly chugging their way through the Industrial Revolution.

The Franco-Prussian War did not, of course, end hostility toward Britain. Indeed, her studious neutrality during the war and the peace negotiations had fueled resentment: Britain, exclaimed

Michelet, had allowed herself to be chloroformed while France was executed. Ahead lay colonial rivalry culminating in the confrontation between Colonel Marchand's expedition and troops led by Kitchener at Fashoda, on the Upper Nile, in 1898. The political path toward even the modest rapprochement of the Entente Cordiale in the early years of the next century was long and strewn with difficulty. Yet it could be pursued because the focus of French anxiety had shifted decisively. And with the change in policy went a much larger change: Germany now served as the major point of reference in national self-definition and self-evaluation.

The French themselves came to call the combined results of this process *le couple France-Allemagne*. In using the phrase as the title of a collection of essays about Franco-German relations published in the 1930s, Jules Romains defined it in terms strikingly similar to those Michelet had used to describe the relationship between France and the old anti-France, Britain. The word *couple*, he reminded his readers, carries at least two levels of meaning. As in English, it usually refers to a husband and wife or male and female pair but, in the specialized language of physics, it also denotes two equal forces pulling in opposite yet parallel directions. The former meaning interested him most, as if the very passion and intimacy of the antagonism between the two nations were a sexual feeling transferred to the collective level: "A badly matched couple. . . . A couple despite themselves. . . . A couple whose quarrels resound throughout the whole of Europe and the whole of the world." At the same time, "the profound differences, the contrasts, that set these two countries against each other could equally well join them."

The dynamics of this coupling expunged previous views France had taken of her neighbor. At times these had been sympathetic and even admiring. Near the beginning of the century, for example, Madame de Staël had praised the German states as the cradle of Kant's idealistic philosophy and the poetry of Romanticism, the congenial home of noble and exalted feeling. The German character might thus embody a different principle, but it was a welcome

196 +   THE ROAD TO VERDUN

counterbalance to the French habit of pursuing abstract logic to its extremes. "France and Germany are Europe," said Victor Hugo, "Germany the heart, France the head." Liberals and republicans of his generation, and Michelet's, could look approvingly on the German impulse for unification as an example of another nation attempting to follow the lead that France herself had given. Had not there been an attempt at revolution in 1848 across the Rhine as well as in France? Like the Poles and the Italians, the Germans were struggling to escape the prison of the past and achieve liberty. Straightforward, sturdy and energetic, the Protestants of the north German states could even remind observers of France's own revolutionaries—and, as such, appear an implicit rebuke to the jaded overrefinement of the French under their Second Empire.

Prussia's victory over Austria in 1866 sounded a note of alarm in some quarters, at least, at the character of the new Germany that might emerge from unification and the threat that it would pose for France. It certainly set the seal on the disillusionment of Michelet's friend and fellow historian Edgar Quinet, a former Germanophile responsible for bringing the philosophy of Herder to the attention of French readers. And it led the elderly François Guizot to warn against Prussia as a "warlike power, ambitious and clever." But exploring the full implications of the discovery did not start until after the Franco-Prussian War. Then, few writers were more influential in forming the impressions of those otherwise without information than Victor Tissot in his immensely popular *Voyage au pays des milliards* (*Journey to the Country of the Billions*).

Forget the picturesque banks of the Rhine, said Tissot at the beginning of his account: unless the Germans started building fortresses there, they held nothing to interest the French and said nothing about the character of the new nation which had replaced the old place of romantic dreams and ideals. It was, above all, a brutal and efficient machine, militaristic in its values, centrist and authoritarian in its government, with a highly industrialized economy and an increasingly urbanized population. His account of the cities stressed their materialistic character and laid salacious emphasis on the prevalence of crime and prostitution, to quell forever any hope that the old Protestant virtues of the Germans might still have lingered. Yet his opportunistic, scattergun denunciation—deliberately seizing on every conceivable ground for despising and fearing Germany—managed to reiterate at least one continual theme. Germany was not just new in being different from her older and unthreatening self, or new in literal fact of her political unification. She embodied the very spirit of modernity.

The same reaction informed more sober and responsible French appraisal than Tissot's trashy account. Just as the war itself had seemed to the French almost a collision with the realities of the modern world, so the contrast between the two nations now looked like the contrast between modernity and obsolescence. Germany had mastered the new sciences not just in the abstract but in their practical application to industry and technology; she had an appetite and confidence in all the skills that brought power. France had clung to the arts that brought grace, and these now looked like weakness and attenuation. In no particular did the sense of being old where Germany was young, in decline where Germany was in the full bloom of vigor, preoccupy the French more than in the matter of population growth. The Germans were multiplying at a faster rate than the French.

In fact, population growth throughout western Europe was slowing down in the course of the nineteenth century, while remaining stronger in Germany than most of her neighbors. Yet the disparity between Germany and France was particularly striking. Between 1871 and 1911 the German population increased by more than 50 percent, from 41 million to 65.3 million; during almost the same period, between 1872 and 1911 the French population increased by only a fraction over 10 percent, from 36 million to 39.5 million. For Germany the result strained her productive capacities, made her people migrants both inside and beyond her borders, and gave added stimulus to calls for territorial expansion, in Europe or by colonization. It increased her sense of *Einkreisung*, of being encircled and hemmed in like some latecomer to the feast of nations forced to make do with too small a seat.

Yet Germany's problem was for France the occasion of envy and dread. It could appear to confirm by statistics the larger fear, never entirely banished from her perceptions of herself, of the end of France. The cause for her diminished growth, particularly marked among the populations of her cities, lay partly in a high mortality rate but chiefly in a low birth rate. It was not that the French were less given to marriage than they once had been or the Germans still were: in that respect the French stood close to the top of the European table. The plain fact was that they were growing less fertile. Attenuation or degeneration, it seemed, was not just a malaise to be read in the cultural or political life of the nation. It was literally a malaise, enacted in the bodies of the people and to be pursued by medical diagnosis and inquiry into drunkenness, prostitution, sexually transmitted disease, cretinism—all the symptoms that miserably throng the pages of Zola.

From such preoccupation emerged the theory of *neurasthénie*— a weakened constitution marking the onset of degeneracy—that would be invoked to explain battlefield stress in the First World War. Yet French anxiety, never simply a matter of national pride, had had its military aspect from the start. The most tangible issue raised by the population figures was the size (and health) of the army France could hope to muster by mass conscription, and above all its size (and health) in comparison to the German army. So the nightmare of the opening days of Verdun had been long in the gestation: not just an artillery bombardment that spoke of technological efficiency in a voice of thunder, but the infantry advancing in numbers so huge that it seemed to swarm, from every direction, like insects.

It was only natural that the French should have spent the decades before Verdun wishing, and seeking, to be as numerous and healthy as the Germans. In terms of public policy, it is quite possible for one nation to regard another as both potential model and potential enemy, even as essential model and essential enemy: an example to be emulated and a foe to be faced on some future battle-field. The views, indeed, are mutually reinforcing, and particularly so in a defeated nation. If we are to beat them next time, we must learn strength from them, learn how to be better at their game. That is why France in the closing decades of the nineteenth century so frequently echoed to calls, if not official at least from respected sources, to adopt a spirit of modernity, a scientific spirit, a habit of methodical efficiency and so forth. Of course, the calls were usually accompanied by some warning or reassurance that she need not and should not abandon the other characteristics, sometimes anti-thetical, on which she prided herself: warmth, imaginativeness, wit, a lightness of touch that would always save her from dullness. If she heeded the lesson—as Zola sought to teach it to the young—perhaps she might have grace with power.

Yet the paradox of regarding the same neighbor as both enemy and model works far less happily at the deeper levels of national psychology. There Germany was *l'anti-France* in a sense more complete and violent than Michelet had intended when he pinned the label on Britain. In war she had sought the end of France; in peace she had not abandoned the goal. She remained the embodiment of an opposite principle, not complementary but antagonistic. She was different, so alien that the possibility of even wanting to grow more like her, much less being able to, was simply out of the question. This level of difference and inherent antagonism the French expressed most consistently in their description of the nation-state that had emerged from the process of German unification. France, as Michelet had taught, was an organism; France had a soul, indeed in a sense France was a soul. In Michelet's generous inter-pretation, she had achieved her present form through natural fu-sion, Paris and central France leading the way in modifying the other parts of her body and in turn being modified by them. At ear-lier points in the nineteenth century Germany, or so French liber-als sympathetically hoped, had promised to achieve a similar fusion. But something had gone radically, fundamentally wrong. The Ger-many that had emerged from the patchwork of German states was soulless and mechanical. The adjectives crop up time and again in French description, and they are far from being casual terms of abuse.

They refer at root to a centrist and authoritarian mode of government which made the rest of Germany not natural limbs of a real body, or voluntary members of a federation, but almost victims of internal conquest as brutally subjugating as the external conquest of France. Modern Germany was thus not a nation, as France conceived it and conceived herself to be, but a grotesque facsimile of a nation. One hears the charge quite clearly in Tissot's contemptuous account of Berlin, written as if in deliberate contrast to Michelet's hymn of praise to Paris, the neutral "head and thought of France":

> Berlin has usurped the place of the head and the heart: it is Berlin that thinks, conceives, reflects, conspires, commands, leads, it is Berlin that gives and takes away, which distributes justice and glory; it is to Berlin that the life and warmth flow of this Germany which is no longer the Germany of naïve legends, gentle ballads, Gothic dreams and godly cathedrals, but the Germany of blood and iron, cannons, shells and battle . . .

German historians since the Second World War have come to speak of their nation's *Sonderweg*, or special path of development. The *Sonderweg* distinguished Germany from nations such as France or Britain; the *Sonderweg* was aberrant. German nationhood, indeed, always contained its own catastrophe. Such ideas have grown familiar, not merely in academic analysis but in modern Germany's own self-doubting perceptions of itself and its past. They echo what detractors had always said, and they echo the old charges most strikingly in agreeing that the heart of the German malaise was Prussia. Prussia, so the diagnosis ran, had not just led German unification, but by its dominance set the nation on its warped path. The indictment was given formal status in the law promulgated by the Allied Control Commission in 1947 abolishing the state which "from early days had been the bearer of militarism and reaction in Germany." This is why Prussia no longer exists as a province of contemporary Germany. "Many states have changed their identity, some states have been expunged from the map altogether," comments a British historian, "but no state—to my knowledge at least—has been formally abolished on the moral grounds that it was a menace to humanity."

French observers had been sure from the start that Prussia was a menace to humanity. Prussia was always the focus of their anxiety. The original dispute in 1870 might have been between Napoléon III and the Prussian ruling family of Hohenzollerns, but the war that resulted was never just with Prussia and, before the peace was brokered, it was with Germany. Yet the English journalist Ernest Vizetelly reported "a curious circumstance" from his observation of Paris:

> from the beginning to the end of the war the French persistently ignored the presence of Saxons, Württembergers, Hessians, Badeners, and so forth in the invading armies. Moreover, on only one or two occasions . . . did they evince any particular animosity against the Bavarians. I must have heard "Death to the Prussians!" shouted at least a thousand times; but most certainly I never once heard a single cry of "Death to the Germans!"

The curious circumstance long outlasted the war. French writers would learn to refer to the new nation as "Germany" but more often than not they labeled her character "Prussian" and called her people "Prussians."

Prussia, then, had not led the German states to unification but imposed it on them. "Do you call it *unity* to bring together, in so bizarre, hasty and violent a manner, warring elements in a cruel circle that imprisons, smothers, smashes them all?" Michelet asked the angry question in 1871, and he was directing it at the lesser German states which had accepted the Prussian yoke. He offered to summarize their reasoning:

Greater Germany will absorb Prussia, as Italy is absorbing Pied-
mont. What is she by itself, except for her cadre of soldiers? Without us she is nothing. The spirits who shine in Berlin are Rhenish,
Swabian, Saxon. Even in war the Prussians live by borrowing. Their
supreme chief is a Dane.* We surround, invade Prussia by our
strength in the arts. If she thinks, if she governs, it is thanks to us.

And then he dismissed the reasoning as deluded: "It is precisely because Prussia is dry, intransigent, sterile and inferior, that her hard
kernel will never be digested."

There is real horror in the denunciation, with its vision of the
Prussians as unchanging and unchangeable, forever sucking energy
from their neighbors to make themselves stronger. Far from being
a temporary product of bitterness after the Franco-Prussian War, it
became something like dogma among French commentators on the
new Germany. Prussia, one writer reminded his audience during
the First World War, "is an artificial State, whose boundaries have
been slowly extended by annexations effected at the expense of peoples sprung from various sources." By then it was a cliché to claim
that the new German state was merely the latest result of these
Prussian annexations—artificial because Prussia itself was artificial—
and that the thirst for annexation remained unslaked.

At its core the indictment of Prussia had nothing to do with the
modernity that had given it mastery of the new sciences; nor was it
just a matter of traditions, real or alleged, of authoritarianism and
militarism. The indictment went deeper than that. What Michelet
and those who followed him were talking about was *barbares*: barbarians. The term of abuse, extended to cover the rest of the Germans whom the Prussians dominated, quickly became universal in
France. It expressed a sense of something ancient and terrible about
the new Germany, as if there had sprung up in contemporary Eu-

* The jibe refers to the elder Moltke: born in Mecklenburg, he had spent part of his youth in
Holstein (with Schleswig, territory then disputed between Germany and Denmark), serving
at court in Copenhagen and holding a commission in the Danish army before entering the
service of Prussia.

rope a nation which, despite its appearance of newness and youthful vigor, was really a survival from the primitive past. In their hatreds the Prussians and the Germans, said Paul de Saint-Victor, "cling to all sorts of ancient Gothic quarrels which we, with our French lightness, have forgotten." They were, said Renan, "men of iron . . . whom our century has seen with terror emerge from the entrails of the ancient Germanic world."

The spectacle did not inspire terror alone, but also an intermittent frisson of envy. Renan himself, in one of his outbursts of contempt for the decadence of the older established nations, had suggested: "If the leprosy of egoism and anarchy causes our western states to perish, the barbarian will rediscover his function, which is to rebuild virility in the corrupt civilizations."* Yet the proper stance of older established nations such as France was, of course, contempt. All the German talk of the Gothic past, all the rhetoric claiming continuity with the tribes from the forests of Tacitus' Germania, was no more than a mark of crudity and inferiority, a further proof (if it were needed) that the Germans were not yet civilized. It went with the emphasis—the Prussian emphasis—on uniformity rather than variety, on group strength rather than individual liberty, on the *Volk* rather than the citizenry. The French were a nation; the Germans were, or thought they were, a race. Some such formula was common, and Michelet himself had been among the first to use it.

Yet no single formula could ever adequately address a concept as potent as tribal identity or a term as slippery as race. Michelet's own dismissal of them had never been entirely wholehearted or consistent; it had, after all, been local in its purpose, as a means of getting the discord out of French history as much as he could. Now they had surfaced again—not domestically but internationally—and he was among those to appreciate how convenient they were in the rhetoric of abuse at a time when he felt the need for abuse. Yet the abuse that nations utter, particularly in a context of such inti-

---

* Marc Bloch commented that one could not read these words in the light of later experience without astonishment.

mate hostility as *le couple France-Allemagne*, has a terrible habit of re-coiling on its authors' heads. The conceptual framework you invoke to describe your enemy will affect how you describe yourself. So tribal identity and race returned—if indeed they could be said ever to have gone away—to modify the theories or ideals of themselves and their own nationhood which the French had constructed. The result would help to take their armies to Verdun and to keep them there with such determination, to die.

5

---+---

"WHAT IS A NATION?"

I put the title of this chapter in quotes because I have borrowed it from the title of an essay by Ernest Renan. Delivered as a lecture in 1882 and published later the same year, *Qu'est-ce qu'est une nation?* is one of the few works to have endured from the vast body of writing about nations and nationhood in the late nineteenth and early twentieth centuries. Reviewing this literature in his own recent study, Eric Hobsbawm can find only Renan's essay, and the pertinent chapter of John Stuart Mill's *Considerations on Representative Government*, to recommend as being of more than just historical interest. It is not difficult to see why. *Qu'est-ce qu'est une nation?* shows Renan, still under the influence of Herder, as much preoccupied with the cycles of life and death determining the fate of nations as he had been at the time of the Franco-Prussian War, but far less inclined to read them with the gloomy fatalism or the antidemocratic bias that had then gripped him. Indeed he seems lucidly detached, not just from the pressure of events but from the assumptions about history and society that could imprison his contemporaries. At times he anticipates the very different language in which we talk about nations today.

Nineteenth-century discussion often began by proposing language, or "natural frontiers," or race, or some combination of all three, as the unifying principle of nationhood. Renan avoids this treacherous ground altogether. To him, nations are neither natural objects nor creations of destiny. The world and history show human society to be various in its ways of organizing itself; the concept of the nation is local to western Europe and, relatively speaking, its recent past. The modern nations are "a historical result brought about by a series of events converging in the same direction." Far from being engraved by Providence or the inexorable logic of river, sea and mountain, the divisions of Europe's present map reflect a particular and temporary arrangement: "They had a beginning, they will have an end. A European confederation will probably take their place."

Of the possible end of the European nations in confederation Renan has little to say apart from this brief prophecy—even less than he has to say about their beginnings in the mists of tribe and race. His real interest is in "the law of the century in which we live," and hence in what has perpetuated nations and given them validity. They are held together, he argues, by history and by consent. The two forces are linked. Rather than simply possessing a shared inheritance of history, as a matter of given, objective fact, the nation has to agree in defining the inheritance that it does share and in emphasizing the bonds of history that unite it. And so, as Renan memorably remarks:

> Forgetting, and I would even say errors about history, are an essential factor in forming a nation, and so it is that the progress of historical studies often poses a danger. In fact, historical investigation unearths the acts of violence that occurred at the inception of any political unit, even those which have had the most beneficial consequences. Unity is always achieved brutally.

That, recognizably, is a shrewd commentary on the uses of patriotic history as advocated by Fustel de Coulanges, supplied by Michelet, and disseminated by the Third Republic through its official iconography and its educational system. Those absorbed in the *mystique républicaine* did not normally spell out with such frankness what building and maintaining the nation required; they preferred to treat nations as being given rather than being built or even manufactured. Yet Renan's point is by no means hostile. The nation might not be natural or eternal, as more simpleminded thinkers liked to maintain, but he plainly believes that while it exists in its present form it can work and had better be made to work. His emphasis on consent marks a common ground with the French tradition of insisting that the nation—the French nation, at least—had its basis in a social impulse, a habit of federation, a common love binding people together. Consent, to Renan, makes what might otherwise seem a mere arrangement into "a soul, a spiritual principle." The phrases echo Michelet's own passionate lyricism. For him, as for Michelet, nations come into being and nations survive because people want them to; they work because people agree to belong to them.

It is always unwise to praise a thinker for transcending the spirit of his time in some miraculous fashion. Historians sometimes make the mistake, of course, and historians of nationalism have often made the mistake of trying to detach Renan's *Qu'est-ce qu'est une nation?* from its context. Yet what I have already said suggests how deeply immersed it is in the ways of thinking about France I have sketched in previous chapters, albeit in its own complex and highly intelligent manner. It belongs to its time in another respect as well, though so covertly that the modern reader can easily miss the contemporary reference. Renan's emphasis on consent has a direct bearing on the fate of Alsace and Lorraine. "A nation never serves its real interests by annexing or holding on to a region against its wishes." This, plainly, is a rebuke to the violent and peremptory way in which the Germans had annexed the provinces. So, even more clearly, is this: "Should doubts arise over frontiers, consult the populations in dispute. They certainly have a right to an opinion in the matter."

Renan is virtually repeating what he had already written in his angry exchange with the German scholar David Friedrich Strauss in 1870–71 and what other French writers had then said in protesting the annexation. Yet the tone of *Qu'est-ce qu'est une nation?* is utterly different from the pamphlet war of the previous decade. The later essay is deliberately general in its approach and theoretical in its preoccupation. Its argument leads unmistakably toward Alsace and Lorraine but then stops short without even mentioning the provinces by name. Those who now hold supreme power in politics would smile at what he has said, Renan concludes, with a smile of his own: "Wait, gentlemen; let their reign pass; know how to suffer the disdain of the mighty. Perhaps, after a lot of useless fumbling around, people will come back to these modest empirical solutions."

His original audience would have had no difficulty in recognizing the rhetorical strategy. *N'en parlez jamais; pensez y toujours*, Gambetta had advised the French in coming to terms with the disasters of 1870–71: "Never talk about them; think about them always." Of all the wounds inflicted on France the loss of Alsace and Lorraine was the deepest; of all the humiliations she had to suffer it was the most tangible and, as it proved, the most abiding. Nothing in the war or the peace that concluded it left the French feeling at once more angry and yet more helpless; nothing made them more convinced of the need for *revanche* and yet more convinced of the impossibility of *revanche*. These tense, paradoxical feelings accompanied the birth of the Third Republic out of the wreckage of the war, and they would remain its burden until the outbreak of the next war in 1914. For much of the time the burden was borne in grim silence; to break the silence often required the careful obliquity that Renan adopted.

The provisional government from which the Republic emerged had been formed in September 1870, immediately after the surrender after Sedan and on the eve of Eugénie's flight. Léon Gambetta's militant rhetoric and his daring escape from the besieged capital epitomized the mood of the moment. Hope lay in mass resistance, the *levée en masse*, and in *jusqu'au boutisme*, the determination to fight to the end—in the whole spirit of revolutionary patriotism revived from the 1790s. Yet by March 1871, after the failure of the *levée en masse* and the fall of Paris, a different mood prevailed in the nation at large and among the deputies elected to the first National Assembly of the Republic at Bordeaux. Realism compelled an acceptance of defeat and the terms imposed by the victor. "It may be horrible," George Sand wrote, "but it's no longer war and one can breathe again."

The Germans had made their intention to annex French territory clear from the time of their first victories in August 1870 and, such was their position of strength, the extent of their demand altered very little. It was marked by an infamous "green line" on the map which Bismarck laid before Adolphe Thiers and Jules Favre, leading the French delegation sent to Versailles to agree the preliminaries of the peace in February 1871. The line sheared almost two provinces away from France: the whole of Alsace, with its provincial capital at Strasbourg on the Rhine, and the northern part of Lorraine, with her capital at Metz on the Moselle. Both had once lain in the short-lived Lotharingia, and both had later belonged to the uncertain patchwork of the Holy Roman Empire. France had achieved sovereignty over them through the expansionist policies of Louis XIV, who had done more than any other postmedieval leader to give his country its present shape on the map.

Der Rhein, Deutschlands Strom nicht Deutschlands Grenze, the title of the pamphlet published by the poet Ernest Moritz Arndt in 1813, had given the rhetoric of German nationalism an enduring slogan: "The Rhine, Germany's river not Germany's boundary." So, even as she achieved unification, Germany had fulfilled a historic goal: her border with France would stand not on the Rhine but, much farther west, on the blue line of the Vosges mountains. For her part, France had suffered her largest loss of territory since the Hundred Years War, a huge bite from a country whose unity, Michelet and others had said, was perfect and indivisible. About a million and a half people—two-thirds of them from Alsace and one-third from northern Lorraine—had been forcibly deprived of their citizenship in the voluntary compact.

Jules Favre turned up to the armistice negotiations at Versailles in January 1871 looking "miserable," or so Bismarck thought, conscious of his own splendid appearance in the dress uniform of the White Cuirassiers. The elderly General Beaufort d'Hautpoul, who had burst into tears on being appointed French military delegate to the mission, delivered an angry tirade against the Germans over lunch. The Germans said he was drunk; the French said he was an outraged patriot, but promptly replaced him. Expressions of helpless grief had grown ceremonial by 1 March, when the National Assembly at Bordeaux sat down to ratify the peace by an overwhelming majority: delegates from the annexed provinces delivered their solemn protest and walked out of the meeting. By a coincidence that seemed like symbolism, Émile Krüss, the staunchly republican mayor of Strasbourg, died of a heart attack the same evening. His body made the journey from Bordeaux back to Strasbourg by train, and at the railway station Gambetta made an impromptu speech in which he spoke of "a revenge that will be the protest of right against force and infamy."

Thereafter, France's helplessness to do anything about the annexation became a fundamental axiom of the Third Republic. The fate of the lost provinces might be a cruel injustice, but it was not one that politics could remedy. Renegotiating the peace treaty was plainly impossible, but so was taking military revenge. The war had convinced politicians that the days when it had taken virtually a pan-European alliance to defeat the first Napoléon had gone forever. France could no longer go it alone in a major European war, and above all not in a war with her newly powerful neighbor. Her task—and it would not be quickly or easily fulfilled—was to end the isolation in which defeat had left her. In the long term her security depended on understandings or alliances, even if they had to be sought in unlikely quarters, with Britain, *ennemi héréditaire* and colonial rival, and Russia, whom Bismarck had made an ally in the *Dreikaiserbund*.

Yet courtship of Britain and Russia, indeed the success of France's whole foreign policy, depended on reassuring Europe—past enemies, potential allies, perceived or future enemies alike—that she would never again be the arrogant and vainglorious nation she had seemed in their eyes when Napoléon III had gone to war with Prussia. Launching, or even risking, a war over Alsace and Lorraine would cause her friends to melt away and guarantee that the *débâcle* was repeated. So, the more tense international relations grew and the more peace became just a synonym for "war expected," the more essential it was that France avoid the least hint of aggression. The fortresses on her eastern border were not just there to calm domestic anxieties; they were there to reassure the other European nations that she was planning only for defense.

So, far from making it a policy to seize Alsace and Lorraine back from the Germans, governments of the Third Republic made it a policy not to do so and not even to be suspected of harboring the intention. *Revanchisme* had no place on their agenda. General Boulanger unwittingly demonstrated the fact when, as Minister of War in 1887, he seized on the Schnaebelé affair as an excuse for saber-rattling. The German authorities, or at least an overzealous police commissioner in the lost provinces, had enticed Schnaebelé, a French frontier official, over the new border and arrested him for spying. Boulanger's proposal to withdraw the French ambassador to Berlin and mobilize 50,000 troops on the border caused turmoil in the cabinet and brought Prime Minister Goblet's government down. Boulanger himself sank into a marginal role of man on horseback and would-be Napoléon.

The crisis had merely endangered the reputation that France wished to cultivate on the international scene—not least by serving Germany's interest in portraying her as incurably bellicose and Bismarck's interest in getting the Reichstag to accept his military budget. "I could not invent Boulanger," the Chancellor remarked, "but he happened very conveniently for me." Yet, before he disappeared into obscurity, Boulanger enjoyed his brief hour in the sun. Out of government, he managed to get himself elected as a deputy and acknowledged as something of a popular hero. To monarchists, as well as elements in the Church and the army, he appeared to epitomize national pride; crowds in the Paris streets hailed him as *Général Revanche* or *Général Victoire*. Plainly he had struck a chord. He drew support from those unreconciled to the Republic, to be sure, but also briefly from those reconciled to the Republic except in their

feelings about the annexation—feelings which the Republic had
done nothing to satisfy and could do nothing to satisfy.

Popular sentiment, historians know, is elusive: hard to locate,
hard to measure, hard to evaluate. It is sometimes fickle and often
self-contradictory. Indeed, it is perhaps in its contradictions that its
real character is to be found. And this means, among other things,
that its voice does not necessarily belong to those who make the
loudest and most emphatic claim to speak on its behalf. Maurice
Barrès, I have already suggested, was hardly the authentic voice of
the *poilu* in the First World War. Yet Barrès was undoubtedly right
to identify the Boulanger crisis as a turning-point not just in his
own attitude to *revanche* but also in what has come to be called a nationalist revival in France. Boulanger revived anger at the loss of the
annexed provinces, which had cooled since its first outbursts in the
immediate aftermath of the war and the Treaty of Frankfurt. And
Barrès was right, as well, to see this revival as the first of several, repeated at roughly regular intervals in each succeeding decade until
the First World War, like exclamation marks recalling the French
to the problem they could not leave unresolved. The last revival
was the one we have already heard Péguy signal in denouncing the
defeatism of those leaders and teachers who had made his generation a *génération sacrifiée*. With grim irony, Péguy professed himself
reluctant to break silence on the question of Alsace and Lorraine:
"Families have these shameful secrets. And so it's best to keep quiet
about them." Yet the question, he insisted, had "emerged from its
long sleep" or, rather, been born again after its long death.

Yet Barrès and Péguy both exaggerated the revival and distorted
its real nature. Gambetta's counsel of silence, like Renan's obliquity,
stood in reminder that the French had not necessarily forgotten or
forgiven the annexation when they were not openly talking of it.
And when they did speak about it, they were not necessarily calling
for *revanche*: diehard, militant *revanchistes* were always compara-
tively thin on the ground. The public mood certainly hardened
from the turn of the century onward, but before then it had not
described a simple cycle of forgetfulness and recall to duty. Pre-
dominantly the mood was always one of grief and mourning tem-

pered by the faith that the wrong would one day be righted. The loss of Alsace and Lorraine was a wound: *la plaie béante, la plaie saignante* and *la blessure toujours douloureuse* (the gaping wound, the bleeding wound, the wound that always hurts). Implicitly, France was an organic whole or body—just as Michelet had envisaged her—and the annexation an act of brutal surgery lopping off two vital limbs. As for the future, the provinces would certainly be returned to France. How this would happen was usually not spelled out—though since it is hard to think of any means other than military action, aggressive threat or relish at the opportunity for war was never completely absent. When it would happen was made even less clear, beyond a general agreement that it would not be today nor even soon. Paul Déroulède, more militant than most, was nonetheless typical in preferring metaphor to specific prophecy in "Vive la France!," a poem from the volume *Chants du soldat*: "It's for the reaper to judge when the field is ripe." The metaphor was typical too, perhaps, in sounding not grandly ominous, as its author hoped, but more than a little evasive.

We have already encountered Louis Madelin as a staff officer at Verdun and a historian of the battle. In the 1890s he was studying at the University of Nancy. His teacher Christian Pfister, an *émigré* from the annexed territory, took him and a party of students to stay at the little village of Brin, where the Seille (a tributary joining the Moselle at Metz) marked the new border with Germany. After breakfast one day Pfister sat looking across the river, and said:

> You see, Monsieur Madelin . . . we need to come back to look at this temporary frontier every once in a while; we need to turn the knife in our heart a little. Do you believe that the brave folk who farm the land over there aren't French? And yet the young men wear the pointed helmet because Moltke wanted them to. Isn't that outrageous? But, just you see, the story will have its end!

Turning the knife dutifully in the heart, taking consolation from the knowledge that the story was not yet ended: these were characteristic ways in which the French sought to come to terms with their loss. They joined denunciations of Prussian brutality and tributes to the virtues of Alsatians and Lorrainers as recurring themes in the popular art of the day—in, for example, Alphonse Daudet's much-anthologized sketch "La Dernière Classe" (about the last lesson conducted in French in an Alsatian school), the cartoons of Hansi, the novels by the collaborative team of Erckmann-Chatrian, and a thousand fashionable songs.

It was easy to dismiss the whole cult. Maurice Barrès accused it of reducing a "grave national theme" to "mawkish sentimentalities smacking of the aesthetic of the café-concert." Yet its clichés were hard to avoid, as he himself demonstrated only a page or so later in the same essay from *Scènes et doctrines du nationalisme* with a panegyric to the sufferings of Metz under German rule, envisaged as a "barracks inside a graveyard" or, more poignantly, as Sleeping Beauty's castle:

> She moves us all the more, this slave who keeps the traits and charms that her friends and her sons loved in the free woman. Recognizing her still as French, belonging to Lorraine and to herself, we feel, so strongly that it disturbs, a host of sensations rising out of the uniforms, the Prussian faces, the official signs.

So it was not just France whom the French portrayed in female imagery—Liberty leading the people, Marianne presiding over the Republic, the princess in the stories capturing the young de Gaulle's imagination—but her constituent parts as well, above all the lost provinces of Alsace and Lorraine. If France was the mother, they were the two beautiful young daughters, lost, abandoned, orphaned, imprisoned, even violated or raped by the brutal foreigner.

The symbolic description of their fate anticipated what would soon, in the First World War, be alleged as literal fact in atrocity stories about the fate of territories occupied by the German armies. Here—said rumor, orchestrated and backed up by propaganda—children were maltreated, even mutilated, and women raped. As

Marc Bloch insisted, the false reports of war derive from collective perceptions that precede their birth. Once roused, these collective perceptions were also ready in February 1916 to crystallize around the fate of Douaumont—another fair captive, taken by the brutal intruder—and of Verdun itself—the queen with the trembling heart, as Paul Voivenel put it, whom the children of France rushed to defend.

Unable though it might have been to appease popular grief by political action, the Third Republic could not ignore it. Like the cult of Jeanne d'Arc, the feeling pressed for recognition and expressed itself in imagery crying out to be incorporated in public rhetoric and ceremony. In tracing this process of adoption, one could not do better than start with the Place de la Concorde, the very center of monumental Paris, where the stone pavilions house statues personifying the great provincial capitals, Strasbourg among them. In September 1870, when the Germans had already overrun Alsace and Lorraine and were making clear their intention to annex them, the statue of Strasbourg became what Paul de Saint-Victor called a "holy idol":

> She has been clothed in a glorious robe, a heroic costume made of flags, and its red bands seem like huge drops of the blood she is so valiantly shedding for France. A garland of leaves and flowers crowns her embattled head; more wreaths and innumerable bouquets lie in a jumbled heap between her knees; Venetian lanterns* hang at her feet; enthusiastic inscriptions, professions of love and grief, patriotic songs, and verses have been pasted on the pedestal. In the evening pieces of coloured glass, haphazardly arranged, light up the statue as if it were an altar. You would think it the martyred city's fervent chapel.

What started as spontaneous demonstration continued as an official act: the statue was draped in black through the years of annexation, until crowds tore off the mourning at the outbreak of

---

* Made of translucent colored paper.

war in 1914. Elsewhere the popular symbolism was enshrined in commemoration. At Mars-la-Tour, where Bazaine's troops had been defeated in their attempt to break out from Metz, the monument depicted a woman holding a dead soldier in her arms; in obvious allusion to the lost provinces, two young children played at her feet. The annual ceremony held at Mars on 8 August always featured a young girl from Alsace and a young girl from Lorraine dressed in mourning. A mourning contingent of local women, personifying the suffering but resistant spirit of Lorraine, played a prominent part in the annual mass for the dead French soldiers celebrated in Metz cathedral on 8 September, a service tolerated though hardly welcomed by the German authorities.

At Belfort a massive lion sculptured by Auguste Bartholdi in rose-colored stone from the Vosges remembered the successful defense of the city by Colonel Denfert-Rochereau and his troops.* Here in 1895 the mayor told the crowds gathered to observe the 25th anniversary of the war: "The government of the Republic has made good all the disasters, sealed an unbreakable alliance with a great and chivalrous nation, organized a national army ready to defend the sacred soil of the *Patrie* and to repel the invader." If these grandiose words showed how thoroughly the Republic had co-opted patriotic memory, they also inadvertently served to underline what the Republic could neither promise nor achieve: recovery of the lost provinces. Raymond Poincaré, senator for the Meuse shortly to become Prime Minister and then President, labored under a similar difficulty as guest of honor at the 40th-anniversary ceremony at Mars-la-Tour in 1910. He struck a personal note, speaking as one who had grown up in the shadow of defeat, hoping for "restorative justice," but went on to temper the hope with political caution and to cloud it with language that stopped well short of anything that could be construed as a promise of *revanche*: "France sincerely desires peace. She will never do anything to

---

* Bartholdi was also responsible for the Statue of Liberty in New York Harbor, presented by France to the USA in 1885—the French Republic thus giving the American Republic its only major female emblem.

disturb it. To maintain it, she will always do everything that is compatible with her dignity. But peace condemns us neither to forgetfulness nor to disloyalty."

Such, then, was the burden that the loss of Alsace and Lorraine imposed on the Republic, its politicians and its citizens—a burden too heavy to be lightened by any convenient rhetorical formula. The loss was no *casus belli*. War was impolitic and undesirable on any count, but particularly on this one; its threat was to be averted by the best efforts of government. Yet the loss of Alsace and Lorraine was at the same time a wrong that would one day be righted, a wrong that would have to be righted, and such strokes of justice usually fall only to the victors in war. The paradox lies close to the heart of France's mood in the years leading up to the First World War. A war would come, but not today; it was to be dreaded as a calamity yet also welcomed as an opportunity. Given how long the French inhabited such a paradox, it was no wonder that when war did actually come in 1914 their reaction should have been ambivalent. War was a shock and no occasion to rejoice, but also the fulfillment of prophecy, the long-awaited signal for action.

Nor, of course, did such ambivalence end when war became a reality to be suffered. France at war was still identifiably the nation that had planned for peace while regarding *revanche* as a due that history owed her. She was still the nation that had built fortresses along her eastern frontier, as if the war she envisaged would be a siege. Yet she was also still the nation whose graduates from cavalry school had ritually visited the blue line of the Vosges, marking the border with the annexed territories, so that they could view the slopes down which they would one day charge. Confused impulses to attack and defend, and eventually notions of attack and defense so confused that they blurred the line distinguishing them, were not peculiar to the generals nor local to the field of Verdun. They had been long in the making, and Verdun was simply the arena where they would be acted out in their largest and most terrible form.

✢ ✢ ✢

The profound differences existing between the mental constitutions of the various peoples result in these peoples viewing the
world in very dissimilar lights. The consequence is that they feel,
reason and act in very different ways, and they therefore find,
when they come into contact, that they are in disagreement on all
questions. Most of the wars that take up so large a portion of
history are the outcome of these dissentiments. Wars of conquest, wars of religion, wars of dynasties, have always in reality
been wars of races.

> Gustave Le Bon,
> *Les Lois psychologiques de l'évolution des peuples*
> (*The Psychological Laws of the Evolution of Peoples*), 1894

Of Paul Déroulède's Ligue des Patriotes, a right-wing group given
heart by the Boulangist crisis of the 1880s, the journalist Séverine
remarked that all its thoughts were like storks: they took refuge on
the rooftops of Alsace. Strictly, this was not true. Like Boulanger
himself, and like similar groups that came into being from the 1880s
onward, Déroulède's league quickly broadened its agenda to include
an anti-Republican call for constitutional change—in effect, for
abandonment of the constitution and the Republic. Yet in a larger
sense Séverine was right. The fate of the lost provinces gave the impulse to the league, and all the other symptoms of what Barrès and
others would hail as a "nationalist revival," and it always remained
their obsession. And, however marginal militant *revanchisme* might
have looked, a great deal of French thought in its milder complexion took refuge on the rooftops of Alsace as well. The fate of the
lost provinces affected how the French thought about themselves
and their nation more deeply than my discussion has so far suggested. It even bit into the way they addressed the large question
that Renan posed: what is a nation?

Obviously, the large question had been present in the particular quarrel from the start. Whatever Gambetta might have counseled for the future, the annexation had not been greeted with silence when it happened in 1870–71. French intellectuals—Michelet and Renan among them, of course—had rushed into print protesting it; their German counterparts, equally distinguished, had rushed to justify it. The argument forced each side in the pamphlet war to spell out its deepest assumptions about what nations were and how they were, or should be, constituted. The fact that the French worked from an awareness of political impotence—the provinces were lost, no matter what they said—made them all the more eager to pursue the local issue into its most abstract implications. Theory, reason and justice were on their side, even if political circumstances were not.

When writers returned to the theory of nationhood in future decades—and it remained, of course, a continual preoccupation in French as in all European writing—they never forgot the circumstance of Alsace and Lorraine, even if they dealt with it only obliquely or by implication. Confessedly or not, all speculation had to be referred back to the provinces, originally the proving ground and still the final test of the endeavor. Never ideal for clear or detached thought, the context was not congenial for the liberal, Republican values I have described in previous chapters. And so, rather than summing up the entirety of what the French thought about their nation, these values were both challenged and changed.

The process was a complex one, not least so for being in part at least subterranean. Yet some of its consequences can be easily recognized and have often been remarked by historians. In summing up the typical form that pride in their country and love of their country took among the French in the first half of the nineteenth century we tend, virtually without thinking, to use the word "patriotism." In summing up their form at, let us say, any point after the Boulangist crisis of the 1880s we tend, again by instinct, to use the word "nationalism." Michelet was a patriot and proud of the word; Barrès was a nationalist and made use of the word in this sense current.

The distance can be measured in strictly political terms. Patriotism was of the left and nationalism was of the right. Michelet stood in a Revolutionary tradition wedded to a social vision with the ideals of liberty, equality and fraternity at its core. Its international vision could include dislike or contempt for other nations; it could certainly recommend pursuing quarrels with them *jusqu'au bout*. The supreme fulfillment of citizenship was embodied in the patriot-soldier fighting tyrannical foreign enemies—the very spirit of *La Marseillaise* in action. Yet Michelet's values were also internationalist in aspiration, or at least they remained so until the shock of the war. He looked forward to harmony and cooperation between nations, prevailing eventually by the same operation of progress that would make liberty prevail at home. Barrès' nationalism, by contrast, rejected the tradition of the Revolution and the Republic. His social vision was traditional and hierarchic: fidelity to history was society's best support, the Church and the army its truest bastions. Abroad lay nations hostile by nature to what France was by nature, and these enemies had a host of allies and coconspirators at home among the Dreyfusards and Jews. Patriotism, one might say, was inclusive and given to invoking love as its central impulse; nationalism was exclusive and prone to the language of hatred.

Another, and crueler, way of describing the shift in French thinking is to say that theorists moved closer to their German counterparts. They were influenced by the very things that France had identified, and professed to despise, as "Prussian." This should not surprise us. A belief in the need to borrow from the Germans, or emulate them, had played its role in French response from the moment of defeat. It is also in the nature of a relationship such as the *couple France-Allemagne* that it should develop a common language, even while denying the very possibility of its existence; perhaps, indeed, such a relationship implies the existence of such a language from the start. Certainly French and Germans had shown striking points of agreement all along, from the time when the provinces were annexed and the intellectuals fought their bitter war of pamphlets.

To explore these points of agreement requires some consideration of what my discussion has so far overlooked: the German point of view. Why did the Germans annex Alsace and Lorraine? And, which is a rather different matter, how did they present and justify their action? The largest answer to the first question is that they acted from an uneasy mixture of motives, reflected in the differing views their leaders adopted as to how much territory should be annexed. Somewhere in the mixture lay an observable disparity between the practical calculation of political factors and the operation, in part spontaneous and in part orchestrated, of popular sentiment. This is why the result was so unhappy—for, though it was never the brutal disaster depicted by French propaganda, the annexation always caused Germany more trouble than satisfaction. Indeed, the acquisition of Alsace and Lorraine proved almost as much a burden for Germany as their loss did for France.

The most striking feature of German motives is that they were not economic except in the most general sense. Extra land was always welcome to a nation with a rapidly expanding population, and particularly welcome if some of the present inhabitants of the land might be expected to emigrate. The Germans certainly encouraged emigration from Alsace and Lorraine, by an arrangement allowing people to opt for French nationality but requiring them to live in France.* But economic considerations of a more precise sort did not enter into their thinking. Reports of exploitable iron deposits in the Longwy and Nancy basins of western Lorraine did not influence the contours of the green line drawn on the map. In later decades such blindness would irritate German industrialists and advocates of expansion, whose remarks were sometimes remembered and selectively quoted by French and British propagandists in proof that economic greed had dominated policy from the start.

The most solid part of Bismarck's reasoning was defensive.

* Estimates of the numbers registering for the option were hotly contested, with French sources quoting a total of 378,000 and German sources, apparently rather closer to the truth, quoting a total of 160,000. Of course, not all those who registered did actually emigrate, and among those who did the desire to avoid military service was a major consideration. Emigration was highest in urban and non-Protestant areas, and among the Alsatian Jewish community. Examples from the last group included the families of Alfred Dreyfus, Marc Bloch and the anthropologist Claude Lévi-Strauss.

Germany needed Alsace and Lorraine, he said, as a glacis to protect
herself from French aggression in the future. By no means all the
German talk—Bismarck himself started it at his meeting with
Napoléon III after Sedan—of Louis XIV and Napoléon I, of France
having made war on the German states 30 times in the previous two
centuries, was just bluster meant to cow the losers further into submission. It reflected a deeply held preoccupation that had already
played its role in the impulse toward German unification. The
French might have been busy persuading themselves that Prussia,
and hence the new Germany, was *l'ennemi héréditaire*; Germans
were already settled, and by no means irrational, in the view that
France was *der Erbfeind*. No leader of the new Germany was about
to forget Jena, or would be allowed to forget it by his people. Nor
would he be likely to forget the casual way in which Napoléon III
had embarked on the Franco-Prussian War. Already aware that the
federation he presided over was fragile, if only because so recently
forged, Bismarck could not afford to overlook the danger from his
troublesome neighbor.

Defense was therefore a legitimate need to consider. Shifting the
Franco-German border westward, locating it further from Berlin
and closer to Paris, pushed back the starting-point from which any
French army could launch an attack. In a larger sense, too, annexation helped to further Bismarck's goal of ensuring that France,
suddenly weakened by her defeat, would stay weak in the future.
But, of course, he did not wish her to be too weak. A France collapsing into chaos—for which history offered precedent and the
Paris Commune gave new warning—would not have helped Germany's security. Nor would it have helped Germany's security to
take on the task of assimilating, or even just administering, too large
a tract of territory: whatever German apologists might claim about
the character of the provinces in question, political realists never
doubted that they would prove, in some degree, refractory.

These considerations made Bismarck moderate in his demands,
at least by comparison with his military commanders. The position they adopted was as hard-line as one would expect of recently

victorious generals. The Kaiser's close adviser General von Alvensleben, for example, wanted to annex France right up to the
Marne. Moltke, a national hero whose voice carried considerable
weight, focused his gaze on military fortresses such as Belfort and
Metz. Bismarck originally demanded Belfort but later yielded it—a
token concession which the French seized on with relief, since the
city's stubborn defense had made it a glorious symbol in a war that
had otherwise left them without glorious symbols. Metz, which Bismarck originally included in his demands for bargaining purposes,
was annexed in deference to Moltke's stated opinion that it was
worth an army of 120,000 men.

On this point Bismarck was also deferring to the Kaiser, who
loved a parade and took particular pride in the scenes of his recent
victories. Just beyond Metz lay Gravelotte, on the disputed road to
Verdun where the Germans had put paid to Bazaine's attempt to
break out. It lay just inside the region annexed, and the Germans
made it one of their chief commemorative sites. On the 25th anniversary of the war, in 1895, veterans gathered to see the new
Kaiser, Wilhelm II, open a special Hall of Memory and museum;
two years later, on the centenary of the first Kaiser's birth, a young
oak was planted from the Sachsenwald, the forest which had been
presented to Bismarck in the name of the newly unified Germany.
A few kilometers beyond Gravelotte and the new border lay Mars-
la-Tour, where the French had put up their monument and were
busy holding their ceremonies, and not far beyond Mars-la-Tour
lay Verdun. So the road between the two cities linked a cluster, not
just of battlefield sites but of commemorated sites: what French
rhetoric had come to call *lieux sacrés*, "holy places" or "sacred soil."

Nations, or even armies, had not always treated such places with
respect. In previous ages the dead had sometimes been left on the
battlefield to rot into the soil, their names unrecorded and their
deeds unmentioned, and the soil had usually been allowed to revert
to anonymous farmland. The English poet Southey made just this
point about Marlborough's "famous victory" at Blenheim, to illus-
trate how transitory was military glory and how ephemeral were the

quarrels that led to battle. But in giving Europe a foretaste of total war, the Franco-Prussian War introduced the reverential cult of the war dead and the places where they died which (ironically, one might say) goes with total war. In my prologue I argued that ground always has an emotional content in battle, usually invested in it by what has happened there before. The commemoration of sites such as Mars-la-Tour by the French and Gravelotte by the Germans had begun to give ground exactly the sort of emotional content that would help shape the particular course of the First World War.

Bismarck privately doubted the wisdom of annexing Metz because he feared the French traditions of its citizens would make it "indigestible." The same realism made him aware that the whole annexation needed to be defended at the bar of international opinion, and in a language other than that of the political calculations among the German leadership. Ideological justification was required, and was of course to be found in the ideology of nationalism. Bismarck himself viewed with amused condescension the "professors" who acted as Germany's apologists. Historians have been divided in their opinion as to what degree he orchestrated them and the sentiments they appealed to, to what degree he merely accepted them as useful, or to what degree—as in his disagreement with the Kaiser over the fate of Metz—he ended up being led further than he really wished to go. One thing is clear, at any rate: if Bismarck regarded the rhetoric of nationalism and the wells of sentiment it could open up as mere taps to be turned on and off at his convenience, he was far from being the only leader mentioned in this book to make the mistake.

In fact, the annexation occurred at a critical moment in the development of nationalist thought. It had already put an end to the time when territories and their peoples could be transferred from prince to prince simply as the rightful spoils of victory. Too much importance was now attached to peoples and too little to princes for this to pass muster. Yet territories and peoples were still bound to be transferred, if only because at this stage of the nineteenth century the nationalist drive was, above all, a drive to build big nations.

Its impulse was to confederate and unify on the grand scale, though always in the name of reconstituting some preexisting entity, ancient or natural. The creation of Germany herself was one result. So was the way France was praised by her admirers: not too far beneath Michelet's tribute to her harmonious variety was a recommendation of the special advantages, the special destiny, of the nation as large bloc.

Nationalism as Balkanization or separatism still lay in the future, its advent to be signaled by the Treaty of Versailles. Meanwhile, small territorial units were too insignificant to be nations; the dismissal usually depended on the idea that nations had to be capable of economic self-sufficiency. Belgium could be derided as an absurdity, which was also roughly the view that Mazzini, the apostle of Italian liberty, took of Ireland. Napoléon III had profited from his intervention in Italian affairs to acquire Nice and the Savoie, and he sought to profit from the Austro-Prussian War by acquiring Luxembourg. German writers dug up these examples as evidence that French protest over Alsace and Lorraine was hypocritical. For their part French writers would stress how easily Nice and the Savoie had been assimilated—how greatly their peoples appreciated French liberty and how quickly they had been charmed into becoming French. In due course, they would point with delight to the difficulties that the Germans encountered in Alsace and Lorraine by their disregard for liberty and their lack of charm. But beneath the spiteful point-making lay a common assumption: Alsace and Lorraine rightfully belonged in a larger unit. If they were not French, they were German.

John Stuart Mill and some British liberals favored the idea that the disputed territory might become another Belgium, a neutral buffer state between France and Germany. Bismarck was aware of the proposal but dismissed it. He, like all the other leaders in Germany and France, ignored the separatist tendency in Alsatian politics, though its presence would cause the Germans problems after the annexation. (For that matter, it would cause the French problems after the Treaty of Versailles ended the annexation in

1919.) Nobody bothered to remember, much less ponder, Voltaire's opinion that the Alsatians were "half-German, half-French and completely Iroquois." Local particularity was ignored in arguments that dealt in large, emphatic concepts of "French" and "German."

To take an obvious example, both sides soon stopped referring to the provinces by their separate names, let alone specifying that only part and not the whole of Lorraine was at stake. Instead they agreed in creating a hyphenated entity—Alsace-Lorraine to the French, Elsass-Lothringen to the Germans—summoned into being not just by the circumstances of the dispute but by the very assumptions of nationalism. It lumped together two regions that, though neighboring, did not possess a common identity. In practice, when Germans spoke of Alsace-Lorraine they usually meant Alsace: on the Rhine directly opposite Baden, with a significant proportion of Protestants and what were called "German speakers" (though they really spoke a German *patois*). By the same token, when the French spoke of Alsace-Lorraine they usually meant Lorraine: a province with a strongly Catholic tradition and few German speakers except on the border with Alsace (though its French speakers really spoke a French *patois*). The result was a shared habit of distortion: proffered generalizations about Alsace-Lorraine commonly referred with any accuracy only to one of its component parts.

It was not the only habit of distortion shared by French and Germans, though it took some time for the full extent of the similarity to emerge. German apologists usually began by invoking justice as it applied to modern history. The annexation, they argued, righted the wrong done by France when it took advantage of the weakness of the German states in the age of Louis XIV and gained sovereignty over the provinces in the first place. "The feeble policy of our forefathers betrayed our land, our faith, and our language," wrote Theodor Mommsen, the distinguished historian of classical Rome (and, in political matters, a liberal not usually in sympathy with Bismarck):

They left us this burden, and we have borne it as best we could; but now, when the fortune of war, not of our own seeking, has

given us back our own, were we in our turn to act the same cow-
ardly part, we should not even have the plea of *non possumus* [we
cannot] to excuse us to the generations that are to come after us.

Such arguments from history can still bedevil territorial disputes
between nations; in the 1870s they were as much a blind alley as
they are now. Renan, as one would expect, had dismissed the whole
question with contempt long before *Qu'est-ce qu'est une nation?*, in
the second of his letters to David Friedrich Strauss: "With this
philosophy of history, the only legitimate rights in the world will
be those of the orang-outangs, unjustly dispossessed by civilized
man."

Yet, when it came to matters involving the identity of nations,
history could never be so easily brushed aside. And of course the
history that Mommsen and other German apologists invoked went
back far beyond the age of Louis XIV. The annexation was "not
conquest, but restoration" in a deeper sense. In this view of history,
the territories and peoples over which nations enjoy sovereignty are
not shaped by accidents of war or political circumstance but by ancient (indeed primordial) kinship. And so a nation like Germany
could never really be new, only newly reconstituted; German unification was, proclaimed the historian Heinrich von Treitschke, a
"great resurrection." The philologist Friedrich Max Müller* could
portray it virtually as a natural event, and as such beyond criticism:

> There are in the history of all countries great convulsions which
> one cannot criticize according to the ordinary rules of right and
> wrong. We do not criticize thunderstorms that darken heaven and
> earth, strike down palaces, and carry off the harvest of peaceful vil-
> lages. We stand in awe while they last, but we know that Nature
> cannot do without them, and that when they are past, the air will
> be purer, and we shall breathe again more freely than before.

Of course, this did not mean that Germany's actions could not
be justified in detail. Max Müller, the most effective of those who

---

* An expatriate, at this time Professor of Comparative Philology at Oxford.

put the German case for the annexation, summed it up in a sentence. The people of Alsace and Lorraine "are all German by blood, many by language, and, what is most important, they are still German by the simplicity and honesty of their religion." It was not just his own bias as a philologist that made him attach so high an importance to language. To Germans, language had always been a central issue. Germany, which was already tempted to define itself by race and would at a later point define itself by racial mission, had first defined itself by language. The fact of the German language itself had, after all, been the most tangible evidence for the common identity, discrete yet waiting to be reconstituted, of the various states which unification had brought together. Germany reversed the usual process of European nations in taking its name, *Deutschland*, from its language; usually languages took their name from the countries where they were spoken.

French writers denouncing the annexation usually rejected the argument from language. The fact that Alsace and Lorraine contained German speakers was irrelevant, they argued, since the kinship binding a nation together was not linguistic. They pointed to the lack of correspondence, in Europe and elsewhere, between national and linguistic boundaries: Switzerland was one nation with several languages, English a language spoken by more than one nation. To this point they could add, in the years after 1870, derisive attack on the policy of "restoring" the German language in the annexed provinces. It, and the whole campaign of *Germanisierung* of which it was a major part, simply demonstrated the ironfisted despotism that came so easily to the Prussian temperament. The French took good care that nobody forgot Treitschke's ineffably tactless description of what *Germanisierung* would involve for the people of Alsace and Lorraine: "Against their will we shall restore them to their true selves."

Such argument seemed to fit the liberal theory of nationhood that the French had developed. Yet in fact they did not always regard nationhood and language as so easily separable. They had assumed that the Jacobin goal, proclaimed at the Revolution, of making France "one and indivisible" involved monolingualism; indeed they had assumed that it depended on monolingualism. In endorsing the ideas of the prelate Henri Grégoire, the Convention of 1794 declared that all children of the Republic must learn "to speak, read and write in the French language." Was not French, after all, the language of Voltaire, the Declaration of Rights and the Code Napoléon? The rich variety of languages, *patois* and dialects persisting throughout the country even at the turn of the nineteenth century was evidence of incomplete nationhood or, worse, disaffection.

The slur of disaffection had been cast directly at the German speakers of rural Alsace in the First War of the Coalition following the Revolution. "Who, in the Departments of Haut-Rhin and Bas-Rhin, has joined with the traitors in appealing to the Prussian and the Austrian on our invaded frontiers?" a report to the Committee of Public Safety had asked in 1794. "It is the inhabitant of the countryside, who speaks the same language as our enemies and so considers himself much more their brother and fellow citizen than the brother and fellow citizen of Frenchmen who speak to him in another language and have other customs." Nor did such attitudes change in the nineteenth century, when French was vigorously promoted as a central component of nationhood.

So the German policy on language in Alsace and Lorraine was no more than a mirror version of what French governments had, in their campaigns of education, been doing there before the annexation and of what the Third Republic was continuing, in its yet more strenuous campaign, to do elsewhere in France. French equivocation over the matter involved a familiar tension in their attitude to what the Germans did. It was at once practice to be condemned, as it duly was in most French commentary on the annexed provinces, and yet, in other contexts, an example to be emulated. Rector Baudouin of Rennes invoked it in the latter spirit when he reported in 1885 on the—to him, unfortunate—survival of the Breton language. And naturally, by way of riposte, advocates of Breton culture could criticize the Third Republic for being as dictatorial in its

language and educational policy as the Germans were in Alsace and
Lorraine. Their protest brought a useful challenge to Michelet's
poetic insistence that France had been formed by natural fusion—
and a useful reminder, too, that the brutality to which Renan conceded a role in forming nations did not all belong to ancient times.

A similar habit of equivocation increasingly pervaded the French
attitude to race—the "blood" that Max Müller, with Treitschke and
all the other German apologists, used to express the kinship of the
people of Alsace and Lorraine with Germany and, of course, the kinship that gave a nation its identity. Race was a concept that had refused to be banished from the arena of debate, despite Michelet's
emphasis on fusion and variety or Renan's emphasis on shared history and consent as the basis of nationhood. Michelet himself was
only one of many French commentators who found in 1870 that they
could not resist the temptation to talk of tribe and kinship, if only as
a stick with which to beat the Prussians for their inferiority. The
question of Alsace and Lorraine, and the "kinship" of its peoples
with either France or Germany, made the issue of race unavoidable.

Nor did the age wish to avoid it. Constructing theories of race
was a major project of science, arguably its central project, at exactly
the point in history when science became the dominant intellectual
discipline and source of ultimate authority, even in social and political thought. By the late nineteenth century the major fruit of
their speculation was the Aryan theory. It originated in the work of
philologists investigating the idea of an ancient Indo-European language, the common parent of later and apparently unconnected
world languages. They posited the existence of an Aryan tongue
which had been transmitted westward from Asia to Europe. An-
thropologists developed the hypothesis into a theory of race and
racial migration. The dolicephalic, or long-headed, Aryans were the
ancient antitype of the Semites, or "Jewish race." Migrating from
the plains of northern India, they had invaded Europe, overcome
its original brachycephalic, or round-headed, inhabitants, and established themselves as ancestors of modern white Europeans.
(Following the work of the Swedish scientist Anders Retzius, an-
thropologists sought the key to racial identity in the shape and size

of skull, presumed indicators of intelligence; craniometry was their most prized method of research, the cephalic index their most authoritative evidence.) The results of their inquiry agreed with the conclusions of philologists in finding the purest traces of Aryan descent among the Nordic or Teutonic tribes, ancestors of the modern Germans.

This is merely the baldest outline of a theory that managed to enjoy a long and sinister life in western-European thought without ever achieving a single form on which the experts of the time could agree. Instead it was propounded in rival versions and with fanciful variations: the Aryans had migrated from west to east and not the other way around, the Aryans had come from Germany in the first place, and so forth. None of them gained anything like universal scientific assent; the scientific community never agreed on any particular racial idea, only on the importance of race and the value of constructing racial ideas. Even in Germany, where scholarship gave the Aryan theory its most congenial home, it was far from being received without challenge.

A fundamental critique came from none other than Max Müller, whose own work as a philologist had contributed to its development. He warned against the easy translation science had made of a theory of language into a theory of race:

Language and *Volk* [people] are certainly in ancient times virtually synonymous, and what creates the ideal unity of a *Volk*—and a *Volk* is an ideal unity—lies far more in spiritual factors, in religion and language, than in blood relationship and community. But even on these grounds great caution is needed. It is too easy to forget that, if we speak of Aryan and Semitic families, the basis for the classification is entirely linguistic. There are Aryan and Semitic languages, but it is unscientific, or rather it would be allowing science some freedom in its terms, to speak of Aryan race, of Aryan blood, or of Aryan skulls, or to attempt ethnological classifications on linguistic bases. At least at the moment these two sciences, linguistics and ethnology, are not strong enough separately, and many misunderstandings, many controversies have their origin in drawing inferences from language about blood, or from blood about language. When both sciences have independently carried out their classification of peoples and languages, then the time will have come to compare the results, but even then one could as little speak of an Aryan skull as of a dolicephalic language.

It was not hard, then, to pick holes in the Aryan theory even from inside the assumptions of nineteenth-century thought. Yet that did not check its life, or even confine it to the sphere of academic controversy, as the role it played in Nazi ideology offers all too ready a reminder. Like racial purity, racial descent and race itself, the Aryans may have been chimeras, but nineteenth-century science remained dedicated to their pursuit. "Race in the present state of things is an abstract conception, a notion of continuity in discontinuity, of unity in diversity," remarked the French anthropologist Paul Topinard. "It is the rehabilitation of a real but directly unattainable thing." Despite the act of reification to which they owed their existence, the Aryans were real enough to the nineteenth-century mind, providing authoritative justification for imperialism abroad and anti-Semitism at home.

An acknowledgment that scientific ideas were political instruments was built into the occasion that Max Müller chose to recant the Aryan theory and rebuke the racial notions of the *Volk* it had helped to promote. He did not choose an academic journal or a learned conference. He chose a public address at the newly Germanized University of Strasbourg (Strassburg) in early 1872, a time and place when his audience had every reason to feel confident of Germany's destiny and Germany's future. His academic warning was linked to a broader political warning, made explicit when he turned his gaze beyond the confines of philology and ethnology:

Abroad, you know, people are not prophesying a great future for us. They are saying that the old, straightforward German customs will fall into disuse, that our ideals in life will be forgotten, that we will abandon satisfaction in Truth and Beauty, as other countries

have done, in pursuing pleasure, greed for money and political
vanity. It is worth all my skill to bring these prophecies to shame,
and to hold the banner of the German spirit higher than ever.
Germany can remain great only through those things that made it
great: through simplicity of life, through frugality, through dili-
gence, through modesty, through high ideals in life, through contempt for luxury, debauchery and boasting: *Non propter vitam
vivendi perdere causas* ["Not to let life make us forget the reasons
for living"], this should be and should stay our motto.

Apparently it was time, amid the triumphalist mood of the new Germany and the triumphalist mood of the scientific ideas associated
with the new Germany, to reassert the values of the old Germany.

The French, of course, were among those certain that the old
Germany was dead. It had been killed by dominance of Prussia—
Prussia with her barbarian anger and her tribal ways of defining
herself, Prussia with her talk of *germanische Frühzeit* (Germanic beginnings) and the *Volk*, the people conceived not as a democratic
community of individuals, or even a community bound together by
spiritual ideals, but increasingly as an involuntary "blood" unit. But
who were the Prussians? Michelet put the question scornfully in the
preface to his pamphlet on the Franco-Prussian War, *La France devant l'Europe*. "Do the Prussians really exist? I doubt it. All their
names are Slavic, Swedish, Danish, Swiss, French, and so forth.
Prussia is a framework that absorbs, a stomach with claws, like the
octopus. And without a body." This takes the familiar charge that
the Prussians had swallowed the other German states in the new
Reich beyond the realm of current politics. Yet it is not merely angry abuse. It deliberately invokes the racial thinking of the day in
order to turn it against the Prussians: far from being pure or Aryan
or descended from Aryans, they are scavenging mongrels with a history of eating up the peoples around them.

Michelet wrote these words in January 1871, and at virtually the
same time a strikingly similar angle of attack was being explored by
Jean-Louis Armand de Quatrefages de Bréau, in an extraordinary

pamphlet called *La Race prussienne*. Its purpose was no less angrily polemical and its language no less extreme, but it made a more careful show of scientific argument. A zoologist, physical anthropologist and hence craniometrist, Quatrefages served as director of the Musée National d'Histoire Naturelle. It was the damage done to his museum by German bombardment during the siege of Paris—he was sure the shells were not random but deliberately aimed—which prompted him to invoke his science in explaining the singular nastiness of the Prussians. What he proposed was essentially a modification to the Aryan theory.

The Aryans had migrated from somewhere on the banks of the Ganges toward the shores of the Atlantic. Their descendants included the Slavs and the Goths, and hence most of the people now called German. But not the Prussians. They came from another people (Quatrefages calls them Allophyllic) pushed by Aryan migration to the shores of the Baltic, where their descendants included the Estonians and the Finns. Some of the Finns crossbred with Slavs to create the dominant racial stock of the Prussians. Neither element made for a promising family tree, since the Finns were irredeemably vengeful and the Slavs aggressive and deceitful. The mixture of the two, together with later elements contributing to the Prussian racial character, made the Prussians unique ("the Prussians are the Prussians")—though not, of course, in anything like the sense that the French had in mind when celebrating the fusion that made themselves so admirably unique a people. The Prussians were a bastardized cross-race, an unstable mix: "In spite of a varnish of civilization, borrowed especially from France, the race is still in its middle age. This will explain some of its hatreds and violence."

My summary does not do justice to Quatrefages's argument; no summary could. The important point to remember is that racial theorizing of this sort was not in its time regarded as eccentric or dismissed as pseudoscience. Bad science though it undoubtedly was, it was also respectable science and as firmly established in the mainstream of scientific thought in France as it was in Germany. This does not mean that Quatrefages's particular theory was widely accepted; the scientific racists never agreed sufficiently among themselves for that to be possible. But it does mean that his pamphlet was reviewed with a show of scholarly disinterestedness in Germany. There, the pathologist Rudolf Virchow greeted it with a combination of rebuke and reassurance:

> Ought we, as we construct our state, ask everyone what their ancestry and racial origins are? No, Herr de Quatrefages, we will not undertake such policies. Modern *Deutschland* is not the old *Germania*. It is fortunately no longer the Holy Roman Empire of the German nation, and that means France should not fear an intention to establish a universal state.

At such moments in the debate about race and nation, the roles we might expect French and German scientists to play seem to have been inverted, with a German adopting a liberal position and a Frenchman an illiberal one. This should not really surprise us. Scientific racism was never exclusively German, much less Prussian; nor of course did it entirely dominate German thinking. Yet by the 1870s and the quarrel about the nationality of Alsace and Lorraine, it had left a perceptible mark on French thinking. The mark was even more apparent in the next century, when the approach and outbreak of war prompted a second pamphlet war between polemicists of a later generation. In contributions from the French side it was by no means unusual to find casual reference to the race of the people of Alsace and Lorraine, along these lines: "the ancestry of the population is Gallic, just as in the rest of France." The co-author of the pamphlet from which this quotation comes was Ernest Lavisse, author of the textbook histories by which the Third Republic promulgated its doctrines of history and nationhood, as well as wartime propagandist who steeled the French to face *l'épreuve de la durée*.

Other pamphlets of the day invoked racial argument with greater determination. One writer, for example, began by dismissing the German attempt "to justify a political demand made in the nineteenth century by ethnographic signatures from the Merovingian period" but was soon assuring his readers that "the measurement of skulls is often in our favor, not only in Lorraine, but even in Alsace; and even the 'Germanic elements' in Alsace are 'strongly mixed with Romano-Celtic blood.' " Another writer, conceding that Alsace "presents a mixed population composed of Celtic and Germanic elements," went on to cite "the latest scientific researches" as demonstrating that "the shape of the German skull, which the Germans love to indicate as the sign of the superiority of the German race, is represented in Alsace only in the proportion of one to three, and the so called Germanic type (blue eyes and yellow hair) is nowhere predominant."

These are just short quotations, taken from a large pamphlet war which in turn belonged to a long dispute, but together they help to indicate the changed temper of French argument. Their ambivalence is particularly striking. Scientific racism had not carried the day so completely as to stifle the old desire to banish prehistory and race from discussion altogether. Yet "the latest scientific researches" had become an authority too strong to be ignored: they must be shown to serve the French case. Plainly polemicists in the First World War wanted to have it both ways; indeed they wanted to win the argument in every possible way they could think of. And as the glibness of reference to concepts such as the "Gallic ancestry" of the French suggests, the idea of race had become attached to the idea of nation in a manner that was no less firm for remaining, in any particular context, casual and unexplained.

In recent years, a good deal of scholarship has been devoted to the French traditions of racist thought linking the ideas of 1870 with the ideas of 1914–18. The Comte de Gobineau, we now know, was not a disregarded eccentric awaiting adoption by the National Socialists but a thinker engaged in correspondence with de Tocqueville and Renan. Later theorists such as Georges Vacher de Lapouge and Gustave Le Bon might have been marginal, but they still influenced a discernible body of right-wing thought.* It is no

* At least one of Le Bon's books was not marginal by any stretch of the imagination. *La Psychologie des foules* (*The Psychology of Crowds*), originally published in 1895, left its mark on Freud and is still sometimes described as a classic of social psychology.

part of my purpose to rehearse any of their arguments in detail. The detail does not matter; the detail of scientific racism never does. The larger assumptions do matter, for they touched a mainstream of thought which was not avowedly scientific or racist. Of course, the largest assumption behind scientific racism was that a scientific view of mankind largely exposed difference rather than similarity, and that in practice its job was to concentrate entirely on difference. Next in importance stood the belief that racial difference, as a fact of nature embodying the laws of nature, was fixed. Except through crossbreeding, which destroyed its original purity and could cause degeneration, race was immutable. Race, in other words, was destiny.

Such ideas were easily applied to the relations between western Europe and those regions of the world that western Europe sought to rule by colonization. They could also be applied to the relations between western and eastern Europe—the latter inhabited by the Slav (whose very label proclaimed enslavement) and connected with the dreaded hordes of Asia. Applying them to the nations inside western Europe was always more problematic and more tentative. Few, if any, French thinkers argued that the French were a race. The French never made themselves prisoners of heredity, as extreme forms of scientific racism would have had them do. Theories of race were too mazelike and various to make a reliable buttress, much less a single buttress, for definitions of the nation and its character. But if they treated specific argument from biology with caution, and were often content to let the matter remain in the vaguest and most general forms, the French showed less reserve in adopting biology's general argument from natural law. In the process they certainly came close to making themselves prisoners of history.

The proud cry that France was not a race but a nation was repeated without challenge from Michelet to Maurice Barrès; if Germans were a race, or thought of themselves as a race, that was a sign of their undeveloped crudity. The French never denied their mongrel ancestry, though Lavisse was typical of his time in preferring to single out the Gauls as their ancestors, or their first ancestors. (In similar fashion the English liked at the same time to call themselves both mongrels and Anglo-Saxons, and sometimes just Saxons.) Most writers on France continued to celebrate the happy fusion that had made the French what they were, and given them their history, their character and their achievements in civilization. And yet increasingly they treated the nation resulting from the process as if at a certain historical point, too early to be specified, it had assumed the status and properties of race. It was taken to be fixed and immutable; its character could degenerate, and needed to be protected from degeneration, but was not otherwise susceptible to change.

To Michelet and Renan, among many others, nationhood was a voluntary act continually reaffirmed; free will and consent always remained its vital principles. The harsh determinism of later generations found nothing voluntary in nationhood. "Nations are not societies that one joins by choice," insisted Vacher de Lapouge, "nor associations of interest that one enters by taking an action, or quits as one might abandon a bill of exchange." People had no choice but to be born into their nation and, while among the living, were always a minority by comparison to the dead who had shaped it. Gustave Le Bon elaborated the implications:

> Infinitely greater in numbers than the living, the dead are also infinitely more powerful. They rule the vast domain of the unconscious, that invisible domain which holds in its power all manifestations of character and intelligence. It is by its dead, far more than by its living representatives, that a people is led. It is by them alone that a race is founded. Century after century, they created our ideas and our feelings, and as a result all the motives of our conduct. The vanished generations do not merely impose their physical constitution on us; they also impose their thoughts. The dead alone are the undisputed masters of the living. We carry the burden of their faults, we reap the reward of their virtues.

"To this infinite power of ancestors, man can only submit," added Vacher de Lapouge by way of summary. It had transformed a people such as the French, whose diversity of origin deprived them of any claim to being a "natural race," into what Le Bon called a "historic race."

In its way the argument ruled out speculation about ancient origin and laid emphasis on the recorded history of later times as emphatically as Michelet's view of the French had done. Yet it did so to different effect. Michelet had conceived history as operating through change and progress; he had celebrated organic growth. To later writers history had become simply a dead weight, expunging the deficiencies and inconsistencies left by biology, welding the nation into a unit with a "soul" as unalterable as any genetic endowment. Quite deliberately, the description robbed the concept of "the people" of those connotations with which thinkers in the republican tradition had sought to endow it. Emphasis shifted from the individual to the group. Individual variation, individual liberty, the power of the individual idea were made to look negligible; they were dwarfed by mass identity, mass character, mass behavior, and above all, by the subservience of the mass to forces too great to be altered by any single act or moment in history. Never had *le peuple* been made to sound so like the German *Volk*.

This vision was by no means limited to forgotten writers like Le Bon or Vacher de Lapouge. It became a central tenet in a good deal of the thinking marshaled, in the late nineteenth and early twentieth centuries under the banner of "nationalism." It certainly animated the work of Maurice Barrès, who gave the word *nationalisme* its currency during the prewar years and, during the war, took it upon himself to speak on behalf of the "soul" of the French. To him, as much as to Le Bon and Vacher, the French were always a *bloc*, their destiny, their character and their relations with other peoples somehow settled before they were born. (So of course were external enemies, such as the Germans, and internal enemies, such as the Jews.) To him, the whole point of nationalism was that—like religion—it brought release from an individuality he conceived largely as shallow and frivolous egotism. "A nationalist," he wrote, "is a Frenchman who has become aware of how he has been formed. Nationalism is the acceptance of a determinism."

Barrès' wartime propaganda would praise self-sacrifice on behalf
of the nation as the noblest gesture to which the individual self
could aspire. Yet before the war came, his work was already a prolonged hymn to the necessity, and the pleasure, of merging with a
force larger than the individual, a unit larger even than its living
members. *La terre et les morts*, the soil and the dead: the phrase rang
through his work in repeated, definitive summary of where the
essence of the nation was to be found. It was the soil of its territory,
the soil where its people were born, the soil where the countless
dead already lay. The graveyard preoccupation was entirely appropriate to a style of thought that would find characteristic and congenial expression in contemplating the cemeteries of war dead, like
those already scattered on the road from Metz to Verdun.

✛ ✛ ✛

Monsieur Dunoyer believes in the new system that ingenious
writers have established for describing the difference between the
races. There is a measure of truth in this system; it is interesting
to examine, and can be of value to science, but we believe that
care must be taken to exclude it from politics. Power is only too
ready to represent its own excesses, its capricious and wilful excesses, as a necessary consequence of natural laws.
    Benjamin Constant,
    "De M. Dunoyer et de quelques uns de ses ouvrages"
    ("On Monsieur Dunoyer and Some of His Works"), 1826

"How ruined are the noble and generous prospects that once lay before us!" exclaimed Émile Littré in despair at the effect of the Franco-
Prussian War on the values of liberal Republicans like himself:

We who brought our children up in well-meaning respect for
foreign peoples! We must change all that; we must bring them up
in defiance and hostility; we must teach them that military training is the first of their duties; we must instil in them constant

readiness to kill and be killed. That is the only way to avoid the fate of Alsace and Lorraine, the saddest of misfortunes, the most poignant of sorrows.

It was not just the temporary bitterness of defeat in the war itself, but the permanent humiliation represented by the lost provinces that altered values. The quarrel with Germany over Alsace and Lorraine itself showed the French view of nationhood and the differences between nations growing harder, more narrow and more hostile. Science helped to lend an air of authority to the change. At the same time the desire for *revanche*, though stifled by political circumstance, took comfort from the sense that a future war with Germany was inevitable and, in some measure, desirable. Science had something to say on this subject too, and people were increasingly ready to listen.

The liberal Republican values whose sudden death Littré lamented had been part of a larger intellectual project common to the various nations of Europe since the age of Kantian idealism and the Enlightenment. In practice it had never been wholehearted in its dedication to peace, of course, any more than it had been as respectful and generous in its view of foreign peoples as its believers might sometimes have liked to claim. Aggressive militancy had always played its part; in France, the cult of the citizen-soldier ready to fight tyranny *jusqu'au bout* enjoyed a career from the early days of the Revolution to Gambetta's call to arms during the Franco-Prussian War. Yet at the same time this tradition of thought had always paid something more than lip service to a dream of peace between nations. Progress would render war unnecessary and eventually extinct.

Most nineteenth-century people who could loosely be called liberals subscribed in some measure to this hope. It formed a major article of belief to Saint-Simon and his followers—as in Britain to politicians of the Manchester school, such as Richard Cobden and John Bright, who exercised considerable sway in Gladstone's administrations. Both groups stated their case in economic terms, connecting the triumph of peace with the growth of international prosperity. The links forged by trade and finance would make waging war less and less in the self-interest of nations. The long decades of peace following the Napoleonic Wars were a particular point of pride; the nineteenth century was, above all, to be the century of trade exhibitions. Theoretically war might even become impossible, at least between the developed nations of Europe.

Despite Littré's outburst of despair these beliefs did not die in 1870, in France or anywhere else, much less die suddenly. They were still alive in 1910, when Norman Angell attracted attention in Europe and the USA as well as his native Britain by restating them in his book *The Great Illusion*. By that date, of course, a belief in internationalism and hence international peace was also receiving support from other quarters. Socialism found difference and antagonism between class and class rather than nation and nation; the wars that the governments of states waged against each other were capitalist impositions on their peoples. Several strands of opinion could thus in practice join to deplore the current level of armaments and to advocate international law as a means of containing hostilities. In all, there was as much talk of peace as of war in the early years of the new century. So it was appropriate that, just when Maurice Barrès was giving the word *nationalisme* its modern shade of meaning, contemporaries should also have found another coinage necessary: *pacifisme*.*

The word did not then necessarily denote an objection to all war on ideological grounds but, more loosely, an emphasis on the virtues of peace. Careless historians, bent on portraying the outbreak of the First World War as an unexpected shock, have sometimes dwelt on these "pacifist" tendencies of the prewar years in isolation. They make the mistake of looking for the temper of an age in a single belief or attitude, rather than in the character of the conflict between different beliefs or attitudes. The attention accorded to Norman Angell, in particular, is often taken as evidence

---

* The word seems to have appeared first in French—as used by Émile Arnaud at the tenth Universal Peace Congress, 1902—and thence migrated to English.

of a prevailing complacency. In fact, it was nothing of the kind. Angell certainly argued that war no longer served the interests of the European nations, but he did so in a spirit of urgent warning. By 1910 his values had been thrown almost as much on the defensive as Littré had felt his values to be some 40 years before.

The threat Angell saw came partly from Germany and Prussian militarism, which could not be relied on to pursue self-interest in a rational or enlightened way. In this respect he was merely voicing an anxiety commonly felt by the older established nations in the prewar years; wartime propaganda would promote it to shrill accusation and the postwar history books would enshrine it as emphatic condemnation. Yet German and Prussian irrationality was not the only challenge to the vision of peace and prosperity. More pervasive, Angell thought, was a new climate of thinking throughout Europe. Its attitude to war was "based on the alleged unchangeability of human nature, on the plea that the warlike nations inherit the earth, that warlike qualities alone can give the virile energy necessary for nations to win in the struggle for life."

The key phrase here is obviously "the struggle for life." It needed no gloss, since it had long since been made familiar beyond Britain and the English language, whether as *la lutte pour l'existence* or *la lutte pour la vie* in France or as *der Kampf ums Dasein* or *der Daseinskampf* in Germany. It belonged to the theory of evolutionary biology that Darwin had proposed some 60-odd years before, and had been rendered particularly memorable by the closing paragraph of *The Origin of Species*. Here, in a rare moment of larger reflection, Darwin had paused to consider an ordinary hedgerow "clothed with many plants of many kinds, with birds singing on the bushes, with various insects flitting about, and with worms crawling through the damp earth." Beneath the surface of even so apparently peaceful a scene "a struggle for life" was being enacted, as it always was throughout the natural world: a never-ending competition between too many beings for too little food and too little territory. The losers in the struggle, whether individuals or species, went to the wall; the winners survived to reproduce and so transmit to future generations those features which had made them best adapted to the conditions of the struggle. This mechanism, which Darwin called "natural selection," was the fundamental law driving the process of evolution. "Thus," he concluded, "from the war of nature, from famine and death, the most exalted object which we are capable of conceiving, namely, the production of the higher animals, directly follows."

"Survival of the fittest," the alternative and soon the more famous label for "natural selection," was coined not by Darwin but by Herbert Spencer. Darwin himself adopted it as a synonym from the fifth edition of his book onward—a huge mistake for a theorist already doomed to misinterpretation, since it encouraged the mistaken popular assumption that the big and the strong won the struggle for life. Contemporary interest in science guaranteed that scientific theories never kept their original precision for long; nor were they allowed to remain very long confined to the issue they sought to address. Though considerably more precise and more cautiously limited in its application than any of the ideas behind scientific racism, Darwin's theory suffered the same loose and happy translation that was busy, during the same period, turning philological into ethnological speculation and both into historical facts illuminating contemporary differences in national character.

Social Darwinism had begun its career. Without encouragement from Darwin or authority from his text, it appropriated not his idea but rather his slogan as an explanatory key to human activity. Natural law licensed competition, not cooperation, as the norm of relations inside the social group. The norm of relations between groups was not peace but war. Far from being the true goal of civilization, peace on any permanent basis was not even an ideal. Indeed, in a sense, civilization itself was no longer an ideal; it was a dangerous illusion. It softened people, weakened them to the point of degeneracy, by making them forget or ignore the underlying laws of nature. Nature, in this sense, was a force at once external and internal: it was both the harsh but exhilarating realities of life itself and the innate, animal self that made surviving them possible. War exposed these realities and tested this self. It restored man to his noblest, and most natural, sphere of action.

Such a call, inevitably, struck the deepest chord among the officer class in the army; it is no accident that so many of the writers who recommended "the struggle for life" as a doctrine of warfare should have been military men. It gave them an extra argument for the need to maintain a state of military readiness in time of peace. Soldiers always have a vested interest in putting such a case, since it involves the practical question of the military budget as well as less tangible but no less important matters, such as the esteem attached to their profession and the quality of men it can recruit. These were of particular urgency in a French army overshadowed by its record of defeat, embarrassed by its performance in the Dreyfus Affair, trying to find its place in the ethos ushered in by the Third Republic. On all these counts the slogan "struggle for life" gave timely help. Most specifically, it served to justify precisely the code of warrior values—disciplined brutality and disciplined sacrifice—that the army in France, as in Britain, believed would overcome the challenges posed by the new technology of war.

In France, as elsewhere, it was not only soldiers to whom the slogans of Social Darwinism appealed. "War, why, life itself is war!" exclaimed Zola, significantly on the 21st anniversary of the fall of Sedan:

> Nothing exists in nature, nothing is born, nothing grows, nothing multiplies except by combat. For the world to live we must eat and be eaten. And warlike nations alone have prospered; a nation dies as soon as it gives up its weapons. War is a school of discipline, sacrifice and courage.

Between nations there was no law except force, insisted Vacher de Lapouge a few years later: "All men are brothers, all animals are brothers, but being brothers is not likely to prevent us eating each other. Brotherhood, perhaps, but the devil take the losers. Life is perpetuated only through death. To live one must eat, to eat one must kill."

It would be easy to extend such quotation into an unpleasant anthology. Indeed such anthologies were offered by French and British propagandists during the First World War, the contents carefully selected to disown the sentiments and present them as uniquely German. The writings of Treitschke and Count von Bernhardi proved a particularly rich trove. Yet even a full collection compiled along international lines would not add much to the quotations I have just offered. Its central core of ideas would still be extremely limited and its rhetorical tone gratingly monotonous. It would, moreover, serve to emphasize that there was nothing inherently new in the position Social Darwinism took. Long before it came on the scene, well-established traditions of thought had already maintained that war was an inevitable fact of life, that war could have a regenerative effect and that force was the arbiter of international relations. To some, the essential conditions of life had always been those holding sway on the raft of the *Medusa*.

Such ideas were at least as old as Machiavelli or Thomas Hobbes. Clothing them in the language of Social Darwinism did not lend them new precision; if anything, it robbed them of the precision that earlier generations of political philosophy had achieved. Wars, after all, do not usually help the fittest to survive. Wars kill them; it is the weak whom armies reject from their ranks. Even Vacher de Lapouge, extremist though he was, acknowledged this elementary truth. A writer like Captain André Constantin, determined to affirm that war served a principle of collective selection, was left trying unhappily to bury the objection beneath qualifying argument: only long wars kill the fittest, or indeed kill people on any great scale, and even then they still somehow promote the moral and intellectual health of the group. The poverty of such reasoning would soon be underlined by the survivors of the First World War, lamenting that it had been the best among their contemporaries who had died.

Yet to let the matter rest here would be to miss the potency that slogans can possess, and the particular potency that the slogan "struggle for life" could hold for an age in the habit of concealing its muddles and prejudices beneath a cloak of scientific authority. To talk of "the struggle for life" as natural, inevitable and hence somehow legitimate might never have come close to being a precise scientific recommendation of war, but it was devastatingly effective in crystallizing discontent with peace on the terms that recent history had given it to France—and, indeed, to Germany. To Germany, peace before 1870 had meant living with Napoléon I's victories unappeased and the impulse to national unification unrealized; after 1870, as the glow of victory faded, it had meant all the frustrations of being a newcomer among the European powers, hemmed in by those who had arrived at the feast before them. To France, peace before 1870 had meant living with the shallow materialism of the Second Empire; after 1870, it had meant living with a Republic which could neither forget nor avenge the humiliations of defeat.

So the lessons of history whispered the same message as the slogans of Social Darwinism. Peace was weak and ignoble, to be endured as a temporary expedient or necessity of political life but not to be embraced as the permanent destiny of nations, much less of civilization. Significantly, the word "civilization" was less and less often heard in the years before the First World War and, when it was heard, it sometimes designated a state of disease or enfeeblement. The keystone of values increasingly resided in the word "nature." Conflict was nature's norm. In war men and nations became most effectively themselves, the individual setting aside the self-interest that flourished in peace and cultivating instead the virtues of duty, obedience and sacrifice. This did not mean that war was to be carelessly sought or rashly provoked, or even that the moment and occasion of its coming could be predicted with any exactitude. Yet it would come, and it should come.

"Even if it destroys us," said Falkenhayn when war did break out, "it would still be wonderful." For several decades a yearning for the savage poetry of war had been part of the mood of the times, and surprise at the specific turn of events in August 1914 was mixed with something like relief that the yearning was at last to be answered. In Munich the photographer Heinrich Hoffmann snapped the glowing face of the young Hitler, among the crowds gathered in the Odeonsplatz to sing *Die Wacht am Rhein* and *Deutschland über alles*. In France the train carriages filled with troops had *À Berlin* chalked on their sides, and the dissenting voice of an intellectual like Romain Rolland was quickly cried down. We are all familiar with at least some of these various signs of enthusiasm, if only because contemporaries took such good care to record and emphasize them. This in itself should make us wary of accepting the enthusiasm completely at face value. Nationalism has always been suspiciously fluent in creating images of itself as a universal and irresistible force. In France *revanchisme* had never achieved the status of policy, any more than expansionism had in Germany. In neither country had people been offered, or persuaded by, detailed scientific argument for the necessity and benefits of warfare *per se*. Indeed, acceptance of war in 1914 was almost always conditional, predicated on the belief that it would be short and decisive. Part and parcel of this mistaken belief was the assumption that the war would also be bloody in its effectiveness, and this prospect alone could temper enthusiasm.

Misleading though it might be to speak of mass enthusiasm, much less hysteria, as greeting the war, there is still no doubt that its coming was accepted, and accepted with active determination rather than mere resignation. To this degree, at least, nationalism and science had together done their work in persuading people of the ingrained difference and hostility between nations, and of the outcome to which they led. And so to contemporaries the events of August 1914 carried with them an air of inevitability. "Everyone heard, rediscovered and listened to, as known and familiar, this deep resonance, this voice which wasn't external, this voice of memory buried and piled up, nobody knew why or for how long." These are Péguy's words, but they were written in 1905, during a crisis of Franco-German relations too passing to be mentioned in all but detailed accounts of the buildup to the First World War. The crises over Morocco and Agadir were still to come, let alone the assassination of the Archduke Ferdinand, when the inner voice of which Péguy wrote at last announced a return to reality after decades spent in the refuge and illusion of peace. After all the years of uneasy waiting, it brought relief; it promised satisfaction.

PART THREE

THE MILL ON THE MEUSE, MARCH–DECEMBER 1916

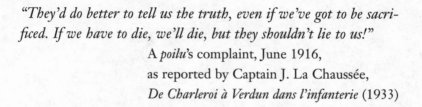

"They'd do better to tell us the truth, even if we've got to be sacrificed. If we have to die, we'll die, but they shouldn't lie to us!"
A poilu's complaint, June 1916,
as reported by Captain J. La Chaussée,
De Charleroi à Verdun dans l'infanterie (1933)

✞   ✞   ✞

They know that they are saving France, but also that they are going to die on the spot.
Report by the French postal censor on morale
at Verdun, 16 July 1916

6

———✛———

HOLDING VERDUN

Dedication to Generals de Castelnau, Pétain and Nivelle and to the generals at Verdun:

I offer this book to you in the combined spirit of manly resignation and melancholy frankness which, in the infantry, characterizes those who have been fighting for 20 months. . . . The war has made us surgeons in some degree, and also, by keeping the same thoughts in our heads day after day, turned us into psychologists.

A soldier from Verdun

> The dedication proposed by Raymond Jubert
> for his memoir *Verdun (mars-avril-mai 1916)*, 1918,
> cut in the published version to the
> salutation and signature

Second Lieutenant Raymond Jubert learned a great deal about the satisfactions of war on 9 April 1916. He was 27 years old, and in civilian life a lawyer nursing literary aspirations; though exempt from military service, he had enlisted at the outbreak of the war. Some 20 months later he was no novice, for he had seen action at Les Éparges and in the Champagne, and no stranger to Verdun, for he had spent a large part of March fighting on the cold plateaus in front of the Fort de Douaumont. Now his regiment, the 151st Infantry, was on the left bank of the Meuse, holding a reserve

position on the southern slopes of the twin-peaked hill known as Le
Mort-Homme: Dead Man's Hill. The troops had not given the
place its name, which was traditional and, so local legend said, referred to the fate of a traveler lost in the winter snow in some previous century. Each day of the battle lent it new meaning.

When the colonel of the regiment put the 151st on alert, Jubert
greeted the news with a mixture of relief and cynicism. "This'll
calm us down," he remarked to a fellow officer: "We were starting
to get out of the habit of dying." That was on Saturday 8 April. He
woke early on the Sunday to a clear, bright dawn and sat alone
watching the sun chase the mists from the peaks of Le Mort-
Homme above him. Like many of those who recorded their impressions of the battlefield, Jubert always responded eagerly to
whatever vestiges of natural beauty somehow managed to coexist
with man's destructiveness. This morning the sunlight acted on him
as a tonic; he thought it like drinking at the Fountain of Youth.
Nevertheless, when he looked at the men around him he saw only
the presentiment of danger: "They were sleeping, with no suspicion
that death was nearby; in the manner of condemned men, they
could be woken up only so that they did not have to die any more."*
Nature, he decided, was like a young consumptive, "never so close
to death as on the day when it is most greedy of life."

The strange mixture of beauty and destruction intensified dramatically when the German guns opened up at seven o'clock. Dark
smoke from exploding shells and yellow smudges of shrapnel
floated over the top of the hill where the morning mist had so recently lingered. It was in fact the heaviest bombardment since the
start of the battle on 21 February, and other witnesses described Le
Mort-Homme as looking like a volcano in eruption. Captain Augustin Cochin, taking the brunt of the firing on nearby Cote 304,
found it the worst ordeal he had ever undergone. He soon reached

* The phrase echoes the exclamation attributed to one of the *grognards* in Napoléon's Grande
Armée on his return from the disastrous Russian campaign: "Now I won't die any more!"
Louis Madelin had also been reminded of it when he saw the survivors straggling out of the
Bois des Caures on 22 February: see Chapter 1.

the end of his tether: "Like the poor beggars in the Gospel, I pleaded not to die so senselessly, I and my poor *biffins*, who were driven half mad: round-eyed, no longer answering when I spoke to them." From his position below, Jubert could make out two zones of fire: one covering the French lines from the crest of Cote 304 along to Le Mort-Homme, and a second barring the likely route by which the French might try to bring up reinforcements.

This soldierly appraisal took second place to sheer awe. Jubert, who had arrived at Verdun after the battle had begun, had never seen anything on quite this scale before, and he found the spectacle romantic in its grandeur. Out of the immediate danger, he described it as if it were a painting, a great canvas of battle actually being painted in front of his eyes:

> Brushstroke was being added to brushstroke in quick succession, dozens at a time. So heavy that they could suffocate you if you were close, from a distance they looked fresh, harmonious to the eye. Thunderclouds floated across the sky, touched with the colour of morning. The sun has this virtue: beneath its rays death takes on pure beauty.

At one o'clock the German guns fell silent. Thinking the attack had been checked, Jubert's company gave vent to hysterical relief. The men sat down to lunch with vast appetites, basked in the sunshine and started to play cards. Jubert himself was enjoying a run of luck when a message arrived from the regimental command post. The crest of Le Mort-Homme had been overrun and his company was ordered to retake it immediately; worse still, it had to launch the counterattack over open ground, since the winding communication trenches leading up the slopes would take too long to negotiate. Nobody hesitated, Jubert stressed; nobody panicked. As soon as the sergeant had been given the orders, men went silently about gathering up their packs, filling them with spare ammunition and an extra day's rations.

They set off, a handful of officers and NCOs leading about 100 troops in straight skirmishing lines up the hill. Occasionally they exchanged encouraging shouts:

"We'll show them what men from the Nord are made of!"
"And men from the Ardennes as well!"
"And Paris!"

For the most part, Jubert noted, the men's faces were grave, though some of them managed a smile when he caught their eye. The smiles, of course, had nothing to do with the cheerfulness which Henry Bordeaux described, from his staff officer's desk, for the benefit of the home front—the cheerfulness, he alleged, of men going into action as if setting out on an excursion from Paris to Saint-Germain or Versailles. "Oh, how often I've seen that smile," exclaimed Sergeant Guy Hallé, "that pale smile, with its slight tremble, pulled toward the corners of the mouth: you have to be-have properly in the presence of death." Some officers regarded it as essential to be seen smiling, though Jacques Péricard (who, for all his habit of promoting battlefield myths, could be engagingly hon-est about his own emotions) admitted to finding the task so hard that he went around with a cigarette permanently hiding the ner-vous falsity of the result.* Morale was always at its lowest in the first stages of an assault, as Jubert knew well: the prospect of danger could be more frightening than danger itself. It made men ask themselves questions like those that flickered through the mind of Jacques Férol, the central character in René Naegelen's auto-biographical novel, *Les Suppliciés* (*The Victims*):

Was he going to be one of those who would one day say, "I was at Verdun"? or one of those of whom people said, "he was killed at Verdun"?

---

* Generals, of course, had to be seen smiling all the time. Kathleen Burke, an English nurse who visited the battlefield, found Pétain smiling; he promised she would find Nivelle smiling too, as indeed she did.

O God, I haven't done anything, I'm not guilty, please spare
me, let me come out of this alive, make them call the attack off,
make the bloody war end!

At least the heat of the action occupied the mind and helped to
banish fear. Jubert was reminded of this psychological truth when
his company reached the first of a series of ridges and looked into
the ravine below, so saturated by artillery fire that it seemed as if a
steel barrier blocked the way. When he entered the danger zone he
quickly discovered another truth of the battlefield, this time a practical one which the commanders should have kept in mind as well.
Long-range bombardments were always less effective than they appeared at first glance. Few of the shells were targeted with any precision and a good proportion (sometimes as many as one in three)
were duds, so that large pockets of safety could remain among the
deafening noise and the flying earth. As he advanced, a shell ex-
ploded behind Jubert, throwing a man several meters in the air;
while his body was still falling, it was jerked upward again by the
force of another explosion. Nearby, a whole section of men lay flattened on the ground. Yet as soon as the explosions had passed, they
got up again and resumed their place in the line. Death might have
visited Jubert's company but so far it had claimed only one victim,
and the company's order still held.

Near the top of the next ridge a lieutenant had been left in position by the battalion commander, waiting to give last-minute in-
structions and point out the final objective of the assault. Yet the top
of Le Mort-Homme was by now so enshrouded in smoke that
he could not offer much help. When Jubert asked exactly where the
Germans were, he got the reply: "That's for you to tell us." The
company split into four sections, one to follow the communication
trench—or what remained of it—up to the crest and the other three
to attack across open ground, but obliquely from the left. Jubert
himself took charge of one section, while Second Lieutenant Noël,
Officer Cadet Buisson and Sergeant Dudot were put in command
of the others.

A mood of exhilaration had now taken hold. Some men were laughing wildly. "We're going to beat them," one shouted: "The bastards won't get past us." Another began to sing a popular song and the rest took it up. It was all bravado in the face of death, Jubert knew, but it gripped him too. The attack, he found, had grown into something deeply satisfying, even beautiful. He remained acutely aware of the spring sunlight around him and the new grass beneath his feet, even as he dodged the machine-gun bullets throwing up spurts of soil and heard his fellow officers crying out in agony when they were hit. Only a remote part of his mind could register their fate, or even the danger to himself: his concentration was focused on covering the hundred, then fifty, then twenty paces of ground ahead.

"With *élan* carrying us forward, we reached the crest." By *élan* Jubert meant sheer physical momentum, but also much, much more than that. The French had long since fixed on the word in pinpointing their leading characteristic, the very quality that gave their national life its violent ups and downs. It was the enthusiasm that made France capable of great achievement yet also, in its fractious energy, allowed France to plunge into the abyss. The years spent in the abyss after 1870–71 had brought self-critical comment on the gulf separating *élan* from the steady, methodical application that the French took to be the core of the German mentality. Yet in *élan* also lay, eventually, the recovery from humiliation. Once war came, it would be the strength of the warrior unleashed—a sheer animal will that could triumph over machinery, however well-built and well-deployed. And for Jubert and his company on the crest of Le Mort-Homme that April morning, *élan* had worked.

It was not the only time that it worked at Verdun, of course, or the only time that men felt their misery and fear dissolve in heady excitement and their excitement rise eventually to some nervous pitch, be it of savagery or quasi-religious exaltation. Finding himself and his unit directly confronting the Germans in February, Sergeant Paul Dubrulle had realized:

It was a beautiful spectacle, and the most beautiful thing about it was the attitude of the men around me.

The beauty immediately gripped me and lifted me high above the miseries of ordinary existence. In the depth of my being I felt I was experiencing one of the great moments of my life, an epic moment, when what was selfish and pedestrian was left behind for good, in the service of great causes.

At almost the same time that Jubert was launching his counterattack on Le Mort-Homme, Second Lieutenant Robert Desaubliaux found himself crouched in another part of the battlefield, waiting for a German attack on his unit of machine-gunners:

After several minutes I rose to my full height and looked, hoping to see them coming; it gave me such profound, savage joy to think of mowing them down in front of me like a harvest, of showing them that, despite all their firing, the French were still here, alive, hanging on to their trench. Nothing mattered any more, not tiredness, nor hunger, nor thirst, nor lack of sleep, nor the bullets ringing in my eyes by the hundred, nor the explosions of shells that whistled and fell like drops of rain.

Everything I had gone through, everything I had suffered, was forgotten; my whole being was possessed by the attack which was about to start. I was waiting for it impatiently, full of the need to kill . . . to kill without pity.

In the event, the Germans did not oblige by attacking and Desaubliaux's need to kill—as he so frankly called it—went unsatisfied. Such moments of wild *élan* were always bound to be brief, and whatever followed them was bound to be anticlimactic. So it certainly proved for Jubert and the remnants of his company when they reached the crest of Le Mort-Homme, leaping over the parapet to find the trench empty for several hundred meters in either direction. The Germans had made a quick tactical withdrawal, leaving behind only their dead and the corpses of the French Zouaves and *chasseurs* who had been defending it at the start of the day.

Jubert took stock of the situation with growing anxiety. In an effort to keep up morale, he seized an envelope he found lying on the ground—it had German writing on it—and made a ceremony of noting down the names of all the survivors, to make sure that they were proposed for commendations. Out of the 100 men who had started out, there were now only 10 left: a couple of sergeants, a corporal and a handful of inexperienced *bleusailles* from the class of 1916. Soon afterward Dudot arrived, bleeding from the chest, and joined Jubert in making a quick reconnaissance. It confirmed that no French units were nearby and that the Germans still occupied an adjoining trench, as yet unaware of their presence. Because they had so few men an artillery bombardment need not be fatal—they could easily play hide-and-seek with the shells in so long a strip of entrenchment—but an infantry assault would have no difficulty overwhelming them. In all, Jubert decided, the position was far too good to abandon.

He scribbled a brief report to his colonel, admitting that he did not know exactly where he was but urgently requesting two companies be sent to support him. The first messenger entrusted with the note was wounded almost as soon as he set out. Dudot insisted on taking his place, arguing that his wound had left him in no state to help in any other fashion. As they shook hands, Jubert was struck by how weak and stiff the sergeant's hand felt, and, as he watched him climb over the parapet, he thought: "There goes another dead man." Dusk fell and the German bombardment grew in violence. At eight o'clock Jubert decided to try reaching the regimental command post himself. On his way down the hill he found Second Lieutenant Noël lying at the bottom of a shell-hole with a broken leg, and managed to direct a party of stretcher-bearers to the spot.

At the command post Jubert was greeted, like a man returning from the dead, with amazement and congratulation but no practical help. His colonel had no reinforcements to offer, and the most that Jubert could wring from him was the promise that a company would be sent as soon as one became available. With this small consolation, he began his journey back up the hill. On the way he passed the stretcher-bearers carrying Noël, white-faced and obviously dying. They embraced without speaking, and Jubert was still too preoccupied with the fate of the rest of his men to spare any time for tears. In fact he found them still nervously hanging on to their position. Another 30 hours of almost continual bombardment and machine-gun fire passed before anyone came to relieve them.

Then they found themselves heroes. It had, after all, been resistance such as they had shown to the German attack on 9 April that led Pétain to issue the cautiously triumphant Order of the Day invoking Jeanne d'Arc's words at the siege of Orléans: *Courage, on les aura!* The company received an honorable mention in dispatches—which took care to record that they had made their attack singing and laughing—and Jubert himself received a medal. Yet by May, when he was again posted to Le Mort-Homme, he saw the battlefield in a different light and took a different view of what it was like to be a hero. In the memoirs which he began around this time and completed during a spell in hospital, he presented the change in himself by an ironic self-catechism:

"What sublime feeling took hold of you as you went into the attack?"

"I was thinking only of pulling my feet out of the mud they were stuck in."

"What heroic cry did you utter when you had recaptured the crest?"

"I resurrected Cambronne* because I thought I was done for."

"What feeling of power did you have when you had defeated the enemy?"

"I was annoyed, because the grub wouldn't get to us and I'd be spending several more days without any *pinard* [wine]."

"Was your first act to give thanks to God?"

"I went off by myself to answer a call of nature."

Anyone who has even dipped into the literature of the First World War will find the note that this passage strikes familiar.

---

* According to legend, General Cambronne refused to surrender at Waterloo with a single word: *Merde*. His name, or the phrase *mot de Cambronne*, thus did service as a polite euphemism.

Indeed, to later generations who had not taken part in the war it often seemed the fundamental note, announcing the real discovery made by the men who fought, the real burden of what they had to say. Most memoirs written by the combatants are, in some fashion, narratives of disillusionment. They record the disparity between the war as it had been imagined or expected—which was also, of course, the war still being described for the benefit of the home front—and the war as it had actually been experienced. On the one hand there was the myth, romantic and glorious, and on the other, the reality, miserable and squalid. Those who had been at the sharp end and lived through the experience were thus men doubly alienated. (The word would soon grow fashionable.) They were alienated both from their innocent prewar selves and from the people—politicians, journalists, families and friends at home—who had not shared their experience.

Of all the battles that French troops fought, Verdun was the greatest crucible where this transformation was wrought. "I am dreadfully changed," wrote Sergeant Marc Boasson to his wife toward the end of a long tour of duty. "Since Verdun my thinking has been very different," the novelist Jean Giono reported in a letter home shortly after he had been invalided out of the action in June. The new direction in which his thinking would eventually take him was spelled out very clearly in his pacifist writing of the 1930s, but his correspondence in 1916 offered barely a clue to what was on his mind. Boasson was hardly more communicative. He went to Verdun in April an ardent Catholic, monarchist and nationalist, but what exactly had Verdun made him when he left in August? His letters to his wife confided little beyond the mere fact of his anger and depression, and this only with reluctance: "I would rather tell you nothing of the terrible weakness that the war has bred in me. It's as if I were crushed, diminished."

Such reticence was typical. Most of those who recorded their experience of Verdun on the spot, or even a good number of years after the event, were as silent about what it had changed in them as the columns of troops making their way back down the Voie Sacrée.

Some of their reasons for it were circumstantial: letters home were read by the postal censor and, anyway, the feelings of their relatives had to be spared. Yet this consideration did not always stop their letters home from being graphic about the physical horror of Verdun. The psychological horror was a different matter, for the journey out of shock was much longer than the journey away from the battlefield. Even when men did attempt to convey what they felt, there could still be the wartime censor to reckon with. But most important of all was their sense that what they had been through was not just *inénarrable*, in the sense that it was too revolting to describe, but in a larger sense *indescriptible*: beyond description. The word and all its synonyms echo through the writing about Verdun by combatants and veterans, not in casual hyperbole but in repeated warning of what lay beyond their powers—perhaps, indeed, the limits of articulacy. And to the sense that what they might wish to tell was probably untellable, and would anyway not be understood by anyone who had not been there, was added another belief: that what they had learned should remain a secret among the initiates. What Verdun did to men was a masonic rite, fierce and exclusive.*

So Raymond Jubert was in a sense breaking the code when he tried to set down as clearly as he could the difference between the battle he had come to fight and the battle he had found himself fighting. As the epigraph to this chapter testifies, he was also running the risk of making the wartime censor angry and his publisher nervous: junior officers were not supposed to talk to generals about psychology. This is not to claim that the disillusionment he had suffered somewhere between his first and second tours of duty on Le Mort-Homme was either complete or ideologically pointed. He had not meant to be subversive, nor did he yet know quite how far toward subversion his new perspective might lead. Verdun must be

---

* The writer Gabriel Chevallier (of *Clochemerle*) did not fight at Verdun but his experience at the Chemin des Dames in 1917 taught him a stance toward the uninitiated that any veteran of Verdun could recognize. "We tell them the story of *their* war, the one that will keep them happy, and guard our secret," says the narrator of his autobiographical novel *La Peur*. And so: "On top of all the concessions we have granted the war, we are adding that of our sincerity. Since the value of our sacrifice cannot be recognized, we feed the legend, and snigger."

held: there was still no question in his mind about that. Verdun must be held because France must hold; to him the war was still a necessary task. Yet the determination to fight it had been severed from its familiar moorings in the imagery and rhetoric that supported pious nationalism and even the idea of war itself.

Previously Jubert's notion of battle, he admitted, had been nourished by what the French call the *imagerie d'Épinal*, the town of Épinal being famous for producing cheaply colored prints of military scenes:

> I used to imagine the magnificent part played by the infantryman, heroism in battle every day, the bitter joy of combat, danger defied and overcome, the brilliant leading role of the man who hurls his chest against the bullets, the heroic charges, the uniforms giving colour to the field of death and, amid all this vast, brightly lit activity, little scenes in which men's lives are made glorious and brought to an end, the blood blossoming in the sunlight, the river Meuse running red with corpses, and when the moon rises in the evening, the white faces of the dead covering the ground in their thousands.

This is certainly every bit as overdrawn and overcolored as anything that came out of Épinal, and no doubt a good deal cruder than Jubert's imaginings had really been. It is in the nature of disillusionment to caricature the illusion that went before. Yet even on 9 April, when he had looked up at the bombardment of Le Mort-Homme, Jubert's eye had still sought out beauty and the sort of beauty, moreover, appropriate to a picture on the grand scale. By May he had given up the attempt. Battle, he had faced, was not made up of "those great tragic tableaux, boldly outlined and brightly coloured, in which death is just a brushstroke, but of melancholy little scenes and, in obscure corners, of little heaps in which one cannot be at all sure if the mud is flesh or the flesh is mud."

This was certainly faithful to the infantryman's experience. The infantry glimpse the big picture only from time to time, if at all;

usually they see only the detail. And in seeing that at Verdun, they were seeing into the heart of the battle. The commanders planned and directed it on the grand scale, and historians often still describe it in terms of sheer size: so many troops, so many guns, so many dead. But the statistics of Verdun disguise its real character. Typically, it was fought by small units of men in small actions, like Driant and his *chasseurs* in the Bois des Caures or Jubert and the handful left of his company on Le Mort-Homme. Often they did not know where the enemy was, or even exactly where they themselves were. For much of the time they were out of contact with their regimental commanders and, even when they were not, they got little help or information to relieve their sense of isolation.

"The infantryman has no function except to get himself crushed," Jubert had concluded: "he dies without glory, without any feeling of *élan* in his heart, at the bottom of a hole, far away from any witness." The opening bombardment of 21 February had driven home to the front-line troops their utter insignificance and powerlessness; the realization would stay with them, as the most humiliating part of their ordeal, throughout the fighting. Jubert was ready to raise it to the status of a new military doctrine: even when the infantry go on the attack "all they are doing is to act as a standard-bearer marking the zone of superiority established by the artillery." Stated thus baldly, this smacks of the infantry's traditional prejudice against gunners, raised in the First World War to a new pitch of mingled envy and resentment. The gunners had an easy time of it, so the common account from the *poilus* ran: they rode up to the battle on horseback while the *poilus* had to slog through the mud, they stayed safely behind the front lines while the *poilus* were exposed at the sharp end, they wielded all the real power while avoiding all the real suffering.

It was, of course, an exaggeration. Though their casualty rate was lower than that of the infantry, gunners suffered and died too. Captain Pierre de Mazenod, who lost half his unit in the two weeks it spent with the other gun batteries on the southern slopes of the Côte Saint-Michel, recorded:

> The men are stretched to the limit. They move like automatons from the shelters to the guns, then from the guns to the shelters, doing this ten, twenty times a day, beneath a raging, relentless bombardment. In this short journey, I have seen men collapse with exhaustion and lie there, exposed to the shelling, until a comrade goes to find them and carries them back to the guns, where they resume the same routine as the rest.

Firepower might kill, as Pétain insisted, yet it was always less crushingly effective than the weight of the guns and the caliber of the shells promised. Jubert himself had discovered on the way up Le Mort-Homme in April that the steel barrier of shells seeming to bar his way was in fact random and patchy enough to be penetrated. Gunners like Mazenod knew how often the artillery was "blind and impotent." They knew what it was like to discover that the range they had been using, based on garbled or mistaken or outdated intelligence, was too long or, even worse, too short. They knew what it was like to be unable to answer the distress signals sent up by their infantry or, most disconcerting of all, to find that the enemy was too close to be fired on.

Yet, even when these qualifications have been registered, Jubert's discovery of powerlessness—the powerlessness not just of the infantry but virtually of the whole army at Verdun—remains true in a deeper sense, as a description of both a psychological ordeal and a tactical dilemma. *Élan*, so dear to the French soul, and all the other warrior virtues no longer decided anything. The French occupied a trench on top of Le Mort-Homme until the April morning when the Germans drove them out; Jubert and his men recaptured it. And a month later he was posted back to the same sector to fight essentially the same battle over essentially the same small patch of ground, pushing forward and being pushed back, in the same ebb and flow.

All that was left, it seemed, was *tenir*. The word had begun its life in February in announcing both a large strategic decision and a precise local order: telling the nation and the world that Verdun must and would be held, ordering the troops to hold the ground where they stood regardless of the cost. As Jacques Péricard remarked, it soon grew into a mantra: a word endlessly repeated, a word whose meaning lay increasingly in its repetition. By the time Jubert returned, disillusioned, to Le Mort-Homme it signified simply a blind commitment to endure. *Tenir* was more and more becoming *se tenir*, the verb that Guy Hallé used in the description I quoted earlier of the men's forced smile as they went into action. "On doit se tenir correctement devant la mort," they reminded themselves: "You have to behave properly in the presence of death." If Verdun had any grandeur or any beauty left for men like Jubert, it lay in the long effort to keep going. The real contest, he had come to believe, was not about ground after all—which might seem a bizarre conclusion to reach of a battle so deeply invested in ground and every shade of significance that ground could hold. Yet he had a point and a reason for making it through hyperbole: Verdun was not "an effort in space" but "an effort in time."

✛ ✛ ✛

Mangin's boys are terrible boys
Who never flinch from a fight!
Mangin's boys attack furiously,
Ready to die *pour la Patrie*!
>> Refrain of "Les Gâs d'Mangin," 1916,
>> by the patriotic songwriter Théodore Botrel
>> (to music by André Caplet)

You did your duty and I cannot blame you. You would not be the man you are if you had not acted in the way you did.
>> Pétain to General Charles Mangin,
>> on the attack on the Fort de Douaumont,
>> 22–24 May

Whether regarded in terms of space or time, Verdun was always a shapeless battle. The Germans had given it a definite, dramatic start with their opening bombardment in February. Their capture of the

Fort de Douaumont a few days later had set the final seal on both sides' commitment to the struggle. To the Germans it had come as an augury of victory, albeit a victory that might take longer than they had hoped. To the French it had come as a blow to national pride, making any lingering thought of withdrawal impossible. Yet what followed at Verdun obeyed no discernible pattern of development, certainly none apparent to those trained in classic notions of how battles unfold their story. The Crown Prince had always wanted such a story, arguing that the attack should be launched against both banks of the Meuse at once. To make sense, Verdun should be a proper "battle of the wings." Pétain agreed, fretting for the battle of the wings to start. He made a point of asking his staff first thing each morning what was happening, not on the right bank, but the left. Something was bound to happen there, if the Germans knew their business.

The Crown Prince did know his business. He began his attack there on 6 March and for the next month made it his particular goal to capture Cote 304 and Le Mort-Homme, the two hills commanding the terrain—and the approach to the city of Verdun—in the same fashion that the Fort de Douaumont and its plateau commanded the right bank. By then the Prince had managed to winkle out of Falkenhayn at least some of the extra reserves he had always wanted, the reserves whose absence had delayed his progress even in the opening days of the battle. But his second hammer-blow, like his first on 21 February, fell just too late and too lightly to have the impact he desired. The French defenses were still patchy and, particularly in the woods at the base of the hills, relied on soldiers who had spent too long in what had so far been quiet positions; some had been there virtually since the outbreak of the war. Yet Pétain was determined to prove that every inch of ground would be bitterly disputed: of the ten counterattacks he personally ordered during March and April, six were made on the left bank. So the Germans had broadened their front without furthering their goal. By 6 March hope of a quick victory had already begun to fade; even the aggressively optimistic had been adjusting their ideas of

(Right) The Crown Prince with Lieutenant von Brandis.

(Below) Kaiser Wilhelm II and the Crown Prince at the Western Front.

POILUS

(Right) Poster by Abel Faivre.

(Below) Corporal Marc Stéphane

(Right) Detail from a drawing by J. Simont.

(Left) Napoléon I.

(Right) Napoléon III.

(Above) Marianne the republican.

(Left) Marianne the revolutionary.

One of Géricault's early sketches for the Raft of the Medusa.

The Eternal Quarrel: French or German?

"What French elegance there is in her beauty . . . Ah! These Alsatian girls are of real French blood!"

"The blond hair, the upright bearing, the confident walk . . . That Alsatian girl has a truly Germanic figure. Everything is German, real German, right to the marrow."

The Germanization of Alsace.

THE LANDSCAPE OF DEATH

(Above) Corpse in a ravine near the Fort de Vaux.

(Left) Malancourt, c. March 1916.

(Right) Le Mort-Homme, April 1916.

(Left) French troops in the Bois de la Caillette.

(Below) French troops at the entrance of Fort de Douaumont, October 1916.

(Below) The destroyed village of Ornes.

(Above left) General Mangin at his headquarters, June 1916.

(Above) Lieutenant Alfred Joubaire.

(Left) La Défense, ou l'Appelle aux Armes by Auguste Rodin.

when victory might come. Now decisive advantage was growing elusive.

A battle without apparent development, even development favoring his own side, was agreeable to Pétain. He had come to Verdun ready to play a waiting game, neither expecting nor wanting the lines marking the front on the map to alter greatly from day to day. Once the first crisis on the right bank had passed and the assault on the left bank been met, time lay on the defenders' side. More troops and fresh troops had to be brought up, not once but in a regular flow down the Voie Sacrée; artillery strength had to be built up, starting from a desperately low base. Guns and ammunition had to be hauled from other sectors of the Western Front, deployed and set to work, stopping the Germans in their tracks, hammering away at their weak points. If the work continued long enough, then the day would come when the initiative would pass to the French and they could push the enemy back from Verdun.

This was Pétain's plan, his definition of *tenir*, and it promised a bloody and exacting battle. The positions he had fixed were to be defended *coûte que coûte*: regardless of cost. If essential positions were lost, they had to be recaptured as soon as possible, *coûte que coûte*. Attacks, though local and precise, were to be launched where tactical interest made it desirable or further proof of French determination was needed. But local and precise attacks do not move the broad lines of the front on the maps, and the prospect of waiting patiently for the day when Pétain judged that those lines could be moved did not appeal to those above or those immediately below him. It did not satisfy the spirit of *élan*. In Joffre *élan* combined with jealous fear that Verdun was sucking away resources earmarked for the Somme. In commanders on the battlefield *élan* combined with personal ambition and the thirst for glory. Their pressure stopped Pétain from developing the battle as he had wanted. Day by day its story grew yet bloodier and more demanding; week by week and month by month it grew more shapeless. The result came close to throwing the army at Verdun into crisis.

The pressure from above had been present from the start.

Indeed, it was inherent in the very decision to defend the right bank, leaving Pétain's resources stretched so thinly over a front offering only the narrowest margin of ground for fixing his vital positions. It continued to make itself felt on even local decisions. When he reported, for example, that a German push near Béthincourt (on the left bank) had in fact eliminated a useless salient in the French lines, Joffre told him to retake the ground with "a vigorous and powerful offensive to be carried out as soon as possible." Pétain reminded him that "the choice of positions is of the highest importance. I therefore ask you to have confidence in me, and not to allow yourself to be alarmed by a few partial withdrawals which have been planned in advance."

He made this weary and stubborn plea in the first week of April. At the beginning of the month the pressure from below had intensified with the arrival of Generals Nivelle and Mangin. Nivelle commanded 3rd Corps and his subordinate Mangin the 5th Division, known throughout the army for capturing the village of Neuville-Saint-Vaast in the Artois offensive during the summer of 1915. Both men put their faith in *élan* and the doctrine of attack, though the difference in their personalities gave their beliefs a rather different flavor. At 58, Nivelle was a coming man with a gift for disguising old ideas in new formulae. His rise had been greatly helped by the suavity and confidence he brought to bear on superior officers and politicians; to the men in the ranks, or so one of them said, he appeared as stiff as if he had swallowed a sword. Several years younger than Nivelle, Mangin was a colonial veteran who had cut his teeth with the expeditionary force which had confronted the British at Fashoda. In 1916 he still breathed energy, daring and a burning hope of promotion; he reminded Henry Bordeaux (though the historian kept the impression for his private diary) of a wild boar about to charge.

Mangin usually was about to charge. He had barely got the 5th Division into position before he threw it into action. It was posted to the Souville sector, which guarded the ravines below the heights where the Fort de Douaumont stood, and its job was to plug the gaps in the lines that German sallies from the fort had been busy opening up. Jean Tocaben, captain in a regiment that had taken the brunt of the attacks, was admirably placed to appraise the situation, and knew the Germans were so well consolidated in their newly captured trenches that it would take a carefully planned bombardment to begin the business of dislodging them. He was eager to see how a general of Mangin's reputation and his troops, battle-hardened yet fresh to the field of Verdun, would handle the task.

Early on the morning of 3 April he watched in amazement and horror as a unit from Mangin's 9th Brigade advanced, not just without artillery preparation but without any clear idea of where the enemy was—unsupported, headed in the wrong direction, exposed to the light of the rising sun. It went, he said, "blindly to the slaughter":

> And on its polished helmets the morning sun broke in splashes of light and, clothing in splendour the men, the young men going to their deaths, covered them with a nimbus of glory and crowned them with a crest of fire. What a sublime, what a poignant sight!

His sense of the romantic, even religious, glory in the sacrifice did not prevent Tocaben from knowing what it must have seemed like to the Germans: "It's certainly a rare piece of luck to see troops coming at you deployed as if they were on maneuvers, and to shoot them at your leisure, without running the slightest risk."

Dangerously swashbuckling even by the standards of the day, Mangin's style of generalship always had its detractors as well as its admirers. He had been at Verdun less than a month when he was already complaining, in a letter to his wife, of his "ostracism" by fellow commanders in the field; a fortnight later he noted that people in Paris (he didn't know exactly who) were attacking him for getting too many men killed. A controversial reputation was one thing: Mangin plainly relished it, while still resenting the blight it might cast on his chances of promotion. Doubt or faintheartedness in those assigned to carry out his commands was another matter: *le mangeur des hommes* (the eater of men) he might be, but Mangin always prided himself on their enthusiastic loyalty. He made the same strenuous demands on himself that he made on them, and deliberately courted the same risks, refusing to stay safely behind the lines in the manner of other generals. His *poilus*, so he liked to claim, said: "He gets us in a pickle, but nobody is better at getting us out of it again."

Verdun was quickly eroding this belief, if in fact the men had ever held it. On the night of 4 April Mangin launched another attempt to dislodge the Germans and to push his line up to the plateau above. It made a particularly strenuous demand on Major Paul Lefebvre-Dibon and his unit, the 3rd Battalion of the 74th Infantry, part of the 9th Brigade whose troops Tocaben had seen being sacrificed only shortly before. Lefebvre-Dibon was new to his position in the Ravin du Bazil, which the men—like virtually all the other men in virtually all the other ravines at Verdun—knew as the Ravin de la Mort: the Ravine of Death.* His orders arrived in the early evening, only 35 minutes before he was due to start, leaving him no chance to make the preliminary reconnaissance prescribed for night attacks.

At 7:30 he duly set out with his men along the Ravin de la Caillette, struggling to advance over terrain made slippery by rain, pockmarked by shell-holes, littered with debris and raked by an intense barrage. On one flank they could not make contact with the 1st Battalion; on the other a company got mixed up with troops from the 2nd Battalion. By the early hours of the morning they had covered only about 400 meters of ground and reached the point of exhaustion; none of the men had any water and some had not eaten a proper meal for the last 48 hours. Worst of all, they were virtually lost. Starting out without any real sense of their bearings, they had missed the opening to a smaller gully which would take them up to the Bois de la Caillette, and now all they knew was that first light would probably find them sitting targets. Lefebvre-Dibon called off

* The only one to which the name stuck after the war is the Ravin de la Dame, north of Thiaumont and the present Mémorial-Musée.

the operation and turned back. The two adjoining battalions followed suit.

The Major was no panicky novice but a 50-year-old reservist; his
regimental colonel had already recommended that he be made a
chevalier of the Légion d'Honneur. Experience had probably told
him from the start that the hastily organized operation bore all the
signs of being a feint and that Mangin intended his real blow to fall
elsewhere. Even so, experience also made Lefebvre-Dibon fully
aware of the gravity of what he was doing—if you were ordered to
attack, you kept attacking until you reached your objective, got
killed or were told to stop—and he made no attempt to shirk responsibility for the decision. It earned him a stinging rebuke from
Mangin, delivered in writing to make clear it would be entered on
his record. Mangin noted sarcastically that, though Lefebvre-Dibon
claimed to have found it difficult rallying his men to get them to advance, he had no difficulty getting them to withdraw; he should
have stayed where he was and secured the ground he had taken. Ordered back into the attack, Lefebvre-Dibon did manage to reach the
Bois de la Caillette a few days later. His success had no tactical
meaning—Germans and French would continue to ebb and flow
over the ground for several months to come—but at least it removed some of the slur on his name. For the rest, all that he could
do was to take consolation from the support of his junior officers,
preserve the diary he had kept in the field and publish his own account once the war had ended.

For Lefebvre-Dibon the experience might have been important
enough to leave him anxious to vindicate himself, but at Verdun it
was no more than a detail—just another of those melancholy little
scenes acted out in obscure corners, of which Jubert wrote, and by
no means the most melancholy that the battlefield could show. By
itself it had little significance and no impact. Only later would it become clear that it had been a straw in the wind: a sign of how easily
the ordeal of holding Verdun, and holding it under bad generalship,
could breed doubt and disaffection among regimental officers, the
very men charged with ensuring that orders were carried out in the

field. For the time being, like the murmuring against him in Paris, it did no damage to Mangin. His bandwagon was firmly hitched to Nivelle's star, and Nivelle's star was rising.

At the beginning of May Joffre promoted Nivelle to Pétain's job commanding the armies at Verdun and kicked Pétain upstairs to General Langle de Cary's old job commanding the Groupe d'Armées du Centre, thus distancing him from the day-to-day running of the battle. Pétain knew exactly what his promotion meant. "Here you see a general who has just been relieved of his command. . . . I'm being told I'm not needed at Verdun any more," he exclaimed in an uncharacteristic outburst of public bitterness, in front of both Nivelle and a politician visiting his headquarters on the Voie Sacrée at Souilly, the headquarters he was about to leave for Bar-le-Duc. With his departure the *tourniquet*, assuring that regiments spent as short a time as possible in the firing line at Verdun, was abandoned. The measure, so fundamental to Pétain's waiting game and so exasperating to Joffre, was no longer deemed necessary. Nivelle—with Mangin, of course, backing him to the hilt—was confident that he could achieve quick results.

The immediate prize at which they aimed was the Fort de Douaumont. Its capture had put the Germans at a tactical advantage since February, giving them an observation post, an artillery position, a place of refuge and a jumping-off point for attack virtually on their front line. Yet to the French the fort had never been just a military position but (as Henry Bordeaux remarked in his diary) the object of a "cult," magnetizing their gaze. Like everything about Verdun, it had become a symbol; indeed, it lay close to the heart of the entire symbolism of Verdun. Its loss echoed the losses that France had suffered as a result of the Franco-Prussian War—the city of Metz, the rest of the annexed provinces—and reverberated with them in the imagination, summing up the humiliations that cried out to be avenged. Sullen lump of concrete and metal and earth though it might be, Douaumont was spoken of as if it were a living thing: a hostage, a captive taken by the enemy and suffering at their hands. Above all, Douaumont was as a woman: a beautiful French woman, another daughter of France abused and defiled.

Mangin had already made a hasty and futile sally at Douaumont in April, when the handful of men who got near the outworks and roof were easily brushed off by the defenders. Now, with Nivelle promoted, he soon found additional encouragement to hand. On 8 May a series of explosions wracked the depths of the fort, spreading from a box of hand grenades to the petrol canisters used in flamethrowers and, finally, to a magazine of artillery shells. Some 650 German soldiers died—underground, in darkness, blown to pieces, seared by fire or choked by smoke—in the worst disaster of its type that either army suffered at Verdun.* Mangin had no means of knowing exactly what had happened, but he recognized the dark plume of smoke rising above Douaumont as a signal of distress, proclaiming its vulnerability. The temptation was irresistible.

His plan of attack called for four divisions; in the event he was assigned only two, his own and, in reserve, General Lestoquoi's 36th. The reason given for withholding the others showed that Joffre's preoccupation could curb enthusiasm as well as patience at Verdun: "And what would be left for the Somme if so many men were used for this local objective?" The artillery at his disposal was less niggardly; indeed, at 300 pieces, it was the largest concentration that the French had so far mustered for a single operation at Verdun. Yet it was weak in the 75s needed to flatten the German trenches around the fort, and the new 370mm mortars which Mangin trusted would shatter the building itself lacked the weight for the job. A commander of one of the other forts, who knew from personal experience what pounding they could withstand, contemptuously asked one of Mangin's staff just how flimsy the General believed Douaumont was.

Mangin was the last man to appreciate the point and remained

---

* It was rivaled in horror on 4 September by the fate of the French soldiers using the Tavannes railway tunnel as command post, emergency hospital, garrison and place of refuge. In the fire set off by the explosion, men tried to scramble up the air vents and exposed themselves to German artillery at the tunnel mouth. Between 400 and 500 died.

confident. He enjoyed a reputation for the grim relish with which he spelled out the ordeal to come in briefing his officers. "Gentlemen, we attack tomorrow," he was supposed to have announced on one occasion:

> "The first wave will be killed.
> "The second also.
> "And the third.
> "A few men from the fourth will reach their objective.
> "The fifth wave will capture the position.
> "Thank you, gentlemen."

But this May he took a breezy tone, claiming that "the artillery preparation will allow us to reach the fort with our rifles over our shoulders, since the fort will be completely destroyed." The assurance proved as hollow as such assurances always did. All the preparation achieved was to give a final signal to the defenders of Douaumont, already alerted to French intentions by poor security, that the infantry assault would soon begin.

The infantry moved forward just before midday on 22 May. Mangin watched its progress through binoculars from the roof of the Fort de Souville, standing out in the open with his usual defiant negligence of his own safety or that of his staff officers. Four of them got hit by a German shell. Unhurt himself, the General was soon cheered by the sight of his men on the roof of Douaumont— so cheered that he rashly announced the successful recapture of the fort to Nivelle and thus, by the evening, to the world. He seems still to have believed in his victory the next morning and imagined that the reinforcements he threw in were merely consolidating it. In reality, the previous day's action had been a chaotic failure. The supporting attacks on the flanks had failed and the troops making the frontal assault on Douaumont had been caught in a narrow salient of their own making, exposed on three sides. Those who had actually managed to get on to the roof were steadily wiped out by sallies from below.

Just how completely the flank attacks had failed Major Lefebvre-

Dibon could, and did, testify. His regiment and the 274th, its sister regiment in the 9th Brigade, stood on the right of the line. The objective assigned jointly to his battalion and that commanded by Major Schaeffer was a cluster of trenches and a turret—the military maps label it Tourelle 3212—some 250 meters northeast of the fort. Neither Schaeffer's battalion nor the 274th regiment could even start out: they quickly found that the German positions immediately ahead of them were still intact and unleashing a withering fire which kept them, in a phrase that crops up dispiritingly often in stories of the battle, "nailed to the ground." At first Lefebvre-Dibon's battalion fared better, though one company was soon knocked off course and another reached Tourelle 3212 only to find itself pinned down by the defenders of the fort. At the cost of 10 of the 20 men in his immediate party, Lefebvre-Dibon himself managed to get to the large concrete depot which he had selected in advance as his command post.

"A horrible sight greeted my eyes," he later wrote. The depot was choked with splintered ammunition boxes, straw bedding, broken bottles, discarded rifles and the dismembered corpses of Germans who had sought refuge from the bombardment: "here a head, there a foot." Some wounded French troops had managed to drag themselves inside, and were soon joined by more wounded and by a party of Moroccan *tirailleurs*. One whole side of the depot had been hit by a shell and stood open to machine-gun fire, so Lefebvre-Dibon set about building a barricade with the debris. There was not much else he could do. He was under heavy fire, unsupported on either side and in only fragile, occasional contact with French lines. It was not reassuring to learn, in the course of the afternoon, that about half the men in his battalion were now dead, wounded or missing. Nor was it helpful, shortly after dark, to be ordered by the colonel of his regiment to continue the attack. Soon after midnight the Germans surrounding the depot began to close in. "How on earth is my poor battalion, crushed, decimated, going to manage to hold?" Lefebvre-Dibon asked himself, and then added, drawing from the memory of Sedan that still haunted the French imagination: "We're caught in a mousetrap!"

And so the men in the depot held the same sort of desperate, hasty conference that Lieutenant Robin, Corporal Stéphane and their little group of *chasseurs* had held in the Bois des Caures, the same conference held in a thousand obscure corners at Verdun. Lefebvre-Dibon made his position clear: "Fight, fight, right to the end, wait for reinforcements or a counterattack from our lines. There can be no question of surrendering." Surrender had no place in the rulebook; surrender was the ultimate shame. "A French officer dies but does not surrender!": more than one account of Verdun attributed these dying words to more than one hero, and the sentiment still weighed heavily on the Major. Yet surely the demands of *tenir* must end somewhere? Nobody believed that they could hold on to the depot by themselves. Nobody really believed that reinforcements would come to the rescue. And nobody really wanted to die. One man pleaded with Lefebvre-Dibon to surrender. He refused. Another took out his handkerchief and tied it to the end of his rifle. Lefebvre-Dibon hurled himself on the man, revolver in hand, and would have shot him—so he still believed afterward—if one of the junior officers had not intervened.

The group, Lefebvre-Dibon knew, had only a few minutes left to live. "I was fully aware of confronting the most frightful responsibility imaginable. I had to face it and I accepted it squarely." It was the same responsibility he had faced in the ravine, rendered graver and more urgent. And again his concern for the lives of those around him triumphed over orders, the rulebook and the code. He surrendered. Or so one gathers from his account, for despite his proud and honest words Lefebvre-Dibon still found the word almost too shameful to write, the act far too shameful to describe. This task was left to one of the junior officers present: "Major Lefebvre-Dibon headed for the German lines, holding up his revolver in a gesture of complete despondency. He threw it down and made a sign that he was giving himself up."

When it came to record his act, the regimental history was respectful and sympathetic: his battalion had suffered casualties of more than 70 percent and, rather than losing its honor, had "held to the limit of human powers." Major Lefebvre-Dibon was careful to cite these words and these figures in his account. The figures were not much worse than those recording what had happened to the 5th Division as a whole in the attempt to take Douaumont, the bloodiest engagement it fought in the entire war. Out of 12,000 men it had lost almost 5,500: nearly 900 killed, nearly 2,900 wounded and another 1,600 reported missing (many of them, like Lefebvre-Dibon, taken prisoner). Just how little he had left was growing apparent to Mangin in the course of 24 May. In the morning he threw in his last reserves and appealed to Nivelle, without success, for two more battalions. In the afternoon General Lebrun, who had stepped into Nivelle's shoes as commander of 3rd Corps, telephoned him to order a new attack. "With what?" he tersely replied. Lebrun repeated the order and Mangin lost his temper: "I don't make second-rate attacks, I don't attack without attacking, really attacking up to the hilt." Lebrun relieved him of his command.

Though Mangin thought it "odious," Lebrun's action was not nearly so grave as the rebuke Mangin himself had delivered to Lefebvre-Dibon. It merely brought forward arrangements already in place for General Lestoquoi of the 35th Division to take over command of the battle at the end of the day. Nor did it leave Mangin lingering in disgrace, for he was soon back in action, unrepentant. "My *poilus*, reduced by half, want more," he boasted in a letter to his wife: "They are saying that with their general at the head they'd go back in again. They were magnificent." However magnificent they might have been, the burden of extreme and inflexible generalship had already been growing intolerable—and not just for the *poilus* in the ranks but also for the junior regimental officers charged with making sure that the generals' orders were carried out, to the hilt, to the end, regardless of cost. Now the cracks were starting to open up among the generals issuing the orders.

All these signs of strain could only multiply in June. In March and April the Germans had turned their attention to the left bank, and been met by the French. Then the French had pushed forward on the right bank, and been met by the Germans. Now, in a battle always costly, never static, never decisive, it was the Germans' turn to push forward on the right bank. Just as the immediate French goal had been Douaumont, so the immediate German goal was its neighbor, the Fort de Vaux. After enduring a week of siege in the most desperate conditions, the fort's commander was forced to yield on 7 June. He passed into honorable captivity—the Crown Prince granted him an audience to salute his bravery—still proudly insisting that it was not the Germans who had made him surrender: it was thirst.

Thirst and the huge flies gathering on the corpses gave this middle period of the battle its distinctive flavor of suffering, just as cold and mud had typified its start. They could somehow blend together in the minds of those who suffered: even the water ration (when it finally came) tasted of dead men, or so Captain Charles Delvert thought. Yet the essentials of his ordeal would have been all too familiar to Jubert, stranded after his victory on Le Mort-Homme, or Lefebvre-Dibon, struggling to convince himself he could hold the depot near Douaumont. Delvert and the company he commanded in the 101st Infantry were sent to the front on 31 May in the attempt to save Vaux. His position, on the edge of the plateau a couple of hundred meters from the fort, was known to the men who made the decisions as R1: *Retranchement*, or Entrenchment, 1. What Delvert found was a chunk of concrete wall split by a shell (from a French 75, he was sure) and some collapsed trenches choked with dead (the company that he was relieving had lost 15 men in the previous four days). The Germans were occupying the trench only about 20 meters ahead and beyond that, across the ravine, he could see them advancing across the Plateau d'Hardaumont "like ants when you kick an anthill over."

Delvert and his company spent five days at R1, three of them without any sleep at all, and several of them without food. Reinforcement or relief, like food, was always being promised but never seemed to arrive, except for a young lieutenant persuaded that his 40 or so men amounted to a full-strength company. The shells that rained down came from French as well as German guns. Most worrying of all, the Germans were gaining hold of the ravines to his left and penetrating the heights of the Bois Fumin to his rear without challenge from French artillery. "Are we going to be caught in a mousetrap?" he worried, summoning up the terrible, abiding memory of Sedan, the same chord of national memory that Lefebvre-Dibon had struck.

In the event he was not surrounded, though the units defending the *retranchements* lower down the side of the plateau were. Relief at last arrived, and Delvert took his company back: jumping from shell-hole to shell-hole, passing trenches filled with French dead, negotiating the Bois Fumin with particular care since he had, as he put it, "no wish to go to Baden-Baden." So few had survived that the company was, in the military phrase, rolled up; its remnants were absorbed into other units. Delvert himself was made a chevalier of the Légion d'Honneur, but at the time the only reaction to reaching safety which he troubled to record in his diary was: "End of martyrdom." At Verdun it was the habit of those who came through to speak of themselves as if they had actually died.

Reports, not of Delvert's martyrdom in R1 but of the dangers threatening the men in nearby R3, had prompted Nivelle to order General Lebrun's 3rd Corps to mount a relief operation. It failed in the early hours of 2 June and again in the early hours of the next day. Lebrun pleaded for fresh units and got his wish, but also a note from Nivelle which demanded to be read with some care:

> I do not doubt that, despite the darkness, the barrage might have been violent enough to stop the progress of a unit firmly resolved to achieve its objective at any price, since it consisted of reopening contact with our own men surrounded by the enemy.
>
> It would not enter my mind to reproach units which have proved their bravery and skill so many times that nothing now justifies me in doubting them. Yet perhaps these men and these commanders had not been sufficiently filled with the importance of their mission, of its sacred character, since it consisted of going to the help of comrades still valiantly standing up to the enemy.

To these reflections may be added others still more important arising from the general situation. It will be your responsibility to make the importance of this mission understood, to raise the morale of the units which will be charged with restoring normality and whose action should be launched with all the power and speed required to assure its success.

When Lefebvre-Dibon, a major in charge of a battalion, had judged the order he received impossible he got a stinging rebuke from Mangin, a general in charge of a division. When Mangin, now in charge of a group of divisions, had judged the order he received impossible he got a mild rebuke from Lebrun, a general in charge of a corps. Now Lebrun in his turn found on his desk what was, for all its suavity, still identifiably some sort of rebuke. At the higher levels of military command an etiquette of courtesy usually prevails, and Nivelle—proceeding by a series of elaborate disclaimers—had been careful not to breach it. Yet his note also made clear that the process of recrimination was spreading to those higher levels.

It had progressed up the ranks because frustration and unease, too obvious to be ignored, were taking hold of the army at Verdun. Virtually all observers were agreed on that. Nivelle's own view of the problem was, predictably, that somebody somewhere was not trying hard enough. His diagnosis proceeded directly from the military doctrine of will and the narrow conception of morale it entailed. If orders were not successfully carried out, the fault lay not in the orders but in the spirit in which they had been carried out. This did not mean that the men in the ranks were made to shoulder the blame. Indeed, Nivelle's note is striking evidence that, however misunderstood and ill-used they might have felt themselves to be, the *poilus* at Verdun had by their suffering already gained a reputation that made them virtually sacrosanct.

Generals might privately judge this unit or that to be weak, or (as Pétain himself would do in June) lament that the best troops had already died and that those who remained were second-rate. Yet, when a difficult action had failed, they pointed the finger of accusation elsewhere. Commanders like Nivelle believed that the problems in their army stemmed from poor leadership, though not of course the leadership they themselves were providing. It stemmed from the regimental officers and particularly the junior regimental officers—men like the earnest Lefebvre-Dibon, and perhaps the disillusioned Jubert—who were failing to strike the right patriotic, aggressive, or inspirational note and instill it in their men.

Not everyone could be expected to agree with this simple diagnosis and the remedy it so readily suggested—the remedy that Nivelle, for all his roundabout style, firmly instructed Lebrun to put into immediate effect. The *poilus* and the men who led them in the field could not: they were already sick of people who combined large tribute to their suffering with failure to understand its nature. Nor could those in Paris who had been murmuring against commanders like Mangin for getting so many of the *poilus* and their junior regimental officers killed. In their different fashions, both groups were growing more determined to be heard. Their voices— as much as anything the Germans did, though the Germans were far from inactive—would make June a month of crisis at Verdun.

✛   ✛   ✛

"The patience of Europeans in this war says a lot about the debasement into which they have sunk. They have grown profoundly lax and they have lost any sense of what is human. Imagine what Socrates or Montaigne would have done at Douaumont. People no longer know what war is, any more than they know what architecture or love are."

> Spoken by the title character in
> Pierre Drieu La Rochelle, *Le Lieutenant de tirailleurs*
> (*The Lieutenant of Colonial Infantry*), published with
> *La Comédie de Charleroi*, 1932

Défaillance is a large word, meaning "breakdown" or "weakness." The French used it for a whole range of offenses against military discipline, great and small, which might variously indicate inadequacy or disaffection: anything from failure to return from leave to desertion, abandonment of post, and open mutiny. In the widest sense, it could be applied to an army that did not look up to its job. *Défaillance* entered the vocabulary of Verdun early on. How could it not have done? The German attack fell on an army which still prided itself on the doctrine of attack, but found itself defending inadequate trenches and undermanned forts. It fell on a nation which still prided itself on its greatness, now suddenly reminded how close lay the abyss. There was no reassurance to be had in the first days when Germans advanced and the French retreated or died, when Douaumont was taken. Nor did the fear of *défaillance* ever recede as the army and the nation began to measure the cost of *tenir*, in simply hanging on to what they held, and measure too the cost of *élan*, in trying to get back what they had lost.

The Germans' delay in widening their front to the left bank gave Pétain a vital chance for preparation, yet the defense he mustered there was still fragile. An attack on the Bois des Cumières and the Bois de Corbeaux, offering access to Le Mort-Homme, easily overwhelmed the 67th Division on 6 and 7 March. Men fled crying "Sauve qui peut!" and, though some were regrouped, more than 3,000 of them were taken prisoner. On 20 March the 29th Division fared no better in the Bois de Malancourt and the Bois d'Avocourt, west of Cote 304, collapsing almost as completely and offering almost as many prisoners to the Germans. From such disasters came, in part, Pétain's readiness to authorize counterattack more freely on the left bank than the right, but also talk of *défaillance*. To be sure, some units had simply lost their edge by being left too long in inactive sectors; others had arrived to take up their positions already worn down by the fighting of 1915. These points were made—and would continue to be made—by generals sympathetic to the difficulties of their men or eager to excuse themselves. The extenuation helped to deflect a good deal of the blame from the *poilus*. Yet the conduct of the 29th Division, in particular, prompted darker rumors and more sinister charges. Men, it was said, had been deserting in droves before they were attacked; men had been in touch with the enemy, arranging their surrender in advance. An entire regiment had simply "given up."

This blunt phrase, and the pressure for official inquiry, came not from the generals at Verdun but from President Poincaré in Paris. His attention frequently turned to the possibility of *défaillance*, as it did to the precise extent of the losses, and he appreciated that in such matters he needed to know more than Joffre chose to tell him or he himself could pick up on his own, largely ceremonial, visits to the battlefield. He quizzed his liaison officer at Joffre's headquarters and cultivated his own sources of information. They did not greatly help him gauge the losses. The last week of May found him skeptical of the casualty figures Pétain had supplied, grim enough though they were and inclined though he was to trust Pétain. The battle so far, it appeared, had left 600 officers and 22,743 men dead, 1,944 officers and 73,000 men wounded, 1,000 officers and 53,000 men missing. (The last category, of course, included those taken prisoner.) But another source suggested that the wounded came to a much higher figure of 103,000. Were the wounded sometimes included among the missing, or did they leave the battlefield without being counted at all? There was no way for Poincaré to tell.

Other politicians, and historians after them, have wrestled with just such problems in finding out how many casualties a given battlefield has claimed. But before then Poincaré had already made his mind up about *défaillance*. There was definitely a problem of morale at Verdun and the answer to it lay in officers maintaining closer contact with their men, to make sure they understood how vital their task was to the nation. The conclusion was the same as Nivelle's and hence open to the same objection. It was precisely those officers who were closest to their men—indeed, identified with them rather than with the superiors giving the orders—who were most likely to husband lives in operations that seemed futile. By abandoning an attack that stood no chance or surrendering when defense had become meaningless, they contributed to what was labeled *défaillance*.

Joffre differed from Poincaré and Nivelle in the view he reached at the beginning of June. Brought grudgingly to acknowledge that "symptoms of lassitude and discouragement" were making themselves felt, and brought grudgingly to concede that tiredness, depression and heavy losses had played their part, he reserved the real blame for the press. Morale was being lowered by remarks in the newspapers criticizing French weaponry and, worse still, French generals. Such criticism was by then an extremely sore point with him. In the middle of May two articles—slipping past the censor, to everybody's surprise—had publicly challenged his conduct of the battle in February and alleged that he had been willing to see the right bank of the Meuse overrun. One had even credited General de Castelnau alone with saving the day. Few people seem to have known who the pseudonymous "A Combatant" and "One in the Know" really were, but the rumors flying around in political circles showed just how deep discontent now ran and how widespread the urge to recriminate had grown. General Galliéni, the Minister of War willing to question Joffre's judgment, had died in the spring but his friends survived and were being joined by other enemies of Joffre. "It's enough to make one weep," exclaimed Poincaré in his diary.

Neither he nor his Prime Minister, Aristide Briand, could resist the pressure, and on 16 June the Chamber of Deputies began meeting in secret session to conduct its own inquiries. In these Comités Secrets, which extended over many months, the main concern was always Joffre's conduct of the war. In June by far the most powerful attack came from André Maginot: not just the voice but the living embodiment of disillusioned and outraged patriotism, no mere politician but Sergeant Maginot, still walking on sticks from the wounds he had received near Verdun in 1914. According to him, Joffre's *gringotage*—the nibbling away at the enemy which was the Commander-in-Chief's own version of *usure*—had proved both a failure and sham: "a war interrupted by partial offensives resulting in no significant strategic gain but, on the contrary, in the most murderous losses." The casualty rate, even as officially conceded by both sides, showed the French losing almost as many men on their single front as the Germans were in both the west and the east.

This massive indictment took force and precision from Verdun, "symbolic" to Maginot as it was in one sense or another to everybody, but in his case as "the proof of inadequacy and short-sightedness in our High Command." The plain truth, he charged, was that Verdun had been "a huge failure" in which the only ray of hope came from "the heroism of our troops." In support of his charge he made the assembled deputies privy to the letter Colonel Driant had written in August 1915 and to Joffre's lordly dismissal of its warning. The standing ovation which greeted the mention of Driant's name did not just pay tribute to a dead hero but also acknowledged Maginot as his heir. Nor was it just dead heroes who informed his words. He and the other critics who joined their voice to his knew what the men still fighting said. They knew all about the appalling conditions, the pitiful pay, the leave promised and delayed. Above all, they knew all about the feeling among the troops that "for the last 18 months they have been thrown, time after time, into the furnace, with no result."

The Comités Secrets left Joffre's reputation fatally wounded. The time had long since gone when he could brush aside questions from a Minister of War; the time he had left in power was drawing to its close. Yet his slow and majestic fall did nothing for the troops at Verdun in June, when his critics were only beginning their work. There the anger grew but so did the sense of helplessness. Both feelings were expressed in the way the troops were coming to use the word "sacrifice." In their mouths it could take two forms: *on se sacrifie* or *on est sacrifié*, one sacrifices oneself or one is sacrificed. To sacrifice oneself is a voluntary act, requiring consent if not exactly choice. Muenier had seen the men of 20th Corps, from all the different regions of France, preparing for just such an act in February. Instinctively, he had found in them an epitome of France, at least in one tradition of how the nation understood itself: a voluntary group, brought together by its awareness of the need to be a group and the importance of its common ideals. Even Barrès' deterministic view of the nation—as a group made and shaped by forces beyond the power of its members—still in practice demanded some sort of acceptance, some degree of awareness. ("A nationalist," he had written, "is a Frenchman who has become aware of how he has been formed. Nationalism is the acceptance of a determinism.") But being sacrificed demanded nothing, except one's death: it was blind, brutal, and perhaps pointless.

How, then, could discontent and disillusionment express themselves beyond the small shift in usage that increasingly transformed *on se sacrifie* into *on est sacrifié*? The place to look for signs of *défaillance*—as the generals were looking, in growing nervousness—was not the battlefield itself. The battlefield was no place to register deliberate protest. There the etiquette of *on ne lâche pas en ligne* (you don't give way when you're at the front) still kept a good deal of its force, sustained by personal pride and group loyalty if by nothing else. Surrender was usually the only form of *défaillance* likely to be available—and the question of surrender, as we have seen, was broached in terms of sheer survival, not protest, and even then only with anguish. What happened at the base camps when men learned they were being posted to Verdun, or the barracks when men learned they had to return, was another matter. The incidence of desertion increased. Mutinies occurred, though they were small and short-lived, like that involving 50 men from the 140th Infantry Regiment in the middle of May.*

It was enough, at any rate, to guarantee that commanders already alarmed grew more so. Robert Desaubliaux, second lieutenant in a machine-gun unit, recorded several incidents illustrating the mood of the men. Since they occurred in April and concerned troops of the 5th Division they showed how unlike the loyal warriors of Mangin's imagination some of them had always been. When the division was posted to Verdun the troops in Desaubliaux's unit got drunk, sung patriotic songs and wept. One followed the column

---

* That culprits received short sentences, and that sentences were usually suspended, showed the dilemma in which the authorities stood, not their leniency: the best way to punish men who did not want to fight at Verdun was to make them fight at Verdun.

as it marched along, making bleating noises: "Baa . . . Baa . . . I'm a sheep being led to the slaughter!" But he seems to have been the group's clown and Desaubliaux did not take him seriously. A few days later, however, other men were starting to say things like, "I'd rather clear out, it doesn't matter where." These he did take more seriously. "Come on, comrades," he remonstrated, "let's not forget we're here for the sake of France." In other words he attempted just the sort of invigorating reminder that Nivelle would shortly urge on junior officers. The irony was that Desaubliaux himself, like Jubert and so many other junior officers, was already on his way to disillusionment.

Neither Desaubliaux nor any of his men did clear out, or show any real sign of trying to. If anything, men in action grew not less but more concerned to carry out their orders, however great the burden of their absoluteness. On the face of it, of course, military orders are always absolute. They do not tell men to do such and such a thing if they can, or to do the best they can; they tell them to go and do it. Yet below the language of command there lies, implicitly, a certain leeway of tolerance—the leeway, in fact, where both men and armies survive. Men ordered to do the impossible can still be praised for doing the best they can; even those who surrender can still receive an honorable mention in the regimental history. But at Verdun this leeway of tolerance, already reduced by the military ethos of the day and the special urgency of the battle, was shrinking almost to nothing. The characteristic reaction of the troops, for all their discontent and even anger, was a particular sort of terrified compliance.

Before Captain Jean Tocaben watched men from the 5th Division marching like lambs to the slaughter, he had already undergone his own ordeals in the front line. "As always, the order was to hold our position until relieved." When one section of his trench came under bombardment, he moved his men to a safe stretch, and when this came under bombardment in its turn, he moved them out altogether and waited for the danger to pass. There might seem nothing remarkable about these expedients, but Tocaben agonized about them both, particularly the second. It offended against the prevailing wisdom that once men are allowed to start moving back, they can be difficult to stop. (On this score, Tocaben shrewdly remarked: "Under fire, any movement naturally takes on the character of flight, even movement forward.") Far more grave, his action infringed the letter of his orders. And at Verdun any infringement of the letter, however obedient it might still be to the spirit, required the most elaborate and careful justification:

> The responsibility I had just taken on myself was formidable, and besides, for me, unprecedented. Here the order was: hold the position. In executing a shifting manoeuvre, I had interpreted the order. I had a right to. The order to hold, which is completed by the obligation to retake lost ground, includes the possibility of moving and even, momentarily, of moving backwards.

Captain La Chaussée encountered a similar case of nerves when he was fighting near Fleury in the third week of June. A German attack began and La Chaussée ordered one of his men to report it to the colonel in his regimental command post. The man refused to go unless he had the order in writing. He was, quite simply, scared of being found moving away from the action without proof that he was obeying a command rather than abandoning his position. Nor in this case was the precise reason for fear far to seek. As La Chaussée's unit was going up to its position a week earlier, it had encountered a party of gravediggers at work by a railway embankment and heard the story they had to tell. The story was making the rounds of the battlefield—changed, mutilated, quite possibly exaggerated in the telling—and, since it was excised from the official record, its details are still hard to reconstruct.

Lieutenant Herduin, a career soldier who had won the Médaille Militaire, and Second Lieutenant Milan, a graduate of Saint-Cyr, fought with their regiment for five days near Thiaumont. It suffered 20 hours of German bombardment, French artillery fire, and a German assault that dislodged it from its position. With about 80 percent of its men dead, wounded or missing, it was not just "ineffective": it was virtually wiped out. When Herduin called for reinforcements on the afternoon of 8 June he was simply instructed to retake his original position. By nine o'clock that evening the unit due to relieve him had not arrived and Herduin conferred with Milan. They probably suspected that they had been forgotten when the remnants of neighboring units from their regiment had been relieved, and they were probably right. They took their surviving men—about 40 in all—back to barracks in the suburbs of Verdun. There Herduin wrote a letter to his wife hinting at how grim the last few days had been and expressing relief at still being alive. The next day they discovered that what remained of their battalion was in the Bois de Fleury and set off to rejoin it.

On their arrival Herduin and Milan learned that their brigade commander, Colonel Bernard, had ordered their immediate execution for abandoning their post. Both men were plainly surprised to find themselves charged with any offense and Herduin, at least, seems to have believed himself the victim of a misunderstanding that could be cleared up. Given what is known of his record, it seems unlikely that he was simply being naïve. It is surely more probable that he was ignorant of the special circumstances of Verdun, and that his experience as a soldier made it hard for him to adjust to a battle where there was none of the usual leeway of tolerance, no room for the sort of initiative he had tried to exercise. He was certainly in no position to grasp the background to the fate of his regiment. The division to which it belonged was one of those dispatched in answer to General Lebrun's plea for reinforcements on 3 June and, as well as this tangible help, Lebrun had also received his rebuke from Nivelle. Neither the extra divisions nor the rebuke had produced anything like the results desired. Far from improving, the tactical position had grown worse with the loss of the Fort de Vaux; as for the psychological position, junior officers had not yet got the message. In other words, it was time to find scapegoats.

Herduin and Milan's fellow officers were sympathetic enough to spend the rest of the day in communication with Bernard, who in turn got in touch with the divisional commander, General Boyer. The next morning Herduin wrote to his wife, assuring her that "my comrades who know me know that I was not a coward" and asking her to protest against the injustice. In the afternoon he and Milan were shot. According to one report, the medical officer refused to attend the execution, apparently out of disgust, and Herduin himself had to give the order to the reluctant firing squad, with these words:

> My friends! We have been accused of not doing our duty, it seems we didn't hold our position strongly enough, we did carry out our duty and we don't deserve this, we are not cowards, this will be acknowledged one day.
>
> And now, you too, do your duty. Don't make us suffer, aim straight for the heart. My wife, my son, goodbye! . . . Fire!

The medical officer, on the other hand, reported that Herduin had encouraged his executioners to "keep on holding, right to the end, for the sake of France." Dying speeches are always easy to write or rewrite after the event, and there are well-worn rhetorical formulae available to suit any taste. So often the dead say what the living want them to have said.

At least Herduin's message to his widow had been clear. After the war she did protest, bringing legal actions against Colonel Bernard and a newspaper which had defended him. In 1921 the Minister of War acknowledged Herduin to have been a "courageous officer" and offered civil damages, while explaining that the law did not allow the case to be reopened. In 1926, after the law had been changed, Herduin and Milan were exonerated. The legal phrase used in describing the fate of men like them, unjustly punished for failing to obey their orders, was that the orders had made demands "beyond the limits of human endurance."

7

---✛---

ENDING VERDUN

This year is going to be idled away in blood.

> General Erich Ludendorff
> in conversation with Paul Rohrbach,
> summer 1916

The German attacks following on the heels of Mangin's failure to retake Douaumont signaled the buildup to a major new offensive. Its focus was the right bank and its aim, greatly helped by the fall of the Fort de Vaux on 7 June, was to push south along the plateaus which could at last be made to grant access to Verdun. From the high point where the Fort de Douaumont commanded the battlefield the ridge of the plateau sloped gently southwest down to the Côte de Froideterre—cold earth indeed for those who died there—via the Ouvrage de Thiaumont, a large concrete bunker lacking only the fixed artillery emplacements to make it a fort. The *ouvrage* commanded a critical junction from which another ridge led southeast to join the southern reaches of the plateau where Vaux stands. Along its course were two insignificant spots which the fighting would make into famous names: the village of Fleury and the Chapelle Sainte-Fine, as it was still called even though the chapel itself had disappeared before 1916. Beyond them lay the Fort de Souville, the immediate prize in the German lines of advance from both Douaumont and Vaux. Behind Souville, to be sure, stood the forts of Belleville and Saint-Michel on the inner-most ring of defense, but by themselves they would not have been enough to protect the suburbs of Verdun, the river, the cathedral and the Citadelle.

Within days of Vaux's capture the Ouvrage de Thiaumont had become the center of fighting which fell into the familiar pattern of attack and counterattack characterizing the whole battle: a tidal ebb and flow wearing landmarks beyond recognition, almost out of ex-istence. The Germans made the customary preparation for the last stage of their all-out push on the evening of 22 June. This time, however, it was marked not by a violent intensification in the bom-bardment but by an apparent lull. Marcel Dupont, who had grown used to the racket of the artillery and the trembling of walls, trees, even the ground beneath his feet, ventured out from the safety of the Caserne Marceau, near the Fort Saint-Michel:

> The sky is clear, all the stars are bright. And in this calm air thou-sands of soft whistling noises go past, past, past; one would think that countless swallows are flying about in search of food. Behind us, in the distance, we can hear the dull rumble of the guns, but in front of us, where this nocturnal flight is coming from, we cannot hear any explosions.

Soon, from the ravine below him, rose "an acrid, nauseating smell, a smell of rottenness mixed with vinegar dregs." The shells were gas shells, whose small bursting charge made them land almost as in-nocently as if they were duds.

Verdun was fought at a turning-point in the development of chemical weaponry. By 1916 gas was being fired in shells rather than sprayed in clouds which a change of wind could easily make fickle, and a new generation of lethal gases was steadily replacing tear gas. The French had already experimented with phosgene at Verdun in February or March, rushing it into use in the panicky days after the first German attack. Since the spring the Germans had been eager to test their latest refinement, soon to be known to the French as *surpalite* and to the British as diphosgene, but they did not have it in sufficient quantities until 22 June. By the next morning they had fired 116,000 diphosgene shells, aimed largely at the French artillery positions near where Marcel Dupont stood. The toxic concentration overwhelmed gas masks, and the attack claimed some 1,600 casualties. Not all of them were gunners but, as the night wore on, the infantry in the front lines became aware that the guns behind them were ominously falling silent.

To Pétain the next day, 23 June, marked the greatest crisis since his arrival at Verdun. Punching a hole in the French lines, the attack captured the Ouvrage de Thiaumont and reached the Ouvrage de Froideterre on the southern tip of the plateau; worse still, it swept down to Fleury and beyond, to the little Chapelle Sainte-Fine. It brought the Germans only just short of the Fort de Souville and within five kilometers of Verdun. The chaos in the French lines looked like the first days of battle all over again, only this time it had fallen on an army already tired and discontented, an army already feared by its commanders to be approaching *défaillance*. Again, some four months after the fighting had started, the prospect had to be confronted of losing the right bank, and losing it not by tactical withdrawal or planned evacuation but simply by being pushed back in disarray. Joffre and Nivelle afterward took care to distance themselves from such fears, dismissed as typical of Pétain's tendency to imagine the worst, but Mangin left on record his respect for a general who looked them squarely in the eye while managing to appear calm to the men around him.

The worst did not happen. Far from sweeping further ahead, the German advance stalled—only just short of Souville but still short of it. The Chapelle Sainte-Fine could not be held more than briefly. From the German point of view as well as the French, the results of the June fighting looked like the first days of battle all over again. Again they had attacked on a narrow front, so that breakthrough cut itself into a narrow salient. And again, for all their apparently massive strength, they lacked the resources to exploit their first gains. No more diphosgene shells were to hand; even water supplies for front-line troops suffering in the summer heat were running out. Another massive attempt to get the advance moving again on 11–12 July, when more diphosgene shells were ready, briefly reawakened hopes. Souville was almost cut off from French support and the gas cloud behind it stretched down to the streets of Verdun, as it had in June. A few troops managed to get on the roof of the fort, like Mangin's men at Douaumont in May, but, like Mangin's men, they were brushed off.

Among those German troops the exhilaration they had felt at clearing the French out of the Bois d'Avocourt in March had disappeared, let alone the hopes they had entertained when the battle had started in February. Many were as tired as the French and, because they had been kept longer in line, some more so; the 15th Corps had been there from the start. Their rate of desertion and surrender betrayed the same mood which was overcoming the French. Disillusionment had infected the higher reaches of command too. Falkenhayn had always been ready to waver in his commitment to the battle he had conceived; the Crown Prince, no optimist in February, had by March lost heart. It was only at the insistence of Knobelsdorf, the Prince's chief of staff, that the June attack had been launched and nothing less than the capture of Souville, to add to Douaumont and Vaux, would have given his voice further authority.

So the gains on 23 June marked the furthest point that the German advance at Verdun ever achieved, and the date and the place would come to be remembered by the French as marking the turning-point of the battle. The site of the Chapelle Sainte-Fine would be commemorated by a stone monument of a lion—alluding to the Lion of Belfort, that earlier monument to the only place where France had successfully resisted the Prussians in 1870–71, the city which had been reprieved at the last minute from annexation by the Treaty of Frankfurt. Veterans would choose 23 June as the anniversary when they returned to the battlefield for ceremonies of remembrance. *Ils ne passeront pas!* (They shall not pass!), Nivelle's Order of the Day celebrating the close shave that the

French army had survived on 23 June, would be added to Pétain's *Courage, on les aura!* in the list of unforgettable slogans from the battlefield.* On this date and in this place the rocklike strength of France withstood the might of Germany and broke it, decisively. It was all wrong, of course, and wrong in more than just the inappropriateness of the rhetoric to two stumbling, punch-drunk heavyweights. Always shapeless, Verdun could never generate its own decisions. For Verdun, the decisive event happened elsewhere on the Western Front and happened the day after 23 June. It came the next morning, when the guns opened up at the Somme.

Even before it started, the Battle of the Somme had already become the ghostly twin of Verdun. Their rival claims on French resources, and how they would so often be decided, had been announced in February when Joffre assigned Pétain and his Second Army, preparing for the Somme in training camp at Noailles, to Verdun instead. Yet the relationship between the two battles went deeper than that. Both had been conceived in December 1915— when Falkenhayn recommended the attack at Verdun in order to forestall a Franco-British offensive, and Joffre convened a meeting with Sir Douglas Haig, newly appointed to succeed Sir John French as commander of the British forces, to propose just such an offensive. The two plans, moreover, belonged to the same style of military thought; quite as much as Falkenhayn, Joffre confused *percée* and *usure*, breakthrough and attrition. The muddle survived all the subsequent changes which the pressure of Verdun forced on plans for the Somme; it was still apparent after an attack, in which the French were to have taken the lion's share of the burden, had grown into a largely British operation.

Pétain resented the plan for the Somme, or so it was widely believed. It would certainly have been understandable if he had, given how often its name was in Joffre's mouth when refusing demands

---

* Memory, even among veterans and historians, would sometimes attribute the phrase to Pétain. In fact, the slogan was circulating among the troops long before Nivelle took it up. Anatole Castex, determined optimist but no phrasemaker, wrote to his wife as early as 23 February that the German attack had failed: "maintenant ils ne passeront pas."

for Verdun. Yet, whether it signaled a change of heart or just clari-
fied a misunderstanding, what Pétain told a meeting of generals and
politicians in mid-May amounted to an endorsement almost as
complete as Joffre's. "Verdun would be brought to an end only by
an Allied offensive elsewhere on the front," so Poincaré's diary reported him as saying. "To him this offensive seemed indispensable."
The waiting game Pétain had originally wanted to play was in expectation of the day when the French would be strong enough to go
on the attack. Yet the extra resources (particularly the all-important
artillery pieces) had arrived in so slow a trickle, and the clamor from
Nivelle and Mangin for action had grown so insistent, that instead
he settled down more pragmatically to wait for the Somme. So the
two battles were now linked, and not just in Pétain's understanding,
by another dimension: Verdun was a holding action for the Somme,
and the Somme was a relief action for Verdun.

Pétain's support carried one predictable rider: the all-important
burden of Verdun did not allow the French to undertake other ven-
tures on the Western Front, and so the Somme should be a completely British operation. It seems unlikely that he ever expected his
condition to be met, and in the event some 14 of the 40 divisions at
the Somme were French. Since Joffre had begun by promising a
full 40 divisions, the figure marked a drastic reduction in France's
commitment—though the commitment was still big enough to ensure that men who had survived Verdun fought at the Somme, and
in some cases died there.* It was also big enough to ensure that the
rivalry between the claims of the two battles continued. The buildup of German attacks in June found Pétain still pleading for, and
Joffre reluctantly conceding, divisions earmarked for the battle that
was about to start.

Exactly when it would start was the question, and no longer a
question that the French could settle for themselves; decisions of
this nature had passed into Haig's leisurely hands. Joffre had origi-

---

* Of the witnesses I refer to, those who went on to the Somme include Louis Botti, Pierre
Bréant, Robert Desaubliaux, Paul Dubrulle, Raymond Jubert, Pierre de Mazenod and René
Naegelen; Augustin Cochin died there.

nally spoken of a summer offensive. Haig timed it for 1 August. Near the end of May, soon after he had given his endorsement to the Somme, the date seemed dangerously remote to Pétain. He pleaded with Joffre—for once a willing listener—and Haig agreed to 1 July. During the terrible day of 23 June Pétain telephoned General de Castelnau urging that the date be brought forward again. Prime Minister Briand put the request to Haig the next morning. Nothing could be done to change the timing of the infantry assault, but Haig agreed to start his artillery bombardment on the spot. It lasted for seven days, longer than the German bombardment at Verdun and longer than any other which the war had seen. It proved no more effective than usual in destroying the enemy's positions but every bit as effective as usual in confirming the enemy's suspicions of the blow about to be delivered.

The impact of the Somme on the higher levels of military command in both France and Germany was far-reaching. Because the battle proved a bloody and costly failure for France, it sealed Joffre's fate. In December he lost his position as Commander-in-Chief, though of course a concern for morale prevented him falling into official disgrace. Instead the man whose purge of his generals at the end of 1914 had originated the word *limoger* was himself *limogé*; Joffre was given a marshal's baton and ceremonial duties. Yet because the Battle of the Somme had happened at all, thus underlining the German failure at Verdun, it cost Falkenhayn his job by the end of August. He did fall into official disgrace, and soon into obscurity as well; his curt description of the manner of his going makes one of the most severely tight-lipped moments in his unrevealing memoirs.

Within a few days of his departure the order had gone out from Hindenburg and Ludendorff, his joint successors, that the Crown Prince suspend the offensive at Verdun and regard his present lines as permanent. Yet long before September it was obvious that the last flicker of German hope had died at Verdun. The battle that was supposed to bleed the forces of France to death, and had at times come close to doing just that, had also come close to bleeding the forces of Germany to death. By 12 July Knobelsdorf's gamble had been abandoned and the order to return to the defensive had gone out. The regimental colors, brought forward in anticipation of victory, were discreetly returned to headquarters; a visit by the Kaiser was canceled. These rituals of failure had been enacted before at Verdun and were already familiar, yet this time they were, in a new sense, permanent. The Germans were never going to get to Verdun: in the shadow of the Somme this was privately, though not publicly, accepted. From now on they would reckon, with growing distress, the cost they had paid even to get where they were at Verdun and the cost they would have to pay to stay where they were.

The impact of the Somme on the French at Verdun was more subtle. Indeed, it was too subtle for some of the troops, who were soon openly cynical of promises that German artillery was being drained away to the new battle in significant numbers. They had heard too many promises before, and found them to be lies used by generals to justify pointless sacrifice. Yet the Somme strengthened Pétain's hand. Between 23 June and 11 July Mangin had launched a vigorous series of counterattacks, with some success as well as Pétain's approval. This did not prevent Pétain from condemning the attempt to retake Fleury on 15 July as rash and ill prepared. Three days later he made his general position known, in a fashion summarized later in his own book on the battle:

> In future our attacks were to be organized by commanders above
> divisional level who, because of their knowledge of the terrain and
> the strength of the forces permanently at their disposal, were best
> qualified to direct the infantry and give it the necessary support.
> They would pay particular attention to the best use that could be
> made of the artillery, in choice of objectives, regulation of fire and
> liaison with assault troops.

The message was clear, not least in emphasizing yet again the vital importance Pétain had always attached to the proper deployment of artillery. What was new—or renewed by the relief that the

Somme had afforded—was his confidence in enforcing an approach that entailed slow preparation for the long-term goals ahead: getting back Douaumont and Vaux, and returning the French lines to their positions in February. Mangin would continue to have command in the field, grumbling in letters home that Pétain was "too defensive, too timid" and prone to start nervously at the very mention of the word "attack." Nivelle would continue to organize tactics on the battlefield, devoting himself to getting rather more of the credit for success than this contribution justified. But timing, the vital element, would be in Pétain's control.

✣　✣　✣

What a strange life, and yet how dull everything was before this war! Afterwards how will those who come through it handle everyday life, life in short? Yet, naturally, there isn't one of them who doesn't want to last until then, to see.

   Pierre Bréant, *De l'Alsace à la Somme: Souvenirs du Front (août 1914–janvier 1917)* (1917)

French restraint and German dejection might have begun to change the temper of battle, but Verdun would always remain a restless and bloody affair. The fighting still ebbed and flowed over the plateaus south of Douaumont and Vaux; the ravines that fringed them still earned their indiscriminately applied nickname, the Ravin de la Mort; for that matter Le Mort-Homme was still, to those who fought there, Dead Man's Hill. For the troops in the front lines, French and German alike, Verdun remained the supreme ordeal, not least because to them—as indeed at times to their commanders—it could still look endless.

Pétain's intervention might have prevented a particular edge of discontent in the French army growing yet sharper; it certainly helped to consolidate the respect the troops accorded him, alone among the high-ranking generals at Verdun, as *un vrai chef*, a real leader. It did not, however, stop him worrying about *défaillance*

(September found him closely inquiring into its causes) or having good reason to worry. When President Poincaré paid a visit near the beginning of November, to award a medal to Mangin, he drove up the last stage of the Voie Sacrée with Nivelle. Some of the troops who recognized them cheered; others hurled insults and threw stones. The word they used was *embusqués*. Literally, it described men lying in wait or ambush, but by 1916 it was universally applied to men in uniform, usually with medals on their chest, who took care to fight their war as far away from the front as possible.

The word found its mark, like the stones, but it did not sum up even the troops' discontents, much less their whole mood. Anger at bad generalship had contributed to the discontents, not formed them. As for the larger mood, it had less to do with generalship of any sort than the generals supposed. Certainly, their names are virtually absent from the diaries and recollections of the fighting men. Philippe Glorennec's illuminating study of the eyewitness accounts assembled by Jacques Péricard for his history reports that, in all 1,200 items, Pétain's name is mentioned only 10 times. Troops at the sharp end, to be sure, do not often meet their generals; usually they do not even see them; they get their orders from officers much lower down the chain of command. But at Verdun the almost complete lack of interest in the generals—barely a hint of gossip, speculation or vulgar jokes—is particularly striking. It reminds us of a truth encountered from whatever angle we view the battle: that for the men who fought, the reality of what they suffered and what it did to them lay somewhere below the official version, the public account, not necessarily challenging its basic premises yet definitely not connecting with them either.

Take, by way of a simple example, the case of Anatole Castex. He was already at Verdun when the battle started, and rose later to be a captain in charge of a machine-gun unit. When I first mentioned him in a footnote a few pages ago I called him a determined optimist. The letters he wrote to his wife in the darkest days of February reaffirmed exactly what the Paris press was telling its readership: that the Germans could not possibly succeed, that the force of their attack had already been broken, that they would not pass, and so on. As for how he and the other troops felt the day after Douaumont had fallen, he claimed: "Morale is very good and everybody is really doing their duty." Given that Castex did not hesitate to include in his letters frank and sometimes gruesome description of the physical horror of Verdun, and by implication the risk to himself, there is no special reason to suppose that here he is simply trying to reassure his wife. Presumably he believed, or wanted to believe, what he wrote.

Belief had grown harder when he was posted back to the battle in August. "So it's Verdun we're off to next," he wrote in breaking the news to his wife, and then added: "I must tell you that it doesn't frighten me and that I go with a calm and tranquil spirit. This time we'll just have to fight a bit harder than we've done so far." There was nothing to alarm the postal censor here. All the words were right and proper, yet somehow the effort of writing them showed through. The result conveyed more of tired resignation than it did of determination, and it failed to conceal the fears of a man who had done his best and found that it was not yet enough. Time had done that to him. Time was often the essential factor in shaping the mood of the men—the real dimension in which the battle was being fought, as Raymond Jubert had suggested. What time might have continued to do to Anatole Castex we do not know: he was dead within two weeks of writing these words.

It did not always require time for Verdun to work its changes. Second Lieutenant Alfred Joubaire arrived on 17 May. "There's no longer any doubt of the position we're going to take up," he wrote in his diary the day before: "it's Verdun, it's the big one, real carnage, real slaughter. Everybody is very calm and very happy." Those words "carnage" and "slaughter" do little to ruffle the lightness of the entry; indeed, they are lightly used. Verdun, after all, still had a reputation that could inspire youthful excitement and bravura. No grizzled *poilu*, Joubaire had only just turned 21: his birthday photograph showed a boyish face desperately proud of the wispiest of mustaches. On 21 May he wrote a letter to his parents, to be sent in the event of his death, telling them: "I will have shed my blood joyfully, and joyfully given my sufferings and sacrifices for this noble cause which lifts up my heart." A sacrifice not just voluntary but joyful, a noble cause, an uplifted heart: the rhetoric and doctrine of nationalism remained immaculately in place, at least on paper. Whether they were really in place, or so immaculately in place, is another matter. "We tell them the story of *their* war," Gabriel Chevallier testified of the *poilu* etiquette toward civilians, "the one that will keep them happy, and guard our secret." Presumably it never had more binding force than in posthumous utterance.

Yet there is no evidence to suggest that Joubaire yet had any clear notion of a disparity between their war and his war—or indeed that he even harbored a suspicion that the war might initiate him in a secret unknown to the public rhetoricians. Certainly there is nothing in his private diary to show him prepared, or to prepare the reader, for the entry he wrote on 22 May, just a day later:

> How long is this going to last? Anguish makes me wonder when and how this gigantic, unprecedented struggle will end. There's no resolution in view. I wonder if it won't just finish for lack of men left to fight. It's no longer one nation fighting another. It's two great blocs fighting, two civilizations colliding. The peoples have been touched by the madness of death and destruction. Certainly, humanity has gone mad! It must be mad to do what it's doing. Such slaughter! Such scenes of horror and carnage! I can't find the words to convey them. Hell could not be worse. Men are mad!

Just what had happened to make five days, at the outside limit, seem an age in experience? Just what had disordered his brave and youthful certainties?

He had spent the last two of those days at a forward observation post, supporting Mangin's attack on Douaumont. The place was like a slaughterhouse: when he arrived there, Joubaire counted 18 corpses, some splattered over the floor, others hanging from exposed bars of iron sticking out of the reinforced concrete, all starting to rot in the mild weather. While he was still there, he had learned the fate of most of the fellow officers in his regiment whom he called friends: "Jacques killed,—Sevin killed,—Pautrel killed,—Crescini killed,—Dubray killed." Sevin had died as a hero should, fighting off attacks until his ammunition ran out and then hurling insults at the enemy. Yet he "slept on the spot where he fell," his body unburied, unreachable, lost somewhere in the disputed ground, like the bodies of the rest:

> One can't even say that they're resting in peace. They fell in the thick of the fighting and, after death, they're still being subjected to insult from bullets and shells! Poor Jacques! Now you're an inert mass, in a blue uniform, on the plain. You were one of the first to fall, hit by a bullet. Where? I've no idea.

These are the facts as Joubaire gave them. A larger and more detached account of what had happened to him than he was in any position to attempt would run rather differently. He had gone to Verdun equipped with all the attitudes of nationalism, fluent in how they were conventionally expressed. He had held a certain set of beliefs about France and hence, presumably, a corresponding set of beliefs about Germany, though his diary is silent on that point. The silence does not matter, because what Joubaire had experienced had, really, little or nothing immediately to do with what he felt about France or Germany. It did not come as a direct challenge to those beliefs, which is why the familiar nationalist talk of civilizations colliding could still float vaguely about in his cry of distress. In this cry of distress there was no sign of disillusionment with his idea of France, no suggestion that he loved her the less. If, by the same token, he had arrived at Verdun hating Germans, then nothing had occurred to make him hate them the less. Like so many of the French troops, he had seen Germans hardly at all and only from a distance.

What he had seen close-up was war. And this meant that he had encountered death as intimately as anyone could without actually dying. How he would have dealt with the shock, beyond an almost incoherent page in his diary registering its first impact, and how it might eventually have affected his beliefs, there is no means of telling. Joubaire returned for a second tour of duty, near his original position, on 31 May. After being caught up in Mangin's attempt on Douaumont, his unit now found itself on the receiving end of the Germans' big gamble in June. At about nine o'clock on the morning of 2 June Joubaire was hit by a shell which ripped open his stomach and left the bones of his right leg showing through the flesh. He spent the rest of the day dying in agony, tended by comrades who could do little to help but could at least save his body from the fate that his friends' bodies had suffered.

The one thing we can never really imagine is our own death. So Freud had argued the year before in "Thoughts for the Times on War and Death." This truth, he concluded, was the secret of heroism. In war men do not go to meet death on the basis of a "decision that the personal life cannot be so precious as certain abstract general ideals" but rather because they can never quite banish the sense that "Nothing can happen to *me*." That was indeed a timely thought for Verdun, where talk of sacrifice, voluntary or involuntary, in the name of ideals greater than the individual life had risen to a special pitch. What else is Joubaire's letter to his parents but the work of a man aware that he might die yet still, really, unable to imagine his own death? By the same token Verdun, that great laboratory of death, would have offered a psychologist like Freud further chance for observing all the ways men think, feel and behave as they get closer and closer to what, at root, they still cannot imagine.

The experience of living with *mort de près* (to borrow Maurice Genevoix's phrase again) took so many forms as to make it highly significant which aspects men chose to dwell on and which they let pass in silence. Of the fear of dying, we have already seen, they left an eloquent record. Corporal Stéphane tried his hardest to evoke what it felt like to sit under bombardment in the Bois des Caures, wondering whether he would be pulverized by a shell arriving with the force of an express train hitting the buffers at 90 kilometers an hour. René Naegelen described Jacques Férol, waiting to go on the attack, praying that it would be called off, that something would happen to end the bloody war. Even Jacques Péricard, eager though he was to promote a myth of heroism, made no secret of the need to hide his trembling smile behind a cigarette. Troops, sensibly, are usually not ashamed of such feelings and the more battle-hardened they grow the less shame they feel.

Troops at Verdun were more discreet when it came to the sense of calm or of wild exhilaration that could succeed fear once they had started to move forward or were about to receive the advancing enemy. Raymond Jubert described it in himself and his men dodging machine-gun bullets on the last stage of their way up Le Mort-Homme and Robert Desaubliaux, yet more frankly, in his eager anticipation of the German night attack that would fall under the muzzle of his machine-gun. At such moments—and they were just moments—they felt death so close, so completely around them, that they accepted, even embraced it. This, at least, is the implication of their accounts; as readers we are more likely to be struck by their belief in their invulnerability, as if being there and still somehow being alive proved they were untouchable, immortal. Waiting for the Germans to attack his position was not the only time that Desaubliaux felt himself in close proximity to death, and his account of the second occasion was even more revealing. For a start, it was not so much he who embraced death as death which embraced him:

I have the sense of marching toward Death. It scares me; but a mystical force pushes me forward all the same.

In the expressions of everyone around me, I read the same confused feelings.

The instinct for self-preservation speaks loudly on the eve of attack. But you are changed, ennobled, by the sense of Death—the soul of the brave knights of old, the soldiers of the Revolution and the *grognards* of the Empire, the soul of a whole people shaped by

20 centuries of struggle and outlasting us in France, made greater, more lovely and more glorious by our death.

The idea that dead soldiers could lend support to the living in their hour of trial had already formed the basis for the *Debout les Morts!* incident which Jacques Péricard had allowed Maurice Barrès, among others, to promote to the status of supernatural legend.* The dead who stiffened Péricard's resolve were fallen comrades immediately around him, not warriors from the great phases of French history, let alone all the French from all the phases of their history. By broadening the perspective in which he stands, the context to which his individual life and death belong, Desaubliaux underlines how directly his experience, like Péricard's, stems from the account of nationhood that Barrès had promulgated before the war. This account always stressed that the dead outnumbered the living. Indeed, the dead had already outvoted the living, determining the living so that the individual had no choice, no real significance, but in submission to the collective destiny. Here these dead command the same power over Desaubliaux, summoning him, impelling toward not just submission but sacrifice.

Some of those who died at Verdun might well have done so in just this spirit of self-transcendence. Desaubliaux, obviously, did not die and so his vision, stopping short of realization, loses its force. It is reduced to a moment, overheated and hallucinatory, in a narrative otherwise as scrupulously honest and questioning as Jubert's and headed, like Jubert's, toward a different and more prosaic affirmation. His experience of marching toward Death, glorious yet literally morbid, has none of the authenticity of his relief at not dying after all. And this sensation dominates what all the survivors have to say of their encounters with death. Their tone ranges from Captain Delvert's curt phrase, "End of martyrdom," still numb with shock and heavy with grief after his experience at R1, to this passage by Lieutenant Louis Botti about his return from fighting on Cote 304:

* See Chapter 2.

I'm back, my hands stained with blood and covered with things that would be revolting if they did not come from the suffering of heroes; everything in my pack shattered by exploding shells; a hole ripped in one sleeve of my great-coat and a piece of shrapnel stuck in the back, as if it had been woven into the fabric.

I'm back, after the early-morning attack, lacerated by the wire, after the terrifying bombardments, after having been subjected to the filthy stench of their gas shells, after going through hell! . . .

I'm back, with an immense pride.

His pride was chiefly in his men, both those who survived and those who did not: "I led them to their death and I'll not forget them!" Out of such near-hysterical relief a good part of the intense bond between the *poilus* was formed and with it, by natural corollary, the *poilus'* common preoccupation with those who had died. Botti has, after all, their blood on his hands, and not just their blood but other traces and fluids from their bodies that would be revolting—*innommable*, literally "unspeakable"—if they did not come from the suffering of heroes. Plainly, he intends the detail as symbolic. It is also symbolic, or at least typical of how the troops write of their encounters with death, in another sense that he did not intend. Botti has just seen the Germans close up, which by no means all the French troops at Verdun did, though perhaps still from the distance of a grenade's throw rather than the length of a bayonet. Presumably he has just killed some of them. And yet of Germans he has in general little to say and of the act of killing them, in this passage or elsewhere, nothing. None of the blood on his hands is German; all of it is French.

Botti's silence on this point is, of course, part of the larger silence of armies, even armies that seek to inculcate the warrior spirit in its most savage form. Killing is the act they are least willing to specify. Except in bayonet-drill and sometimes even in this specific and gruesome exercise, killing is approached through euphemism: the talk is of knocking out positions, flattening defenses, rendering the opposition ineffective or (in Vietnam) "wasting" the enemy.

That soldiers should not have spoken of killing in their letters home might not seem remarkable, though at Verdun it stands in contrast to the willingness of a man like Anatole Castex to go some way toward indicating how the French were suffering and dying. That they should have written so little of killing in their private diaries stands in even greater contrast to their willingness to describe a shell burst making the man a few paces away vanish in a smear of blood or a bullet making the man beside them lean forward as "the blood gushes out like a fountain" from his temple.

Jean Tocaben is the only soldier from Verdun (or at least the only one I know of) whose account breaks the silence in more than a passing comment. I think it significant that he was writing long after the event—his book appeared in 1931—and even then wrote about killing by way of digression, albeit a lengthy digression, from the main burden of what he had to recall. He hated Germans before the war, he says, but not during the war itself. Indeed, he goes out of his way to cast doubt on the atrocity stories then so widely circulated and to stress that he came to respect them as enemies. Nevertheless, the starting-point of his digression is to insist that he felt no remorse at killing them, though he had always felt some remorse at killing animals when he was out hunting. Killing Germans, it seems, was a different matter from hating them. It was part of the job and in no way remarkable, even though watching Frenchmen die and particularly watching General Mangin send Frenchmen to die a useless death still seemed remarkable—at once outrageous and poignant—years later.

There is a certain courage in what Tocaben wrote but also an uneasy defiance. He knew that he was breaking taboos both of speech and act—taboos that belonged in part to 1931 and in part to 1916. The spirit of reconciliation that flickered during the interwar years bred precisely the suspicion of atrocity stories and the respect for former enemies which he expressed. Yet they also demanded, if not exactly repentance for killing, at least a degree of retrospective anguish which he refused to claim for himself. Shameful things had been done in 1916 in the climate of war and the heat of battle. Even then they had not seemed routine or ordinary, for in that case they would have taken their place in the contemporary record, at least the private record of diaries, prosaically beside the complaints about the food and the pay and the mud. At the time they had been accepted, if only provisionally and by an effort of self-censorship; the real struggle came later, in memory.

Maurice Genevoix's account of his experience fighting at Les Éparges, near Verdun, in the opening months of the war casts a little more light on what the men of 1916 did, and how they felt about it then and how they came to feel about it later. In its original form *Sous Verdun* was a testament to remarkable self-honesty, and in its later forms it grew into a testament to the difficulties of remaining honest. The first edition, published in 1916 from the diary he had kept in the field, contains this brief passage:

> Before I reached the *chasseurs* I passed four more Germans, by themselves. Running at the same speed but keeping a pace behind, I gave each of them a bullet from my revolver in the back or the neck. They fell to the ground, with a long choked cry.

This is indifference, but in a man and a writer used to noting even his indifference laconically and exactly. Genevoix cut the passage when *Sous Verdun* was reissued in 1929, but restored it when he brought the book together with his later war writings as a single volume, *Ceux de 14*, in 1950. His preface called this final version of the text "definitive." Some passages had been trimmed, but simply to create unity and for no other reason. His original purpose in writing had been to set down his "spontaneous reaction to the facts of war." He believed then and he still believed that his subject was "a reality so particular, so intense and dominating that it imposed its own laws and demands on the chronicler," and it was to this reality, rather than to any second thoughts, that he had tried to be faithful.

Despite this assurance, Genevoix did in fact systematically censor the "definitive" text of *Sous Verdun*. Painfully honest though he was in restoring the record of killing Germans, he cut or diluted passages expressing attitudes to Germans which went with the killing. When a German prisoner brought in from the battlefield is greeted with a joke "he smiles all over his plump and ruddy face, happy at a familiarity in which the good will alone matters to him, vile and loathsome like almost all his kind, once they are captured and know that they are at the mercy of a victor." At least this was what the first edition, and presumably Genevoix's field diary, said. By 1950 it had become: "he smiles all over his plump and ruddy face, happy at a familiarity in which the good will alone immediately lets him know that he is safe."

In October 1914 he had fancied that the bells in a local steeple were addressing the German invaders: " 'I know that the day will come when the cock on the steeple, which all the time inspects the horizon, will witness your headlong flight and the innumerable bodies of your dead rotting throughout our countryside!' " By 1950 the passage had disappeared. Genevoix could no doubt have defended his changes on the grounds that *jejune* reflection had no rightful place in a book dedicated to "the facts of war," but the justification would not have been quite convincing, if only because *jejune* reflection had obviously played a part in the facts of his war.

He did not mind killing Germans and in retrospect he felt no regret, said Tocaben, but he did not hate them as he had done beforehand and he did not believe the wartime propaganda about them. He killed Germans indifferently, said Genevoix, and, with some hesitation, stuck to the record, while still wishing to expunge the stereotyped view he had of his enemy. Somewhere in these shadowy transactions between honesty and shame, between what men did and thought and what they later remembered or wanted to be remembered, there was some diminution of the violent hatreds in which nationalism had educated them during the prewar days. But it occurred after the event and probably because of the sheer scale and horror of the event as much as anything else. Thinking about Germans was never a major preoccupation of the French at Verdun. Killing Germans was certainly not the most sensitive or intimate aspect of their encounter with death.

This, of course, came with the death of friends, of other soldiers in the same unit, of other Frenchmen. Where the record is virtually blank when it comes to Germans dying, the record of Frenchmen dying is virtually the main burden of what the combatants have to say. How comrades died is often described in fluent and appalling detail; when it cannot be, there is often some reference to the author's attempt to find out the exact circumstances. Grief is expressed, in few terse words and exclamation marks by the diarists, at more florid length by the writers of memoirs. Almost always a vow never to forget the dead is made. Celebrating the *poilu* sense of fraternity, I suggested earlier, was the motive the writers themselves most commonly proffer for writing about Verdun at all. Plainly the dead were the members who most demanded celebration.

There is nothing surprising about this. What may be less expected is that the focus of the writing should so often have been the same as Alfred Joubaire's in his cries of distress in May. Then the death of his friends came as a great shock, for all that he thought he knew of war, and an occasion for grief. Yet what turned his sense of tragedy into a sense of sheer horror was the thought of their bodies lying unburied, unreachable on the battlefield: "One can't even say that they're resting in peace." To treat with respect the bodies of those we have known, or at least of those whom we acknowledge as part of the same community, is one of our most elaborately developed instincts. The conditions of battle, which make showing such respect more difficult, do not make it seem less important: here of all places, for these people of all people, the rituals take on extra meaning.

The hospital where Georges Duhamel was posted in February subjected patients, and doctors, to the most appalling conditions. Men lay in dirty field dressings for several days awaiting treatment; the surgeons who operated on them discovered open wounds crawling with lice. Yet the staff still took time to make provision for the corpses that went beyond mere sanitary concern. "They were laid on the ground, side by side, and carefully buried in their shrouds, feet together, hands crossed on their chest," Duhamel recorded,

adding laconically: "when they still had hands and feet." The Abbé
Thellier de Poncheville spent much of his long tour of duty—from
March 1916 until January 1917—conducting burial services, not in
safety well behind the lines, but at the most exposed and dangerous
parts of the front: hasty, clandestine affairs, carried out at night,
showing as little light and making as little noise as possible, yet services nonetheless. The Abbé's diary, with its account of his continual journeys around a battlefield where those in motion were often
most in danger, is more than a record of priestly obligation fulfilled
under the most extreme conditions. It also conveys how much his
arrival, with his prayer book and the authority of his office, meant
to those who still survived.

Yet he and others like him, and the parties of gravediggers, could
do little. The unburied became as much a feature of the battlefield
as the shattered trees and the overlapping shell-holes. In winter
they lay on the frozen soil. With the spring rains they began to sink
into the mud. Then the sun dried the mud, fixing them as if in
cement. The Abbé saw many in this state, and described one in
particular:

> Some of his comrades recognized him and mentioned his name:
> "Hang on, look at him; that's so-and-so." They didn't even try to
> get him out, because they didn't have the tools and they didn't
> have the time. You can't hold up the circulation in a spot where the
> food-carriers pass and the shells fall continually. So the remains of
> this poor man will stay here until the feet of passers-by have worn
> them away or the mud has completely enshrouded them.

In fact, it took longer than the Abbé seemed to imagine it would
for the dead to disappear in this fashion—for death, as André
Bridoux put it, to become "discreet." In the summer, continual
shelling sifted the dry soil time and time again, scattering the
corpses, mutilating them further, disinterring even those which had
once received some sort of burial. Many witnesses remarked on the
way they appeared or disappeared from one day to the next, but

none more memorably than Major Roman on arriving at his position in the Bois Fumin during the second week of July:

> At the entrance to my shelter the earth has been so crushed and turned over that it looks like a dune of coarse sand. On my arrival the body of an infantryman in his blue great-coat is sticking halfway out of this mixture of earth, stone and unspeakable debris. But things are different a few hours later. He's gone, making way for an infantryman from a colonial regiment, in khaki. More and more corpses come and go in succession. The shell that buries one makes the next appear. We get used to the sight, however; we put up with the appalling stench of this charnel house we're living in, but after the war our *joie de vivre* will be poisoned for good.

This description carries a forcible reminder why so many men compared Verdun to Dante's *Inferno*, and why they did not always make the comparison simply as a way of saying that it was hell or evoking what the battlefield looked like at night. If, as Freud maintained, our own death always lies beyond the last reach of the imagination, one cannot speak of the survivors as having encountered death. Yet, like Dante in the *Inferno*, they did encounter the dead. Like the poet, they found the dead thronging around them, pressing in on them with the force of live presences, bearing the stories of who they had once been and how they had died. The experience became so much a part of their daily life that it became, in so far as such an experience ever could, familiar. With Colonel Roman, men got used to it while still occasionally pausing to worry what it all might be doing to them—how both the experience and familiarity with it might have changed them.

"Coming out of the shelter, I realize that I'm walking on corpses, from the way the soil gives under my feet, and feels slippery and soft," wrote Captain La Chaussée, setting down a newcomer's disgust. Yet he arrived in June, and by then thousands of men had already made the same discovery and felt the same disgust—including, quite possibly, the men whose corpses he now found himself walking over. One difference between newcomers and veterans was that the veterans did not break their stride or change their course to avoid treading on a scrap of uniform, or a leg, or a face. Occasionally they might exclaim: "Ah! If our poor wives could see us now!" But if they bothered to remark such details any longer, it was usually with jokey familiarity: "The arm of a corpse appeared yesterday from the parapet of a communication trench through which a relief unit passed; a lot of the men shook the bloodless hand and said, 'Goodbye, old chap! Good day to you!' "

It is not hard to hear the unease in this bravado. Jacques Péricard, honest as he so often was about his own feelings, gave it a precise voice as he looked over the corpses lying around the village of Douaumont in February:

> When it's my turn to be laid low as well, my head smashed in like this man here or my stomach opened up like that one there, will my men take the time to put me somewhere out of the way, in the shelter of a hedge, or behind a pile of ruins? . . . How cold I shall be! . . .
>
> And men will march over me and the nails of their boots will rip up my face, as just a moment ago I ripped up the face of that corporal when I stumbled over him in the snow . . .

"How cold I shall be!": even that brief comment again shows how impossible it is truly to imagine one's own death, to feel in anticipation what it might be like to be beyond feeling. Yet Péricard has obviously been brought as hard up against the fact of his own mortality as living man can get. More than the sound of the shells or the near-misses, more even than the fear preceding action or the grief following the death of friends, the sheer litter of corpses on the battlefield was always the best *memento mori*.

The *memento mori* has a long tradition in religion and philosophy, as well as art and literature. Some of the troops were fully aware of it. Here is Georges Gaudy—whose memoir turned the troops on their way down the Voie Sacrée into a painting of the

Descent from the Cross—contemplating one of the many corpses in his view:

> Through some mental aberration, it soon seemed to me that I was seeing myself in the future, that the body was what I would be in perhaps a few days' time. I looked at the blackened hand with its clenched fingers; then I looked at mine and flexed the muscles. Was this what became of man? And I examined the wide-open eye as if to read some secret frozen there, some memory of things gone by. Now cold, the corpse's heart had been beating a few weeks ago, perhaps no more than a few days. The skull where the cropped hair stuck hideously up had been teeming with thought!

This, perhaps, benefits rather too much from Hamlet's colloquy with Yorick's skull; it smacks of being written up after the event. Robert Desaubliaux was altogether more direct, and at the same time more directly evocative of the horrors to be found on some churchyard monuments and gravestones:

> I dozed for a few seconds last night without meaning to; as I woke up, I thought I heard a cry: "Watch out!" I gave an involuntary start . . . in a daze; the arm of a corpse lying on the parapet hit me in the face. I thought it had moved and was clawing me; its contorted face seemed to be laughing and its open mouth shouting at me: "Run for it! . . . Run for it while you can; in no time you'll be a foul wreck like me!"

The *memento mori* is meant to shock and terrify; its whole purpose is to jolt people out of their ordinary preoccupations and begin to see themselves in the context of time and eternity. Yet further along this train of thought lies solace, or at least it does in the tradition which developed the *memento mori* into precise emblem and instrument. Fragile and brief though the individual life may be— so much so that the lesson of the skull makes it appear without meaning—it belongs to a larger pattern, a larger purpose, which gives it significance. We have already heard Desaubliaux attempting this consolation, as he marched toward Death supported by the souls of dead warriors and of generations yet to be born. Yet this other "hallucination" (the word is his) lacked the sheer intensity, and the staying-power in memory, of the moment when the rotting face of the corpse seemed to be screaming at him a message of panic and despair.

For all the fevered imagining that surrounded it, the face was not a hallucination or a work of art contrived to make a point. It was a fact and a fact of daily life. And the message it carried for men like Péricard or Gaudy or Desaubliaux was not, after all, quite the usual burden of the *memento mori*, but far more particular to the occasion and the place. It was not that men died and their bodies rotted before disappearing into nothing. It was that here men died and their bodies were left to rot and disappear without the usual rituals, the decencies, of civilization. The appalling indignity of their fate contained nothing to challenge the devout in their religious faith, however much it might disgust them or add to their grief. But it dealt a blow to men accustomed to expressing their devotion to France in terms borrowed from the language of religious faith. The distance between the noble rhetoric of death in war, so easy on the tongue, and the obscene reality, so hard to bear, seemed too great. It strained their relationship to breaking-point, in just the same way as Jubert's discovery of the difference between the *imagerie d'Épinal* and what he had seen on the top of Le Mort-Homme.

France should be loved and worshiped with the same force as the objects of religion. Indeed, so the Republic had insisted, France was virtually a religion—offered in substitute, partial or total, for the religion from which the Republic kept its wary distance. In time of war, the insistence grew stronger and religious language dominant—above all, with words like "sacred" and "sacrifice." Even the wartime truce between political parties could not remain just a *Union Nationale*, the term which Poincaré had used in proposing it; it had to be labeled a *Union Sacrée*. The road to Verdun, of course, was the Voie Sacrée; for those on the way up, it marked an Ascent to the Cross and for those on the way down, a Descent from the Cross. When it was not openly compared to Calvary and the Crucifixion, the battle was still an "altar" or a "martyrdom"; the fate of the dead was always "sacrifice."

I have already remarked the difference between *se sacrifier*, sacrificing oneself, and *être sacrifié*, being sacrificed. The register of the word's meaning included other, even darker, possibilities as well. Jacques Péricard had called himself and the other men thrown into battle during the darkest days of February "sacrifices chosen for the salvation of Verdun": chosen rather than choosing, one notes, and not strictly "sacrifices" but in the original French *holocaustes*, or burnt offerings. The word *holocauste* no doubt seemed appropriate to a battle which it was becoming commonplace to describe as a "furnace," yet it had less strictly Christian connotation than "sacrifices." It belonged to an ethos that Péricard himself would no doubt have labeled pagan or primitive—the ethos of the Canaanite god Moloch, for example—whose rituals were to the Christian or civilized mind savage, senseless and disgusting. So, though Péricard did not choose it carefully or deliberately, the word was also appropriate to a battle where "sacrifices" were left, unhallowed and unburied, to rot and suffer insult.

Here is Augustin Cochin, a man of impeccably conventional views, not announcing a change of heart but simply making a terse and hasty comment about the unit—a pathetic little platoon of *chasseurs*—which relieved his own on Cote 304: "They're the next course; it'll be time to serve another before long, since the ogre has a taste for the sport." The imagery of eating comes easily to soldiers, I suggested in introducing Joffre's choice of the term *gringotage* for his version of attrition: they like to talk of biting and gulping and swallowing the enemy. Such words were often merely euphemisms, to help them avoid the terrible word "kill," but not always. Sometimes they expressed the savage hatreds between armies and the antagonistic nations they represent. In 1870–71 the Prussian soldiers had boasted of being *Franzosenfresser* (French-eaters), or so Paul de Saint-Victor claimed. Michelet expanded the charge, when he rephrased his analysis of Prussia as "a framework that absorbs" in language quite literally visceral, calling it "a stomach with claws, like the octopus."

Nations and their armies, then, eat their enemies. A certain sort of general, not hard to find in the First World War, eats his own men—for it was French troops, as much as German, of whom Mangin was said to be a *mangeur*. Yet however palpably the familiar usage lies behind what Cochin said of death on Cote 304, it does not convey what Cochin really meant. The ogre who had eaten most of his unit and would eat the platoon of *chasseurs* and then would need yet another course was not a bad French general, or even the German artillery. It was the battle itself, come to monstrous life of its own, exacting its own primitive and disgusting sacrifice.

This vision impressed even those who did not intend deliberately or systematically to reject conventional attitudes and the rhetoric that went with them. I pointed out in my Prologue that the troops tended to avoid calling the road to Verdun the Voie Sacrée: not the least of their reasons was how much the label conflicted with their own more immediate perception. Pierre de Mazenod saw columns of lorries carrying "human flesh towards the great eater." To Jean Tocaben (uncannily though perhaps accidentally adapting Michelet's phrase) the battle was already, even in distant prospect, "the hungry octopus." To all the troops, at one point or another, Verdun seemed *l'abattoir*, the place where animals were slaughtered to be eaten. By the end of 1916 the words *Chemin de l'abattoir* had been chalked on a wall in the suburbs of Verdun.

✥ ✥ ✥

Douaumont is like those distant and disdainful women who seem impregnable but yield in an instant.

Henry Bordeaux,
diary entry for 25 October 1916

Meanwhile, there was a battle still to finish, and Pétain for one was determined to bring it to the tidiest and most methodical of ends.

His directive in mid-July had announced his intention of curbing the *élan* of men like Nivelle and Mangin, as much as that was possible, until the moment arrived to unleash it in a final counter-assault. Mangin was assigned three front-line divisions, with three more in support and two held at his disposal in reserve. The troops charged with spearheading the operation rehearsed on a simulated version of the battlefield near Bar-le-Duc. Artillery was built up until it achieved the superiority which Pétain had so long desired and so long lacked: 650 pieces, of which almost half were heavy.

Two new 400mm guns—the heaviest France had fielded, and virtually as big as the German Big Bertha—soon proved their worth. During the preparatory bombardment of Douaumont, on 23 October, one 400mm shell achieved what the Big Berthas (let alone Mangin's 370mm mortars) had failed to do. It penetrated the concrete roof of the fort. About 50 Germans died, mainly staff and wounded in the sick bay, and the rest of the garrison was left unnerved at this unexpected proof of vulnerability. The success was only one proof of how carefully the French guns were deployed. Halfway during their bombardment they deliberately fell silent, making the Germans believe that the infantry assault had started and tempting them to betray their own artillery positions by opening fire. Of 158 German batteries which fell for the trick, only 90 remained in action after the French response. When the infantry assault really did start, the troops moved forward under the protection of a *barrage roulant*, or creeping barrage: a curtain of artillery fire steadily lengthening its range to keep slightly ahead of the advancing lines.

The advance began shortly before midday on 24 October, in a lingering fog that seemed at first to favor the defenders rather than the attackers. Yet before the day was over it had covered three kilometers—a remarkable achievement in a battle where gains were usually measured in meters. Above all, the Fort de Douaumont was once again in French hands. The honor of being first to enter it was amicably disputed between men from the 321st Infantry Regiment and Major Nicolay's battalion from a colonial regiment, the Régiment d'Infanterie Coloniale du Maroc. Gaston Gras, a sergeant in

Nicolay's battalion, set aside the rival claims—and set aside, too, the role of the Moroccans who had suffered in the brunt of the fighting—to award the honor to France:

> Steel-skulled Bretons, calm and obstinate men from the Auvergne, clear-eyed men from the Vosges, Gascons talking like d'Artagnan, idle men from Provence who put their back into it at the right moment, wolf-hunting men from the Isère, cynical and dandified Parisians, people from the plain or the mountain, from the city or the hamlet. The same fervour welded them into a matchless whole.

It was the same matchless whole that Muenier the ambulance driver had found embodied in the troops who had come to the rescue in February, the same matchless whole that Michelet had taught generations of the French to celebrate.

Yet, in truth, the recapture of Douaumont came as something of an anticlimax to an army which had spent seven months hoping for the event—let alone to a general like Mangin who had made it the focus of his frustrated quest for glory. The fighting in front of the fort had been severe by the standards of a severe battle but what went on inside proved virtually a repetition of what had happened when the Germans arrived in February. Then, successive parties of Brandenburgers had found the building manned only by Sergeant-Major Chenot and his ill-prepared Territorials. By 24 October the German garrison had been hastily evacuated in fear of more carnage from another 400mm shell. When the French got into Douaumont they found only a party of about 20 signalers, seeking refuge from the battle outside, vainly summoning reinforcements.

In military terms this was no check at all; it was certainly no disappointment to a general like Pétain, who liked his battles to end as undramatically as possible. Far more serious was the French failure on 24 October to reach the second goal of their attack, the Fort de Vaux. It did not fall for more than another week, and then only to cautious assaults from the flanks. The closer they got, the more the

French found themselves advancing through the worst debris of battle. In every shell-hole, one stretcher-bearer reported, there lay at least one corpse:

> some on their back, others on their stomach. Some, mown down in a bayonet charge, still clutch their rifle butts. Others have been felled at their machine-gun posts. Human remains everywhere, mangled limbs. Sticking out of the half-flattened trench we are following, here, there, an arm, a leg, a head.

Worse horrors lay in store for the men cutting forward trenches toward Vaux from the line of *retranchements* where Captain Delvert had fought at the beginning of June. One party reported that they were digging not soil but "viande": meat. "Don't pay any attention to it," replied their lieutenant. "Keep on digging."

When the French finally entered Vaux in the early hours of 3 November, it was empty. The Germans were conceding the battlefield, if not the battle. The French lines kept on moving and on 15 December reached Bezonvaux and Louvemont, taken in the first days of the fighting. But by then winter had set in, forcing an end to operations. Jean de Lattre de Tassigny, a commander of de Gaulle's Free French forces in the Second World War but in 1916 a captain posted to Verdun for a second tour of duty, found

> a terrain which was just a half-frozen charnel house. Impossible to make any attempt at digging trenches. The men were split up into small combat groups on the edges of the few shell-holes where there was no risk of getting too badly bogged down. Every night men disappeared into the icy mud.

The New Year arrived, then spring and summer, without engagements on the scale of the previous year. In July the pilot Jacques Boulenger got a bird's-eye view of the landscape which 1916 had made:

> The long white ribbon of the Voie Sacrée, Verdun, half encircled by the open knot of its river, passed beneath my silver wings, and

then I saw the vast grey arena with its countless winding ravines, the ground cracked and ravaged, more pockmarked with shell-holes than a face with small pox; on the left bank of the Meuse, a white and stony desert: that's Cote 304; a few furrows on the right bank, like wrinkles half wiped away: these are the noble remains of Douaumont and Vaux, no longer recognizable except by their geometric outlines.

Only a few moments after getting this view Boulenger was hit in the leg by a machine-gun bullet. Even in its inactive phases Verdun was never a quiet sector.

The next month Raymond Jubert returned for a second tour of duty and was killed in the Bois des Caurières—another melancholy little scene in an obscure corner, though according to a posthumous commendation he "died gloriously" as he reached the German position he was attacking. His death belonged to the last major counterattack that the French launched at Verdun, an operation showing a good deal about what had happened to their army. It had been Nivelle, not Pétain, who took the lion's share of the credit for recapturing Douaumont and Vaux, indeed for holding Verdun. (In his memoirs an unrepentant Joffre would describe Nivelle, "happily assisted" by Mangin, as Verdun's "real savior.") So it was Nivelle, not Pétain, who succeeded Joffre as Commander-in-Chief in December 1916. Not a man given to self-doubt, he took from Verdun increased confidence in his grasp of formulae that would unlock the stalemate of the Western Front. It was based in part on a failure to appreciate what a difficult and dangerous tactic the *barrage roulant* could prove in a war still bedeviled by the lack of reliable communication between artillery and infantry. The disastrous offensive at the Chemin des Dames in April brought his army to the verge of mutiny. Of the three divisions worst affected, two—the 18th and Mangin's old division, the 5th—had fought and suffered at Verdun.

Pétain, brought in to replace Nivelle, relied on the same combination of compassion and sternness he had shown at Verdun to handle the mutinies. He also relied on Verdun. It was, after all, a glorious name and the place where he had made his own name glorious. Properly approached, it was also the closest thing to a soft target that the Western Front offered the French army. His autumn offensive was essentially a demonstration of his own style of generalship, so reassuringly different from Nivelle's: maximum deployment of artillery and minimum risk to the infantry, limited goals and tangible gains. The result certainly had the right effect on Harry Crosby, one of the American ambulance drivers serving on the Western Front in increasing numbers. He arrived already convinced that Verdun was "the most famous place in the history of the World" and found the sight of the Voie Sacrée, again thronged with traffic as it had been in the busiest days of 1916, profoundly satisfying: "This is War all right. I've never been so impressed in all my life. . . . It is thrilling living amidst such surroundings and taking an active part in events that are making history."

The previous history of Verdun teaches one to expect a certain naïvety from noncombatants, including noncombatants on the very edge of the action and even *poilus* who have not yet become combatants in this particular battle. But the novelist John Dos Passos, Crosby's friend and colleague in the ambulance service, saw a rather different Verdun. While knowing little or nothing of the problems in the French army, he recognized troops in a ragged state of morale when he saw them. Men at Verdun had always relied heavily on their *pinard*, the wine ration, for in any battle alcohol plays a role in dulling the senses and blunting the perception of danger. In August 1917 Dos Passos found the men lacing their *pinard* with *agnol*, a mixture of rum and ether. Discipline was much weaker than it had been the previous year, so he was told by a schoolmaster whose house stood by the side of the Voie Sacrée. He spent an afternoon with the schoolmaster and his wife in what had once been their garden, listening to the thunder of the wheels and the grinding of the gears as he watched: "Huge trucks packed with young men, all drunk and shouting and excited and waving their canteens, or else silent and sullen—looking as ghastly as dead men in their shroud of white dust." It sounds very like the desperate, oblivious gaiety that Zola had conjured up at the end of *La Bête humaine*, as the trainload of soldiers hurtled toward the disaster of the Franco-Prussian War.*

Despite the condition of the troops, the offensive proved a success bearing all the hallmarks of Pétain's approach. Its target was Pétain's old preoccupation, the left bank, and it gave the French undisputed possession of Le Mort-Homme and Cote 304, as well as the chance to take about 10,000 prisoners. Dos Passos saw the fighting for the Bois d'Avocourt, beneath Cote 304, where the ease with which the Germans had taken French prisoners had first prompted serious concern about *défaillance* back in March the previous year. He found the wood, if it still deserved the name, "ghoul-haunted," smelling of "poison gas, tangled with broken telephone wires, with ripped pieces of camouflage." But it would still be a long time before the French again saw their original lines up in the Bois des Caures, where Colonel Driant and his *chasseurs* had taken the brunt of the German assault at the start of the battle. And even then the troops who recaptured this sector on 8 November 1918—only three days before the armistice ended the war—were not French but Americans, from the US 26th Division.

So, somewhere between autumn 1916 and November 1918, the Battle of Verdun had ended. Exactly when, or where, it is impossible to say: of all the battles in the war, it was the least capable of reaching a clean and shapely finish. Yet the question of an end mattered greatly to the French, eager to proclaim a victory and to reassure themselves that the long ordeal of suffering was over. The recapture of the Fort de Douaumont provided an obvious opportunity, only partly spoiled by their failure to get Vaux back at the same time. The largest fort on the battlefield and a vast tactical asset to its possessor, it also held a significance beyond the purely military. To the French, it symbolized Verdun—which is to say it had become the symbol of a symbol. Gloomy labyrinth of concrete

---

* For Dos Passos one legacy of Verdun appears to have been a recurring nightmare, described in his private journal, of a sun which "was filmed over like a bloodshot eye and began to sway and wobble in the sky as a spent top sways and wobbles, and whirling rolled into the sea's vermilion waves so that pitchblackness covered me."

though Douaumont might have been in reality, it had become in imagination the fair captive, the daughter of France in German hands—its fate fraught with overtones of the fate that Metz and the annexed provinces had suffered, the fate that Verdun (and France) could but must not suffer.

Henry Bordeaux, who entitled his history of the Verdun forts *The Deliverance of the Captives*, was particularly determined to find these overtones in the prosaic details. A diary entry made as the details of Douaumont's recapture began to filter through to staff headquarters noted with gratification: "Astonished to find themselves entering so formidable a place, the men adopted an expression of reverence, a religious expression. They stopped, gazed around them, forgot the battle." Such feeling was in sharp contrast to the German attitude, as witnessed by the "dismal" state in which they had left it:

> Visitors are met by a sickening smell. The corridors are in a disgusting state of filth. The rooms are in complete chaos: abandoned weapons and equipment lie in heaps. . . . Here is a room where they tried to make a stand; it is jammed with half-burnt corpses, still wearing their gas masks—a nightmare vision of horror.

Thus *The Deliverance of the Captives*, contriving to make the detritus of battle sound like poor housekeeping. Lest the reader fail to take his point, Bordeaux quoted Douaumont's new commander, Major Nicolay—"As for the dirtiness of the rooms, it's inconceivable: they are virtually dunghills"—and emphasized the "German filthiness" that the French found in the Fort de Vaux as well: "No tenant ever left things in a state so detrimental to his reputation." Plainly, the Germans were animals, defiling what they touched, violating what was holy to the French.*

* The accusation that the Germans defiled what they occupied, in the crudest manner, enjoyed a long career. During the Second World War a British writer claimed that Germans who had commandeered châteaux in France "deposited their excrement on the dining-room table. This strange and barbarous habit has been practiced by the Germans in the last three wars: in the last war we used to call it 'the mark of the beast.' I know of no other race which indulges in such practices."

In fact, this propagandist message had no basis in the impressions that Bordeaux himself had formed when he visited Douaumont for the first time after it had been liberated, on 2 December. His diary certainly mentioned the smell of corpses—the 50 or so Germans whom the 400mm shell had killed—but no dirt. Rather, it noted the telephone and radio communications that the Germans had installed, and took a certain wry pleasure in finding a fat gray cat, previously a German mascot, wearing a *tricolore* ribbon round its neck. Moreover, the claims Bordeaux went on to make in print were challenged by Fernand Ducom, a sergeant in the Engineers who had been one of the first to enter the fort on 24 October. He had not noticed even a smell of corpses, much less dirt: "I must admit I did not see anything disagreeable about Douaumont. In fact the Germans, with their characteristic concern for comfort, had administered their conquest in an admirable way." His awe, rather than being the religious awe of a man entering a French holy place, was reserved for the improvements the Germans had made: electric light in corridors that had previously been lit by kerosene lamps, comfortable beds, a proper isolation ward in the sick bay, even a casino for the men in their free time.

Modern efficiency, and hence a concern for comfort, accorded with one stereotype of the Germans, albeit a stereotype different to the one that Bordeaux chose to discover fulfilled at Douaumont. Sergeant Ducom also had the chance to get a glimpse of what might lie behind the stereotypes. The little fraternization between French and Germans that did occur at Verdun usually took place between captives and captured. Ducom spent the night after the fort fell guarding Captain Prollius, commander of the party of signalers which had taken refuge in Douaumont, and so in practice though not in title the last German commander of the garrison. Prollius, it turned out, was talkative and fluent in French. In speaking of Verdun, he grew thoughtful: "a good loser, he acknowledged our success but, despite everything, believed Germany would soon muster a decisive blow." Clearly he felt on safer ground appraising the soldiers from the various nations ranged against Germany: the Russian was brave and could endure terrible losses; the Englishman was no good as a fighter and, moreover, cordially detested; the Frenchman was the best of all. Ducom agreed. But then, he reflected, in the circumstances Prollius would say that, wouldn't he?

In the event, the French did not even wait for the recapture of Douaumont to proclaim victory. So great was their eagerness to proclaim an effective end to a battle that had already lasted so long that they arranged what was in effect a victory celebration for the end of August. Renewed worries for Verdun's safety, particularly because of the men and guns being drained away to the Somme, postponed the ceremony until 13 September. Then Generals Joffre, Pétain, Nivelle and Mangin gathered in the crypt of Verdun's Citadelle with politicians including André Maginot, present in his capacity not as scourge of the generals but as one of the deputies for Lorraine. Representatives of the nation and its allies honored the city with a long list of medals: the Military Cross from Great Britain; the Cross of Saint George from Russia; the Cross of Leopold I from Belgium; the Gold Medal from Italy; the Gold Medal from Serbia; the Ohilitch Gold Medal from Montenegro; and the Cross of the Legion d'Honneur, presented by President Poincaré in the name of France.

It had apparently been intended that Britain's Military Cross would be presented by Lloyd George, appointed Minister of War after Kitchener's death in July and already on his way to succeeding Asquith as Prime Minister. The change of date came too late to adjust his schedule and Lloyd George went ahead with his visit on 3 September. A photograph shows him on the walls of the Citadelle, with field glasses slung around his chest, looking over the roofless shells of the houses toward the hills. Beside him stands Albert Thomas, Undersecretary to the French Minister of War, whose nephew—a lieutenant in the 18th Infantry Regiment—had taken part in Mangin's assault on Douaumont in May. After this distant inspection of the battlefield Lloyd George was guest of honor at a dinner held in the crypt by the Citadelle's commander, General Dubois.

At the end of his speech he raised his glass in a toast and solemnly intoned the name of France three times. The gesture had a great effect. In the few words that preceded it Lloyd George showed himself fluent in the rhetoric commonly applied to the battle—the victory, as it was now being openly called. Verdun had held and, by holding, had vindicated France from the reproach—and self-reproach—of weakness and division which had haunted her since the Franco-Prussian War. So it was appropriate for a visitor from across the Channel to praise a France "strengthened by a *sang-froid* and tenacity which yield nothing to British phlegm." It was also fitting to speak of "the evil force of the enemy" as having been broken "as an angry sea breaks upon a granite rock." In the rhetoric of victory, Verdun was always a rock, its strength residing not so much in the walls of the Citadelle or the forts on the battlefield as in the *poilus*, their chests a human wall, as firm as natural objects in resisting the enemy.

Despite this fluency in what was fitting to say on such an occasion, Lloyd George's speech was bedeviled with language difficulties. His Welsh accent and his rapt style of oratory baffled those Frenchmen at the dinner who flattered themselves that they understood English; and several times even his official interpreter was defeated. But this, it proved, did not matter. The precise details of the rhetoric of war and patriotism never do matter, and the speech had a tremendous impact on its immediate audience and, through reports in the press, on the French public at large. As one officer present in the crypt told Henry Bordeaux: "We had no need to understand what he said to guess that his theme was sacrifice and glory."

——— ✣ ———

THE ROAD FROM VERDUN

A battlefield today is just a field like any other; it's just something
to be turned over. Its soil is ploughed more deeply than in other
fields; its furrows aren't straight; you have to look very closely to
get any idea of the corpses it holds.

Raymond Jubert, *Verdun (mars-avril-mai 1916)* (1918)

M y prologue drew attention to the length at which diarists and
memoirists described their approach to Verdun. Sometimes
they gave almost as much space to the journey down the Voie
Sacrée—let alone the business of getting into position on the battlefield—as they did to the actual fighting. By comparison, they had
little to say about leaving the battle: Captain Delvert's terse "End of
martyrdom" when he came back from defending R1 in June is typical. So all-engulfing and self-contained was the world of Verdun
that its effect was virtually incommunicable. The difficulties of leaving it and returning to ordinary life (or what might pass for ordinary life in wartime) could barely be hinted at, even if they could be
foreseen.

Paul Dubrulle's memoir offers a rare exception to the rule
of near-silence. A Jesuit priest serving as a sergeant in the infantry, Dubrulle arrived in the chaos of late February and served an
eight-day stint at the front—the ideal length specified in Pétain's
tourniquet—before being relieved. He gave few details of the route

his regiment took out of the battlefield; his interest lay entirely in expressing the relief that the men felt at being back in barracks where they could enjoy "an almost completely animal existence: eating and sleeping!" Eventually they boarded a train. The fact that they had to travel in cattle trucks, squatting on the floor amid straw crushed flat by previous occupants, was no cause for complaint:

> It was delightful to find ourselves moving: it had been so long since we had travelled by railway, such a long time that we had been leading the primitive life of men of the woods! We felt a naïve pleasure, like a child taking its first outing. Another feeling filled our hearts: at last, we were leaving Verdun, the realm of horror.

The mood changed when the train arrived at Bar-le-Duc and stopped next to an express filled with civilians. The sight gave the men a sudden, unexpected glimpse of the world they had been fighting for and longing to return to:

> At first its huge carriages filled us with respectful fear. To us poor savages—being moved about in cattle trucks, as if we were parcels—it was like civilization suddenly appearing before our eyes in all the prestige of its superiority. Then, quite naturally, we made the comparison between the two trains. It was striking. On one side, strong men, the nation's treasure, brave men who had risked themselves and everything they had on behalf of others. And opposite? . . . Who were these people leaning out of windows down the whole length of the train, staring at us with curiosity?

It is a finely observed moment, expanding on Jubert's brief description of how he had felt at the smart restaurant in Bar-le-Duc. "We were Red Indians," he exclaimed as he suddenly realized what he looked like in the eyes of the other diners, also instinctively perceiving the contrast between *l'avant* and *l'arrière* as the gulf between

savagery and civilization. His first reaction had been embarrassment, almost shame, as if the marks of battle were something to be
apologized for. Yet the pride of the *poilu* reasserted itself in him, and
with it all the contempt the *poilus* so readily felt for all those who did
not share their own exclusive, masonic experience: the gunners, the
staff officers, the *gendarmes* who policed the Voie Sacrée, let alone
the civilians of the home front, apparently pursuing their normal
lives undisturbed by suffering.

So what did Dubrulle and his comrades think of the people who
were looking so curiously at them?

> We studied them for a while in frigid silence. So this was
> the flower of the much-reviled *arrière*. Who made up the crowd?
> Pleasure-seekers, perhaps, taking advantage of our sufferings and
> our blood to enjoy themselves. Those plump, respectable men?
> Weren't they the industrialists who were growing fat at our ex-
> pense? Those gilded stomachs? Weren't they the shameless fi-
> nanciers who were speculating in our lives? And above all, those
> immensely insignificant figures, weren't they politicians, the sol-
> dier's greatest enemy, the cabinet strategists, the faint copies of
> Gambetta, who vetoed sensible tactics and decided on disastrous
> attacks?

"A dull anger rose in us," added Dubrulle. The anger is familiar
from the literature of Verdun, like the list of grievances and the
stereotypes of the home front on which it depended. Usually, however, it was provoked by reading the newspapers; diatribes against
the press are a common feature of diaries and memoirs. Only occasionally did a *poilu*, like Jubert, describe how he reacted to finding
himself actually among noncombatants and civilians again. Lieutenant Fonsagrive (ironically, a gunner and hence himself in a class
despised by the front-line infantry) left an account of a confrontation with a railway ticket collector who told him that his certificate
of leave did not entitle him to travel on express trains. Fonsagrive
harangued him:

Sir, consider that you are younger than me, that you look as if you're doing very well for yourself, that since mobilization you've kept your peacetime job while I've had to give mine up, and that I live where danger is as great as comfort is small. Really, you could be more easy-going. After the war I hope that the relative contributions everyone has made to national defence will be examined. Scores will have to be settled.

One does not have to believe that he really made so tidily phrased a speech—it obviously smacks of being written up after the event—to accept the authenticity of his feelings. It said what Fonsagrive had wanted to say at the time, and what thousands of *poilus* had wanted to join him in saying: "Scores will have to be settled."

And now it looked to Sergeant Dubrulle and his fellow soldiers at Bar-le-Duc station as if the opportunity to settle scores had arrived. "The silence grew threatening," he remembered, "the tension extreme; the least incident could have unleashed a storm." Yet what happened next suddenly cleared the air. One of the troops got out of his truck, went up to one of the open windows on the express, and timidly asked: " 'Sir, do you happen to have a newspaper?' "

The traveller withdrew into the compartment and, a moment later, reappeared with the most gracious smile, carrying an armful of papers. His action lit a trail of powder. Heads and shoulders disappeared from the windows down the whole length of the express and people carrying papers immediately appeared at the doors. The effect was magical. From our train, from every truck, men jumped out on to the platform, bounded across the tracks and besieged the doors. The newspapers scattered. Conversations started, one after another: "You're coming back from Verdun? What happened to you there? Where were you? Was it dreadful?"

Soon the men were being showered with fruit and cakes, cigarettes and cigars.

"The soul of France hovered around us," Dubrulle's account

concluded, taking flight into lyricism, "and the smile that she gave us was only a pale sign of the immense love she bore us." However sharply observed his description of the *poilus'* resentments might have been, he was determined to provide a happy ending—an ending, indeed, pregnant with large and reassuring symbolism. The determination was congenial to a writer such as Henry Bordeaux, who, in contributing a preface to Dubrulle's memoir, singled out this "meeting between *l'avant* and *l'arrière*" for special praise. By showing what happened after the troops returned from the battlefield, it completed the public, or official, myth of Verdun that was being constructed.

The battle had reaffirmed the strength and greatness which France had signally failed to demonstrate in the *débâcle* of the Franco-Prussian War. It had shown, moreover, that these qualities came, as they always did, from the people: the unity willingly forged out of variety which Pierre-Alexis Muenier had seen in action among the troops of 20th Corps, brought in to save the day in February, and Gaston Gras had again found among the troops (except the poor forgotten Africans) who recaptured Douaumont in October. Even if they were acknowledged, the resentments that their deprivation and suffering had instilled in the troops did not need to be dwelt on. Any division between *l'avant* and *l'arrière* could be healed virtually on the spot, as civilians embraced the combatants on their return, absorbing them back into the larger unity of the French people. Presiding over this "union of hearts" (as Dubrulle called it) was the soul of France, like the Pentecostal spirit, animating and blessing the French as they fulfilled the destiny of their nation.

Such was the vision preferred by the Republic, conforming to the idea of France it had always sought to nurture. Yet, of course, it was far from being the only way to interpret Verdun. There were other lessons to be drawn from the battlefield or discovered on the return home. If anything, time multiplied them and enlarged their scope until they touched the largest issues of nationhood and war at stake during the interwar years. On the whole, time also exposed the inadequacies of any single reading. The process began at the strictly military level, when Nivelle took from Verdun to his job as Commander-in-Chief a large confidence in his powers which the Chemin des Dames attack soon discredited. Thereafter, it appeared, Verdun taught a lesson of the defensive rather than a lesson of the offensive. The strength that the despised forts had shown during the battle was widely admired, and even Mangin declared himself a convert to fortification in the history of the First World War he published in 1920. Concrete and armor plating would continue to play a role in warfare, he argued, and went on to envisage forts with all the technological improvements which the Germans had sought to make at Douaumont during their brief tenure. From such conversions came the faith that France chose to place in her Maginot Line, even its name, let alone its purpose and its design, declaring its descent from the lesson of Verdun.

So France hesitated, after Verdun as she had done before, between a military stance of attack or defense. Yet by the time the Maginot Line itself had been discredited in 1940, the question had already been subsumed into the larger question of the stance that nation should adopt toward nation. Was Verdun, as a victory over the hostile might of Germany, a vindication of militant nationalism? Or was it rather, as a tragic sacrifice, an indictment of militant nationalism? It is not difficult to find politicians taking one or other of these positions during the interwar years; indeed, during the war itself the first had been represented by France's President, Poincaré, and the second by her Prime Minister, Briand. Yet somewhere between these extremes lay a complex and more revealing body of opinion epitomized by the veterans, among whom the veterans of Verdun played a particularly prominent role.

In his impassioned, magisterial survey of their writings Jean Norton Cru chose to call the veterans' characteristic stance as *anti-patriotisme* and to describe it as shaped "by an infinite misery, by the spectacle of the egoism of those who escaped the ordeal of the trenches, by the absurd and murderous conduct of the war." Unsurprisingly (for the refrain is by now familiar) he added: "I do not believe that this feeling has ever been understood by noncombatants, since it did not stop the *poilus* from holding their ground, defending themselves, even attacking, and from having a sort of manly honor that was different in its nature from the honor that the books tell us about." More recently, Antoine Prost has revived the title of a conference held by a veterans' group in the 1930s to call the veterans' attitude *patriotique pacifisme*. It celebrated both France and peace, though not necessarily in a manner that patriots and pacifists (particularly noncombatant patriots and pacifists) could easily recognize. France needed to remain strong among nations, as she had proved herself to be at Verdun, but the nations also urgently needed to reconcile, so that Verdun need never be repeated.

Always a point of reference, Verdun gradually became a generic term. Yet the meaning that *un Verdun* held would always remain equivocal: emphasis could be placed on France's greatness and her need to be great, or on her suffering and her need not to suffer again. This did not diminish Verdun's power as a national symbol for, as I have argued, national symbols do not mark agreement so much as establish a territory where differing shades of meaning can cohabit and disagreement achieve special focus. Its status, however, did warn that Verdun would never be politically decisive any more than it had been decisive in its own avowed military terms, of victory or defeat. The greatest and most expressive arena where the *couple France-Allemagne* had yet been enacted, it could not in itself end that terrible coupling. To Verdun men had brought complex and bitter memories of 1870–71; from Verdun they took memories yet more complex and bitter, to fuel the next stage in the cycle of national confrontation.

For the veterans least of all was Verdun a simple lesson or a decisive political event. To them it was never a generic but a specific place, the witness to experience and the focus of memory. In a very real sense, the men who had come back down the road from Verdun did not ever quite leave Verdun. How could they not linger in imagination, or not return in literal fact, to a place where they had left a part of themselves? How could they not return to a place which, in its physical appearance alone, bore witness to something not yet completed? Even President Poincaré, prematurely celebrating victory in his speech presenting the Cross of the Legion d'Honneur, had made a politician's acknowledgment that the battlefield had a future as well as a past:

> Yet Verdun will again be born from its ashes: the destroyed and deserted villages will rise afresh from their ruins; too long exiled, their inhabitants will come back to their rebuilt homes; under the protection of a victorious peace, this ravaged countryside will recover the laughing face it wore in happy times.

Whether interpreted as promise or as prophecy, the claim was appropriate to the public mood and rhetoric of September 1916. Like almost everything else said about Verdun on that occasion, it was symbolic. France had not just triumphed over the threat of disaster; she would recover, healed and perhaps even strengthened by her ordeal—just as France had emerged the greater, so the Republic insisted, from the *débâcle* of the Franco-Prussian War. Yet at the same time, the words had an obvious and literal application to the future of the battlefield, and this is in itself was to his listeners a matter of deep emotional resonance.

A staff officer who had arrived the day before Poincaré's speech voiced a newcomer's shock at what the battlefield now looked like: "No longer a leaf, no longer a patch of grass; the woods have been razed to the ground, the roads destroyed . . ." To a man such as Henry Bordeaux, who had already spent months at Verdun and formed part of Poincaré's audience in the crypt of the Citadelle, the spectacle was familiar yet no less tragic. Discreet though his accounts of the battle might have been about the suffering of the troops and the mood it engendered, his descriptions of the sheer violence done to the landscape were unsparing. On his first visit to the Fort de Douaumont after its liberation in November he was struck yet again by "this ravaged soil, devoid of vegetation, this lunar landscape, this dead world." It still inspired him with anger as well as sorrow: "This is what men have done, this is what the

Boches have done to our French soil. It cries out for vengeance, it shows us its wounds."

This outburst might have fallen rather too easily into the rhetoric of nationalistic propaganda; it certainly contrived to echo the terms in which it was by then customary to speak of the lost provinces. Yet there is no reason to doubt that Bordeaux's reaction had a spontaneous origin in outraged pastoralism. On a much earlier visit to the Fort de Vaux before it fell to the Germans he had paused with less rhetorical fuss and quite genuine surprise to note that a skylark was singing, "beating its wings and shaking its feet, suspended in the rosy air." Skylarks, indeed, seem to have been particularly stubborn in their refusal to quit the battlefield, for Jean Tocaben also heard them singing above the trenches near Douaumont in March. He was only one of many soldiers to clutch gratefully at the smallest sign of nature amid the destruction, as Raymond Jubert did when he sat alone watching the sun rise on the morning of his counterattack on Le Mort-Homme. Yet soon all they had to clutch at were the place names, now gruesomely inappropriate, which spoke of woods and ponds, forests and farms: "pretty names, conjuring up bucolic freshness, an undulating countryside dense with plants and trees. . . . But the muffled noise of the guns warns us what is left of it."

No name conjured up bucolic freshness more than Fleury, and no place offered a more poignant instance of destruction. The village lay on the ridge of the plateau linking the Fort de Douaumont and the Côte de Froideterre with the forts of Vaux and Souville. Before the war it had boasted about 500 people, their farms and houses standing on either side of a long, straggling main street, in the fashion of Lorraine villages. It had still been a working community when Henry Bordeaux visited it with the historian Louis Madelin in the spring of 1915. The last inhabitants left in the nervous days before 21 February and, when he passed through a week later, Jacques Péricard saw the food on the tables and the unmilked cows in the barns bearing witness to the haste of their departure.

He also saw the holes ripped in the walls by German shells. In

the weeks that followed roofs caved in and houses collapsed altogether. Passing Fleury in the moonlight near the end of March,
Jean Tocaben found its remains a strange "apparition," piles of
gleaming white stones looking more like a quarry than a village.
Soon only the foundations of the houses could be seen and not long
afterward, according to the priest Thellier de Poncheville, even
these had been reduced to "heaps of white foam." The pilot
Bernard Lafont agreed: from the air Fleury was just "a white smear,
a ploughed field enriched with lime." So the village had almost disappeared even before the summer, when the German attack on
Souville from Douaumont and Vaux made it a cockpit of the fighting. Between 13 June and 17 July, one modern historian has calculated, it changed hands 16 times. After that, it was no longer even a
landmark, much less a village, just a position on the military map.
In September Henry Bordeaux could walk over the site without
even realizing that Fleury had once stood there. In the words of
Louis Gillet, another staff officer who wrote a history of the battle,
it had become "nothing": "The whole place has returned into dust,
with the bones of the thousands of adversaries who rushed here
pell-mell, a chaos of shadows in this village of shadows."

It would remain nothing. Poincaré might have looked confidently forward to the day when the destroyed and abandoned villages would rise again from their ruins, and Bordeaux might have
joined him in the hope, but neither Fleury nor eight other villages
in the battle zone were ever rebuilt or resettled.* It would not have
been hard to put up new houses, of course, but regenerating the
countryside on which the villages depended was a different proposition. Though they had never exactly worn "the laughing face"
with which Poincaré's rhetoric embellished them, the hills round
Verdun had at least yielded a meager livelihood to farmers, foresters
and hunters. Now the soil had been sifted to the texture of a sand
dune and choked with the litter of battle. Unexploded shells were a
continual hazard as well as a powerful pollutant, joined in their nox-

---

* The others were Douaumont, Vaux, Bezonvaux, Louvemont, Ornes, Haumont, Beaumont
and, on the left bank, Cumières. The Mémorial-Musée stands on the site of Fleury.

ious effect by rusting metal and traces of chemicals like diphosgene, which had killed even the flies on the battlefield. Several attempts to reforest Le Mort-Homme were doomed to failure.

So the battlefield was, after all, to remain the "dead world" which had grieved and angered Henry Bordeaux in November 1916. To many, and to the veterans above all, this fate seemed not just inevitable but appropriate. For all the rhetoric of the speech-makers, talk of recovery and regeneration would always mean less at Verdun than acts of remembrance and commemoration. Even in 1916 the troops had sometimes paused to wonder what sort of monument could adequately mark the place where they fought; the question was a natural result of their feeling that their acts were making history. To Pierre Teilhard de Chardin, serving as a stretcher-bearer with a colonial regiment, "a great Christ" belonged on Froideterre: "Only the figure of the One who was crucified can gather together, express and assuage all the horror, the beauty, the hope and the deep mystery in such a torrent of conflict and sorrows." In this suggestion he was out of tune with the feeling of most *poilus*, sometimes tinged but never dominated by religious imagery. Nor would the Republic have endorsed monuments exclusively Christian in their reference. It would have been willing to waive its prohibition against statues of the living in the case of Pétain—or so it was widely assumed during the interwar years—but he wisely refused to countenance the proposal.*

The battlefield belonged to the generals no more than it did to the theologians. It belonged to the dead, left where they had fallen without burial. Charles Delvert's last thoughts had been of them when he looked around R1 at the end of his martyrdom: "Alas! what mournful sentinels we're leaving behind! There they are, lined up on the parapet, stiff in their canvas sheets, dripping with blood, fierce and solemn guardians of this patch of French soil, which they still seem, in death, to seek to deny the enemy." Here the sentiment

* After his trial and official disgrace at the end of the Second World War, his body was refused burial in the spot reserved in the cemetery at Douaumont and, in at least one instance, his name was chiseled off a monument he had unveiled.

is plainly ambivalent: that his comrades should remain where they had died struck Delvert as at once indecent yet fitting. If their fate remained troubling because it was somehow incomplete, it could be brought to real completion only on the battlefield itself. These two reactions, working together, tell us a great deal about why, even after the journey back down the Voie Sacrée, the official attempts to declare the battle over, the armistice of 1918 and the victory parades of 1919, Verdun still appeared unfinished in the imagination of the veterans. It still beckoned for them to return; it demanded more if it was to be brought to anything like closure.

When the 137th Infantry Regiment was posted back to Verdun in January 1919 its commander, Colonel Collet, took particular care to inquire into the fate of its soldiers who had died there in 1916. His most curious, and soon most famous, discovery concerned the 3rd Company, which in the early hours of 12 June had been defending a position in the Ravin de la Dame near Douaumont. Here a row of bayonets was found sticking from the soil, and below it the bodies of the men from 3rd Company still standing in their trench with their rifles in their hands. They had been buried by a German shell as they fought to the last. So, at least, it was widely assumed, for the Tranchée des Baïonettes appealed so vividly to the imagination that the story of their fate seemed to demand reverential embellishment. Articles in the press were followed by an account in Colonel Henri Bouvard's *La Gloire de Verdun*, originally published in 1922, which lent a stamp of authority to the legend. By then an American millionaire had donated the money for the site to be roofed over and preserved, as it had been found, for posterity.

Yet examination of the legend soon raises doubts. That a shell should have buried men standing in a row was unlikely; that they should have been buried alive in soil as fine as sand added to the implausibility. The lack of any contemporary reports, or even rumors, hinting at the fate of 3rd Company was curious, and by no means all the postwar testimony which thronged to confirm it was reliable. Some stories told by men claiming to have witnessed similar incidents elsewhere on the battlefield sounded fanciful and opportunistic. Only the most credulous could swallow Lieutenant Gaudy's account of finding, in the same action that had killed 3rd Company, more than 50 men in both a front and a reserve trench still standing at attention, dead without a mark on them. Though both were cited as crucial witnesses, neither Major Dreux nor Lieutenant Polimann of the 137th Infantry claimed to have seen what had actually happened in the Tranchée des Baïonettes. Significantly, Polimann was most preoccupied by his lingering shame at being forced to surrender while other men had fought and died heroically.

Obviously men had fought and died heroically in the Tranchée des Baïonettes. In all likelihood they had died in all the various ways in which other men, before and after them, died at Verdun. The soil had probably been thrown over their bodies by the Germans who took the trench. The rifles and bayonets may have been left where they had been found leaning against the trench wall, or the bayonets may have been deliberately placed as markers, in a hasty gesture of respect. All these suggestions were made in the postwar years by veterans alarmed at seeing the sufferings of their comrades overlaid by melodrama and superstition, and these in turn fueling what was identifiably growing into battlefield tourism. "Let's have done with this childishness which makes us a laughing stock," protested Joseph Bayon, former chaplain to the 137th Infantry. Jean Norton Cru, a debunker of legends particularly hostile to legends involving bayonets, treated the Tranchée des Baïonettes with withering scorn in his survey of veterans' writing.

It should come as no surprise that Jacques Péricard was not among the skeptics. The Tranchée des Baïonettes was, after all, virtually an appendix to the story of *Debout les Morts!* which he himself had set in motion in 1915. Indeed, he adopted virtually the same approach to the two legends: sticking modestly to the known facts himself while contriving to smile on the exaggerations and embellishments that others cherished. The story of the Tranchée des Baïonettes as it had been promulgated might not be true, but why quibble in the presence of such undoubted heroism? Why challenge a particular monument when the whole battlefield should be a monument? In this respect his history of Verdun reads like the work of a Catholic theologian determined neither to endorse nor to challenge a doubtfully attested miracle. He himself would probably not have resented or denied the comparison.

The whole battlefield should be a monument: most of the veterans could assent to this, at least. In 1916 Verdun had been a charnel house, as the troops often put it; after the war a charnel house, literally, was needed. In the 1920s the bones were gathered from the soil and placed in the crypt of the gigantic Ossuaire built on the site of the Ferme de Thiaumont, not far from where the Fort de Douaumont still stands. The number of these anonymous dead runs perhaps to 75,000, perhaps to 150,000, depending on which tourist brochure or guidebook you read. Most of them remember to specify that all the bones are French. The building above them combines, in glum uncertainty, the ecclesiastical and the military style. A tower rises where a church tower should rise, but contrives to look like a gigantic artillery shell. It looks out over a spreading military cemetery and, beyond, a host of smaller graveyards and monuments, like the little chapels marking the sites of the abandoned villages. Even now that the grass and the forests have at last grown up again, the landscape is still visibly marked by craters and trench lines. Here the dead will always vastly outnumber the living.

In the city of Verdun itself Poincaré's promise could be fulfilled, though the style of the rebuilding turned a dull provincial city into a place inexpressibly drab. Despite the dedication to peace it has proclaimed in recent years, it still feels like a garrison town that has died. Here the monuments predominate: a gloomy congress of military commanders outside the Citadelle, a stalwart row of soldiers on a bastion of the rampart protecting the bridge. The Victory Monument in the main thoroughfare is topped by the figure of a Gallic warrior, mustaches curling, hands resting on the hilt of his two-handed sword. Only near the Porte Saint-Paul is there a monument that speaks of the battle which the *poilus* described in the witness they left.

The Porte itself, a reconstructed medieval gateway to the city, bears a plaque listing all the dates when Verdun was besieged, damaged or destroyed, from the fifth century to the twentieth century. The list is incomplete since the plaque was put up before 1940, when the city fell to the Germans after the briefest of engagements, and 1944, when it was liberated by General Patton's Third Army.* Symbolically positioned just outside the gate stands Rodin's bronze, *La Défense*. Its composition, a female figure with a dead or wounded soldier on her knee, echoes the medieval Pietà, which showed the Virgin Mary cradling the crucified Christ. Rodin's woman combines a winged Victory and Marianne or Liberty, with her bare breasts and Phrygian cap, though her ruffled wings and contorted figure express neither triumph nor repose. Her face, like that of François Rude's "La Marseillaise" on the Arc de Triomphe, is vibrant with emotion and her mouth is open. What issues forth is no patriotic anthem: she is screaming in grief and anger at the sky.

---

* The future President Mitterrand was among the French soldiers taken prisoner in 1940. Patton's campaign in 1944 marked his second tour of duty in Lorraine, for he had taken part in the Saint-Mihiel Offensive and the Meuse-Argonne Offensive in September 1918. After liberating Verdun in early September 1944 Patton was stalled outside Metz until December; his chief obstacle, the linchpin of the fortifications which the French had built between the wars, was Fort Driant.

SOURCES AND NOTES

—— ✛ ——

A SUMMARY OF THE MAIN SOURCES

Like many English people, I first read about Verdun in Alistair Horne's *The Price of Glory: Verdun 1916*, originally published in 1962 (the latest revised edition was published by Penguin, 1993). I remain indebted to it for its incisive narrative and the many occasions it offers for disagreement. For the rest, the literature of Verdun, the First World War and its background is too vast for me to attempt to mention here all the books I have found useful. Instead I list below the works I have found particularly important, in the following categories:

    1) Diaries, letters, memoirs, fiction, etc. by combatants at Verdun;
    2) Works about Verdun by generals, politicians and journalists;
    3) Early histories of Verdun (pre–World War Two);
    4) Official military histories of Verdun;
    5) Later histories, collections of essays, etc., dealing with Verdun;
    6) Studies of the First World War;
    7) Studies of French and European history, 1870–1914.

The first category is by far the richest. Other works on which I have drawn in my text are identified in the notes to each chapter.

1) Diaries, letters, memoirs, fiction, etc. by combatants at Verdun:

Jean Norton Cru's *Témoins: Essai d'analyse et de critique des souvenirs de combattants edités en français de 1915 à 1928* (Paris: "Les Étincelles," 1929) goes far beyond its function as a bibliography of combatants' writing; Cru's commentary (much of it deriving from his own experience and testimony) makes it in its own right a major achievement in the literature of Verdun and the First World War.

Émile Baumann, *L'Abbé Chevoleau, caporal au 90e d'infanterie*. Paris: Perrin, 1917.

Marc Boasson, *Au soir d'un monde: Lettres de guerre de Marc Boasson (16 avril 1915–27 avril 1918)*. Paris: Librairie Plon, 1926.

Louis Botti, *Avec les zouaves: De Saint Denis à la Somme. Journal d'un mitrailleur (1914–1916)*. Paris: Berger-Levrault, 1922.

Jacques Boulenger, *En escadrille*. 5th edition. Paris: Librairie Gallimard, 1930.

Pierre Louis Georges Bréant, *De l'Alsace à la Somme: Souvenirs du Front (août 1914–janvier 1917)*. Paris: Librairie Hachette, 1917.

André Bridoux, *Souvenirs du temps des morts*. Paris: Albin Michel, 1930.

Henri Castex (editor), *Verdun, années infernales: La Vie du soldat au front d'août 1914 à septembre 1916*. [The letters of Anatole Castex.] Paris: Albatros, 1980.

Pierre Chaine, *Mémoires d'un rat*. Paris: À L'Oeuvre, 1917.

Augustin Cochin, *Le Capitaine Augustin Cochin: Quelques lettres de guerre*. Preface by Paul Bourget. Paris: Bloud & Gay, 1917.

Charles L. Delvert, *Histoire d'une compagnie: Main de Massiges–Verdun, novembre 1915–juin 1616. Journal de marche*. Preface by Ernest Lavisse. Paris: Berger-Levrault, 1918. (The full version of the diaries from which Delvert drew this account later appeared as *Carnets d'un fantassin* [Paris: Albin Michel, 1935].)

Robert Desaubliaux, *La Ruée: Étapes d'un combattant: La Meuse, L'Yser, L'Artois, La Somme, Verdun*. Paris: Bloud & Gay, 1919.

André Dollé, *Le Cote 304 et souvenirs d'un officier de zouaves*. Paris: Berger-Levrault, 1917.

Pierre Drieu La Rochelle, *Le Chien de l'écriture* and *Le Lieutenant de tirailleurs*, collected with *La Comédie de Charleroi*. Originally published 1920. Paris: Gallimard, 1970.

Paul Dubrulle, *Mon régiment dans la fournaise de Verdun et dans la bataille de la Somme: Impressions de guerre d'un prêtre soldat*. Preface by Henry Bordeaux. Paris: Librairie Plon, 1917.

Georges Duhamel, *Vie des martyrs, 1914–1916*. Originally published 1917. 111th edition. Paris: Mercure de France, 1938.

Marcel Dupont [pseudonym of Marcel Ernest Béchu], *En campagne:*

L'Attente: Impressions d'un officier de légère (1915–16–17). Paris: Librairie Plon, 1918.

Lieutenant Fonsagrive, *En batterie! Verdun 1916—La Somme—L'Aisne—Verdun 1917*. Paris: Librairie Delagrave, 1919.

Georges Gaudy, *Souvenirs d'un poilu du 57e Regiment d'Infanterie: Les Trous d'obus de Verdun (fevrier–août 1916)*. Paris: Librairie Plon, 1922.

Gaston Gras, *Douaumont, 24 octobre 1916*. Paris: Imprimeries Vieillemard, 1934.

Guy Hallé, *Là bas avec ceux qui souffrent*. Paris: Garnier Frères, 1917.

Louis Hourticq, *Récits et réflexions d'un combattant: Aisne—Champagne—Verdun, 1915–1917*. Paris: Librairie Hachette, 1918.

Alfred Joubaire, *Pour la France: Carnet de route d'un fantassin*. Preface by Fortunat Strowski. Paris: Perrin, 1917.

Raymond Jubert, *Verdun (mars–avril–mai 1916)*. Preface by Paul Bourget. Paris: Payot, 1918.

Capitaine J. La Chaussée, *De Charleroi à Verdun dans l'infanterie*. Paris: Eugène Figuière, 1933.

Capitaine Georges de La Tour du Pin, *Le Creuset*. Paris: Librairie Plon, 1920.

Bernard Lafont, *Au ciel de Verdun: Notes d'un aviateur*. Paris: Berger-Levrault, 1918.

Commandant Paul Lefebvre-Dibon, *Quatre Pages du 3e Battalion du 74e R.I.: Extraits d'un carnet de campagne 1914–1916*. Preface by Louis Madelin. Second edition. Nancy: Imprimerie Berger-Levrault, 1920.

Henri Libermann, *L'Infanterie héroïque et douloureuse: Thiaumont—Moronvilliers juillet–août 1916—mars–avril 1916. Récits vécus d'un officier de ligne*. Paris: Perrin, 1918.

Jean Limosin [pseudonym of Georges Maurice Ardant], *De Verdun à l'Yser: Notes d'un aumônier militaire*. Paris: Bonne Presse, 1917.

Pierre Mac Orlan [pseudonym of Pierre Dumarchey, or Dumarchais], *Les Poissons morts: La Lorraine—L'Artois—Verdun—La Somme*. Paris: Payot, 1917.

Capitaine [Pierre] de Mazenod, *Étapes du sacrifice: Souvenirs d'un commandant de batterie (1915–1917)*. Paris: Librairie Plon, 1922.

César Méléra, *Verdun (juin–juillet 1916), La Montagne de Reims (mai–juin 1918)*. Paris: Les Éditions de la Lucarne, 1925.

H. Morel-Journel, *Journal d'un officier de la 74e Division de l'Infanterie et de l'Armée française d'Italie (1914–1918)*. Montbrison: Imprimerie Eleuthère Brassart, 1922.

Pierre-Alexis Muenier, *L'Angoisse de Verdun: Notes d'un conducteur d'auto sanitaire*. Preface by Victor Giraud. Paris: Librairie Hachette, 1918.

René Naegelen, *Les Suppliciés*. Originally published 1927. Paris: Éditions Colbert, 1966.

J.-L. Gaston Pastre, *Trois ans de front: Belgique—Aisne et Champagne—Verdun—Argonne—Lorraine. Notes et impressions d'un artilleur*. Paris and Nancy: Berger-Levrault, 1918.

Lieutenant Jacques Péricard, *Ceux de Verdun*. Paris: Librairie Payot, 1917.

Colonel [Sylvain-Eugène] Raynal, *Le Drame du Fort de Vaux*. Originally published 1919. Verdun: Éditions Lorraines, 1996.

Paul Simon, *Fanion-Bleu-Jonquille: Carnet de Campagne d'un Chasseur de Driant 1914–1918*. 6th edition. Paris: Éditions Argo, 1930.

Marc Stéphane [pseudonym of Marc Richard], *Verdun: Ma dernière relève au Bois des Caures (18–22 février 1916): Souvenirs d'un chasseur de Driant*. Paris: Librairie René Liot, 1929.

Abbé Charles Thellier de Poncheville, *Dix mois à Verdun*. Paris: J. de Gigord, 1919.

Jean Tocaben, *Virilité*. Preface by André Tardieu. Paris: Flammarion, 1931.

Dr. Paul Voivenel, *à Verdun avec la 67e DR: Notes d'un médecin-major*. Edited by Gérard Canini. Témoins et Témoignages. Nancy: Presses Universitaires, 1991.

Jules Romains was not a veteran of Verdun but made careful use of combatants' writing for *Prelude à Verdun* (1937) and *Verdun* (1938), novels in the sequence *Les Hommes de bonne volonté*. Two further books offer classic accounts of the combatants' experience of the war: Andre Pézard's *Nous Autres à Vauquois, 1915–1916*, originally published 1918 (Nancy: Presses Universitaires, and Paris: Sécretariat d'État Chargé des Anciens Combattants et Victimes de Guerre, 1992) and Maurice Genevoix's *Ceux de 14* (Paris: Flammarion, 1960), a collection made in 1950 of *Sous Verdun* (1916), *Nuits de guerre* (1917), *Au Seuil des guitounes* (1918), *La Boue* (1921) and *Les Éparges* (1923); to it Genevoix added *La Mort de près* (Paris: Plon, 1972).

2) Works about Verdun by generals, politicians and journalists:

Maurice Barrès, *L'Âme française et la guerre*, Volume 9: *Pendant la bataille de Verdun*, and Volume 10: *Voyage en Angleterre*. 3rd edition. Paris: Émile-Paul Frères, 1918–19.

General Erich von Falkenhayn, *General Headquarters 1914–16 and Its Critical Decisions*. London: Hutchinson, 1919.

Joseph Joffre, *Mémoires du Maréchal Joffre (1910–1917)*. Two volumes. Paris: Librairie Plon, 1932.

General Charles Mangin, *Comment finit la guerre*. 18th edition. Paris: Plon, 1920.

General Charles Mangin, *Lettres de guerre, 1914–1918*. Paris: Arthème Fayard, 1950.

Henri Philippe Pétain, *La Bataille de Verdun*. Paris: Payot, 1929.

Raymond Poincaré, *Au service de la France: Neuf années de souvenirs*, Volume 5: *L'Invasion 1914*, and Volume 8: *Verdun 1916*. Paris: Librairie Plon, 1925 and 1931.

Raymond Poincaré, *Messages, discours, allocutions, lettres et télégrammes (31 juillet 1914–17 novembre 1918)*. Paris: Bloud & Gay, 1919.

Crown Prince Wilhelm, *My War Experiences*. London: Hurst & Blackett, 1922. (Far more coherent than the scrappy account of Verdun in *The Memoirs of the Crown Prince of Germany*. London: Thornton Butterworth, 1922.)

3) Early histories of Verdun (pre–World War Two):

Henry Bordeaux, *Verdun 1916: Les derniers jours du Fort de Vaux, la bataille devant Souville, les captifs délivrés*. Paris: Librairie Plon, 1936. (Particularly useful in conjunction with Bordeaux's diary, published as *Histoire d'une vie*, Volume 4, *La Guerre incertaine de la Marne à Verdun, 2 août 1914–21 février 1916*, and Volume 5, *Douleur et gloire de Verdun, 21 février 1916–2 janvier 1917*. Paris: Librairie Plon, 1957 and 1959.)

Paul Heuzé, *Les Camions de la victoire*. Paris: La Renaissance du Livre, 1920.

Louis Madelin, *Verdun*. Collection "La France dévastée," Série 1: Les Régions. 3rd edition. Paris: Félix Alcan, 1920. (One of the ablest early histories, in contrast to the same author's hasty propagandist effort, *L'Aveu: La Bataille de Verdun et l'opinion allemande. Documents inédits et fac-similés*. Paris: Librairie Plon, 1916.)

Daniel Mornet, *Tranchées de Verdun: Juillet 1916–mai 1917*. Paris: Berger-Levrault, 1918.

Jacques Péricard, *Verdun: Histoire des combats qui se sont livrés en 1916 sur les deux rives de la Meuse*. Originally published 1933. Paris: Nouvelle Librairie de France, 1997. (Particularly useful in conjunction with Philippe Glorennec, "Le Fonds Péricard," in Canini, *Mémoire de la Grande Guerre*, 313–24.)

Francisque Vial, *Territoriaux de France*. Paris: Berger-Levrault, 1918.

4) Official military histories of Verdun:

Service Historique, Ministère de la Guerre, *Les Armées Françaises dans la grande guerre*, Volume 4: *Verdun et la Somme*. Paris: Imprimerie Nationale, 1926.

Reichsarchiv/Kriegsministerium, *Der Weltkrieg 1914 bis 1918*, Volume 10: *Die Operationen des Jahres 1916*. Berlin: Mittler, 1936.

5) Later histories, collections of essays, etc., dealing with Verdun:

Georges Blond, *Verdun*. Paris: Presses de la Cité, 1961.

Gérard Canini, *Combattre à Verdun: Vie et souffrances quotidiennes du soldat, 1916–1917*. Nancy: Presses Universitaires, 1988.

Gérard Canini (editor), *Mémoire de la Grande Guerre: Témoins et témoignages*. Actes du colloque de Verdun (12, 13, 14 juin 1986). Nancy: Presses Universitaires, 1989.

Alain Denizot, *Verdun 1914–18*. Paris: Nouvelles Éditions Latines, 1996.

Maurice Genevoix (editor), *Verdun 1916: Actes du Colloque International sur la bataille de Verdun, 6–7–8 juin 1975*. Verdun: Association Nationale de Souvenir de la Bataille de Verdun, Université de Nancy II, 1976.

Jacques-Henri Lefebvre, *Verdun: La plus grande bataille de l'histoire racontée par les survivants*. Originally published 1960. 12th edition. Verdun: Éditions du Mémorial, 1996.

Antoine Prost, "Verdun," *Les Lieux de Mémoire*, Part 2: *La Nation*, Volume 3. Edited by Pierre Nora. Paris: Gallimard, 1986.

Malcolm Brown, *Verdun 1916* (Stroud: Tempus, 1999) and David Mason, *Verdun* (Moreton-in-Marsh: Windrush Press, 2000) appeared too recently for me to make use of them.

6) Studies of the First World War:

Paul Allard, *Les Dessous de la Guerre révélés par les comités secrets*. 93rd edition. Paris: Éditions de France, 1933.

Stéphane Audoin-Rouzeau, *14–18: Les Combattants des tranchées*. Paris: Armand Colin, 1987.

Annette Becker, *La Guerre et la foi: de la mort à la mémoire*. Paris: Armand Colin, 1994.

Jean-Jacques Becker, *1914: Comment les Français sont entrés dans la guerre: Contribution à l'étude de l'opinion publique printemps–été 1914*. Paris: Presses de la fondation nationale des sciences politiques, 1977.

Jean-Jacques Becker and Stéphane Audoin-Rouzeau (editors), *Les Sociétés européennes et la guerre de 1914–1918*. Center d'Histoire de la France contemporaine. Nanterre: Université de Paris X–Nanterre, 1990.

Jean-Jacques Becker, Jay M. Winter, Gerd Krumeich, Annette Becker and Stéphane Audoin-Rouzeau (editors), *Guerre et Cultures 1914–1918*. Paris: Armand Colin, 1994.

Correlli Barnett, *The Swordbearers: Studies in Supreme Command in the First World War*. London: Eyre & Spottiswoode, 1963.

Brian Bond and Ian Roy (editors), *War and Society: A Yearbook of Military History*. London: Croom Helm, 1976.

Joanna Bourke, *An Intimate History of Killing: Face-to-Face Killing in Twentieth-Century Warfare*. London: Granta Books, 1999.

Hugh Cecil and Peter H. Liddle (editors), *Facing Armageddon: The First World War Experienced*. London: Leo Cooper, 1996.

Modris Eksteins, *Rites of Spring: The Great War and the Birth of the Modern Age*. London and New York: Bantam Press, 1989.

David Englander, "The French Soldier, 1914–18," *French History*, 1 (March 1987), pp. 49–67.

David French, "The Meaning of Attrition, 1914–16," *English Historical Review*, 103 (April 1988), pp. 385–405.

Martha Hanna, *The Mobilization of Intellect: French Scholars and Writers during the Great War*. Cambridge, MA: Harvard University Press, 1996.

Barry D. Hunt and Adrian Preston (eds), *War Aims and Strategic Policy in the Great War, 1914–1918*. London: Croom Helm, 1977.

Paul M. Kennedy (editor), *The War Plans of the Great Powers, 1880–1914*. London: George Allen & Unwin, 1979.

Eric J. Leed, *No Man's Land: Combat and Identity in World War I*. Cambridge: Cambridge University Press, 1979.

Jacques Meyer, *La Vie quotidienne des soldats pendant la Grande Guerre*. Paris: Hachette, 1966.

Allan R. Millett and Williamson Murray (editors), *Military Effectiveness*. Volume 1: *The First World War*. Boston: Allen & Unwin, 1987.

George L. Mosse, *Fallen Soldiers: Reshaping the Memory of the World Wars*. New York: Oxford University Press, 1990.

Guy Pedroncini, *Les Mutineries de 1917*. Paris: Presses Universitaires de France, 1967.

Guy Pedroncini, *Pétain: Le Soldat et la gloire, 1856–1918*. Paris: Perrin, 1989.

Antoine Prost, *Les Anciens Combattants et la société française, 1914–1939*. Three volumes. Paris: Presses de la Fondation Nationale des Sciences Politiques, 1977.

Gerhard Ritter, *The Schlieffen Plan: Critique of a Myth*. Translated by Andrew and Eva Wilson. Foreword by B. H. Liddell Hart. London: Oswald Wolff, 1958.

Pierre Servent, *Le Mythe Pétain: Verdun, ou les tranchées de la mémoire*. Paris: Payot, © 1992.

Leonard V. Smith, *Between Mutiny and Obedience: The Case of the French Fifth Infantry Divisions during World War One*. Princeton, NJ: Princeton University Press, 1994.

Trudi Tate, *Modernism, History and the First World War*. Manchester and New York: Manchester University Press, 1998.

Tim Travers, *The Killing Ground: The British Army, the Western Front and the Emergence of Modern Warfare, 1900–1918*. London: Allen & Unwin, 1987.

Jay Winter, *Sites of Memory, Sites of Mourning: The Great War in European Cultural History*. Cambridge: Cambridge University Press, 1995.

Robert Wohl, *The Generation of 1914*. London: Weidenfeld & Nicolson, 1980.

7) Studies of French and European history, 1870–1914:

Claude Digeon's *La Crise allemande de la pensée française (1870–1914)* (Paris: Presses Universitaires de France, 1959) is vast, old-fashioned and for my purposes indispensable.

Maurice Agulhon, *Marianne au combat, 1789–1880: L'Imagerie et la symbolique républicaines de 1789 à 1880*. Paris: Flammarion, 1979.

Maurice Agulhon, *Marianne au pouvoir, 1880–1914: L'Imagerie et la symbolique républicaines de 1880 à 1914*. Paris: Flammarion, 1989.

Benedict Anderson, *Imagined Communities: Reflections on the Origin and Spread of Nationalism*. London: Verso, 1983.

Richard D. Challener, *The French Theory of the Nation in Arms, 1866–1939*. New York: Columbia University Press, 1955.

Suzanne Citron, *Le Mythe nationale: histoire de France en question*. Paris: Les Éditions ouvrières and Études et Documentation internationales, 1987.

Linda L. Clark, *Social Darwinism in France*. Alabama: University of Alabama Press, © 1984.

I. F. Clarke, *Voices Prophesying War: Future Wars 1763–3749*. Originally published 1966. 2nd edition. Oxford and New York: Oxford University Press, 1992.

Yvette Conry, *L'Introduction du Darwinisme en France au XIXe siècle*. Paris: Librairie Philosophique J. Vrin, 1974.

Henry Contamine, *La Revanche, 1871–1914*. Paris: Berger-Levrault, 1957.

Paul Crook, *Darwinism, War and History: The Debate over the Biology of War from the "Origin of Species" to the First World War*. Cambridge: Cambridge University Press, 1994.

Ernest Gellner, *Nationalism*. London: Weidenfeld & Nicolson, 1997.

Richard Hartshorne, "The Franco-German Boundary of 1871," *World Politics*, 2 (1950), 209–50.

E. J. Hobsbawm, *Nations and Nationalism since 1780: Programme, Myth, Reality*. 2nd edition. Cambridge: Cambridge University Press, 1992.

Michael Howard, *The Franco-Prussian War: The German Invasion of France, 1870–1871*. London: Rupert Hart-Davis, 1961.

John F. V. Keiger, *France and the Origins of the First World War*. London: Macmillan, 1983.

Martin Kitchen, *The German Officer Corps, 1890–1914*. Oxford: Clarendon Press, 1968.

Herman Lebovics, *True France: The Wars over Cultural Identity, 1900–1945*. Ithaca and London: Cornell University Press, 1992.

Edmond Marc Lipiansky, *L'Identité française: Représentations, mythes, idéologies*. Paris: Éditions de l'Espace Européen, 1991.

Karma Nabulsi, *Traditions of War: Occupation, Resistance and the Law*. New York: Oxford University Press, 1999.

Claude Nicolet, *L'Idée républicaine en France: Essai d'histoire critique*. Paris: Gallimard, 1982.

Robert A. Nye, *Crime, Madness and Politics in Modern France: The Medical Concept of National Decline*. Princeton, NJ: Princeton University Press, 1984.

Léon Poliakov, *The Aryan Myth: A History of Racist and Nationalist Ideas in Europe*. Translated by Edmund Howard. London: Chatto, Heinemann for Sussex University Press, 1974.

François Roth, *La Guerre de 70*. Paris: Fayard, 1993.

François Roth, *La Lorraine annexée (1870–1918)*. Annales de l'Est, Mémoire No 50. Nancy: Université de Nancy, 1976.

David Schoenbaum, *Zabern 1913: Consensus Politics in Imperial Germany*. London: Allen & Unwin, 1982.

Dan P. Silverman, *Reluctant Union: Alsace-Lorraine and Imperial Germany, 1871–1918*. University Park and London: Pennsylvania State University Press, 1973.

Zeev Sternhell, *La Droite révolutionnaire, 1885–1914: Les origines françaises du fascisme*. Paris: Éditions du Seuil, 1978.

Tzvetan Todorov, *Nous et les autres: La Réflexion française sur la diversité humaine*. Paris: Éditions du Seuil, 1989.

Robert Tombs (editor), *Nationhood and Nationalism in France: From Boulangism to the Great War, 1889–1918*. London: HarperCollins Academic, 1991.

Paul Viallaneix and Jean Ehrard (editors), *Nos Ancêtres les Gaulois*. Clermont-Ferrand: Faculté des Lettres et Sciences humaines de Clermont-Ferrand II, 1982.

Eugen Weber, *Peasants into Frenchmen: The Modernization of Rural France, 1870–1914*. London: Chatto & Windus, 1977.

Michel Winock, *Nationalism, antisémitisme et fascisme en France*. Paris: Éditions du Senil, 1982.

Theodore Zeldin, *France 1848–1945*. Two volumes. Oxford History of Modern Europe. Oxford: Clarendon Press, 1973–77.

Unfortunately, H. J. Wesseling, *Soldier and Warrior: French Attitudes toward the Army and War on the Eve of the First World War*, translated by Arnold J. Pomerans (Westport, CT, and London: Greenwood Press, 2000) appeared too recently for me to make use of it.

NOTES TO THE TEXT

Prologue: The Road to Verdun

[1–20]

Valéry (epigraph): *Oeuvres*, Volume 5: *Discours* (Paris: Éditions de la N.R.F., 1935), 72. **Giono** (epigraph): *Refus d'obéissance* (Paris: Gallimard, 1937), 38. **Madelin**: *Verdun*, 10. **"Avenue de l'Opéra"**: Limosin, 50. **378,777 casualties**: *Armées françaises*, 4, Part 3, 509. Recent historians who have refined them or commented on them include Canini, whose preface to *Combattre à Verdun* includes a particularly useful discussion, and Denizot, 188. **one and a half million dead in the whole war**: I am accepting the figure of 1,451,340 offered in revision of earlier estimates by Prost, *Anciens Combattants*, 2, Chapter 1. **Alistair Horne**: *Price of Glory*, 327–8. **reference books**: for example, in its entry for Verdun *The Macmillan Dictionary of the First World War*, edited by Stephen Pope and Elizabeth-Anne Wheal (London: Macmillan, 1995) quotes a "probable" total of 984,000 casualties and claims that about half of them were killed. Colin Jones's *The Cambridge Illustrated History of France* (Cambridge: Cambridge University Press, 1994), 245, speaks of "maybe half a million German deaths." **"Isn't every unit bound"**: Naegelen, 81. **"Our men know"**: Bréant, 150. **"In our old age"**: Dupont, 113. **"The general opinion in the trenches"**: Chaine, 61. **"He was hungry for some clarification"**: Bridoux, 9. *monade de guerre*: Pierre Teilhard de Chardin, *Genèse d'une Pensée*, edited by Alice Teillard-Chambon [sic] and Max Henri Begouen (Paris: Bernard Grasset, 1962), 198. **"As soon as I saw the battlefield"**: Private J. Ayoun, quoted by Péricard, *Verdun*, 535–6. **Genevoix**: *Mort de près*, 18–19. **"I want only to talk"**: Dollé, 5. **"When we get back"**: Jubert, 138–9. **"grim and austere"**: *Les Derniers Jours du Fort de Vaux* in *Verdun 1916*, 30. **"from Paris to Saint-Germain or Versailles"**: *Les Captifs délivrés* in *Verdun 1916*, 270. **"Are they men or lumps of mud?"**: *Captifs* in *Verdun 1916*, 274. **"their features taut"**: Hourticq, 70. **"You don't take up your position"**: Dupont, 222–3. **"What disgrace!"**: Boasson, 127. **"It's a bad one, this spot?"**: Jean Meigneu of the 174th Infantry, quoted by Péricard, *Verdun*, 378. **Naegelen**: *Suppliciés*, 83. **Mazenod**: *Étapes du sacrifice*, 191. **"The very look"**: La Tour du Pin, 222. **"Seeing us, they began"**: Simon, 204–5. *neurasthénie*: I am indebted to the discussion in Nye, which quotes Proust and Ballet on 148–9 and Durkheim on 150. See also Bourke, Chapter 8 ("Medics and the Military"), 246–64.

le cafard: for it and associated terms, see the entry in Gaston Esnault, *Le Poilu tel qu'il se parle: Dictionnaire des termes populaires récents et neufs employés aux armées en 1914–1918, étudiés dans leur étymologie, leur développement et leur usage* (Paris: Éditions Bossard, 1919). I owe the quotation from *L'Écho des marmites* (10 March 1917) to Audoin-Rouzeau, 92.

[21–41]
Ludendorff (epigraph): quoted by George C. Bruntz, *Allied Propaganda and the Collapse of the German Empire in 1918* (Stanford: Stanford University Press, and London: Oxford University Press, 1938), 3. **"a false report"**: Marc Bloch, "Réflexions d'un historien sur les fausses nouvelles de la guerre" (1921), reprinted in *Mélanges historiques* (Paris: École Pratique des Hautes Études, 1963), 1, 41–57; the words quoted appear on page 54. **War has to have a goal**: my discussion of goals is indebted to Hunt, "Introduction" to Hunt and Preston. **"always a serious means"**: Carl von Clausewitz, *On War*, translated by Colonel J. J. Graham, new and revised edition by Colonel F. N. Maude (London: Kegan Paul, Trench, Trübner, 1908), 1, 21. **engulfed by war hysteria**: I have particularly in mind Jean-Jacques Becker's *1914*. **Clemenceau**: article in *L'Aurore* for 19 June 1905, quoted by Digeon, 506, fn2. **Wilhelm II**: quoted by Fritz Fischer, *Germany's Aims in the First World War* (London: Chatto & Windus, 1967), 33. **Churchill**: quoted by John Terraine, *Impacts of War 1914 and 1918* (London: Hutchinson, 1970), 217. **"a war of extermination?"**: quoted by Jean Lacouture, *De Gaulle*, Volume 1: *Le Rebelle 1890–1944* (Paris: Éditions du Seuil, 1984), 62. **Léon Daudet**: quoted by Eugen Weber, *Action Française: Royalism and Reaction in Twentieth-Century France* (Stanford, CA: Stanford University Press, 1962), 101–2. ***Lord Northcliffe's Weekly Dispatch . . .*** **Horatio Bottomley**: quoted by Cate Haste, *Keep the Home Fires Burning: Propaganda in the First World War* (London: Allen Lane, 1977), 125 and 126–7. **"The impression left on one's mind"**: Marjorie Grant, *Verdun Days in Paris* (London: W. Collins, 1918), 126–7. **Schlieffen Plan**: my discussion is indebted to Ritter. ***Deutschland ganzlich einzukreisen***: quoted by Barbara Tuchman, *The Guns of August* (New York: Dell, 1963), 21. ***Feinde ringsum***: Roger Chickering, *We Men Who Feel Most German: A Cultural Study of the Pan German League, 1886–1914* (London: Allen & Unwin, 1984), 123. **Slavic East . . . Latin West**: the elder Moltke writing in 1860, cited by Ritter, 18. **"a great fortress"**: the Great Memorandum of 1905, quoted by Ritter, 144. **"shaped solely by the imperatives"**:

Hunt, "Introduction" to Hunt and Preston, 9. **manifest reluctance by Sir John French**: see Richard Holmes, *The Little Field Marshal: Sir John French* (London: Jonathan Cape, 1981), 225–40. **"fitted into the original Schlieffen Plan"**: L. C. F. Turner, "The Significance of the Schlieffen Plan," in Kennedy, 212. **"I don't know what's to be done"**: quoted by Sir Llewellyn Woodward, *Great Britain and the War of 1914–1918* (London: Methuen, 1967), 39. **"The truth is"** (footnote): Sir John French, "Preface" to Friedrich von Bernhardi, *Cavalry in War and Peace*, translated by Major G. T. M. Bridges (London: Hugh Rees, 1910), xviii. **"rationalization of weakness"**: the phrase comes from John Bowditch, "The Concept of Élan Vital: A Rationalization of Weakness" in *Modern France*, edited by Edward M. Earle (Princeton: Princeton University Press, 1951). The idea is usefully developed by Nye, 313. **"It is always necessary in battle"**: quoted by Contamine, 167. I am borrowing the English translation offered by Barnett, 248. **Charles de Gaulle**: quoted by Lacouture, 1, 46. **Kitchener . . . alone in her cabinet**: on 7 August 1914 he told his colleagues that he based his reckoning on a three-year war needing a British army of a million. Sir Edward Grey, the Foreign Secretary, privately noted that this estimate "seemed to most of us unlikely, if not incredible" (quoted by Philip Magnus, *Kitchener: Portrait of an Imperialist* [London: John Murray, 1958], 284). *l'épreuve de la durée*: Lavisse, "L'Usure des forces allemandes" in Émile Durkheim, Ernest Lavisse, Louis Cazamian and others, *Lettres à tous les Français* (Paris: Librairie Armand Colin, 1916), 32–3. **unreliable statistics of battle**: they are used to good effect in his discussion of attrition by Niall Ferguson, *The Pity of War* (London: Allen Lane, The Penguin Press, 1998), 290–303; Rawlinson's words are quoted from here. *limoger*: see John Keegan, *The First World War* (London: Hutchinson, 1998), 98–9.

[42–57]

Valéry (epigraph): *Discours*, Volume 5 of *Oeuvres*, 70. **ground has an emotional content**: my discussion is indebted to Travers, 255. **"a point of contact"** (footnote): quoted by Martyn Cornick, "Fighting Myth with Reality: The Fall of France, Anglophobia and the BBC," in *France at War in the Twentieth Century: Propaganda, Myth and Metaphor*, edited by Valerie Holman and Debra Kelly (New York and Oxford: Berghahn Books, 2000), 86. **Raymond Poincaré**: *Au service*, 5, 61. **historic associations**: for some of these associations I am indebted to Tuchman, notably 229–30 and 382.

"Verdun exercises a sort of fascination": "La bataille de Verdun" (article of 26 February 1916), *Pendant la bataille*, 3. Historians who followed him include Henry Dugard, *La Bataille de Verdun, 21 février–7 mai 1916* (Paris, 1916), Louis Gillet, *La Bataille de Verdun* (Paris and Brussels: G. Van Oest, 1921) and Mangin, *Comment finit la guerre*. **a draft of the memo**: Falkenhayn, 209–18. In quoting from it I have silently altered the English translator's archaic usage, "moral," to "morale." **philosophy of the defensive**: Brigadier-General Sir John Edmonds, "Preface" to *Military Operations: France and Belgium, 1917* (London: Macmillan, 1940), 1, xi. **German weakness**: for Germany's sense of weakness on eve of war Ferguson, especially 98–9. *Gericht*: Horne, 38. **"Everything is very simple in war"**: Clausewitz, 1, 77.

PART I:

Clausewitz (epigraph): 3, 222. I am grateful to Daniel Pick, *War Machine: The Rationalisation of Slaughter in the Modern Age* (New Haven and London: Yale University Press, 1993) for first drawing my attention to the importance Clausewitz assigned to "friction" in war.

Chapter 1: The Bois des Caures

[61–79]

Driant (epigraph): quoted by Lefebvre, 75. **Madelin**: *Verdun*, 3–4. **General Séré de Rivières**: my account of the Verdun fortifications and their history is indebted to Gérard Canini, "Politique et Militarisation (1870–1914)," Chapter 9 of *Histoire de Verdun*, edited by Alain Girardot (Toulouse: Éditions Privat, 1982); Roth, *Guerre de 70*, especially pages 664–8; and to the vivid chapter on Fort Douaumont in Horne. **the first sentence of Plan XVII**: quoted by Tuchman, 59. **the elder Moltke . . . Ducrot**: quoted by Howard, 207 and 208. **father of a family**: Limosin, 46. **"a very tranquil and peaceful place"**: Étienne Gilson, quoted by Laurence K. Shook, *Étienne Gilson*, The Étienne Gilson Series, No. 6 (Toronto: Pontifical Institute of Mediaeval Studies, 1984), 74. **"We have almost nothing"**: Castex, 130. **"To understand how obnoxious"**: quoted by Gaston Jollivet, *Le Colonel Driant*, 2nd edition (Paris: Librairie Delagrave, 1918), 181. **ready for catastrophe**: see Horne, 51. **adolescent de Gaulle**: The story is reproduced in de Gaulle's *Lettres, notes et carnets*

(Paris: Librairie Plon, 1980–88), 1, 7–8. **"a noble people"**: Clarke, 104. I am indebted to Clarke's admirable discussion of Driant's fiction. **"in an inconceivable aberration"**: Driant, "Comment restaurer l'idée patriotique menacée," conference speech of 16 February 1908, quoted by Daniel David, "Un Officier témoin de son temps: le commandant Driant," in Canini, *Mémoire*, 279. **"Should our front line"**: quoted by Jollivet, 179–80. **Galliéni . . . Joffre**: quoted by Allard, 19–20. **admitted to one of his lieutenants**: Simon, 167. **"You talk to us about heavy artillery"**: de Gaulle ironically quoted the words in *La France et son armée*, originally published in 1938 (London: Hutchinson, not dated), 138. **Voivenel**: *à Verdun*, 26. **Bordeaux**: *Douleur et gloire*, 17. **"In the streets you see"**: eyewitness report noted by Voivenel, 125. **Maurice Barrès . . . Reporting his visit in April** (footnote): "Un voyage à Verdun: II. Les fleurs de Verdun" (article of 15 April 1916), reprinted in *Pendant la bataille*, 167–8. **"Any news?"**: Stéphane, 14. **"a terrible day"**: Pézard, 281. **20 February . . . Bois des Caures**: Stéphane, 32.

[80–95]
Driant (epigraph): quoted by Jollivet, 194. **"Ah! Mon Dieu!"**: Gaudy, 120–1. **"That one's coming straight at me"**: Thellier de Poncheville, 206. **Jünger**: cited by Ferguson, *Pity of War*, 341. **"Imagine, if you can"**: Stéphane, 68–9. **"In the clear air"**: Voivenel, 117. **"A long pool of blood"**: Delvert, *Histoire*, 240. In *Carnets*, 252, the luckless D . . . is identified as Deline. **"A great pile of earth"**: Jubert, 192. **"When a shell bursts"**: Dubrulle, 26. **George Sand**: *Journal d'un voyageur pendant la guerre*, 4th edition (Paris: Michel Lévy Frères, 1871), entry for 25 September 1870. **"Bah!"**: Mazenod, 196; the ellipses are Mazenod's. **openly mad**: my examples of their behavior come from Gaudy, 109–10 and Morel Journel, 266. **"Barely able to hear"**: Stéphane, 80. **"It puts you partly to sleep"**: Maurice Galbrun, quoted by Glorennec in Canini, *Mémoire*, 321. **Private T. Jacobs** (footnote): quoted by Keegan, *First World War*, 427. **"the sensation of being in a cabin"**: Bréant, 154. **"Perhaps the best comparison"**: Dubrulle, 25. **"I never saw the bayonet"**: Cru, 611. Bourke is also useful in considering and exploding the myth of the bayonet: see, for example, page 51, which cites an Australian Army medical services report for 1914–18 as finding bayonets responsible for only 0.5 percent of wounds. **"The two of us"**: quoted by Shook, 81. **clearest version of the incident**: my sources are Simon, 175ff; Georges Becker,

Verdun—Le premier choc de l'attaque allemande (Paris: Berger-Levrault, 1932), 53; Stéphane, 196, n1; A. L. Grasset, *La Guerre en action*, Volume 4: *Verdun: Le premier choc à la 72e Division: Brabant—Haumont—Le bois des Caures (21–24 février 1916)* (Paris: Éditions Berger-Levrault, 1927), especially the map of positions in the Bois des Caures, Map 9, between 66 and 67. The account in Horne, 79–80, is characteristically clear. **official and unofficial accounts of his fate**: Georges Becker, 55; Grasset, 11 and 62–3; Stéphane, 193ff. **"Dreadful, dreadful race"**: Cochin, 55–6. **"wir sind keine Barbaren"**: Gilson, quoted by Shook, 81–2. **"unkillable"**: Louis Papin, quoted in Péricard, *Verdun*, 221. **"like a soul in pain"**: Stéphane, 25. **Driant held a conference**: Jollivet, 205, and Henry Dugard, *La Victoire de Verdun: 21 février 1916–3 novembre 1917* (Paris: Librairie Académique Perrin, 1918), 172. **"whiter than candlewax"**: Stéphane, 108. **"You're all cowards"**: Simon, 195. *l'arrière de l'arrière*: Meyer, 12. **"They fixed their gaze straight ahead"**: Madelin, 55. **"Oh! là, mon Dieu!"**: Sergeant Jules Hacquin, quoted by Péricard, *Verdun*, 24.

Chapter 2: The Fall of Douaumont

[96–118]
Laquièze (epigraph): quoted by Péricard, *Verdun*, 285. **Bréant took stock of the losses**: Bréant, 158. **"converted the beautiful countryside"** . . . **"to break down enemy defenses quickly"**: quoted by Kenneth Macksey, *Guderian: Panzer General* (London: Greenhill Books, and California: Presidio Press, 1992), 17 and 16. **"The unfortunate men apologized"**: Duhamel, 136. **"There were so few"**: Muenier, 75. **"Nothing can stand up against this"**: Muenier, 2. **"It wouldn't take anything"**: Muenier, 47. **On their way into position . . . Of the troops they were supposed to relieve**: the details and quotations in these paragraphs draw mainly on Péricard, *Ceux de Verdun*, particularly 98–129 and 199–201, and *Verdun*, particularly 43–6. **"The soil of the trenches"**: Maurice Barrès, *Les Traits éternels de la France*, 19th edition (Paris: Émile Paul Frères, 1916), 21. **"I seemed to see a furnace"** (footnote): Arthur Machen, introductory note to "The Bowmen" in *The Collected Arthur Machen*, edited by Christopher Palmer (London: Gerald Duckworth, 1988), 195. **Henry Bordeaux suspected**: he kept the suspicion for the privacy of his diary: see *La Guerre incertaine*, 269. **"We had the clear impression"**: Péricard, *Ceux de Verdun*, 129. **"We are lost!"**: Dubrulle, *Mon régiment dans la fournaise*, 34. **"We marched for six hours"**: Drieu La Rochelle, *Le Chien de l'écriture*, in *La*

Comédie de Charleroi, 141–2. My account is indebted to Jean Bastier, *Pierre Drieu La Rochelle: Soldat de la Grande Guerre, 1914–1918* (Paris: Éditions Albatros, 1989). **"These men were no longer men"**: *Chien de l'écriture*, 148–9. **General Deville**: as reported by Jubert, 36. *style Joffrette*: Voivenel, 55. **"It breaks your heart"**: Second Lieutenant de Beaucorps, quoted by Canini, *Combattre à Verdun*, 43. **the work of several historians**: notably Kurt von Klüfer, formerly a major in the 24th Brandenburg Regiment to whom the capture of Douaumont was first reported, in *Seelenkräfte im Kampf um Douaumont* (published in 1938) and Horne, Chapter 9, to which—despite my disagreements—I am greatly indebted. **official communiqué**: *Recueil des communiqués officiels des gouvernements et états majors de tous les belligérants*, Série 26 (Paris: Payot & Cie, 1917), 35–6. **official communiqué**: *Recueil*, 26, 37. **"O Verdun!"**: Voivenel, 68. **curious story to tell**: Péricard, *Ceux de Verdun*, 139–46; reprinted in Lefebvre, 126–33. **August 1792**: see Rodney Allen, *Threshold of Terror: The Last Hours of the Monarchy in the French Revolution* (Stroud, Glos: Sutton Publishing, 1999), 104. **Crimean War**: see Trevor Royle, *Crimea: The Great Crimean War 1854–1856* (London: Little Brown, 1999), 96. **same trick**: see, for example, Bordeaux, *Les derniers jours du Fort de Vaux* in *Verdun 1916*, 62, and *La Bataille devant Souville* in *Verdun 1916*, 182. The accusation that the Germans pretended to surrender crops up in combatants' memoirs (for instance, Botti, 219), but is dwelt on most vehemently by Edward R. Coyle, in *Ambulancing on the French Front* (New York: Britton, 1918), Chapter 16. **German soldiers with the spikes removed**: Horne, 119. **virtually as prisoners**: Barrès, "Pendant la bataille" (article of 1 March 1916), reprinted in *Pendant la bataille*, 10. See also: "The German troops are shut up in the internal shelters of the fort and as a result are prisoners" (article in *La Croix*, 29 February; quoted by Servent, 113). **General Verraux**: quoted by Brunhes, article in *L'Oeuvre* of 28 February 1916, reprinted by Dugard, *La Bataille de Verdun*, as a footnote on 35–6. **"Even if I am killed"**: Péricard, *Ceux de Verdun*, 149.

[118–139]
Chrétien (epigraph): quoted by Péricard, *Verdun*, 61. **"The defense of the Meuse"**: quoted by Péricard, *Verdun*, 71. **defend to the hilt**: Smith, 130, usefully speaks of *defense à outrance* as the counterpart to *attaque à outrance*. **good Republican general**: I am indebted to David B. Ralston, "From Boulanger to Pétain: The Third Republic and the Republican Generals," in Bond and Roy, 178–201. **sabers . . . were sprinkled with**

incense: cited by Michael Curtis, *Three Against the Third Republic: Sorel, Barrès, and Maurras* (Princeton: Princeton University Press, 1959), 39. **"He walked into the meeting room"**: quoted by Péricard, *Verdun*, 71. **"volatile"**: report of 2 November 1915, quoted by Pedroncini, *Pétain*, 137. **"The soldier of 1916"**: Louis Mairet, *Carnet d'un combattant (11 février 1915–16 avril 1917)* (Paris: Georges Crès, 1919), 172–5. **"That isn't French"** (footnote): quoted by Meyer, 175. **Pierre Dreyfus . . . Alfred**: see Michael Burns, *Dreyfus: A Family Affair, 1789–1945* (London: Chatto & Windus, 1992), Chapters 19 and 20. **"I am like my leg"**: quoted by Pierre Belperron, *Maginot of the Line*, translated by H. J. Stenning, with additional matter edited by John E. Cross (London: Williams & Norgate, 1940), 44. **de Gaulle**: for the circumstances of his capture see Lacouture, 1, 70–3; the two legends appear in Edmond Pognon, *De Gaulle et l'histoire de France: Trente ans éclairés par vingt siècles* (Paris: Albin Michel, 1970), 13–14. The quotation from his lectures in captivity appears in Lacouture, 1, 84. **"It is a nation"**: Bordeaux, *Vaux* in *Verdun 1916*, 67. **early Revolutionaries**: Richard Cobb examines the "Thermidorean imagery" of the Revolutionaries in "The Officers and Men of the Parisian *Armée*," reprinted in *The French and Their Revolution*, edited by David Gilmour (London: John Murray, 1998), 72–3. *La Psychologie du soldat*: quoted by Meyer, 81. **"You would think"**: Castex, 129. **"we were Red Indians"**: Jubert, 154. **"immortal heroes"**: Barrès, "Pendant la bataille" (1 March 1916), *Pendant la bataille*, 11. **But for him the turning-point**: Muenier, 119–26.

PART II:

Clausewitz (epigraph): 1, 26. **Freud** (epigraph): *Collected Papers* (London: The Hogarth Press and the Institute of Psycho-Analysis, 1924–50), 4, 303–4.

Chapter 3: The Raft of the *Medusa*

[143–154]
de Gaulle (epigraph): *La France et son armée*, 124. **Michelet** (epigraph): *Oeuvres complètes*, edited by Paul Viallaneix (Paris: Flammarion, 1971–82), 21, 435. **"Three absurd weeks"**: de Gaulle, *Vers l'armée de métier*, first published in 1934 (London: Hutchinson, not dated), 32. **"One should not, in general, rely"**: quoted by Howard, 220. **as if thunderstruck**:

cited by Rupert Christiansen, *Tales of the New Babylon: Paris 1869–1875* (London: Sinclair-Stevenson, 1994), 159. **fate of the *Medusa***: my account is drawn from Michel Le Bris, *Romantics and Romanticism*, translated by Barbara Bray and Bernard C. Swift (London: Macmillan, 1981), 123–5. **"Here we are on the raft"**: quoted by John Bierman, *Napoleon III and His Carnival Empire* (London: John Murray, 1989), 379–80. **"Old age is a shipwreck"**: de Gaulle, *Mémoires de guerre*, Volume 1: *L'Appel (1940–1942)* (Paris: Plon, 1954), 61. **"We will not yield"**: quoted by Robert Baldick, *The Siege of Paris* (London: Batsford, 1964), 26. **"We didn't deserve this"**: quoted by Ernest Lavisse, "L'Invasion dans le département de l'Aisne," in *Essais sur l'Allemagne impériale* (Paris: Librairie Hachette, 1888), 3. **"a truly Hohenzollern idea"**: letter of 13 December 1870 in *Letters to Doctor Kugelmann* (London: Martin Lawrence, not dated), 115. **"France in its entirety"**: the phrase is from the second of Mommsen's two letters to "The People of Italy," dated 20 August 1870, translated in Theodor Mommsen, David Friedrich Strauss, F. Max Müller and Thomas Carlyle, *Letters on the War between Germany and France* (London: Trübner, 1871), 12–13. ***Kriegsverrat***: the doctrine is discussed by Geoffrey Best, "How Right Is Might? Some Aspects of the International Debate about How to Fight Wars and How to Win Them, 1870–1918," in *War, Economy and the Military Mind*, edited by Geoffrey Best and A. Wheatcroft (London: Croom Helm, 1976), 125. **"The very severest treatment of the guilty"**: quoted by Howard, 378. **"The German authorities give notice"**: quoted by Lavisse, "Invasion," 31. **"The war is gradually acquiring"**: Fedor von Rauch, quoted by Howard, 379. **"It will come to this"** . . . **"shot and stabbed to death"**: quoted by Howard, 380 and 381. **"The whole country understands"**: quoted by Howard, 372–3. **"Tout est fini"**: quoted by Digeon, 117. **"It was the end of everything"**: *La Débâcle*, 2, 586, in *Oeuvres complètes*, edited by Maurice Le Blond and Eugène Fasquelle (Paris: François Bernouard, 1927–9). **barbarians want to destroy Rome**: see, for example, Paul de Saint-Victor, *Barbares et bandits: La Prusse et la Commune*, 5th edition (Paris: Calmann-Lévy, 1885), 178: "Just as the Barbarians wanted to destroy Rome, so the extermination of France is the Prussians' avowed goal." **"a wound beneath the wound"**: "La Réforme intellectuelle et morale de la France" (incorporated in *La Réforme intellectuelle et morale*) in *Oeuvres complètes*, edited by Henriette Psichari (Paris: Calmann-Lévy, 1947–61), 1, 366.

[155–159]

Gobineau (epigraph): quoted from *Selected Political Writings*, edited by Michael Biddiss (London: Jonathan Cape, 1970), 225. **Renan**: Preface to *Questions contemporaines* (1868), *Oeuvres complètes*, 1, 28. **by 1848 a political cartoon**: reproduced in Agulhon, *Marianne au combat*, 86. **Louis Blanc**: quoted by Nicolet, 159. **Flaubert**: quoted by Digeon, 166. **"I cannot walk"**: quoted by David Duff, *Eugénie and Napoleon III* (London: Collins, 1978), 249. **"mere general"**: quoted by Frank McLynn, *Napoleon: A Biography* (London: Jonathan Cape, 1997), 112. **"The horse looks intelligent"**: quoted by Zeldin, 1, 596.

[162–171]

Durkheim (epigraph): *Les Formes élémentaires de la vie religieuse. Le système totémique en Australie* (Paris: Librairie Félix Alcan, 1912), 329 and 331. **"The Empress is *légitimiste*"**: quoted by Zeldin, 1, 514. The cousin Napoléon III referred to was the ever-meddlesome Prince Jérôme; the Duc de Morny was his half-brother; the Duc de Persigny had helped bring the Emperor to power. **Aristide Briand**: the calculations are from William L. Shirer, *The Collapse of the Third Republic: An Inquiry into the Fall of France in 1940* (London: Pan Books, 1972), 94. **561 men**: Zeldin, 1, 589. **Clemenceau**: quoted by Shirer, 94. **"the very backbone of the nation"**: *La Débâcle*, 2, 554. **"a Head of State who is not a Head"** . . . **"a useless organ"**: quoted by Nicolet, 169. **Saint-Saëns** (footnote): quoted by Brian Rees, *Camille Saint Saëns: A Life* (London: Chatto & Windus, 1999), 379. **Verlaine**: quoted by Agulhon, *Marianne au combat*, 225. My discussion is deeply indebted to this volume and its companion, *Marianne au pouvoir*. **Treitschke**: *Was fordern wir von Frankreich?* (1870), translated as *What We Demand from France* in *Germany, France, Russia, and Islam* (London: Jarrold & Sons, Allen & Unwin, 1915), 135. **cults of the Sacré-Coeur and Sainte Bernadette**: for a pertinent discussion, see Ralph Gibson, *A Social History of French Catholicism, 1789–1914* (London and New York: Routledge, 1989), 148. **"an enormous festival of the political right"** (footnote): Gibson, 148. **Jeanne d'Arc**: I am indebted to Rosemonde Sanson, "La 'Fête de Jeanne d'Arc' en 1894: Controverse et célébration," *Revue d'Histoire Moderne et Contemporaine*, 20 (1973), 444–63, and to Gerd Krumeich, "Joan of Arc Between Right and Left," in *Nationhood and Nationalism*, edited by Tombs, 63–73. **"What troubled the minds"**: Jean Quercy, *Journal d'un curé de campagne* (1915), quoted by Annette Becker,

70. **"Jeanne d'Arc won"**: quoted by Tuchman, *Guns of August*, 485. **"their older sister"**: Thellier de Poncheville, 166.

Chapter 4: A Certain Idea of France

[173–181]
"All my life . . ." (epigraph): de Gaulle, *L'Appel*, 1. **"fascist"**: see Patrick Marnham, *The Death of Jean Moulin: Biography of a Ghost* (London: John Murray, 2000), 141. **"The sword of France"**: quoted by Alexander Werth, *De Gaulle: A Political Biography* (Harmondsworth, Middx: Penguin, 1967), 65. **"that hidden force"**: de Gaulle, *La France et son armée*, 124. **"deep resources"**: Marc Bloch, *L'Etrange Défaite: Témoignage écrit en 1940* (Paris: Armand Colin, 1957), 218. **Bloch was reminded**: *L'Étrange Défaite*, 212, n1. **"a fire without flame"**: Renan, "La Réforme intellectuelle et morale de la France" (incorporated in *La Réforme intellectuelle et morale*) in *Oeuvres complètes*, 1, 355. **"France can do anything"**: Renan, "La Monarchie constitutionelle en France" (1869), in *La Réforme intellectuelle et morale, Oeuvres complètes*, 1, 520–1. **"Our faults caused our reverses"**: quoted by Michael Biddiss, "Hippolyte Taine and the Making of History," *The Right in France: 1789–1996*, edited by Nicholas Atkin and Frank Tallatt (London and New York: Tauris Academic Studies, 1998), 75. **"It was the scientific spirit"**: Zola, "Lettre à la jeunesse" in *Le Roman expérimental*, 83, in *Oeuvres complètes*. **"This is why we"** . . . **"All we have to do"**: *Roman expérimental*, 88, in *Oeuvres complètes*. **"Young man, young man"**: Barrès, *Scènes et doctrines du nationalisme* (Paris: Librairie Plon, 1925), 1, 288–9. **"We have been continually betrayed"**: *L'Argent (suite)* (April 1913), in *Oeuvres complètes de Charles Péguy 1873–1914* (Paris: Librairie Gallimard, 1917–55), 14, 209.

[182–191]
Fustel de Coulanges (epigraph): quoted by Digeon, 238. **In France . . . traditional accounts**: I have found two older works on French theories and theorists of ancient history still of value: Jacques Barzun, *The French Race: Theories of Its Origins and Their Social and Political Implications Prior to the Revolution* (New York: Columbia University, 1932) and Marc Bloch, "Sur les grandes invasions: Quelques positions de problèmes," *Mélanges historiques*, 1, 90–109. I am also indebted to: Poliakov; Stephen A. Kippur, *Jules Michelet: A Study of Mind and Sensibility* (Albany: State University of

New York Press, 1981); Eugen Weber, "Gauls versus Franks: Conflict and Nationalism," in *Nationhood and Nationalism*, edited by Tombs, 8–21; and the essays gathered in *Nos Ancêtres les Gaulois*. **"The Gauls were lively"**: Pierre Anquetil's *Histoire de France depuis les temps les plus reculés jusqu'à la révolution de 1789* (1803), quoted by Claudine Lacoste, "Les Gaulois d'Amédée Thierry," in *Nos Ancêtres les Gaulois*, 204. **"ferocious beasts in search of pasture"**: quoted by Poliakov, 25. **Abbé Siéyès**: Emmanuel-Joseph Siéyès, *Qu'est-ce que le Tiers État?*, quoted by Barzun, *French Race*, 248. **Augustin Thierry**: "Sur l'antipathie de race qui divise la nation française" (1820) in *Dix ans d'études historiques*, in *Oeuvres complètes* (Paris: Furne & Cie, 1851–56), 6, 240. **François Guizot**: *Du Gouvernement de la France depuis la Restauration et du ministère actuel* (1820), quoted by Bloch, "Sur les grandes invasions," *Mélanges historiques*, 1, 99. **"Such was the accumulation of races"**: Michelet, *Oeuvres complètes*, 4, 182. **"the ingenious races of the Midi"** etc: *L'Histoire Universelle* (1831) in *Oeuvres complètes*, 2, 290–1. **"Here can be found the proof"**: *Oeuvres complètes*, 2, 247. **"the head and the thought of France"**: *Oeuvres complètes*, 2, 291. **"On that day everything was possible"**: *Histoire de la Révolution française* (1847–53), edited by Gérard Walter (Paris: Nouvelle Revue Française, Bibliothèque de la Pléiade, 1961–62), 1, 430. The ellipses are Michelet's. **"Give us festivals!"**: *L'Étrange Défaite*, 210–11. For the affinity between Bloch and Michelet I am indebted to the discussion of "federation and epiphany" in Arthur Mitzman, *Michelet, Historian: Rebirth and Romanticism in Nineteenth-Century France* (New Haven and London: Yale University Press, 1990), 153.

[191–203]
Edgar Quinet (epigraph): quoted by Digeon, 28. **"France certainly undertakes"**: *La France devant L'Europe* (1871), in *Oeuvres complètes*, 20, 658. **Georges Bidault**: quoted by Anthony Beevor and Artemis Cooper, *Paris After the Liberation: 1945–1949* (London: Hamish Hamilton, 1994), 129. **"Doubtless all great nations"**: *Le Peuple* (1846), edited by Lucien Refort (Paris: Librairie Marcel Didier, 1946), 236. *l'anti-France*: *Le Peuple*, 240. **Britain . . . had allowed herself to be chloroformed**: *La France devant l'Europe* (1871), in *Oeuvres complètes*, 20, 641. **"A badly matched couple"**: Romains, Preface to *Le Couple France–Allemagne* (Paris: Ernest Flammarion, 1934), x–xi. **Victor Hugo**: quoted by Hans Kohn, *Prophets and People: Studies in Nineteenth-Century Nationalism* (New York: Macmillan, 1957),

49. **Guizot**: quoted by Digeon, 24. **population growth**: for the figures and pertinent analysis, see: Nye, 134–5; Paul Weindling, *Health, Race and German Politics between National Unification and Nazism, 1870–1945* (Cambridge: Cambridge University Press, 1989), 11–13; Michael S. Teitelbaum and Jay M. Winter, *The Fear of Population Decline* (New York: Academic Press, 1985), 21; and Francis Ronsin, *La Grève des ventres: Propagande néo-malthusienne et baisse de la natalité française (XIXe–XXe siècles)* (Paris: Aubier Montaigne, 1980), 14. **"Berlin has usurped"**: Victor Tissot, *Voyage au pays des milliards*, 4th edition (Paris: E. Dentu, 1875), 2. **"from early days"**: quoted by T. C. W. Blanning, "The Death and Transfiguration of Prussia," *The Historical Journal*, 29, 2 (1986), 442. **"Many states have changed"**: Blanning, 442. **Ernest Vizetelly**: *My Days of Adventure: The Fall of France, 1870–1871* (London: Chatto & Windus, 1914), 108–9. **"Do you call it *unity*"**: *La France devant l'Europe*, in *Oeuvres complètes*, 20, 694. **"Greater Germany"**: *Oeuvres complètes*, 20, 644. **"is an artificial State"**: Gustave Le Bon, *The Psychology of the Great War*, translated by E. Andrews (London: T. Fisher Unwin, 1916), 53. **Saint-Victor**: *Barbares et bandits*, 13–14. **"men of iron . . . whom our century"**: Renan, *La Guerre entre la France et l'Allemagne* (1870), in *Oeuvres complètes*, 1, 433. **"If the leprosy of egoism"**: Renan, "La Monarchie constitutionelle en France," in *Oeuvres complètes*, 1, 513. **Marc Bloch commented** (footnote): "Sur les grandes invasions," *Mélanges historiques*, 1, 99. **Michelet himself had been among the first**: see, for example, "France is not a race like Germany; she is a nation," from the introduction to Michelet's *Histoire universelle* (1831), in *Oeuvres complètes*, 2, 253.

Chapter 5: "What Is a Nation?"

[205–216]

more than just historical interest: Hobsbawm, 2. **"a historical result brought about"**: Renan, *Oeuvres complètes*, 1, 892. **"They had a beginning"**: *Oeuvres complètes*, 1, 905. **"the law of the century"**: *Oeuvres complètes*, 1, 905, **"Forgetting, and I would even say errors"**: *Oeuvres complètes*, 1, 891. **"a soul, a spiritual principle"**: *Oeuvres complètes*, 1, 903. **"A nation never serves"**: *Oeuvres complètes*, 1, 905. **"Should doubts arise"**: *Oeuvres complètes*, 1, 906. **"Wait, gentlemen"**: *Oeuvres complètes*, 1, 906. ***N'en parlez jamais***: quoted by Tuchman, *Guns of August*, 46. **"It may be horrible"**: quoted by Roth, *Guerre de 70*, 474. **About a million and a**

half people: for population figures, see François-Georges Dreyfus, *Histoire d'Alsace* (Paris: Hachette, 1979), 251–2, and Roth, *Guerre de 70*, 497. Roth estimates the total at 1,597,000 inhabitants. **Jules Favre . . . General Beaufort d'Hautpoul**: the details come from Baldick, 224–5, and Alistair Horne, *The Fall of Paris: The Siege and the Commune 1870–71* (London: Macmillan, 1965), 239. **"a revenge that will be the protest"**: quoted by Roth, *Guerre de 70*, 475. **"war expected"**: William James used the phrase in his essay "The Moral Equivalent of War" (1910); it is quoted by Daniel Pick, *War Machine: The Rationalisation of Slaughter in the Modern Age* (New Haven and London: Yale University Press, 1993), 15. **"I could not invent Boulanger"**: quoted by Frederic H. Seager, *The Boulanger Affair: Political Crossroad of France, 1886–1889* (Ithaca, New York: Cornell University Press, 1969), 50–51. **"Families have these shameful secrets"**: Péguy, *L'Argent (suite)* (April 1913) in *Oeuvres complètes*, 14, 117. **"emerged from its long sleep"**: "Deuxième suite de Notre Patrie," *Par ce demi-clair matin*, in *Oeuvres complètes*, 16, 45. Péguy probably wrote the essay in 1906, but it was not published until its inclusion in his complete works in 1952. **"It's for the reaper to judge"**: Paul Déroulède, *Chants du soldat*, 163rd edition (Paris: Calmann-Lévy, not dated [1915?]), 6. **"You see, Monsieur Madelin"**: quoted by Roth, *Guerre de 70*, 663–4. **"La Dernière Classe"**: published in *Les Contes du lundi* (1873). **"grave national theme"**: Barrès, "Une Nouvelle Position du problème Alsacien-Lorrain" (originally a speech delivered in 1899), in *Scènes et doctrines*, 2, 3. **"barracks inside a graveyard"**: *Scènes et doctrines*, 2, 6. **"She moves us all the more"**: *Scènes et doctrines*, 2, 4. **"holy idol"**: "La Statue de Strasbourg" (written in September 1870), in *Barbares et bandits*, 39. **"The government of the Republic"**: quoted by Roth, *Guerre de 70*, 701. **"France sincerely desires peace"**: quoted by Roth, *Guerre de 70*, 706.

[218–239]

Gustave Le Bon (epigraph): quoted from the English translation, *The Psychology of Peoples: Its Influence on Their Evolution* (London: T. Fisher Unwin, 1909), 233. **Séverine**: quoted by Curtis, 25. Séverine was the pseudonym of the journalist Caroline Rémy. **378,000 . . . 160,000** (footnote): Roth, *Lorraine annexée*, 97. **Reports of exploitable iron deposits**: see Hartshorne, especially 221–33. **a glacis to protect**: see Roth, *Guerre de 70*, 666, and Howard, 227, n4. **General von Alvensleben . . . Moltke's stated opinion**: Silverman, 31–2. **"indigestible"**: quoted by Hartshorne,

232–3. **Historians have been divided in their opinion**: for summaries and references see Silverman, 29 and footnote, and Roth, *Lorraine annexée*, 22, n22 and 29–30. **Belgium . . . Ireland**: see Hobsbawm, 30–1. **John Stuart Mill . . . British liberals**: see Dora Neill Raymond, *British Policy and Opinion During the Franco-Prussian War* (New York: Columbia University, 1921), 216–17. **"half-German, half-French and completely Iroquois"**: quoted by Jan Morris, *Fifty Years of Europe: An Album* (London and New York: Viking, 1997), 61. **"The feeble policy of our forefathers"**: Mommsen, in *Letters on the War between Germany and France*, 24. **"With this philosophy of history"**: Renan, "Nouvelle lettre à M. Strauss" (dated 15 September 1871), in *Oeuvres complètes*, 1, 454. **"not conquest, but restoration"**: Mommsen, in *Letters on the War*, 24. **"great resurrection"**: Treitschke, *What We Demand from France* in *Germany, France, Russia, and Islam*, 140. **"There are in the history"**: Max Müller, in *Letters on the War*, 63. **"are all German by blood"**: Max Müller, in *Letters on the War*, 94. **"Against their will"**: Treitschke, 105. **"to speak, read and write"**: quoted by Weber, *Peasants into Frenchmen*, 72. **report to the Committee of Public Safety**: Bertrand de Barère de Vieuzac, quoted by Michel de Certeau, Dominique Julia and Jacques Revel, *Une Politique de la langue. La Révolution française et les patois: L'enquête de Grégoire* (Paris: Éditions Gallimard, 1975), 293. My attention was first drawn to this passage by Hobsbawm, 21. **"It is too easy to forget"**: F. Max Müller, *Über die Resultate der Sprachwissenschaft: Vorlesung gehalten in der kaiserlichen Universität zu Strassburg am 23 mai 1872* (Strassburg and London: Trübner, 1872), 17–18. **Topinard**: quoted by Nancy Stepan, *The Idea of Race in Science: Britain, 1800–1960* (London: Macmillan, in association with St. Anthony's College, Oxford, 1982), 94. **"Abroad, you know"**: *Über die Resultate*, 6–7. **"Do the Prussians really exist?"**: Michelet, *Oeuvres complètes*, 20, 644. **"the Prussians are the Prussians"**: Jean-Louis Armand de Quatrefages, *The Prussian Race Ethnologically Considered. To which is appended some account of the bombardment of the Museum of Natural History etc., by the Prussians in January 1871*, translated by Isabella Innes (London: Virtue, 1872), 66n. **"In spite of a varnish of civilization"**: Quatrefages, 66. **Rudolf Virchow**: quoted by Weindling, *Health, Race and German Politics*, 48. **"the ancestry of the population"**: Ernest Lavisse and Christian Pfister, *The Question of Alsace-Lorraine* (London, New York and Toronto: Hodder & Stoughton, 1918), 1. **"to justify a political demand" . . . "the measurement of skulls"**: Georges Delahache, *Alsace-Lorraine: La Carte* *au liséré vert*, 4th edition (Paris: Librairie Hachette, 1911), 49. His source of quotation is Werner Wittich, "Deutsche und französische Kultur in Elsass" in *La Revue alsacienne illustrée* (1900), translated by André Korn as *La Génie nationale des races française et allemande en Alsace* (1903). **"presents a mixed population"** . . . **"the latest scientific researches"**: Daniel Blumenthal, *Alsace-Lorraine: A Study of the Relations of the Two Provinces to France and to Germany and a Presentation of the Just Claims of Their People* (New York and London: G. P. Putnam's Sons, 1917), 8 and 9–10. **a good deal of scholarship**: my own debt is to Poliakov, Winock and two works by Sternhell: *La Droite révolutionnaire*, particularly for its discussion of Gustave Le Bon and Georges Vacher de Lapouge, and "The Political Culture of Nationalism" in *Nationhood and Nationalism*, edited by Tombs, particularly for its argument that the French sometimes came to treat the nation as a " 'cultural' race" (33). **prisoners of heredity**: I borrow the phrase from Alfred Kelly, *The Descent of Darwin: The Popularization of Darwinism in Germany, 1860–1914* (Chapel Hill: University of North Carolina Press, © 1981), 105. **"Nations are not societies"**: *L'Aryen, son rôle social* (1899), quoted by Sternhell, *Droite révolutionnaire*, 168. **"Infinitely greater in numbers"**: *Les Lois psychologiques de l'évolution des peuples* (1894), quoted by Sternhell, *Droite révolutionnaire*, 150–1. The passage appears in the English translation, *The Psychology of Peoples*, 10–11. **"To this infinite power of ancestors"**: *L'Aryen*, quoted by Sternhell, *Droite révolutionnaire*, 151. **"natural race"** . . . **"historic race"** . . . **"soul"**: For Le Bon's use of these ideas, see in particular *Psychology of Peoples*, Chapter 1, "The Soul of Races." **"A nationalist . . . is a Frenchman"**: *Scènes et doctrines*, 1, 10.

[240–248]

Constant (epigraph): *De la liberté chez les modernes: Écrits politiques*, edited by Marcel Gauchet (Paris: Livres de Poche, 1980), 554–5. My attention was drawn to this essay by Todorov, 46. **"How ruined are the noble"**: Émile Littré, *De l'établissement de la Troisième République* (Paris: Aux Bureaux de la *Philosophie Positive*, 1880), 112. **Angell . . . taken as evidence of a prevailing complacency**: see, for example, Keegan, *First World War*, 10. **"based on the alleged unchangeability"**: Norman Angell, *The Great Illusion: A Study of the Relation of Military Power in Nations to Their Economic and Social Advantage* (London: William Heinemann, 1910), ix. **"clothed with many plants"** . . . **"Thus, from the war of nature"**: *The Origin of Species*, edited by Gillian Beer, Oxford World's Classics (Oxford and New

York: Oxford University Press, 1998), 395–6. **"War, why, life itself is war!"**: article of 1 September 1891 in *Le Figaro*, quoted by Digeon, 278. **"All men are brothers"**: *L'Aryen*, quoted by Sternhell, *Droite révolution-naire*, 25. **Captain André Constantin**: *Le rôle sociologique de la guerre et le sentiment national; suivi de La Guerre, moyen de selection collective par S.R. Steinmetz; traduit de l'allemand par le Capt. Constantin*, Bibliothèque scientifique internationale, No. 58 (Paris: Félix Alcan, 1907), particularly 171. **Falkenhayn**: quoted (with a correction to the translation) from Ferguson, *Pity of War*, 98. **Péguy**: *Notre patrie* in *Oeuvres complètes*, 20, 349.

PART III

La Chaussée (epigraph): 245.
Report by the French postal censor (epigraph): quoted by Pedroncini, *Pétain*, 153.

Chapter 6: Holding Verdun

[253–266]
Jubert (epigraph): reconstructed from the published dedication of *Verdun* and the sketch for a dedication printed as an appendix, 217–18, with help from Cru, *Témoins*, 329. **9 April 1916**: my account is drawn from Jubert, Part 2, Chapter 2, "L'Assaut du 9 avril," 111–29. **"Now I won't die any more"** (footnote): cited by Madelin, *Verdun*, 55. **"like the poor beggars"**: Cochin, 46. **Bordeaux**: *Les Captifs délivrés* in *Verdun 1916*, 270, already cited in my Prologue. **"Oh, how often I've seen"**: Hallé, 31–2. **Péricard**: *Ceux de Verdun*, 63. **Kathleen Burke** (footnote): *The White Road to Verdun* (London: Hodder & Stoughton, 1916), 44. **"Was he going to be"**: Naegelen, 85. **"It was a beautiful spectacle"**: Dubrulle, 15. **"After several minutes I rose"**: Desaubliaux, 291–2. **May . . . again posted to Le Mort-Homme**: my account of Jubert's disillusionment is drawn from Part 3, Chapter 1, "Un deuxième aspect du Mort-Homme," 163–83. **"I am dreadfully changed"**: Boasson, 127. **"Since Verdun my thinking"**: quoted by Pierre Citron, *Giono, 1895–1970* (Paris: Éditions du Seuil, 1990), 75. **Gabriel Chevallier** (footnote): *La Peur* (originally published in 1930), 76th edition (Paris: Le Quadrige d'Apollon, Presses Universitaires de France, 1951), 223. *inénarrable . . . indescriptible*: for examples of the former word, see Baumann, 94–5, and of the latter, see Dubrulle, 26, and

Dupont, 120. **"The men are stretched"**: Mazenod, 215. **"blind and impotent"**: Mazenod, 204.

[267–282]
Botrel (epigraph): *Chants de Bataille et de Victoire (1916–1919)* (Paris: Payot, 1920), 114–16. **Pétain** (epigraph): as reported in Mangin, *Lettres*, 115. **"a vigorous and powerful offensive"** . . . **"the choice of positions"**: the exchange is quoted by Pétain himself in his usually discreet *La Bataille*, 71. **as if he had swallowed a sword**: the impression recorded by Jacques Duclos, Secretary of the Communist Party from 1931 to 1964, in *Mémoires*, Volume 1: *1896–1924: Le chemin que j'ai choisi; de Verdun au Parti communiste* (Paris: Fayard, 1968), 123. **a wild boar about to charge**: Bordeaux, *Douleur et gloire*, 204. **"blindly to the slaughter"**: Tocaben, 269. **"It's certainly a rare piece of luck"**: Tocaben, 271. **"ostracism"**: Mangin, *Lettres*, 108. **getting too many men killed**: Mangin, *Lettres*, 112. **"He gets us in a pickle"**: as reported by Mangin, *Lettres*, 146. **Lefebvre-Dibon**: my account is largely based on Chapter 3, "Prise du Plateau de la Caillette (Secteur de Verdun) Avril 1916." Smith, 134–7, has a useful discussion of the incident; I am also indebted to its discussion of officers identifying downward with their men rather than upward with their commanders. **"Here you see a general"**: Painlevé, the visiting politician, reported the words to Poincaré, who recorded them in *Au service*, 8, 221–2. **"cult"**: Bordeaux, *Douleur et gloire*, 251. **"And what would be left for the Somme"**: quoted by Péricard, *Verdun*, 282. **"Gentlemen, we attack tomorrow"**: quoted by Rimbault, *Propos d'un marmité*, 93. Capitaine Paul Rimbault, *Propos d'un marmité (1915–1917)* (Paris: L. Fournier, 1920), 93. **"the artillery preparation will allow us"**: quoted by Péricard, *Verdun*, 280. **Major Lefebvre-Dibon could, and did, testify**: in *Quatre Pages*, Chapter 4, "Au Fort de Douaumont (Secteur de Verdun)," the basis of my account. **"A French officer dies"**: Péricard, *Verdun*, 111, for example, attributes them to Second Lieutenant Paul Girault, killed in the Bois des Cumières on 10 March. **"Major Lefebvre-Dibon headed for the German lines"**: unidentified officer (perhaps Captain Lanquetot) quoted by Péricard, *Verdun*, 274. **"With what?"** . . . **"I don't make"**: quoted by Péricard, *Verdun*, 279–80. **"odious"**: Mangin, *Lettres*, 115. **"My *poilus*, reduced by half"**: Mangin, *Lettres*, 115. **it was thirst**: Raynal, 175–6. **Delvert**: his account appeared in *Histoire* as Chapter 5, "La Défense de R1 (30 mai–5 juin 1916)," 241–72, and later *Carnets*, 252–80. My quotations

are drawn from the version in *Histoire*, made widely available by Bordeaux, *Vaux* in *Verdun 1916* (though with references to the inaccuracy of the French guns excised), and Lefebvre, *Verdun*, 237–46. **"I do not doubt that"**: quoted by Pedroncini, *Mutineries*, 28. **as Pétain himself would do in June**: see Pedroncini, *Pétain*, 152.

[283–290]
Drieu La Rochelle (epigraph): *Comédie de Charleroi*, 246. **"Sauve qui peut!"**: Péricard, *Verdun*, 107–8, not the sort of detail he usually records. **darker rumors and more sinister charges**: see, for example, Péricard, *Verdun*, 150. For a modern inquiry, see Pedroncini, *Pétain*, 150–3. **"given up"**: Poincaré, *Au service*, 8, 134. **casualty figures Pétain had supplied**: Poincaré, *Au service*, 8, 242–3. **the answer to it lay**: Poincaré, *Au service*, 8, 200–1. **"symptoms of lassitude and discouragement"**: quoted by Pedroncini, *Mutineries*, 27. **two articles**: Allard, 7–8. **"It's enough to make one weep"**: *Au service*, 8, 213. **Maginot**: the account and quotations are drawn from Allard, 15–24. **They knew all about**: for an example of the connection between politicians and the front, see *Nous crions grâce: 154 lettres de pacifistes juin–novembre 1916*, edited by Thierry Bonzon and Jean-Louis Robert (Paris: Les Éditions ouvrières, 1989), a collection of letters—some from Verdun—written to the Socialist deputy Pierre Brizon. **"for the last 18 months"**: Maurice Viollette, quoted by Allard, 41. *on se sacrifie* or *on est sacrifié*: compare Marilène Patten Henry, *Monumental Accusations: The «monuments aux morts» as Expressions of Popular Resentment* (New York: Peter Lang, © 1996), 26–9. **50 men from the 140th Infantry Regiment**: see Pedroncini, *Pétain*, 150–3, and Servent, 91–2. **"Baa . . . Baa"**: Desaubliaux, 255. Smith, 140, n56, records that during the April attacks 11 soldiers in the 5th Division were convicted of abandoning their post, nine of desertion, and one of both offenses. Three were sergeants and one was a corporal. None had a previous record, and 14 had been with their regiments since mobilization. **"I'd rather clear out"** . . . **"Come on, comrades"**: Desaubliaux, 290. **"As always, the order was"**: Tocaben, 71. **"Under fire, any movement"** . . . **"The responsibility I had just taken"**: Tocaben, 141–2. **Captain La Chaussée encountered**: 249. **a party of gravediggers**: La Chaussée, 223. **Herduin . . . Milan**: my account is drawn largely from Jean-Galtier Boissière and Daniel de Ferdon, "Herduin et Milan: Exécution sans jugement," *Les Fusillés pour l'exemple* (special issue of *Le Crapouillot*, August 1934), 43–6, with a few de-

tails borrowed, cautiously, from Henry Andraud, *Quand on fusillait les innocents*, 5th edition (Paris: Gallimard, 1935), 163–74.

Chapter 7: Ending Verdun

[293–301]

Ludendorff (epigraph): as reported by Prinz Max von Baden, *Erinnerungen und Dokumente*, edited by Golo Mann and Andreas Burckhardt (Stuttgart: Ernst Klett, 1968), 120. **"The sky is clear"**: Dupont, 188. **chemical weaponry**: my account is indebted to L. F. Haber, *The Poisonous Cloud: Chemical Warfare in the First World War* (Oxford: Clarendon Press, 1986), 94–5, and William Moore, *Gas Attack! Chemical Warfare in 1915–18 and Afterward* (London: Leo Cooper, 1987), 98–105. **"maintenant ils ne passeront pas"** (footnote): Castex, 148–9. **"Verdun would be brought to an end"**: Poincaré, *Au service*, 8, 224. **Verdun did not allow the French**: see Poincaré, *Au service*, 8, 224. **"In future our attacks"**: Pétain, 126–7. **"too defensive, too timid"** . . . **"attack"**: Mangin, *Lettres*, 145.

[301–320]

Bréant (epigraph): 163. *embusqués:* see Lefebvre, 398–9. **Philippe Glorennec's illuminating study**: "Le Fonds Péricard," in Canini, *Mémoire*, 323. **"Morale is very good"**: Castex, 150. **"So it's Verdun we're off to next"**: Castex, 173. **"There's no longer any doubt"**: Joubaire, 268. **"I will have shed my blood"**: Joubaire, 283. **"How long is this going to last?"**: Joubaire, 276. **"Jacques killed"**: Joubaire, 273. **"slept on the spot where he fell"**: Joubaire, 274–5. **"One can't even say"**: Joubaire, 278. Freud: "Thoughts for the Times on War and Death," *Collected Papers*, 4, 304–5 and 313. **"I have the sense of marching"**: Desaubliaux, 300. **"I'm back"**: Botti, 212–13. **"I led them"**: Botti, 214. **"the blood gushes out"**: the detail is from Delvert, *Histoire*, 248. **Tocaben**: 101–19. **"Before I reached the *chasseurs*"**: *Sous Verdun, août–octobre 1914* (Paris: Librairie Hachette, 1916), 66, and *Sous Verdun* in *Ceux de 14*, 51. My attention was originally drawn to this passage by Servent, 132. **"he smiles"**: *Sous Verdun* (1916), 144–5, and *Sous Verdun* in *Ceux de 14* (1950), 97. The English translation by H. Grahame Richards, *'Neath Verdun: August–October 1914* (London: Hutchinson, 1916), 168, rendered the opening of the sentence as: "an unctuous laugh spreads all over his greasy face." " 'I know that the day' ": *Sous Verdun* (1916), 250, omitted from *Sous Verdun* in *Ceux de 14*

(1950), 156. **"They were laid on the ground"**: Duhamel, 141. **"Some of his comrades"**: Thellier de Poncheville, 118. **"discreet"**: Bridoux, 177–8. **Major Roman**: quoted by Péricard, *Verdun*, 431. **"Coming out of the shelter"**: La Chaussée, 228. **"Ah! If our poor wives could see us now!"**: reported by Vial, 58. **"The arm of a corpse"**: Morel-Journel, 243. **"When it's my turn"**: Péricard, *Ceux de Verdun*, 126; the ellipses are Péricard's. **"Through some mental aberration"**: Gaudy, 138–9. **"I dozed for a few seconds"**: Desaubliaux, 289; the ellipses are Desaubliaux's. *Union Nationale . . . Union Sacrée*: the change of terminology is noted by Henry, *Monumental Accusations*, 15–17, though I disagree strongly with her argument that the sense of nationhood and the nation was too weak for *nationale* to have sufficient rhetorical force. **"sacrifices chosen for the salvation of Verdun"**: Péricard, *Ceux de Verdun*, 129, already quoted in Chapter 2. **"They're the next course"**: Cochin, 47. *Franzosenfresser*: Saint-Victor, *Barbares et bandits*, 13. Travers, xxiii, n8, briefly notes the military habit of using the language of eating. **"a framework that absorbs"** . . . **"a stomach with claws"**: *La France devant l'Europe*, in *Oeuvres complètes*, 20, 644, already quoted in Chapter 5. **"human flesh toward the great eater"**: Mazenod, 191. **"the hungry octopus"**: Tocaben, 53. *Chemin de l'abattoir*: noted by Lefebvre, 398–9.

[320–330]
Bordeaux (epigraph): *Douleur et gloire*, 235. **"Steel-skulled Bretons"**: Gras, 18–19. **"some on their back"**: J. Carafray, of the 118th Infantry Regiment, quoted by Péricard, *Verdun*, 602: **"viande"**: Albert Texier, of the 42nd Infantry Regiment, quoted by Lefebvre, 402. **Jean de Lattre de Tassigny**: *Ne pas subir: Écrits, 1914–1952*, edited by Élisabeth du Réau, André Kaspi, Marc Michel, Guy Pedroncini and Maurice Redan (Paris: Plon, 1984), unnumbered page in the opening "Présentation." **"The long white ribbon"**: Boulenger, 228. **Jubert . . . posthumous commendation**: signed by General Guillaumat on 10 September 1917; see appendix to Jubert, 222–3. **"real savior"**: Joffre, 2, 269. **"the most famous place"** . . . **"This is War all right"**: quoted by Geoffrey Wolff, *Black Sun: The Brief Transit and Violent Eclipse of Harry Crosby* (London: Hamish Hamilton, 1976), 51–2. **pinard with agnol**: Townsend Ludington, *John Dos Passos: A Twentieth Century Odyssey* (New York: E. P. Dutton, 1980), 137. **"Huge trucks packed with young men"**: *John Dos Passos' Correspondence with Arthur K. McComb: or "Learn to Sing the Carmagnole,"* edited

by Melvin Landsberg (Niwot, Colorado: University Press of Colorado, ©
1991), 61. **"was filmed over like a bloodshot eye"** (footnote): entry for
November 1918, quoted by Ludington, 173. (I have silently corrected Dos
Passos' hasty spelling, which Ludington reproduces.) **"ghoul-haunted"**:
quoted by Ludington, 137. **"Astonished to find themselves"**: Bordeaux,
Douleur et gloire, 243. **"dismal"** . . . **"Visitors are met"**: *Les Captifs
délivrés* in *Verdun 1916*, 326–7. **" 'As for the dirtiness of the rooms' "**:
Captifs in *Verdun 1916*, 329. **"German filthiness"** . . . **"No tenant ever
left"**: *Captifs* in *Verdun 1916*, 378. **"deposited their excrement"** (footnote): Neville Lytton, *Life in Unoccupied France* (London: Macmillan,
1942), 23. **His diary certainly mentioned**: *Douleur et gloire*, 266. **"I must
admit I did not see"**: quoted by Péricard, *Verdun*, 584. **"a good loser"**:
quoted by Péricard, *Verdun*, 586. **Lloyd George**: my account of his visit
and the quotations from his speech are drawn from John Grigg, *Lloyd
George: From Peace to War 1912–1916* (London: Methuen, 1985), 380–1.
The photo appears as illustration 14b, between 400 and 401. **In the
rhetoric of victory, Verdun was always a rock**: see, for example, "the
French rock" (Mazenod, ix) and "the unshakeable rock" (Thellier de
Poncheville, 2). **"We had no need to understand"**: Bordeaux, *Les Captifs
délivrés: Douaumont–Vaux (21 octobre–3 novembre 1916)* (Paris: Nelson,
1919), 27. The passage describing Lloyd George's visit and speech was left
out of the slightly shortened version of the book collected in *Verdun 1916*,
but retained in the contemporary English translation by Paul V. Cohn, *The
Deliverance of the Captives: Douaumont–Vaux October 21–November 3, 1916*
(London: Thomas Nelson & Sons, 1919), 27.

Epilogue: The Road from Verdun

[331–341]
Jubert (epigraph): 171. **"an almost completely animal existence"**:
Dubrulle, 68. **"It was delightful to find"**: Dubrulle, 75. **"At first its huge
carriages"**: this and following quotations are from Dubrulle, 78–81. **"We
were Red Indians"**: Jubert, 154, already quoted in Chapter 5. **"Sir, consider that you are younger"**: Fonsagrive, 66. **"meeting between *l'avant*
and *l'arrière*"**: Bordeaux, in Dubrulle, xxxi. **even Mangin declared himself a convert**: *Comment finit la guerre*, 59. **Jean Norton Cru**: *Témoins*,
600. **Antoine Prost**: *Anciens Combattants*, 3, 78. **generic term**: for some
examples of its use as a generic, see Nicola Cooper, "Heroes and Martyrs:

The Changing Mythical Status of the French Army during the Indochinese War," in *France at War*, edited by Holman and Kelly, 131–2. **Poincaré**: *Messages*, 158. **"No longer a leaf"**: Morel-Journel, 242. **"this ravaged soil"**: Bordeaux, *Douleur et gloire*, 249. **"beating its wings"**: Bordeaux, *Vaux* in *Verdun 1916*, 54. **Tocaben**: 101. **"pretty names"**: La Tour du Pin, 217. **Fleury**: my main sources are: Bordeaux, "La Ronde de nuit dans Fleury," Chapter 7 of *La Bataille devant Souville* in *Verdun 1916*; Péricard, *Ceux de Verdun*, 199–201 (already cited in Chapter 2); Tocaben, 81–2; Thellier de Poncheville, 92; Lafont, 64; Servent, 27; Gillet, *Verdun*, 157. **Teilhard de Chardin**: *Genèse d'une Pensée*, 152. **"Alas! What mournful sentinels"**: Delvert, *Histoire*, 269. **Tranchée des Baïonettes**: my main sources are: Henri Bouvard, *La Gloire de Verdun: Les Faits—le commandement—le soldat*, revised edition (Paris: Payot, 1935), 133–9; Péricard, *Verdun*, 368–75; Cru, 33–5 and 85–7; Lefebvre, 289–97; Servent, 157–62; and Winter, 99–101.

ACKNOWLEDGMENTS

—✛—

My researches have been greatly helped by the staff of the following libraries: the British Library; the Department of Printed Books, Imperial War Museum; the library of the Musée de la Guerre; the Universités de Paris BDIC; and, in Cambridge, Churchill College Library, Emmanuel College Library, Seeley Historical Library and the University Library. Dr. P. D. Baker, Major Stephen Casey, Professor I. F. Clarke, Gemma Geoghegan, Marie Christine Lopacuich, Dr. Karma Nabulsi and Francis Pochon have all been generous with their knowledge. I am also grateful to my agent Andrew Lownie and, at Random House, Will Sulkin and Jörg Hensgen for their patience and support. Anna Saunders best knows everything that she has contributed to the making of this book.

INDEX